A Peculiar
Treasure

The Enduring Legacy of
Herbert & Loma Armstrong

Jon W. Brisby

P.O. Box 775
Eugene OR 97440
www.cogeternal.org

Copyright © 2019 by Church of God, The Eternal
All rights reserved. No part of this book may be reproduced or used in any manner without written permission of the copyright owner except for the use of quotations in a book review.

Manufactured in the United States of America
by Taylor Communications

Library of Congress PCN 2019900486

First hardcover, paperback, and ebook editions June 2019

ISBN 978-0-9600289-0-0 (hardcover)
ISBN 978-0-9600289-2-4 (paperback)
ISBN 978-0-9600289-1-7 (Kindle)
ISBN 978-0-9600289-3-1 (EPUB)

Jacket design by Deborah Bussiere

Globe graphic by permission of Shutterstock Stock Images.
Oyster shell graphic by permission of Getty Images
Cover image of Herbert & Loma Armstrong—Ambassador College Envoy, 1961
Graphic of Ambassador College Seal—Envoy, 1969

All Bible citations are taken from the King James Version, unless otherwise noted.

This work is dedicated to the scattered and disillusioned who have not given up on solving the puzzle of their faith.

Retail sales of hardcover and paperback versions of this work make publication possible. All *digital versions* are intended to be free of charge when possible—made available for educational and inspirational purposes—and can be obtained from the publisher at www.jonwbrisby.com

Table of Contents

PREFACE ix

--- PART I ---

GOD'S *PECULIAR TREASURE* DEFINED

CHAPTER ONE
A BIBLE FRAMEWORK FOR REFERENCE 3

CHAPTER TWO
BEHAVIOR OF GOD'S TREASURE—PAST AND FUTURE 17

CHAPTER THREE
TESTING HERBERT ARMSTRONG AGAINST OUR BENCHMARK 31

--- PART II ---

SYNOPSIS OF LIFE AND WORK OF HERBERT & LOMA ARMSTRONG

CHAPTER FOUR
EARLY LIFE AND MINISTRY 1892–1934 47

CHAPTER FIVE
FOUNDING AND GROWTH OF CHURCH AND COLLEGE 1934–1957 77

CHAPTER SIX
KEY DEATHS, NEW MISSION, UNREST 1957–1974 111

CHAPTER SEVEN
TURMOIL, ATTEMPTED RESTORATION, DEATH 1974–1986   135

CHAPTER EIGHT
THE AFTERMATH 1986–1997   167

PART III
"ARMSTRONGISM" EXAMINED WITH RESPECT TO THE ANTAGONISTS

CHAPTER NINE
SOURCES OF INSPIRATION   177

CHAPTER TEN
UNIQUE SALVATION DOCTRINE   191

CHAPTER ELEVEN
ANGLO-ISRAELISM   203

PART IV
IF IT WAS GOD'S *PECULIAR TREASURE*, WHAT WENT WRONG?

CHAPTER TWELVE
TRANSFORMATION OF CHURCH PERSONALITY   235

CHAPTER THIRTEEN
MOTIVES FOR MEMBERSHIP   251

CHAPTER FOURTEEN
THE PROPHECY DEBACLE   265

CHAPTER FIFTEEN
1968 IN PROPHECY   283

CHAPTER SIXTEEN
THE PENTECOST PRECEDENT   295

CHAPTER SEVENTEEN
A TALE OF TWO STUDENTS   313

PART V
IF IT WAS GOD'S *PECULIAR TREASURE*, WHERE IS IT TODAY?

CHAPTER EIGHTEEN
CURRENT STATE OF HIS LEGACY   345

CHAPTER NINETEEN
WHAT ABOUT MISTAKES AND BAD BEHAVIOR?   359

CHAPTER TWENTY
WHAT ABOUT A WORK TODAY?   375

CHAPTER TWENTY-ONE
HALLMARKS OF A FAITHFUL REMNANT   393

Now therefore, if ye will obey my voice indeed, and keep my covenant, then ye shall be a peculiar treasure unto me above all people (Exodus 19:5).

PREFACE

Many authors have written previously about the life and work of Herbert Armstrong. As a polarizing public figure, he has been a lightning rod of controversy, eliciting strong responses both in reproach and in defense. Quite a few therefore have sought to capitalize upon his notoriety, from one perspective or another. What then is the purpose for generating one more book about Mr. Armstrong at this late date? Has not everything been said that can be said? Are there not already enough comprehensive works providing sufficient perspectives from which to evaluate? Is this perhaps just one more attempt by an aspiring author to ride his posthumous coattails into the limelight? These are the questions you will be answering for yourself as you evaluate the material that follows.

By and large, current books about Herbert Armstrong fall into one of two categories: either they seek to laud him as the infallible last-day Elijah, prophesied to restore all things and to warn the world in advance of the return of Jesus Christ, or else they denigrate him, seeking to repudiate his legitimacy as having been an inspired servant of God at all. The former typically include much advocatory rhetoric, matched with an agenda to promote the author as the legitimate successor to Mr. Armstrong. These writers often claim prophetic biblical titles for themselves and seek to parlay an affinity for Mr. Armstrong's work into a following for themselves. On the other hand, the list of derogatory works is long, and often demonstrates an author's desire for some form of personal catharsis—through tabloid character assassination—to deal with scars from past church association. There are some few authors who might be said to constitute a third category of writer. These have attempted to analyze the history of Herbert Armstrong and the Worldwide Church of God from a detached, scientific perspective. Their focus is upon the "what and why" of member reactions, based upon specific stimuli from church association, but they typically concede no personal belief about God's actual involvement one way or another.

What about this author? To make it easier to get the gist of this work from the outset, here is a clear declaration of motive. You are not being asked to sift through hundreds of pages before the author's *real* intent finally emerges. You will receive that explanation right now, up front, and in plain language. There is no need to hunt for it by thumbing through the final chapters out of order.

This author is an admitted partisan, believing that Herbert Armstrong was indeed an inspired servant of God, sent not by his own will, but by the will of God to fulfill key prophecies of the Bible for the last days—before the imminent return of Jesus Christ to this earth. He believes that what emerged from the work of Herbert Armstrong was a manifestation of the true Church of God in this age, a phenomenon unlike any other religious work of our time. He believes that without the work of that particular man, none of us would understand the real keys to Bible truth, including who is God, what is man, and why this whole physical creation exists at all. For that reason, Herbert Armstrong will be considered in this book with the utmost respect and personal appreciation.

Notwithstanding, in contrast to the traditional zealots who have written books thus far, this author will show that Herbert Armstrong—although absolutely called and commissioned by God as an inspired representative of Jesus Christ in this age—departed from the correct path in his old age, not because he became evil-minded, but because of the overwhelming influence of men around him who did not really love the Truth as did he. This, too, was an absolute fulfillment of prophecy for the last-day Church of God, even though very few have ever come to recognize it. There is an absolute reason that God allowed these events to transpire, and in fact He is the One who orchestrated them. It was necessary to prove every one of those whom He had called, to know whether we were merely following a man, or whether we had truly *verified* that Way of Life as a divine gift from God. It is the story of God's ingenious work to test and to prove a called-out people, to prepare them for a glorious future as firstfruits in the Family of God. This book will make the case for the divine nature of Mr. Herbert Armstrong's incredible work, and highlight the positive aspects of that work which endure today.

Another unique aspect of this written work includes shining a very bright light upon Mrs. Loma Armstrong, the faithful wife of Herbert Armstrong, who influenced him more than most begin to realize. It was during the time of her partnership with him that Herbert Armstrong produced such incredible results, and it was after her death that everything began to change. No other writer has noticed this, but ample proof is found in the historical record. More than any seem to realize, she was a key part of his final legacy.

Believing that Mr. Armstrong himself departed under pressure in the 1970s from the very revelation of God which he had once taught us all to hold dear, this author will be ridiculed and rejected by both the worshipful zealots as well as the Herbert Armstrong haters. Because this book will make the case for the legitimacy of his work under the authority of God, the haters will mock. But because this work will also show that Mr. Armstrong made serious mistakes in his old age which triggered the very destruction of the church that he loved, those partisans who accept no other reality than that Mr. Armstrong—as the "last-day Elijah"—was basically infallible, will heap ridicule with perhaps even more vehemence than the others.

The interpretation of church history you are about to explore is truly unique from that which has been published to date by any of these other writers. Whether you ultimately find the arguments credible or not, it is definitely a "different take" from any other major work published in the last forty years. It is not actually a "*new* take" at all, but one that has been much more obscure in comparison to the popular theories that abound today. If enough time has elapsed to allow many to admit to themselves that these other "takes" are inadequate and somehow unsatisfying, perhaps the time is finally right to present an answer which may fill in some mysterious blanks.

What is the real reason for this book at this time? The author is pastor of one of those many remnant groups that came out of the Worldwide Church of God in past decades. He makes no claim to prophetic title nor any other grand commission for self-aggrandizement. He believes earnestly that the portrayal of events and circumstances documented in this work answers the key questions about why the work of Herbert Armstrong was so compelling, yet seemed to disintegrate in the end. Most of the evidence will be presented from the very words of Herbert Armstrong himself. You will not be asked to believe some wild and unsubstantiated theory of the author. When these facts are highlighted, and then organized into proper sequence, you just might be amazed to find that an incredible plan unfolds which reveals a divine tapestry of God's work that has still been operating uninterrupted through all of the seeming chaos. That work is still going on. There is still purpose and direction. That is the very good news.

Surely this author is just trying to get more members for his own church, right? Some will certainly believe that to be so. The community of former members of the Worldwide Church of God has become a very jaded bunch indeed. But come now! If one believes earnestly in a way of life that he thinks will lead to salvation, and he is willing to sacrifice personally to walk in that way, it is natural that he would desire fellowship with others who share in that same belief. And if it might just turn out to be *the right way*—as opposed to one of the myriad counterfeits being sold out there today—of course that would be another strong motivation for publishing. What author writes without the hope of inspiring others to find value in his perspective? Anyone who claims otherwise is being dishonest. Only the reader can determine for himself whether this work has any spiritual substance. Please put it to the test and determine that for yourself.

PREFACE   xiii

There is another reason for this book. It is *not* part of some grand scheme to try to do "a Work" like Mr. Armstrong did, with the hope of copying the success he experienced in building a large religious empire. That principle will become very plain in the following chapters. But there is definitely a spiritual motive: to be acquitted before God as a minister of Jesus Christ—to avoid becoming a hireling, and to seek out the lost sheep who have been scattered due to the corruption of Israel's shepherds (Ezekiel 34:2–5; Jeremiah 50:6). No grand commission to the world is claimed. But a responsibility in good conscience toward those called ones who have become troubled and confused cannot be ignored.

For whom then is this book really written? There are many out there in one of two broad categories who have provided inspiration for this work. The first includes those who were touched by the Worldwide Church of God to some degree in decades past, but who are still very troubled because they have never really found an explanation that makes complete sense of the collapse of that church. If you are one who feels there are still too many loose ends that make these other writers' conclusions seem forced and shallow, then this book is for you. Secondly, if you are one of those who only recently has discovered the teachings of Herbert Armstrong and are finding value in them *for the first time*, and you are struggling to reconcile all you are being told happened during the last seventy years in that original church, this book is likewise for you. Hopefully it will provide another perspective to consider as you seek to verify whether or not there is anything of real value in the unique life's work of Herbert and Loma Armstrong.

PART I

GOD'S PECULIAR TREASURE DEFINED

CHAPTER ONE
A BIBLE FRAMEWORK FOR REFERENCE

To evaluate the potential legitimacy of Mr. Herbert Armstrong's work—or that of any other man or organization claiming God's inspiration—we first have to have a benchmark for comparison. How can one hope to "prove the truth" if he is not really sure what he is looking for? Should he simply employ the proverbial "elephant test"—searching haphazardly for something that is hard to describe in advance, but is hoped to be instantly recognizable when spotted? Or is there perhaps a better strategy to identify the true work of God?

If we trust that the Bible is the inspired word of God, perhaps He has provided some hints to show us what a legitimate work in His name should actually look like. Perhaps He has also recorded information to tell us what befalls His work among men, both historically and prophetically. If so, it may not require such a blind stab in the dark after all to assess objectively whether the empire built under Herbert Armstrong might possibly have had any divine inspiration—or not.

TIME ORDER FOR SALVATION

One of the most distinctive hallmarks of the true Church of God is acknowledgment that God is not trying *presently* to save the whole world. Oh yes, it is His ultimate intent to bring salvation to the world (1 Timothy 2:3–4; 1 John 2:2). But what most self-proclaimed Christians do not understand is that there is a specific *time order* being implemented by God, and that only very few human beings are being offered a close personal relationship with Him *for the moment.* The Bible is replete with confirmations of this fact, yet so few recognize this simple truth:

For as in Adam all die, even so in Christ shall all be made alive. But every man *in his own order*: Christ the firstfruits; afterward they that are Christ's at his coming (1 Corinthians 15:22–23) [emphasis mine].

. . . and they lived and reigned with Christ a thousand years. But the rest of the dead lived not again until the thousand years were finished (Revelation 20:4–5).

No man can come to me, except the Father which hath sent me draw him (John 6:44).

Of his own will begat he us with the word of truth, that we should be a kind of firstfruits of his creatures (James 1:18).

The symbolism of firstfruits—differentiating an early harvest from a latter harvest—permeates the Bible as a hallmark of God's work with man. The majority of those in this world claiming to be Christians share the false belief that anyone who *chooses* can "come to Christ" at any time. They do not ascribe any *serious* relevance to early and late harvests in their theology. In fact, they believe all men alive today are being offered salvation *right now*, and that anyone who does not accept that calling before he dies is doomed. That is why so many religious groups expend enormous energies and resources sending missionaries to all parts of the globe. They are trying to "save" as many people as they possibly can before it is too late. To them, the worst possible end is for anyone to die having never said the magic words, "I accept Jesus Christ as my personal Savior." Couple this with their false notions about the afterlife—believing that the "unsaved" will live forever in the torment of hell fire, suffering in excruciating agony—and you have the answer for how Satan has deceived the whole world (Revelation 12:9).

All of these ideas are completely bogus and totally unscriptural, for anyone who cares to examine them honestly. The Bible is very plain that God did not choose to open salvation to every human

A BIBLE FRAMEWORK FOR REFERENCE

being at any and every given time. God determines the specific time of each one's privileged call, and until that time, no one can force Jesus Christ to receive him. This truth is hated by the majority of those claiming to be Christians in this world, but it is fact nonetheless. It is one of the truths that makes Christian imposters hate the true people of God so much. The world has been blinded by Satan into believing that everyone should have an *equal opportunity* at salvation *on their own terms*, and anyone who advocates otherwise is called discriminatory, hateful, racist, and even dangerous to society. But whether or not well-meaning "Christian" activists want to admit it, Jesus Christ has always shown *partiality* in His work among men. The very role of Israel in this great Master Plan for human salvation is proof of that.

GOD'S PECULIAR TREASURE

Understanding the real work of God begins with understanding the role of Israel. Those who ignore the Israel of God preclude themselves from ever understanding the plan being unfolded step by step to bring salvation to this world. God made Israel special.

> Now therefore, if ye will obey my voice indeed, and keep my covenant, then ye shall be *a peculiar treasure* unto me above all people: for all the earth is mine: And ye shall be unto me a kingdom of priests, and an holy nation. These are the words which thou shalt speak unto the children of Israel (Exodus 19:5–6) [emphasis mine].

Yes, like it or not, God showed explicit partiality to one little group of people out of all who lived upon the face of the earth. He did not treat all men "equally," as political correctness in today's world demands. God loves all men *equally*, and they are *all* special in His glorious Master Plan of love, but that plan is being unfolded step by step according to *His* specifications, not theirs.

For the LORD hath chosen Jacob unto himself, and Israel for his *peculiar treasure*. For I know that the LORD is great, and that our Lord is above all gods. Whatsoever the LORD pleased, that did he in heaven, and in earth, in the seas, and all deep places (Psalm 135:4–6) [emphasis mine].

So God refers to Israel as His *peculiar treasure*. As we shall see, this does not refer merely to those physical descendants of Abraham, Isaac, and Jacob historically. Ancient Israel was the *type*—the physical forerunner—an instructive symbol. But the New Testament Church is the *antitype*—the *spiritual counterpart* and true fulfillment of all that God is doing to bring salvation to mankind (Galatians 6:15–16). Jesus Christ confirmed that salvation is of the Jews (John 4:22). That is indisputable. But He also revealed through the Apostle Paul that a *real Jew* is not just one who has a physical pedigree, but one who is *converted* through *circumcision of the heart* (Romans 2:28–29). Those who are called by God—regardless of race or national heritage—and who accept that calling through baptism and begettal of the Holy Spirit, become spiritual Israelites. The true Church of God—wherever it may be found—is *spiritual Jerusalem*, the mother of us all (Galatians 4:26), and the wife whom Jesus Christ will marry at His Second Coming (Revelation 19:7). The New Testament Church, composed of physical members *of all peoples* according to His pleasure, becomes—through the miracle of spiritual conversion—the true Israel, God's peculiar treasure.

For the grace of God that bringeth salvation hath appeared to all men, Teaching us that, denying ungodliness and worldly lusts, we should live soberly, righteously, and godly, in this present world; Looking for that blessed hope, and the glorious appearing of the great God and our Saviour Jesus Christ; Who gave himself for us, that he might redeem us from all iniquity, and purify unto himself *a peculiar people*, zealous of good works (Titus 2:11–14) [emphasis mine].

A BIBLE FRAMEWORK FOR REFERENCE   7

Given that very brief synopsis of God's plan, what can we discover about the true Church of God from all that God has recorded in the Bible? Remember, we are trying to identify *distinguishing characteristics* of that Church—God's peculiar treasure—which will allow us to test the legitimacy of any modern group claiming to be part of it.

WHY PECULIAR?

Why did God call His chosen people peculiar? The Hebrew word is *cegullah*. It means a valued property, a possession that is distinctively special. It does not denote something that is common or run-of-the-mill. Solomon's use of the word in Ecclesiastes chapter two—describing his search for gratification through the acquisition of unique and precious possessions—provides context:

> . . . also I had great possessions of great and small cattle above all that were in Jerusalem before me: I gathered me also silver and gold, and *the peculiar treasure of kings* and of the provinces . . . So I was great, and increased more than all that were before me in Jerusalem (Ecclesiastes 2:7–9) [emphasis mine].

When human kings become great and marvelously wealthy, they often seek to acquire precious things which are uniquely valuable and awe-inspiring, therewith enhancing their own personal prestige and legacy. Solomon was one such king. Another example familiar to most of us is the Egyptian pharaoh, Tutankhamun, whose vast burial treasures on display worldwide today include incredible jewelry, ornaments, statues, and sculptures. Millions around the world have paid to see the traveling exhibits of this ancient pharaoh's own *peculiar treasures*. Solomon's reference to the *peculiar treasure of kings* uses the very same Hebrew word, *cegullah*, which God uses to describe His own chosen people.

8 A PECULIAR TREASURE

This should help confirm that those who are offered a close, personal relationship with God are not *many*, are not *common*, and are certainly not *unremarkable*. They are *rare* within the population of human beings, they are *unique* in characteristics, and they are *curiously valuable* to God in this world. This very depiction of Israel by God Himself totally undermines the false "salvation-path doctrines" espoused by the majority today. Any group that claims God is not using a *preferential order* in offering salvation to mankind is denying the clear evidence of the Bible.

> For thou art an holy people unto the LORD thy God: the LORD thy God hath chosen thee to be a special [*cegullah*] people unto himself, above all people that are upon the face of the earth (Deuteronomy 7:6).

HATEFUL DISCRIMINATION?

Is not this doctrine just another attempt to twist Scripture to justify divisive, arrogant partiality in order to glorify a very few today at the expense of the many? After all, many hate-filled religious groups have claimed to be "Israel" in order to justify very un-Christian behaviors, disdainfully treating anyone whom they consider to be "Gentile" with gross disrespect, and even violence!

Anyone can pick up a Bible and read that Israel was the special treasure of God, then co-opt that title for selfish reasons and commit all manner of atrocities "in the name of God." Men have been doing that for thousands of years. Satan encourages such abuse as a means to further disparage the truth of God's Master Plan on this earth. But the misdeeds of deceived men will never negate the validity of God's work. So how can you tell the difference? Many claim to be the Israel of God (Galatians 6:16). What are the fruits of the true Church that distinguish it from all the many imposters?

Another identifying mark of the true Church of God is the understanding that they have never *earned* their special favor with God. There is no arrogance involved! They acknowledge that they

A BIBLE FRAMEWORK FOR REFERENCE

are most unworthy among all human beings on earth, and that they now enjoy this special relationship with God only because of His mercy and inexplicable benevolence. Again, God's explanation—in His own Words—reveals much:

> The LORD did not set his love upon you, nor choose you, because ye were more in number than any people; for ye were the fewest of all people: But because the LORD loved you, and because he would keep the oath which he had sworn unto your fathers, hath the LORD brought you out with a mighty hand, and redeemed you out of the house of bondmen, from the hand of Pharaoh king of Egypt (Deuteronomy 7:7–8).

There is no inherent honor in being born an Israelite. The history of the acts of ancient Israel is a testament to that fact. Israel had no qualities that made them better than any other peoples. They never *earned* God's special favor in any way. Furthermore, since they never obeyed God for any length of time, their recorded history is one of national failure. Israel became a reproach because of her stiff-necked arrogance, unchecked personal weakness, and refusal to do things God's way. Anyone who decides to attach himself to Israel as a means of making himself seem "better" should study the abject failure of those very people. Jesus Christ Himself said that taking pride in being an Israelite of the flesh is worthless. In speaking to *bona fide*—pedigreed—Israelites, He said:

> If ye were Abraham's children, ye would do the works of Abraham. . . . Ye are of your father the devil, and the lusts of your father ye will do. He was a murderer from the beginning, and abode not in the truth, because there is no truth in him. When he speaketh a lie, he speaketh of his own: for he is a liar, and the father of it. And because I tell you the truth, ye believe me not. Which of you convinceth me of sin? And if I say the truth, why do ye not believe me? He that is

10   A PECULIAR TREASURE

of God heareth God's words: ye therefore hear them not, because ye are not of God (John 8:39, 44–47).

So being a physical Israelite profits nothing if there is not actual *behavior*—personal fruits—that pleases God. Even as ancient Israel was not picked by God for special favor because of anything they ever did to deserve it, the same is true with those who have been offered special favor in being called to become part of the New Testament Church—spiritual Israel.

For ye see your calling, brethren, how that not many wise men after the flesh, not many mighty, not many noble, are called: But God hath chosen the foolish things of the world to confound the wise; and God hath chosen the weak things of the world to confound the things which are mighty; And base things of the world, and things which are despised, hath God chosen, yea, and things which are not, to bring to nought things that are (1 Corinthians 1:26–28).

If you are one who has been called by God—given an open mind to receive an understanding and appreciation of the real Truth—then you have no cause to gloat. That calling had nothing to do with your inherent worthiness. Much to the contrary, it probably indicates you are one who is *least likely* to be appreciated in this world, according to man's standards. Why would God choose to call primarily the weak and the base?

That no flesh should glory in his presence. But of him are ye in Christ Jesus, who of God is made unto us wisdom, and righteousness, and sanctification, and redemption: That, according as it is written, He that glorieth, *let him glory in the Lord* (vv. 29–31) [emphasis mine].

So now it becomes plain! When people who—by nature—are the off-scouring of the world are given a special calling, and by the power

A Bible Framework for Reference 11

of God's Holy Spirit learn to manifest good fruits which were previously beyond their reach, it is *God* who will get the credit—the glory—for their changed lives, *not the individuals themselves*. Amazing. If it were otherwise, and God chose to call the most respected and revered individuals on earth "naturally," their successes in Christ would easily become attributable to their own inherent abilities. God would receive little, if any, of the credit, and our masterful Creator is too wise to have designed His plan in a way that fosters such a false impression.

The true Church of God does not vilify the uncalled masses of the world. They resist becoming part of the world and its evils, but they recognize that all of these people are likewise beloved children of God, and in His appropriate time, all of them will receive their opportunity to know God. Salvation is only through Israel, but all of those children—some sooner, some later—will receive their chance to become spiritual Israelites through the gift of the Holy Spirit. "It is the spirit that quickeneth; the flesh profiteth nothing" (John 6:63). Therefore, anyone who professes to be of Israel, but shows institutional disdain and hatred toward other peoples—whether in or out of the church—is an imposter. That will never be a trait of the true Israel of God.

Respect for God's Law

What else has God recorded in His Bible to help us identify unique traits of the true Church—God's peculiar treasure? Wherever it exists, it shows sincere respect for the commandments of God.

Look down from thy holy habitation, from heaven, and bless thy people Israel . . . This day the LORD thy God hath commanded thee to do these statutes and judgments: *thou shalt therefore keep and do them* with all thine heart, and with all thy soul. Thou hast avouched the LORD this day to be thy God, and *to walk in his ways, and to keep his statutes, and his commandments, and his judgments*, and to hearken

12   A PECULIAR TREASURE

> unto his voice: And the LORD hath avouched thee this day to
> be *his peculiar people*, as he hath promised thee, and that
> thou shouldest keep all his commandments; And to make
> thee high above all nations which he hath made, in praise,
> and in name, and in honour; and that thou mayest be an holy
> people unto the LORD thy God, as he hath spoken
> (Deuteronomy 26:15–19) [emphasis mine].

Lest anyone believe this was merely a requirement for ancient
Israel but not for spiritual Israel—the Church—let Jesus Christ
resolve that with His own words:

> If ye love me, keep my commandments. . . . He that hath my
> commandments, and keepeth them, he it is that loveth me:
> and he that loveth me shall be loved of my Father, and I will
> love him, and will manifest myself to him. . . . If a man love
> me, he will keep my words: and my Father will love him, and
> we will come unto him, and make our abode with him. He
> that loveth me not keepeth not my sayings: and the word
> which ye hear is not mine, but the Father's which sent me
> (John 14:15, 21, 23–24).

This is the very same standard required of ancient Israel. The
commandments confirmed by Jesus Christ were the very same ones
established by God *from the beginning*, and later codified on two
tablets of stone for Israel at Mt. Sinai.

> Think not that I am come to destroy the law, or the prophets:
> I am not come to destroy, but to fulfil [fill full, magnify]. For
> verily I say unto you, Till heaven and earth pass, one jot or
> one tittle shall in no wise pass from the law, till all be
> fulfilled. Whosoever therefore shall break one of these least
> commandments, and shall teach men so, he shall be called
> the least in the kingdom of heaven: but whosoever shall do

A Bible Framework for Reference   13

and teach them, the same shall be called great in the kingdom of heaven (Matthew 5:17–19).

Jesus Christ never did away with those commandments, but in fact *magnified them* and made their spiritual application even more far-reaching than ever before (Matthew 5:21–28). Therefore, anyone claiming that God's commandments are not incumbent upon Christians today is demonstrating that he is an imposter.

And hereby we do know that we know him, if we keep his commandments. He that saith, I know him, and keepeth not his commandments, is a liar, and the truth is not in him. But whoso keepeth his word, in him verily is the love of God perfected: hereby know we that we are in him. He that saith he abideth in him ought himself also so to walk, even as he walked (1 John 2:3–6).

Jesus Christ set a perfect example by keeping the Ten Commandments. Those claiming that Christ kept them perfectly so that we do not have to are only espousing exactly what the Apostle John said would identify the imposters.

The Sabbath—a Sign

Obedience includes belief and practice of the fourth commandment—keeping the Sabbath. Many will acknowledge the need to avoid murder, theft, and adultery, but for some reason, keeping God's Sabbath is a huge obstacle. Is that not why God said that the Sabbath(s) would become *the sign* between Him and His true people?

Speak thou also unto the children of Israel, saying, Verily my sabbaths ye shall keep: for it is a sign between me and you throughout your generations; that ye may know that I am the Lord that doth sanctify you (Exodus 31:13).

14   A PECULIAR TREASURE

> Moreover also I gave them my sabbaths, to be a sign between me and them, that they might know that I am the LORD that sanctify them (Ezekiel 20:12).

Jesus Christ never did away with the Sabbath commandment any more than He did away with the laws against murder, theft, and adultery. And therefore, one of the key indicators to help narrow our search for the true Church of God today is a respect for keeping His commanded Sabbaths. Any group that repudiates those Sabbaths is automatically disqualified. That single criteria will cull the vast majority of so-called "Christian fellowships" in one fell swoop. It still leaves a number of competing groups today who *do* claim the Sabbath, but it surely helps narrow the field. Sabbath-keeping is certainly a major factor in making the true Church stand out as "peculiar" in this world.

> For thou art an holy people unto the LORD thy God, and the LORD hath chosen thee to be a peculiar people unto himself, above all the nations that are upon the earth (Deuteronomy 14:2).

IN SUMMARY THUS FAR

We began by asking how we might verify the potential legitimacy of that significant and intriguing religious movement begun under Mr. Herbert Armstrong in the twentieth century. Before attempting to make that assessment, we first must have a standard—a benchmark—by which to measure. Recognizing the key criteria for any legitimate work of God *according to God's own definition* is the first step. What do we know so far?

Wherever a true work of God is found, it is a body that acknowledges:

1) God has instituted a time order in offering salvation to men, and no one decides of himself to become a Christian. He must be

A BIBLE FRAMEWORK FOR REFERENCE
15

called. Relatively few are being called now, with the vast majority to be called only after Jesus Christ returns.

2) Israel is God's special people—His peculiar treasure—through whom salvation is being offered to all mankind. They are the firstfruits of His work among men. Ancient Israel was only a physical type. The New Testament Church is the true Israel of God, including members from all races and nationalities, made special—peculiar—by the gift of the Holy Spirit at baptism.

3) Legitimate spiritual Israelites humbly acknowledge their own worthlessness and express their gratitude for being called by God according to His pleasure. They do not justify contempt and disdain for anyone else, either in or out of the Body.

4) The true people of God honor the Ten Commandments. Anyone who claims those commandments were done away is denying the very Savior who confirmed them.

5) The Sabbaths of God are a distinctive sign (out of all of the laws) which acts as a beacon to differentiate the true Church of God from the rest of the world.

These are the important first criteria—straight from the Bible—which form a key part of our benchmark for testing the religious works of men.

Before applying this yardstick specifically to the work of Herbert Armstrong, are there yet other elements that can be added to strengthen our differential analysis? Yes, indeed. Next, we will look at the *historical behaviors* of Israel—God's peculiar treasure—as well as the *prophesied behaviors* of spiritual Israel in the last days. Given what God recorded that ancient Israel actually did, and what spiritual Israel of the first century actually did, are we provided any hints to show what would befall the true Church of God in our very own time? Those words were recorded so that the called of God would have a definite basis for comparison.

> . . . and a book of remembrance was written before him for them that feared the Lord, and that thought upon his name. And they shall be mine, saith the Lord of hosts, in that day

when I make up my jewels [*cegullah*]; and I will spare them, as a man spareth his own son that serveth him. Then shall ye return, *and discern between the righteous and the wicked,* between him that serveth God and him that serveth him not (Malachi 3:16–18) [emphasis mine].

Adding this historical dimension will give us much to compare as we dissect the history of the Radio Church of God (which became the Worldwide Church of God) under Herbert Armstrong.

CHAPTER TWO
BEHAVIOR OF GOD'S TREASURE—PAST AND FUTURE

Is it really reasonable to conclude that the Radio Church of God was actually the work of the Living God in this age? Is there *solid evidence* to support that belief for ones who may be honestly doubtful? We began by profiling the biblical attributes of the true Church of God and what it must look like wherever it may be found. We identified five major attributes that help distinguish the true Church from all other claimants.

With these principles in mind, what other evidence might be available in the Bible to help us identify unique characteristics that differentiate God's true church—His peculiar treasure—from all others? What about the recorded history of the *behavior* of ancient Israel, the *behavior* of the first-century Church, and specific prophecies related to the *behavior* of a last-day Church? Did God prophesy what would actually happen to that Church—God's peculiar treasure? And if so, might any of those detailed events have already transpired?

ANCIENT ISRAEL'S BEHAVIOR

We have already seen that ancient Israel was called out from among all nations to become God's peculiar treasure. He promised to fight their battles for them and to deliver them from any enemy if they would honor their covenant promises to Him:

When thou art in tribulation, and all these things are come upon thee, even in the latter days, if thou turn to the LORD thy God, and shalt be obedient unto his voice; (For the LORD thy God is a merciful God;) he will not forsake thee, neither destroy thee, nor forget the covenant of thy fathers which he sware unto them. For ask now of the days that are past, which were before thee, since the day that God created man upon the earth, and ask from the one side of heaven unto the other, whether there hath been any such thing as this great thing is, or hath been heard like it? Did ever people hear the voice of God speaking out of the midst of the fire, as thou hast heard, and live? Or hath God assayed to go and take him a nation from the midst of another nation, by temptations, by signs, and by wonders, and by war, and by a mighty hand, and by a stretched out arm, and by great terrors, according to all that the LORD your God did for you in Egypt before your eyes? Unto thee it was shewed, that thou mightest know that the LORD he is God; there is none else beside him. Out of heaven he made thee to hear his voice, that he might instruct thee: and upon earth he shewed thee his great fire; and thou heardest his words out of the midst of the fire. And because he loved thy fathers, therefore he chose their seed after them, and brought thee out in his sight with his mighty power out of Egypt; To drive out nations from before thee greater and mightier than thou art, to bring thee in, to give thee their land for an inheritance, as it is this day. Know therefore this day, and consider it in thine heart, that the LORD he is God in heaven above, and upon the earth beneath: there is none else. Thou shalt keep therefore his statutes, and his commandments, which I command thee this day, that it may go well with thee, and with thy children after thee, and that thou mayest prolong thy days upon the earth, which the LORD thy God giveth thee, for ever (Deuteronomy 4:30–40).

But did God really expect that they would be a faithful and loyal people to Him? God was not so naive.

O that there were such an heart in them, that they would fear me, and keep all my commandments always, that it might be well with them, and with their children for ever! (Deuteronomy 5:29)

God knew the end from the beginning (Isaiah 46:10). And lest any should later believe He was surprised by the eventual outcome of ancient Israel, He made sure to prophesy through Moses exactly what He knew they would choose to do:

> For I know thy rebellion, and thy stiff neck: behold, while I am yet alive with you this day, ye have been rebellious against the LORD; and how much more after my death? Gather unto me all the elders of your tribes, and your officers, that I may speak these words in their ears, and call heaven and earth to record against them. For I know that after my death ye will utterly corrupt yourselves, and turn aside from the way which I have commanded you; and evil will befall you in the latter days; because ye will do evil in the sight of the LORD, to provoke him to anger through the work of your hands (Deuteronomy 31:27–29).

God also prophesied what His own response to their faithlessness would be:

> When thou shalt beget children, and children's children, and ye shall have remained long in the land, and shall corrupt yourselves, and make a graven image, or the likeness of any thing, and shall do evil in the sight of the LORD thy God, to provoke him to anger: I call heaven and earth to witness against you this day, that ye shall soon utterly perish from off the land whereunto ye go over Jordan to possess it; ye shall not prolong your days upon it, but shall utterly be destroyed. And the LORD shall scatter you among the nations, and ye shall be left few in number among the heathen, whither the LORD shall lead you (Deuteronomy 4:25–27).

And that is precisely what happened to them over many centuries. The Old Testament is largely an historical record of the failures of God's chosen people. Times of reformation and heartfelt reconciliation with God through the work of faithful champions (judges, kings, or prophets) were all too few and far between. Mostly, in spite of being given every possible advantage, Israel never appreciated it and repeatedly drifted back into lawlessness and idolatry. They did exactly what God prophesied they would do. And very often, it was the leaders of Israel—especially their priests—who were responsible for their national apostasy.

> But they also have erred through wine, and through strong drink are out of the way; the priest and the prophet have erred through strong drink, they are swallowed up of wine, they are out of the way through strong drink; they err in vision, they stumble in judgment. For all tables are full of vomit and filthiness, so that there is no place clean (Isaiah 28:7–8).

> And I brought you into a plentiful country, to eat the fruit thereof and the goodness thereof; but when ye entered, ye defiled my land, and made mine heritage an abomination. The priests said not, Where is the LORD? and they that handle the law knew me not: the pastors also transgressed against me, and the prophets prophesied by Baal, and walked after things that do not profit (Jeremiah 2:7–8).

But surely this failure only occurred with ancient Israel—that physical nation, right? Spiritual Israel—the New Testament Church—with the power of God's Holy Spirit indwelling, would never behave in the same way, would they?

Behavior of the First-century Church of God

Unfortunately, the written history of the first-century church—the true spiritual Body of Jesus Christ—was no better than that of the original *church in the wilderness* (Acts 7:38). Though called out of this world to become God's peculiar treasure, and sanctified by the gift of the Holy Spirit, within forty years of the death and ascension of Jesus Christ, they too corrupted themselves through perversions of the true doctrine and became largely cut off from God. Ironically, the Apostle Paul prophesied in God's name to the Church with an ominous warning about their future, just as Moses had prophesied earlier to Israel.

Take heed therefore unto yourselves, and to all the flock, over the which the Holy [Spirit] hath made you overseers, to feed the church of God, which he hath purchased with his own blood. For I know this, that after my departing shall grievous wolves enter in among you, not sparing the flock. Also of your own selves shall men arise, speaking perverse things, to draw away disciples after them. Therefore watch, and remember, that by the space of three years I ceased not to warn every one night and day with tears (Acts 20:28–31).

Not only did God prophesy through Paul that the true church would begin to champion corrupt teachings, but also that perversion would spring from the faithless acts of church leaders—the elders—who would cease to defend the Truth originally delivered to that chosen Body by Jesus Christ Himself!

Beloved, when I gave all diligence to write unto you of the common salvation, it was needful for me to write unto you, and exhort you that ye should earnestly contend for the faith which was once delivered unto the saints. For there are certain men crept in unawares, who were before of old ordained to this condemnation, ungodly men, turning the grace of our God into lasciviousness, and denying the only Lord God, and our Lord Jesus Christ. . . . These are murmurers, complainers, walking after their own lusts; and their mouth speaketh great swelling words, having men's persons in admiration because of advantage. But, beloved, remember ye the words which were spoken before of the apostles of our Lord Jesus Christ; How that they told you there should be mockers in the last time, who should walk after their own ungodly lusts. These be they who separate themselves, sensual, having not the Spirit (Jude 3–4, 16–19).

So the legitimate Body of Jesus Christ in the first century—the true church of God—actually *abandoned the Truth*, just like the original Israelites did. By the early 90s A.D., the Apostle John had been cast out of the physical assembly of the church, and was forced to minister to only a small scattered remnant left of those who still loved the original teachings.

I wrote unto the church: but Diotrephes, who loveth to have the preeminence among them, receiveth us not. Wherefore, if I come, I will remember his deeds which he doeth, prating against us with malicious words: and not content therewith, neither doth he himself receive the brethren, and forbiddeth them that would, and casteth them out of the church (3 John 9–10).

It was this perverted leader, Diotrephes (as well as many others across Asia Minor), who held sway with the assembly in that region, not the true apostles, like John. The main assembly—within forty years of the beginning of the Christian faith through the gift of the Holy Spirit (Acts 2)—no longer wanted to hear those foundational doctrines confirmed. They had moved on to teachings they considered to be superior, but which God considered to be Baal worship. These were the "Church Fathers" of the late first century and second century who repudiated Sabbath-keeping in favor of

Sunday worship, embraced the Trinity heresy to explain the nature of God, and every other perversion that became ultimately synonymous with *Christianity* so-called from that time down to the present.

But what about God's true church in our own time? Why should there have to be a modern-day parallel? After all, just because the first-century church was seduced from within through the subtleties of Baal worship, should we not expect the *legitimate* church of God in our own time—founded upon the *true* Jesus Christ—to have remained faithful? What does the Bible say?

Prophecies of the Last-day Church

The New Testament not only records a history of what happened to the first-century church, but also many prophecies applying specifically to that Body that would exist *immediately prior and leading to* the Second Coming of Jesus Christ.

Now the Spirit speaketh expressly, that *in the latter times* some shall depart from the faith, giving heed to seducing spirits, and doctrines of devils; Speaking lies in hypocrisy; having their conscience seared with a hot iron (1 Timothy 4:1–2) [emphasis mine].

In fact, the Bible really applies *primarily* to that church of the last days. Concerning all of the events chronicled in the Old Testament, Paul wrote:

Now all these things happened unto them for ensamples: and they are written for our admonition, *upon whom the ends of the world are come.* Wherefore let him that thinketh he standeth take heed lest he fall (1 Corinthians 10:11–12) [emphasis mine].

24   A PECULIAR TREASURE

This includes those very prophecies Moses spoke concerning the "latter days."

> For I know that after my death ye will utterly corrupt yourselves, and turn aside from the way which I have commanded you; and evil will befall you *in the latter days*; because ye will do evil in the sight of the LORD, to provoke him to anger through the work of your hands (Deuteronomy 31:29) [emphasis mine].

Moses was not just speaking and writing a condemnation of the Israelites of his own day. Remember, these were God's inspired words—not his own—and even without Moses' knowledge, God was recording a warning for the Church He intended to raise up in those days *just prior* to the end of this age. Many have assumed that Paul (and other apostles), by such statements about *the latter days*, were mistaken in believing they themselves would live to see the Second Coming of Christ. Is that true? Who is it that wrote these New Testament books, including every word within them? Is it God, or was it fallible men? Who is it that wrote:

> For the Lord himself shall descend from heaven with a shout, with the voice of the archangel, and with the trump of God: and the dead in Christ shall rise first: *Then we which are alive and remain shall be caught up together with them in the clouds, to meet the Lord in the air*: and so shall we ever be with the Lord (1 Thessalonians 4:16–17) [emphasis mine].

By using the pronoun, "we," did Paul really believe that some to whom he was writing in the first century would still be alive *physically* at the return of Christ? What about this warning:

> Now we beseech you, brethren, by the coming of our Lord Jesus Christ, and *by our gathering together unto him*, That ye be not soon shaken in mind, or be troubled, neither by

spirit, nor by word, nor by letter as from us, *as that the day of Christ is at hand* (2 Thessalonians 2:1–2) [emphasis mine].

Was Paul truly mistaken about the time of Christ's return? This is a common conclusion among many. But if that is so, then God allowed human error—the presumptions of false reasoning—to be recorded in His Holy Bible. Do you believe that is true? If not, then what instead must be true? It actually confirms that Paul (as well as the other inspired writers) was only penning the words that God *dictated to him to be carried down to the last-day Church*—God's peculiar treasure—which would exist in the days *just before* the consummation of this age.

And as he sat upon the mount of Olives, the disciples came unto him privately, saying, Tell us, when shall these things be? and what shall be the sign of thy coming, and of the [consummation of the age]? And Jesus answered and said unto them, Take heed that no man deceive you. For many shall come in my name, saying, I am Christ; and shall deceive many (Matthew 24:3–5).

Why did Jesus Christ not only speak these words, but then ensure that they were carried down in writing to our very time? Was it merely an historical record of a one-time conversation He had with those early disciples? Or was He recording a specific message for those He knew would be called in a much later generation? And if Christ's own words were for a last-day Body of believers, why is it so difficult to recognize that the words of Paul, Peter, Jude, and John were *likewise* recorded *by Jesus Christ* for the last-day Church?

What else did God's warnings through the apostles to that last-day church reveal?

This know also, that in the last days perilous times shall come. For men shall be lovers of their own selves, covetous, boasters, proud, blasphemers, disobedient to parents, unthankful, unholy, Without natural affection, trucebreakers, false accusers, incontinent, fierce, despisers of those that are good, Traitors, heady, highminded, lovers of pleasures more than lovers of God; *Having a form of godliness, but denying the power thereof*: from such turn away. For of this sort are they which creep into houses, and lead captive silly women laden with sins, led away with divers lusts, *Ever learning, and never able to come to the knowledge of the truth.* Now as Jannes and Jambres withstood Moses, *so do these also resist the truth*: men of corrupt minds, reprobate concerning the faith (2 Timothy 3:1–8) [emphasis mine].

This is not a condemnation of religionists of the world (Catholic and Protestant) who have *always* been deceived and have never yet been called by God. This is a prophecy concerning God's true people, the ones in the last days *who were called*, and *who did have* a chance to understand. As quoted before from 1 Timothy 4:1, Paul said, "in the latter times some shall *depart* from the faith, giving heed to seducing spirits, and doctrines of devils." A man cannot depart from that which he never first possessed. To depart requires one first to have *known and understood* the Truth, even as Israel of old had been *given* that Truth, but then later forsook it. The church of the last days, wherever it may be, was prophesied to do the very same thing.

Preach the word; be instant in season, out of season; reprove, rebuke, exhort with all longsuffering and doctrine. For the time will come when *they will not endure sound doctrine*; but after their own lusts shall they heap to themselves teachers, having itching ears; And *they shall turn away their ears from the truth, and shall be turned unto fables* (2 Timothy 4:2–4) [emphasis mine].

The true Church of God in the last days either already has, or yet will, turn away from the revealed Truth of God, just as its forerunners did. God said so.

> Let no man deceive you by any means: for that day shall not come, except there come *a falling away* first, and that man of sin be revealed, the son of perdition (2 Thessalonians 2:3) [emphasis mine].

This phrase, "falling away," is the Greek word, *apostasia*. It means, specifically, a defection from the Truth! It is a last-day prophecy confirming that the true Church of God—His peculiar treasure—would *depart* from the Truth upon which that Body would first be founded. That organized church would *begin* with the Truth as a revelation from God, but in time would change its teachings to embrace concepts that God despises.

What does all of this tell us about attributes of the true Church of God in the last days? If we are seeking to find the legitimate work of God, what should we be looking for as far as its prophesied *behavior*? It is not a church that begins with and holds firm to the correct teachings of God. If you are looking for a church that has always set a perfect example and continues consistently in good behavior and positive fruits, you are sure to miss it altogether. God's peculiar treasure of the last days is a body that will do exactly what its historical counterparts have always done. It will begin with the blessings of God in a miraculous work from its inception. But over time, it will allow men with nefarious personal agendas, especially its ministry, to destroy it from within:

> Woe be unto the pastors that destroy and scatter the sheep of my pasture! saith the LORD. Therefore thus saith the LORD God of Israel against the pastors that feed my people; Ye have scattered my flock, and driven them away, and have not visited them: behold, I will visit upon you the evil of your doings, saith the LORD. . . . The anger of the LORD shall not

return, until he have executed, and till he have performed the thoughts of his heart: *in the latter days ye shall consider it perfectly* (Jeremiah 23:1–2, 20) [emphasis mine].

So What About the Radio Church of God?

We are trying to answer the question, is it possible that the twentieth-century work of Herbert Armstrong was actually the inspired biblical fulfillment of God's last-day Church? Could the Radio Church of God potentially have been His peculiar treasure in our very own time? It is certainly a church that began with monumental impetus over the first forty years of its existence, and then gradually began to change its teachings as no other church in history has ever done, ultimately repudiating its very doctrinal foundation. It is also a church that began to splinter in the face of serious turmoil and internal strife, ultimately rejecting those members who still insisted upon holding to the original doctrines, and leaving those former believers scattered and disillusioned.

According to these biblical prophecies, we certainly cannot rule out the legitimacy of that work under Herbert Armstrong at this juncture, because the Radio Church of God experienced exactly the kind of initial blessing and ultimate corruption that God indicated must absolutely come to pass. Perhaps those who are skeptical will still not be convinced. But it still merits following the trail and completing our investigation.

Next, we want to summarize the basic doctrines that set Herbert Armstrong's work apart from all other churches. Did his teachings meet the Bible's *signature profile* of the true Church as opposed to the world's false notions of Christianity? Then we want to summarize some of the key historical events that occurred in the early formation and expansion of the Radio Church of God, likewise examining the institutional forces that came to bear upon that body over time. If it was the true Church of God, then it must have possessed those doctrines that distinguish it from all imposters. Did it? It must also have endured the eventual destabilization and destruction prophesied to befall that last-day Body. Many writers have tried to interpret that history. But all of these other writers have failed to recognize the underlying reasons for much of that which transpired. The true history is there for anyone who desires to confirm the facts and to consider it objectively. When evaluated without the entrenched preconceptions of most former members, or the skepticism of disdainful onlookers, the actual facts are quite startling. It is a story that can be told, and it should be told.

CHAPTER THREE
TESTING HERBERT ARMSTRONG AGAINST OUR BENCHMARK

Wherever that true Church may be found, it is one prophesied first *to possess the revealed Truth of God,* but then *to forsake* those priceless teachings, just as did the ancient Israelites *and* the New Testament church of the first century. Is it possible that the work of Herbert Armstrong indeed may have been the fulfillment of some of those very last-day prophecies? It could only be so if he was called by God and given divine inspiration to proclaim the true tenets of God's plan and purpose for man's salvation. Were Herbert Armstrong's teachings absolutely consistent with those biblical principles that distinguish the true Church of God from the counterfeit religious movements extant in the world today? Let us examine that doctrinal history and then decide. The five *test points* we have already highlighted (chapter one) are certainly not an exclusive list, but they indeed do help to narrow the field remarkably in evaluating all of those religious works that claim to adhere to the Bible as God's revealed Word.

THE TIMES OF SALVATION

What did Mr. Armstrong teach concerning the opportunity to know and accept Jesus Christ? Did he profess the common ideas espoused by most churches, that salvation is open and obligatory for all men right now? From a 1952 issue of *The Good News,* here is a confirmation of his fundamental teaching:

It would APPEAR from the common teachings that salvation is open to EVERYONE *today* and that all one has to do now is to join a church and be "saved." IS EVERYONE FREE

TO ACCEPT SALVATION AND BE SAVED ANY TIME ONE WISHES TO BE? Or are some *blinded* to salvation in this day? . . .

Paul, speaking to the Romans concerning their Gentile forefathers, said: "As they did not like to retain God in their knowledge, God gave them over to a REPROBATE MIND. . . being filled with all unrighteousness, fornication, wickedness . . . full of envy" (Romans 1:28–29). Again, "For God hath concluded them (*all* mankind) all in unbelief that he may have mercy on all," Romans 11:32. The GENTILES were blinded then and THEY ARE BLINDED TODAY! ALL NATIONS are blinded today! ("Is This the Only Day of Salvation?," *The Good News*, July 1952, pp. 5–6)

Was that principle intended to glorify an "elite few" at the expense of the many? In Herbert Armstrong's view, did any human being, Jew or Gentile, have any "natural advantage" in the salvation process? What did he clarify further, in the same 1952 *The Good News* article, p. 6, concerning natural-born Israelites?

A FEW had received the chance of salvation—but notice verse 7 [Romans 11]: ". . . the REST (the VAST MAJORITY) were BLINDED." The same is true today: the few, whosoever *will*, may come to God, but the vast majority *won't* because they are blinded to God's truth by thinking their ways are better. Jesus *never once* said that everyone is in this age called to salvation. Paul said: "Not many wise men after the flesh, not many mighty, not many noble, are called." (I Cor. 1:26). Only those drawn by the Spirit of God and who come through Jesus can approach God, John 6:44.

Did Herbert Armstrong thereby perceive a cardinal principle of the Bible which mainstream Christianity despises and rejects? Yes, indeed. Most professing Christians love to quote John 3:16 as proof that anyone who wishes can accept Jesus Christ at any given time: "that whosoever believeth in him should not perish, but have everlasting life." But it is amazing how they refuse to acknowledge the very *clear and simple* statements of Christ concerning what it means to *really believe* in Him. Herbert Armstrong challenged mainstream dogma by pointing out that Jesus *nowhere* said that all people automatically have salvation opened to them *at every time in every age.* He further proved it by emphasizing texts like John 6:44: "No man can come to me, except the Father which hath sent me draw him." If all men have an *automatic right* to "accept Jesus" whenever *they* choose, why this kind of emphatic pronouncement? In fact, John 6:44 became an "identifying text" expounded throughout Herbert Armstrong's ministry. While other churches avoided it like the plague (as well as 1 Corinthians 1:26, etc.), he fearlessly emphasized *all of the texts* that, assembled together with simple clarity, demonstrate the true revelation of Jesus Christ on this topic of a necessary calling—the choice and timing of God, not man.

What did he teach concerning those who have lived and died in this world, never having been given the opportunity to date of a true calling by Jesus Christ? Are they doomed to eternal oblivion? Continuing from the same 1952 *The Good News* article, p. 7:

> Now, if God is Just and it is He who has blinded most of the people that ever lived, from understanding his laws and the grace which they must accept to be saved, then He will have to remove the blindness to give them a chance—their first chance—will he not? YES!—and he has PROMISED TO DO IT!
>
> "And he will DESTROY in this mountain the face of the COVERING CAST OVER ALL PEOPLE, and the VAIL THAT IS SPREAD OVER ALL NATIONS," Isaiah 25:7. It is no stigma or disgrace to your loved ones or others that they are among those that are blinded *now.* God's PLAN called for the removal of blindness from only a *few* NOW. It is HIS responsibility! . . .
>
> AFTER *blinded* man has had a lifetime of sad *experience* living by *his own* way of life, then is resurrected back to this earth and has *his blindness removed* so that he can SEE and PRACTICE GOD'S WAY OF LIFE—the only way that leads to

happiness, and can SEE HOW MUCH BETTER GOD'S WAY IS THAN HIS OWN—*then*, AND ONLY THEN, it is that God REALLY starts to save the *vast majority* of mankind and give eternal life to those who are willing to come under his loving rule and aid HIM in administering wisely the great power HE will give to them!

So we see that a key identifier of the true Church of God—documented in the Bible concerning multiple and distinct times of salvation for human beings—was certainly taught by Herbert Armstrong. What about our second key identifying mark of the true Church?

THE ISRAEL OF GOD

Did Herbert Armstrong understand the significance of the type/antitype role of Israel in God's Master Plan for the salvation of all mankind? Here is what he wrote in the 1967 edition of his book, *The United States and British Commonwealth in Prophecy*:

We must realize, if we would understand, a peculiar fact. The Holy Bible is the particular Book of a definite nationality—the children of ISRAEL.

It is undeniable! Its history, from Genesis to Revelation, is primarily the history of one nation or people—the Israelites. Other nations are mentioned only insofar as they come into contact with Israel.

All its prophecy, too, pertains primarily to this people of ISRAEL, and to other nations only insofar as they come into contact with Israel.

The Bible tells of these Israelites and their God. It was inspired by the God of Abraham, Isaac and Jacob, committed to writing through Israelites exclusively, and was preserved until after the New Testament was written by these Israelites.

In its sacred passages we read that all the promises and the covenants of God, all the sonship and the glory, belong solely to Israel (Romans 9:4). . . .

In Old Testament times, His people were the people of Israel In New Testament times, His people are those of God's own Church—the truly converted, Spirit-begotten Christians! (Chapters III, p. 14; XI, p. 159)

Herbert Armstrong certainly understood, therefore, the significance that God had placed upon His peculiar treasure—Israel—as an instrument for offering salvation to all mankind. Wherever the true Church of God exists, it will possess this knowledge as a key in applying the physical and spiritual lessons found within God's salvation plan. Any church that ignores the special role of Israel—both physically *and spiritually*—is offering proof that it is not the true Church of God at all.

As mentioned before, the problem with professing belief in the unique role of Israel as God's chosen people is the charge by many of exclusivism, divisiveness, and even racism. To hold to a belief that no one can have a personal relationship with Jesus Christ without being specially called, that few at this time are receiving such a call, and that we are required to become part of Israel to be saved, is guaranteed to elicit charges of hatemongering. The *politically-correct* position, especially in this twenty-first century, is to accept *all peoples, all ideas,* and even while pursuing your own chosen religious beliefs freely, to be sure to allow that *other beliefs* are equally as "right" as yours, and that yours is not "the only way" to salvation. In general, any manner of bizarre beliefs will be tolerated in our modern societies as long as we leave room for the practices of *every other group* as being "right" also, no matter how perverted. In this day and age, about the most criminal label you can receive is that of being *intolerant* or *exclusive.* And the true teachings of the Bible about the singular path to human salvation—through Jesus Christ and His chosen people—is a recipe for controversy, ridicule, and loathing.

There is a reason that Jesus Christ was hated and martyred. It was not that many of His individual doctrines were so intolerable, but that He taught them as the *exclusive* requirement for salvation:

> Then Jesus said unto them, Verily, verily, I say unto you, Except ye eat the flesh of the Son of man, and drink his blood, ye have no life in you. . . . When Jesus knew in himself that his disciples murmured at it, he said unto them, Doth this offend you? . . . And he said, Therefore said I unto you, that no man can come unto me, except it were given unto him of my Father. From that time many of his disciples went back, and walked no more with him (John 6:53, 61, 65–66).

In the same way that Christ's *exclusive* message became the catalyst for His own persecution and eventual martyrdom, rest assured this same dynamic *has been* and *yet will be* a factor for any who will walk *legitimately* in His footsteps:

> Then shall they deliver you up to be afflicted, and shall kill you: and ye shall be hated of all nations for my name's sake (Matthew 24:9).

> They shall put you out of the synagogues: yea, the time cometh, that whosoever killeth you will think that he doeth God service. And these things will they do unto you, because they have not known the Father, nor me (John 16:2–3).

So persecution is assured for those who embrace the real Truth, wherever that may be found. But truth is still truth. How did Herbert Armstrong succinctly describe the makeup of spiritual Israel—the Church—in relationship to that physical nation of old?

> YOU HAVE TO BECOME AN ISRAELITE TO BE SAVED! You have heard a lot of *false* and *anti-Scriptural* teaching leading you to suppose salvation is for Gentiles. IT IS NOT!

TESTING HERBERT ARMSTRONG AGAINST OUR BENCHMARK

All the PROMISES were given to ISRAEL. Why?

Listen! Read carefully, and UNDERSTAND! All nations had gone into anti-God, false, pagan religions. In such a God-rejecting world, God raised up, from the children of Abraham, Isaac, and Jacob, in the days of Moses, a special nation to be HIS nation—to be a *light* to the non-believing Gentiles. Incidentally, the very name *Gentile* MEANS unbeliever.

God gave this special called-out nation HIS right ways of life—and *to them* were given the PROMISES which include salvation. (Romans 9:4.) But, when a Gentile-born person repents, accepts Christ and receives God's Holy Spirit, then he becomes, spiritually, an Israelite, a child of Abraham, and an heir of the promises (Gal. 2:28–29).

Salvation is of the Jews (John 4:24). Salvation, however, is for EVERYONE that believes (in *living* faith, not dead faith)—to the Jew first, and, through Christ, also to the Gentile (Romans 1:16).

YOU can have no salvation *unless* you become, spiritually, a JEW! (Romans 2:28–29.) Of course, through disobedience, all natural-born Israelites have been *cut off* from the Promises and God's Salvation—but they may receive it, like all others, *through Christ!* (Romans 11:17–18, 23–26.) ("Which Day Is the Christian Sabbath?," *The Plain Truth*, October 1962, pp. 41–42)

This leads us to the next important test to identify the true Church of God.

THE TRUE CHURCH IS NOT ARROGANT OR RACIST!

The next key identifier to distinguish the true Church of God is that it does not take credit for its own special place in God's plan, and certainly does not view any other human being as inferior or beyond hope. As mentioned previously, among many who have attached themselves to the idea of being "the Israel of God," you will find many groups that twist this concept to justify persecution or disdain toward those they consider "inferior" (i.e.: the Christian Identity movement). This, too, is a ploy used by Satan to besmirch the truth about God's Master Plan and to make it seem evil. With so many who have justified violence, wars, and even genocide while promoting the cause of "an elect few," it is no wonder there is such a backlash today against *any* who profess belief that *some people* were called out to be "special" to God. But what was Herbert Armstrong's teaching in this regard? Did he consider that a "chosen few" today are better than everyone else? Was his doctrine used to justify hatefulness and intolerance toward the rest of humanity? In the December 1952 issue of *The Good News*, p. 13, we find this citation as an example of his consistent position on this critical point:

> GOD CALLED Israel out of Egyptian slavery to perform the most important mission any nation has been given in all the history of mankind.
>
> Israel is not God's "favorite" people, or "pet" nation. They were not chosen for any goodness of their own (Deut. 7:6–9).
>
> God called them so He could reveal *Himself* as Creator and Ruler of the universe—so that through them He could reveal his *plan*, his laws, and his blessings to all nations (Deut. 4:5–9).

This describes accurately and succinctly what members of the Radio Church of God were taught consistently over many years. They were taught that ancient Israel's failings were a warning to spiritual Israel of today—the New Testament Church—and that we can just as easily become failures if we take our calling for granted or assume any "right" to salvation:

> Let us therefore fear, lest, a promise being left us of entering into his rest, any of you should seem to come short of it. For

unto us was the gospel preached, as well as unto them: but the word preached did not profit them, not being mixed with faith in them that heard it (Hebrews 4:1–2).

Members of the Radio Church of God were taught not to become smug by virtue of being "called." That calling brings serious accountability for acquiring the loving and merciful nature of Jesus Christ, and rejecting the arrogance of those natural-born Jews whom Christ criticized strongly as hypocrites for using their physical pedigree (as children of Abraham) as an excuse to manifest hatred and indifference toward others (John 8:39–41). Herbert Armstrong taught that *the called* are being judged *now*, based upon their works to either please or displease God, while the uncalled world is *not* being held accountable as yet. Therefore, the wise individual will take heed and focus upon overcoming his own carnal nature, learning to show mercy to those who yet have not been offered that priceless opportunity to know Jesus Christ. It is a doctrinal approach that is anything but racist.

WHAT ABOUT THE TEN COMMANDMENTS?

So Herbert Armstrong understood the Bible truth concerning the need for a special calling from God, the fact that there are differential times offered for those callings in His dealing with mankind, and that Israel is the instrument through which that salvation plan is being sponsored. But what did he believe and teach concerning the Law of God? Did he believe—like so many others—that Christ "did away" with the Ten Commandments? Here are some quotations that will confirm the original doctrine of the Radio Church of God concerning sin and law:

NEARLY everyone has been taught that the old covenant was the ten commandment law—that the new covenant contains only grace and promises, but no law. Hence, it is argued that since the old covenant has been abolished God's law has also been abolished.

This teaching would lead you to believe that the law of God was harsh, cruel, and enslaving—that the FAULT of the old covenant was with the law, and since *God* gave the law, the FAULT must have been His! . . .

If the fault were with the law, then the law would *not* have been perfect; but David said, "The law of the Lord *is perfect*, converting the soul" (Psalm 19:7). . . .

There is a great deal of needless misunderstanding about that which constituted the first covenant with Israel. In Exodus, the 19th chapter, God made arrangements to declare the conditions of His covenant to the people. Then in the 20th chapter God spoke every word of the ten commandments.

The ten commandments are a perfect and complete law in themselves. When the Eternal God finished speaking them "HE ADDED NO MORE. AND HE WROTE THEM IN TWO TABLES OF STONE" (Deut. 5:22).

The ten commandments were *a distinct part of* the terms of the old covenant to which Israel agreed. . . .

When God spoke the old covenant to Israel at the time they were brought out of Egypt, He did not command them "concerning burnt offerings and sacrifices: But this thing commanded I them saying, Obey my voice, and I will be your God, and ye shall be my people" (Jeremiah 7:22, 23).

The ceremonial and ritualistic laws were *added later because of transgressions and as a reminder of sin*—after the old covenant was sealed. . . .

Remember that the spiritual and civil laws were not instituted by the old covenant. They were already in existence and had to be included in the covenant. (See Genesis 26:5 and Exodus 16:28 and 18:16). ("The NEW Covenant—Does it Abolish God's Law?," *The Plain Truth*, April 1956, pp. 9–10)

Testing Herbert Armstrong Against Our Benchmark 41

We see then that Herbert Armstrong understood and taught that the Ten Commandments had been instituted *for man's benefit* from Creation, and were not done away by being incorporated *much later* into a special *temporary covenant* with ancient Israel. A body of law can never be annulled by revocation of a *later covenant agreement* having its own *separate and distinct* origin and purpose. That covenant did not bring the Law into existence, so neither can its annulment extinguish the Law. What we find is that Herbert Armstrong taught exactly what Jesus Christ Himself—as well as the apostles, including Paul—taught concerning the spiritual Law of God, that those rules of "right and wrong" for man's own good have *never been abolished.* Any group claiming so is proving thereby that it is *not* a legitimate spokesman for the true Christ at all.

The Sabbaths as a Sign

The final point we initially identified to help distinguish the majority of false churches from those few *that might possibly* represent the true Church of God, is their treatment of the commanded Sabbaths of the Bible. What did Herbert Armstrong teach about the fourth commandment specifically? Again, from the October 1962 issue of *The Plain Truth*, pp. 30–32, 41:

> Later, after both the Ten Commandments and the Old Covenant had been made *complete,* ratified, put in force and effect God made ANOTHER TOTALLY SEPARATE and eternally-binding covenant with HIS PEOPLE. . . .
>
> God, through "The Word" (John 1:1–3) who became Jesus Christ, *made* the Sabbath. He made it *for* man.
>
> But WHY?
>
> What PURPOSE does it serve? . . .
>
> That is why this special, separate SABBATH COVENANT is important. For it reveals THE REASON—the basic *purpose.* . . .
>
> In Exodus 20:8 we saw that He commanded to "keep it HOLY"—God *made* it HOLY TIME, and commanded us to *keep* it holy—NOT TO PROFANE WHAT IS HOLY TO GOD.

Now study this special covenant a little further:

"... for it is a sign between me and you throughout your generations; that ye may know that I am the LORD that doth sanctify you...."

NOTE THOSE WORDS CAREFULLY!! It is the *sign* that IDENTIFIES to them *who is their GOD!* It is the sign *by which we may KNOW that He is the LORD!!* It identifies *GOD!...*

Jesus Christ says "The Sabbath was made for MAN"—for all mankind! Remember? It was made WHEN man was made—at the time of Adam! There were no Jews then! God Almighty does not have one standard for Jews and another for Gentiles. No Gentile can become a Christian *until* he becomes an ISRAELITE—read Ephesians 2:11–22. God says, through the apostle Paul to GENTILES: "There is neither Jew nor Greek . . . for ye are all ONE in Christ Jesus. And if ye (Gentiles) be Christ's, then are ye Abraham's seed (children), and heirs according to the promise." (Galatians 3:28–29.)

This is only a single condensed citation among hundreds which could have been quoted to confirm one of the bedrock doctrines of the Radio Church of God from its inception. Belief in the seventh-day Sabbath as a key identifier of the true Church was one of Herbert Armstrong's most foundational teachings. As you will soon see, it was his wife, Loma—by the rejection of Sunday worship and change to Sabbath-keeping—who originally spurred Herbert Armstrong into his first religious studies. So there is no question that his work was grounded upon respect for this distinctive sign of the true Church of God. Furthermore, his profession of the requirement to keep God's *annual Sabbaths*—the Holy Days listed in Leviticus 23—certainly set his work apart even from those few groups in the early twentieth century that were honoring the weekly Sabbath. More on that later.

The Only Identifiers?

Thus far we have analyzed only one broad category of biblical understanding—and Herbert Armstrong's doctrinal positions on those particular points—to help narrow our search for the true Church of God. That broad category has included five basic points concerning Israel as a firstfruits harvest in God's plan, the Ten Commandments and the Sabbath as a sign marking the true people of God, their orientation to that special calling, and their role within a *much greater plan* that God is orchestrating to bring salvation to the whole world. But are these the only distinguishing marks of the true Church? Not at all.

Historically, Mr. Armstrong listed *the name* of the church as another defining signature of God's true people. He stated that the Bible shows the name should always be the *Church of God*, and that any church not using that name is illegitimate. While it is certainly true that this criterion was useful in the early twentieth century in narrowing the field of religious works, today there are so many groups calling themselves "Church of God" in some form—especially among the many groups that have sprung from the Worldwide Church of God—that *the name itself* has ceased to provide the distinguishing mark that it once did. But are there other indicators that still make God's true church stand out from the others? Certainly.

If your interest is piqued enough at this point to entertain *the possibility* that the teachings of Herbert Armstrong *just might* correspond with real biblical Truth, then it is time that you become familiar with the *actual life and work* of the man in question. In Part II, we will summarize the key events that transpired in the lives of Herbert and Loma Armstrong, providing a basis for continuing our analysis of his doctrine and personal legacy.

PART II

SYNOPSIS OF LIFE AND WORK
OF HERBERT AND LOMA ARMSTRONG

CHAPTER FOUR
EARLY LIFE AND MINISTRY 1892–1934

Before going any further with detailed analysis, it is time to pause and go back to the beginning to provide a *summary* of key events that defined the life of Herbert Armstrong, as well as important benchmarks in the history of the Worldwide Church of God in general. Many who witnessed those significant events in earlier decades are now gone, and newer ones just learning about that history may never yet have heard the story expounded in a succinct manner.

It can be overwhelming to take mountains of facts and figures and make cohesive sense of them all. Reading Mr. Armstrong's autobiography will certainly tell the tale, but that requires digesting over one thousand pages of his writings. During the heyday of the church, members often heard stories repeated of how Herbert Armstrong first became interested in religion, how the Radio Church of God and Ambassador College were founded, and how that work grew over time. But as with all such history, it is easily forgotten, even by those who lived through part of it, let alone cloaked in obscurity for those to whom it is all so foreign. So what follows is a relatively *condensed outline*, taken primarily from the *Autobiography of Herbert W. Armstrong*, of key events in the life and work of the man and his wife.

BEGINNINGS

Herbert Armstrong was born in 1892 in Des Moines, Iowa, to parents who were Quakers. He regularly attended church with his family and was indoctrinated into the most common Protestant beliefs about the nature of God, salvation, and Christian duty, but as a young adult he showed little personal interest in religion.

48   A PECULIAR TREASURE

In 1910, at age 18, his Uncle Frank encouraged him to pursue a career in advertising, rather than go to university. He landed his first job writing want ads for the *Daily Caller* newspaper in Des Moines. Over the years, that advertising experience helped him change his objective from trying to use vocabulary *beyond everyone*, to learning to speak and write so that *all* could understand. He learned to eschew boring outlines and instead to make written concepts "pop" with interest. He applied himself with great ambition to becoming a successful businessman, educating himself, creating his own opportunities by *thinking big*, and working harder than anyone else. He sought to learn from those who had already achieved great success, and he possessed exceptional confidence in his own abilities to achieve anything he chose. More than that, this is how he described himself as a young man:

> In those days I had developed a very excessive case of swelled-head. I was snappy, confident, conceited—yet *sincere*, and intending to be completely honest ("The Autobiography of Herbert W. Armstrong," *The Plain Truth*, November 1957, p. 4).

On July 31, 1917, Herbert married Loma Dillon, a schoolteacher his own age from a very small town in Iowa. In the 1967 revised autobiography, he elaborates that he was introduced to her as his *third cousin*, but also later states that Loma's father was first cousin to his own mother, which if so, actually made Herbert and Loma second cousins (*Autobiography of Herbert W. Armstrong*, 1967, p. 186). He described Loma this way:

> Also, from the instant when she first came *bounding* in at my aunt's farm, I had noticed she was almost something of a tom-boy—active, very alert. Whatever she did, she did it quickly. I learned later that her brothers dubbed her with two nick-names—"She-*bang*" and "Cyclone!" She was full of fun, yet serious—with the unspoiled wholesomeness of an

EARLY LIFE AND MINISTRY 1892–1934   49

Iowa country girl. And, most important of all, strength of character! ("The Autobiography of Herbert W. Armstrong," *The Plain Truth*, July 1958, p. 21)

They married in Chicago, where he was living and working at the time, but expecting that at any moment he would be drafted into the Army (the United States had just declared war on Germany on April 6). Although willing and eager to serve, he had been classified as "Class IV, Noncombatant," not only because he was newly married, but probably more so because they were already expecting a baby in May of the next year. Beverly Lucile was born May 9, 1918, and then Dorothy Jane on July 7, 1920.

Their two sons, Richard David and Garner Ted, were born sixteen months apart, in mid-1928 and early 1930 respectively. These two sons would later become pivotal in the work of their father, as this summary will show. Having been raised during the time of their parents' progressive conversion, that way of life would have a profound effect upon all of the children, although it is Garner Ted Armstrong who would become the key figure in the church storyline from the 1960s onward.

The flash economic depression of late 1920 destroyed Herbert's flourishing advertising business. He was still determined to rebuild it, but had not yet grasped that his future would lead in a totally different direction. Of that time period, he wrote:

For two years I stayed on in Chicago vainly attempting to revive a dead business. I didn't know, then, that God the Eternal was intervening to take from me and destroy my IDOL—the god I was placing before HIM! That false god was the vanity of desiring to be considered "IMPORTANT" and to reap and accumulate a big share of this world's material goods. . . .

From that time on I became like King Midas in reverse.

Everything I touched, as a business enterprise, turned to failure, and always by causes totally outside my control! It was frustrating, humiliating, and exceedingly painful ("The Autobiography of Herbert W. Armstrong," *The Plain Truth*, November 1958, pp. 25–26).

By June 1924, after some minor business successes but many more major setbacks, Herbert consented to Loma's request to make a trip to Salem, Oregon, to visit his parents and younger siblings whom he had not seen since their move out west twelve years previously. He was viewing this as a short-term excursion, fully intending to return to the Midwest by that same autumn, but she was convinced they would not be returning at all (*The Plain Truth*, January 1959, p. 30). After staying a few weeks with family in Salem, Herbert began exploring advertising openings in Portland, Oregon, and Vancouver, Washington. For months he was greatly encouraged, and the business opportunities continued to multiply. He was moving quickly to surpass even his greatest past accomplishments in Chicago, with expectations of even more incredible income within two or three years. And then, once again, by the fall of 1926, the bottom fell out. Here is how he described it:

> Now, with a new business of much greater promise, all my clients were suddenly removed from possibility of access, thru powers and forces entirely outside of my control.
>
> It seemed, indeed, as if some INVISIBLE and MYSTERIOUS HAND were causing the earth to simply swallow up whatever business I started. And indeed, that is precisely what was happening! God was knocking me down! But I was not yet *out!* . . .
>
> My morale was fast descending to subbasement. I was not so cocky or self-confident now. I was being "softened" for the unconditional surrender to God ("The Autobiography of Herbert W. Armstrong," *The Plain Truth*, February 1959, p. 17).

Challenged About the Sabbath

During this very same time frame, Herbert Armstrong was already reeling at home because of his wife's *new discovery* from the Bible concerning the seventh-day Sabbath. This would prove to be the very beginning of a total life change for both of them.

Loma had met Emma Runcorn, who awakened in her an interest in meaty Bible study, rather than just the superficial, socially-focused religion of her Methodist upbringing. Mrs. Runcorn and her husband, O. J., were members of Church of God, Seventh Day, a "Saturday-keeping church," and through Mrs. Runcorn, Loma came to see from the Bible that there was no authority for worshiping God on Sunday. She could not wait to share her discovery with her husband who she was certain would respond with similar enthusiasm. Instead, this is how he reacted:

My wife gone into religious *fanaticism*! I was horrified, outraged! What would my friends—my business associates say? . . .

I had been humiliated, my ego punctured, by unpreventable business reverses. But this was the greatest humiliation of all. This seemed more than my vanity and conceit could take. It was a mortifying blow.

"You can't tell me that all these Churches have been wrong all these years and centuries! They all teach that Sunday is the day to keep and hold church services, all but one strange, queer, fanatical sect."

My wife was broken up, too, when for the first time in our married life I threatened divorce. She was sobbing.

"But I can't help it," she sobbed. "I have seen with my own eyes *in the Bible* that God made holy the hours between Friday sunset and Saturday sunset. I would be disobeying God if I gave it up now—I would be lost!"

I was boiling with indignation and anger.

"I *know* that the BIBLE says we are to keep SUNDAY," I said sternly. "I don't know just *where*, but I do know that all these churches can't be wrong! I'm going to give you just one more chance, before your nonsensical fanaticism breaks up our home! I have an analytical mind. I've been trained in getting and analyzing *facts*! Now I'm going to research the Bible! I'm going to find *where* the Bible commands us to observe SUNDAY. I'LL PROVE IT TO YOU IN THE BIBLE! Will you *then* give up this fanaticism?"

She agreed—*IF* I could prove it, and show it to her *in the BIBLE*. That was good enough for me! I was supremely confident. I knew it was there. I knew I could find it!

And so it came about that in the fall of 1926, with my business gone—with but one laundry client left, whose advertising required only some thirty minutes of my time a week, that I was goaded into my first real study of the Bible ("The Autobiography of Herbert W. Armstrong," *The Plain Truth*, March 1959, pp. 7–8).

Thus, what began as a strategy to defend his own personal pride and reputation in the world would boomerang into a series of events leading him in the opposite direction.

From his sister-in-law's goading during the same time, he also began a study of the theory of evolution, which prompted him to start at the very beginning to either prove or to refute the existence of God. After six months of intensive study, he found that evolutionary theory was a charade, supported only by circular reasoning which could never hold water. He also found no evidence whatsoever in the Bible for worshiping on Sunday. Much to the contrary, he discovered that the real crux of the issue was obedience to the commands of a Creator versus the incessant rejection of any authority except that originating from men's minds. Here is how he described the aftermath of his study:

EARLY LIFE AND MINISTRY 1892–1934   53

IT WAS humiliating to have to admit my wife had been right, and I had been wrong, in the most serious argument that ever came between us.

It was shocking, disillusioning, to learn, after intensive study of the Bible for the first time, that what I had been taught from a child in Sunday School was, in so many basic points, the very opposite of what the Bible plainly states! ...

They had originated, as research in history had revealed, in paganism. Numerous Bible prophesies foretold it. The amazing, unbelievable TRUTH was, the SOURCE of these popular beliefs and practices of professing Christianity was, quite largely, paganism and human reasoning and custom, *NOT the Bible!*

I had first doubted, then searched for evidence, and found PROOF that God exists—that the Holy Bible is, literally, His divinely inspired revelation and instruction to mankind. I had learned that one's God is what a person OBEYS. The word "LORD" means MASTER—the one you OBEY! Most people, I had discovered, are obeying *false* gods, rebelling against the one true CREATOR who is the supreme RULER of the universe.

The argument was over a point of OBEDIENCE to GOD.

The opening of my eyes to the TRUTH brought me to the crossroads of my life. To accept it meant to throw in my lot with a class of humble and unpretentious people I had always looked upon as inferior. It meant being cut off from the high and the mighty and the wealthy of this world, to which I had aspired. It meant the final crushing of VANITY. It meant a total change of life! ("The Autobiography of Herbert W. Armstrong," *The Plain Truth*, April 1959, p. 6)

Finally making the choice to embrace that new path in 1927, Herbert Armstrong was baptized (in either May or June; *Autobiography of Herbert W. Armstrong*, 1967, p. 311) and then sought to pursue something that had true meaning in his life.

There is something interesting that many others have failed to remember or to emphasize in reciting this history. Notice how Mr. Armstrong speaks of the role his wife continued to play in his spiritual growth:

> From the time of my conversion Mrs. Armstrong has always studied with me. We didn't realize it then, but God was calling us *together*. We were always a team, working together in unity ("The Autobiography of Herbert W. Armstrong," *The Plain Truth*, May 1959, p. 10).

This fact will become much more significant in later years as the story unfolds.

Where Is the Church?

It is all very good to acknowledge a Creator God and a need to obey Him, but where to go from there? The very same Bible that Herbert Armstrong came to accept as God's Word also spoke of an assembly of true believers. Where was this "church"?

For some time, he fellowshipped with those families through whom he and Loma had first learned about the seventh-day Sabbath. These people were affiliated with an organization headquartered in Stanberry, Missouri, named Church of God, Seventh Day. But this group's doctrines were not all satisfying to Herbert, which is why he states emphatically that he never became an official member:

> Meanwhile, what was I to do? I was not at all convinced this was the one and only true Church. Yet, if it was not, *which one was?* This one came *closer* to the Bible qualifications than any I knew.
>
> Therefore, I began to fellowship with their scattered and few members in Oregon, while at the same time refraining from acknowledging membership. . . .

EARLY LIFE AND MINISTRY 1892–1934

And so it was, in this detached fellowship, that Mrs. Armstrong and I continued the first three and a half years of my ceaseless night and day STUDY of the Bible—of history, especially as connected with Biblical history and prophecy—and of pertinent allied subjects ("The Autobiography of Herbert W. Armstrong," *The Plain Truth*, August 1959, p. 15).

It was this continued personal study—and then writing his findings in article form—that first catapulted Herbert into greater visibility within that little church, eventually leading to his role as a teacher among them. Ironically, it is also this very same tenacity to study and to "prove the truth" that would eventually annoy those church leaders enough to solicit his expulsion.

TRYING TO BE A BIG SHOT?

Once Herbert Armstrong began to focus upon religion, what was his new personal mission, really? Detractors will argue that he simply co-opted religion as a new outlet to make himself rich and famous. His own account is much different. He describes a sincere and heartfelt desire to get to know the true Creator God and to learn the real truth about man's purpose for existence—to apply himself to something more rewarding than the vanity of the world. His voracious study and the writing of his findings were *foremost* instruments for his own learning, but would lead him nevertheless into the spotlight. He also states that his education took many years, one teaching at a time:

> But, as mentioned before, all this study and research had to be approached a single doctrine at a time. I was to be some years in getting to the very TRUNK of the tree of the very PURPOSE for which mankind was placed on earth, and getting clearly straightened out with a right understanding of God's PLAN.

56   A PECULIAR TREASURE

Nevertheless, having been a trained magazine article and advertising copy writer, the results of these studies were written up, purely for my own benefit, in article form. My wife began showing these articles to some women members of this Church of God who lived in Salem. Soon they began to urge me to preach before them. But becoming a preacher was the very *last* thing I had ever wanted to do. I felt an instinctive aversion to the idea.

Meanwhile, on their urging, a few of these articles had been mailed in to *The Bible Advocate* in Stanberry, Missouri. These articles began appearing on the front page ("The Autobiography of Herbert W. Armstrong," *The Plain Truth*, August 1959, pp. 15–16).

His first "sermon" in the summer of 1928 was a Sabbath lecture to a small group near Salem about a new "discovery" of truth concerning the Covenants. Although amateurish (according to Mrs. Armstrong's critique), it was well received and he was asked to speak on a regular basis to this little group that was without a local minister. Opposition came from Stanberry as church leaders worried that Armstrong was trying to create his own following out of their members. But an attempt to silence him by ceasing to publish his articles met with a significant backlash from the local people. Even though the ministerial leadership acquiesced under this pressure, the spirit of jealousy, competition and distrust among those leaders would be enduring.

INDUCTION INTO THE MINISTRY

In November 1930, many members of the church in Oregon came together in the town of Jefferson to form the Oregon Conference of the Church of God, for the purpose of holding tithes in the local area, rather than sending them to the "General Conference" in Stanberry, Missouri. Although the Armstrongs were not official members, Mr. Armstrong was asked to be the secretary of the meetings leading to

EARLY LIFE AND MINISTRY 1892–1934 57

this new organization. (It was this Oregon Conference that would ordain Herbert Armstrong as a minister the following year, not the Stanberry General Conference.)

After the Oregon Conference was formed, Herbert was asked by the new leadership to hold a public evangelistic campaign in December 1930. Designing a circular to advertise the meetings to be held in Harrisburg, Oregon, was the first time he began to use his twenty years of advertising experience in God's Work (*The Plain Truth*, November 1959, pp. 8–9). The results of this campaign were meager, but four new individuals were converted. They wanted to be baptized. But Herbert was not yet an ordained minister. With approval of a young minister of the Church of God, sent out from Stanberry headquarters, Herbert Armstrong performed his first baptisms.

Here is how he describes the result:

> This brought stern criticism from "authorities" higher up in the church. There was criticism because the Conference paid expenses when I was not even a member. In fact, from this time I was to meet continued criticism, opposition, persecution, and political maneuvering to discredit and remove me from the active ministry ("The Autobiography of Herbert W. Armstrong," *The Plain Truth*, November 1959, p. 31).

> Every person has his IDOL. God cannot receive and convert a human life until his idol has been smashed or torn from him. My idol had been an egotistical sense of self-importance—a cocky self-assurance—a passion to become successful in the eyes of the material world. God is creating in those He calls a righteous character which can be developed only through *experience;* and experience requires TIME. God has a lot of time—He is Eternal—He has always existed—He always will.

> It took *time* to eradicate from my heart the love of the praise of men. God gave me, instead, the false accusations,

the unwarranted oppositions, the scheming persecutions of people. It required *time* to bring me to a place where I no longer set my heart on material possessions and the finer things of this material world.

This process required not one or two years—not seven—but *four sevens!* For 28 financially lean and humiliating years out of *the very prime of life,* God continued to root out of my life and character this vain idolatry!

From the first and for many years I was the *least* of the ministers. I was the green-horn tail-ender among the ministers of the Church of God (world headquarters then Stanberry, Missouri). And I was never permitted to forget that fact! *God knew I needed this* ("The Autobiography of Herbert W. Armstrong," *The Plain Truth*, December 1959, p. 7).

It was Robert Taylor, a minister formerly of the Seventh Day Adventists from California, who began teaching the Oregon brethren in 1931 and who advocated ordaining Herbert officially into the ministry.

Mr. Taylor's suggestion meant a complete change in my life. In former years the idea of becoming a minister was the very *last* thing I should have wanted to do. But by June, 1931, I had been preaching a great deal for three and a half years. By this time my whole heart was in it. . . .

The decision was not difficult. God had now brought me to the place where I really "heard" the voice of Christ as if He were saying, "Come, and follow me, and I will make you a fisher of men" ("The Autobiography of Herbert W. Armstrong," *The Plain Truth*, December 1959, p. 9).

So, in an outdoor meeting in the rural area of Jefferson, Oregon, in June 1931, ministers and laity alike laid hands upon him:

Early Life and Ministry 1892–1934

I am sure it was the weight of the *experience,* from a spiritual and emotional standpoint, rather than the physical weight of hands and arms—but it seemed I was entirely weighted down with the heaviest load I had ever stood up under, as one of the ministers asked God in prayer to ordain me into the ministry of Jesus Christ and His Gospel.

To me this was symbolic of the tremendous responsibility that now came down on my head and shoulders (*The Plain Truth*, December 1959, p. 9).

The Question of Church Government

In the process of learning more of the truth of the Bible, Herbert Armstrong was confronted with questions about proper organization of the church. Once ordained as a minister, he became immersed immediately in the reality of church government as practiced by the Oregon Conference of the Church of God. Here is how he described the question that confronted him in 1931 and would take nearly twenty years to be resolved:

I was especially puzzled over the matter of church organization. Not yet having come to see and understand the plain and clear Bible teaching, I had gone along with the Oregon Conference in its idea of government by the lay members. In the Conference the governing board was composed solely of lay members. They hired and fired the ministers. . . .

But the question of church organization and government was to keep coming up in my mind for years, before it was finally to become clear. Remember, I still was driven by the persistent question: "*WHERE* is the one *true* Church—the same one Jesus founded?" This Church of God, with national headquarters at Stanberry, Missouri, seemed to be closer to it, according to the pattern in the Bible, than any—yet I was unable to reconcile myself that such a small, and especially

60

A PECULIAR TREASURE

such a *fruitless* church, could be that dynamic fruit-bearing spiritual organism in which, and through which CHRIST was working. Surely the instrument Christ was using would be more alive—more productive! Yet I had not found it! ("The Autobiography of Herbert W. Armstrong," *The Plain Truth*, January 1960, pp. 6–7).

So, for a number of years he tried his best to work within the structure that already existed among these Sabbath-keeping brethren. It is apparent that he never sought to make himself the center of attention. He seems sincerely to have desired to achieve "results" in helping the church to grow, and was very willing to "play second fiddle" behind other ministers in order to accomplish that overarching goal.

Poor Results From Collaboration

Both before and after his ordination, Herbert Armstrong worked in several instances with other ministers to organize evangelistic campaigns to spread the gospel. Here is what he said about the fruits of those projects:

My first evangelistic effort was conducted alone, at the end of 1930, in Harrisburg. There were conversions. In 1931 I was teamed with Elder Taylor, who had arrived from California. There were no results, except for the night it stormed the meeting out, and in a private Bible study in my room Mrs. Elmer Fisher had accepted the truth. I was teamed with Elder Roy Dailey. There were no results. He left Umapine. I continued alone, and *there were conversions.* Results then were small—indeed it was a small beginning, compared to the mounting world-wide harvest of today [1967]—but God was using me, and producing "fruit" ("The Autobiography of Herbert W. Armstrong," *The Plain Truth*, January 1960, p. 9).

This was the consistent pattern over those early years. Only when Mr. Armstrong "wound up" working alone did there seem to be any serious response. This seemingly accidental occurrence would become a consistent pattern, leading Herbert Armstrong eventually to conclude that God does indeed sponsor His divine work through particular chosen servants. It is one thing to claim such a role and then seek selfishly to substantiate it. It is quite another to have that role thrust upon one, becoming apparent through repeated events and proofs manifested through undeniable results.

Derailed for a Time

At the end of 1931, there was no salary available from the church to support Herbert and his family full time in the ministry. Although he regretted it later, he allowed himself to be enticed into accepting another newspaper advertising job in Astoria, Oregon. What he intended to be only a short-term position stretched into fifteen months, until the beginning of 1933. During that time he continued to study and learn, although there was no opportunity to focus upon God's work. This is how he described that time:

I found I was caught in a trap. We had 23 men employed. If I left then, the paper would have folded up, and these men would have been out of work. There still was no money in the Oregon Conference church treasury to bring me back into the ministry. I was stuck in Astoria. God intended for me to learn a lesson. It seems that most of the time I have had to learn these lessons the HARD WAY, through experience, and by suffering. This was to be no exception. It was not until the end of February, 1933, that my prayers to be relieved of these newspaper responsibilities, and to be allowed to return to God's ministry, were answered ("The Autobiography of Herbert W. Armstrong," *The Plain Truth,* February 1960, p. 32).

62　　　　　　　　　　　　　　A PECULIAR TREASURE

SON MIRACULOUSLY HEALED

While Mr. Armstrong was working in Astoria, Mrs. Armstrong and the family were still living in Salem, and he was making trips back most weekends. Here is his account of a significant event in their lives which would also impact the future of the church:

Finally, by early July 1932, we decided to move the family to Astoria. This resulted from my wife calling long distance late one afternoon asking me to rush home. Little Garner Ted was stricken with pneumonia! I drove the *Messenger* coupe down to Salem, arriving late that night. The children were asleep. Mrs. Armstrong was still up, beside little Teddy's sofa, on which he was lying. Immediately, we both knelt beside our sick baby. Little Garner Ted was then two years and five months.

And I must explain here that he had been, to that time, dumb—unable to talk. While somewhere between six months and a year old, he had fallen out of his crib-bed head-first onto the hard wood floor. We attributed his inability to talk to this fall, landing on his head. He would point to whatever he wanted to tell us about, making motions, and grunting "Ugh! Ugh!" But he was unable to speak a single word. We were becoming much concerned.

I anointed Teddy and began to claim God's promises to rebuke the fever and heal him. As I was praying, Mrs. Armstrong silently prayed, asking God that, if it was His will to heal our baby of this dumbness at that time, to put it in my mind to ask for this, as well as healing from the pneumonia. . . .

I did also have this in mind—or God put it in my mind—for the very instant she had asked for this, I began asking God to restore Ted's power of speech.

His fever left quickly. The very next day he was able to say a number of single words. In about three days he was talking in whole sentences ("The Autobiography of Herbert W. Armstrong," *The Plain Truth,* March 1960, p.12).

This account shows not only the miraculous way God was working to honor the faith and sincerity of the Armstrongs, but even more particularly, the quiet but strong role that Mrs. Loma Armstrong continued to play as events progressed. This, too, will continue to be evidenced over the next thirty-five years of their lives.

THE TITHING LESSON

In later decades, the issue of tithing would become very contentious, and the Worldwide Church of God would be criticized by the world for its teaching on the doctrine of tithing, among other things. But here is what Mr. Armstrong recounts about the very personal lesson he and Mrs. Armstrong learned from their own experience:

> I have mentioned repeatedly how God had brought me down, reduced us to poverty and want, and how much we had suffered hunger through those years. Much of the time in Astoria, up until about the time of this emergency trip to the Helms farm, we had not had enough to eat.
>
> I have explained in past chapters how, after conversion, I had to come to learn and understand one doctrine at a time. The truth was not acquired all at once. I had known that the Bible had quite a little to say about tithing one's income, and probably had by this time come to understand that it was still in force during the New Testament. Yet somehow it had never become completely clear, and we had never made tithing a regular and strict practice.
>
> At about this time, in the little time I had from my work at the newspaper for Bible study and prayer, I had made a special and thorough study of this matter of tithing. We saw the mistake we had been making, and started a definite

64   A PECULIAR TREASURE

practice of strict tithing. We had only a very little on hand, but we sent a tenth of it, plus an offering, to the Oregon Conference treasurer.

That very day, the way opened for us to be able to stock up at home with a reasonable abundance of food. For one thing, we had a large thick steak. My wife cooked it at low heat with the utensils we had acquired when I had devoted a year to selling them. I shall never forget that steak! It was 'way and by far the best steak I have ever tasted!

Although we still were required to live another 14 years in the barest and most modest financial circumstances, we have never from that day had to be actually hungry, and miss meals, because of financial poverty! We have since heard of scores and scores of case-histories of the experiences of others who were immediately prospered, once they began tithing. But we, ourselves, lived through this same experience. I am very grateful to have been privileged to have been instrumental in bringing countless others into this same divine *blessing!* My wife and I had to learn it the HARD WAY! ("The Autobiography of Herbert W. Armstrong," *The Plain Truth,* March 1960, p. 24)

It was February 1933 when the door opened for Mr. Armstrong to return his attention to the ministry. The Oregon Conference had accumulated enough funds to pay the Armstrongs $3 per week, and sent a member to Astoria to move them back to the Willamette Valley. Since the Astoria newspaper was already virtually defunct by then and the workers already gone, Mr. Armstrong felt comfortable in leaving and resuming his primary mission in the ministry.

LESSON OF FAITH AND DIVINE HEALING

Two months later, in April 1933, the next major lesson would begin. Mr. Armstrong's father had embraced the Truth by this time and asked to be baptized. Having experienced what was thought to

EARLY LIFE AND MINISTRY 1892–1934

be a bad case of indigestion, he had asked to be anointed. It was planned to baptize him the day after this anointing. But by that evening, he had fallen into a coma and never recovered. It was not indigestion, but a heart attack. Mr. Armstrong had full confidence his father would be healed, yet at 9:40 A.M. the next morning he died. Here was the result as it affected his son:

> I *knew* that God could not break a promise. I *knew* God has promised to HEAL—that Jesus took the penalty of physical sickness and infirmities and paid it for us by having His perfect physical body broken by being beaten with stripes!
>
> But WHY, then, did my father die? Through James God instructs us that if any lack wisdom, he shall ask of GOD—asking in FAITH, not wavering or doubting—and God promises wisdom shall be given. I prayed earnestly. I asked God for UNDERSTANDING.
>
> And I searched the Scriptures for the explanation. I did not doubt—but I *did* seek an explanation. Faith must be based on UNDERSTANDING, and I knew there was something I had not yet come to understand. Naturally I soon came, in this search, to the "faith chapter"—the 11th of Hebrews. Then the answer became plain.
>
> God gives us many examples of faith in that wonderful chapter. I noticed the example of Abraham—the *father* of the faithful. He, with Isaac and Jacob and Sarah "all died, *not having received the PROMISES.*" My father, like them, died, not having received God's promise of healing—*AS YET!* Did the death of Abraham, *before* he received what God had unconditionally PROMISED, nullify that promise? Did his death mean that God failed—that God's promise was worthless, not to be kept? NOT AT ALL!
>
> No, it simply meant that, for God's own reason and purpose, the fulfilling of the promise is delayed UNTIL THE RESURRECTION!

In like manner, I could now understand that God has PROMISED to heal—but He has *not* promised how immediately, or by what manner, He will do it. I knew, now, that my father's healing is still absolutely SURE. He will be resurrected—HEALED! I saw, now, that our days are indeed numbered. God has not promised that we shall live in this mortal existence eternally. It is appointed to men once to DIE—and after this the resurrection. I read how the TRIAL of our faith is allowed to work PATIENCE.

God, then, does give us tests of faith. Faith is the EVIDENCE of that NOT seen, NOT felt. Once we FEEL and SEE that we are healed, we no longer need the invisible spiritual evidence of faith. Faith, then, is our evidence—our PROOF of the healing—which God gives us to be exercised and utilized BETWEEN the time we ask, and the time the physical evidence is granted.

We should not *go* to God, asking, unless we have FAITH that God *will* do what He has promised, and what we are ready to ask. Then, after we ask, we should *still* have faith—just as before—that God WILL do as He has promised.

Now I understood! ("The Autobiography of Herbert W. Armstrong," *The Plain Truth*, April 1960, p .8)

This is a succinct summary of the original doctrine about divine healing that would be taught to thousands. It is another teaching that brought persecution upon the church in time, and was eventually altered by the Worldwide Church of God in the tumultuous decade of the 1970s. But this history confirms not only the original teaching that Herbert Armstrong came to understand, but also the *divine means* by which he claims God chose to teach it. This would be the very same pattern that would emerge to confirm *many doctrines* of the church over time. It is also the *foundation of thinking* that would be repudiated in his old age. This is why time has been taken to highlight these details.

EARLY LIFE AND MINISTRY 1892–1934   67

HUMBLE BEGINNINGS OF THE RADIO CHURCH OF GOD

In the spring of 1933, Mr. Armstrong had once again collaborated with another minister (Elder S. A. Oberg) for an evangelistic campaign over several months in the Salem, Oregon, area. Pentecostal elements had, for the most part, hijacked those meetings and chased away anyone who was interested in simple, straightforward Bible instruction (*Autobiography of Herbert W. Armstrong*, 1967, pp. 465–468). Because Mr. Armstrong was still being paid a small salary by the Oregon Conference of the Church of God, he felt obligated to defer to their authority in assigning his duties and to work with these other men, even though he was anxious to pursue other opportunities (p. 474). Mr. Armstrong describes one such opportunity which would mark the beginning of the Radio Church of God:

> The meetings held by Elder S. A. Oberg and me in the "Hollywood" district of Salem, Oregon, ended on July 1st, 1933. Just prior to this date I received an invitation that was to result in the start of the great world-wide work of today.
>
> This invitation came from Mr. and Mrs. Elmer E. Fisher. They were the couple who had been brought into the church by our private Bible study in my room, the night the storm prevented the meeting, during the tent campaign in Eugene, in the summer of 1931. The Fishers were successful farmers, living seven miles west of Eugene. Mr. Fisher was a member of the school board of the one-room Firbutte school, eight miles west of Eugene on the old Elmira road. The Fishers asked me to hold meetings in this country school house, inviting me to be their guest in their farm home during the meetings ("The Autobiography of Herbert W. Armstrong," *The Plain Truth,* May 1960, p. 11).

The Oregon Conference approved the plan for these meetings, and Mr. Armstrong began evening Bible studies almost nightly for

68 A PECULIAR TREASURE

several weeks. There were twenty-seven attendees at the very first meeting, on Sunday, July 9, 1933. Through those initial meetings he was forced to prove himself against particular individuals who attended for the sole purpose of stirring up trouble, making visiting ministers look foolish. But Herbert Armstrong was different, and he successfully weathered these attacks, proving not only the strength of his doctrinal understanding compared to others, but also the ability to think on his feet and to "convince the gainsayers" in a public forum. The result was a nucleus of local attendees that became the foundation of the Radio Church of God.

CONTROVERSY OVER BAPTIZING PORK-EATERS

At the same time, Mr. Armstrong was still dealing with complications from his association with the Oregon Conference. Other men with personal agendas continued to accuse and to undermine him, keeping Mr. Armstrong in a defensive posture. The flashpoint centered around the requirements for baptism. Here is how Mr. Armstrong described it:

> At this Meeting with Mr. Ray and Mr. Oberg, they strenuously objected to my baptizing new converts *before* I had preached to them against pork, and had evidence they had given it up. I knew that Messrs. Oberg and Ray intended to use this against me in the business meeting, as their latest trap to get me ousted from the payroll.
>
> I must repeat that I was receiving a salary of $3 per week! The farmer members provided my family in Salem with a certain amount of food, in addition to the salary ("The Autobiography of Herbert W. Armstrong," *The Plain Truth,* June 1960, p. 10).

In what Mr. Armstrong called the "all-day wrangle," he was forced to defend the fact that he was not making the eating of pork a "test" for baptism. Here was his rationale at the time, which is very revealing in comparison to the policy used decades later in the Worldwide Church of God:

> Since people cannot fully comprehend the truth of the Commandments and the teaching of the Bible until AFTER they receive the Holy Spirit, and since there is no promise God will give the Holy Spirit until after baptism, therefore I baptized them after repentance and faith, just as the Bible instructs—and *then*, after laying on hands with prayer for their receiving of the Holy Spirit (Acts 8:12, 14–17; Acts 19:5–6; I Tim. 4:14; II Tim. 1:6, etc.), I taught them God's Commandments, and not to eat unclean meats, etc. Every convert I had ever baptized had obeyed all these truths as soon as I taught them. They were submissive, teachable, yielded to God, hungry for His truth. The KNOWLEDGE of the Lord is something to teach *converted* people whose minds are opened by God's Spirit. We must continually GROW in this knowledge ("The Autobiography of Herbert W. Armstrong," *The Plain Truth,* June 1960, p. 13).

Ironically, over the next thirty years within the Radio Church of God, this philosophy morphed into something very similar to that of the old Oregon Conference, with ministers requiring potential members to state that they were not eating pork, not smoking, etc., before being baptized. By the 1970s, it became *even more stringent*, requiring demonstration of many "spiritual fruits" before even being invited to attend a Sabbath service, let alone becoming baptized! It is just one more way that the history of Mr. Armstrong's thinking from the early years would be contrasted with that which emerged once that physical church grew in scope and power.

Mr. Armstrong's refusal to depart from this philosophy about baptism in 1933 created a furor among the other Oregon Conference ministers, and they sought to force him to follow their policy. Mr. Armstrong refused to be manipulated. This is how he responded:

70   A PECULIAR TREASURE

> They immediately offered a resolution that I be required,
> if I remained in the conference, to baptize people their way
> instead of the Scriptural way, and those remaining inside the
> church building were swayed into voting for it. . . .
>
> As soon as I heard of the action taken, I immediately
> wrote a letter cancelling the $3 per week salary, and
> suggesting they give it to Messrs. Oberg and Ray, or else go
> throw it in the Pacific Ocean! I did not resign from the
> Conference, nor was I put out. But I refused further salary.
>
> My wife was in complete accord with me (*Autobiography
> of Herbert W. Armstrong*, 1967, p. 492).

This event effectively *set him free* to begin devoting his attentions to the new little flock solidifying outside of Eugene, Oregon, which was growing slowly but surely and showing more serious appreciation for his approach to God's Truth. It was still very meager, with only about twenty firm members after six weeks of Bible studies in the Firbutte schoolhouse. It required a true act of faith on the part of both Mr. and Mrs. Armstrong to stick to their convictions without evidence of any significant physical support:

> My wife and I *knew* we were obeying and serving God. We
> *knew* He was using us. The FRUITS being borne were loud
> testimony of this. Therefore we *knew*, in perfect faith, God
> would supply our need ("The Autobiography of Herbert W.
> Armstrong," *The Plain Truth*, June 1960, p. 14).

THE VERY FIRST RADIO BROADCAST

The opportunity for Herbert Armstrong to take his religious message to a much broader audience *appeared* to happen quite by accident. It was never premeditated on his part to try to utilize anything but print media to advertize the gospel. But this is what occurred:

Late in September someone brought to my attention the fact that the local radio station at Eugene, KORE, then the very smallest minimum-power of 100 watts, had a Morning Devotional program scheduled, but that they were having difficulty getting local ministers to conduct the program. It was free time, carried by the station as a public service sustaining program, of 15 minutes, 7:45 to 8:00 A.M.

Immediately I went to the radio station. A woman secretary told me she felt sure they would be glad to have me take the program for a week. I was to call back later for the exact date.

On my second call I was assigned the week of October 9th.

October 9th was surely a great big day in my life—the day of my very first experience before a microphone, *ON THE AIR*! ("The Autobiography of Herbert W. Armstrong," *The Plain Truth*, June 1960, p. 14)

Even from his first awkward and novice presentation behind a microphone, that short radio program immediately began generating letters to the station. This prompted the station owner to propose a permanent, thirty-minute program on Sunday mornings, at a reduced cost of $2.50 per half-hour. Even though that was still a fortune to the Armstrongs—given their severe financial challenges—in faith they accepted the proposal:

But, $2.50 every week! *WOW*! That was almost as much as my entire salary had been! And I had just previously renounced even that small salary! . . .

Yet I knew this was GOD'S WORK, not mine. I was only an instrument. God had promised to supply every need.

God had OPENED THE DOOR OF MASS EVANGELISM!

He had opened the first radio door (Rev. 3:8). I knew He wanted us to walk through that door. I knew He would somehow supply that $2.50 every week. I knew also that we had to do our part, not lie down, do nothing, and expect God

72 A PECULIAR TREASURE

to do it without any effort from us ("The Autobiography of Herbert W. Armstrong," *The Plain Truth*, June 1960, p. 30, 32).

At the very same time that this new radio experiment was percolating, something else very significant was occurring as well. Mr. Armstrong and his local core of supporters were finalizing plans to formalize their association into a registered church:

> Then, October 21st, at the home of Mr. and Mrs. Ed Smith, just across the road from the Jeans school, 4 miles west of Firbutte, a new Church of God was organized, with Mr. E. E. Fisher as deacon, and myself as Pastor. Meetings continued from that date, three times a week, Tuesday and Thursday evenings, and Sabbath afternoons. Attendance was averaging 22. A first action of the new Church was the decision of whether to go ahead with the broadcast. They all approved it joyfully as an effective evangelistic activity of the Church ("The Autobiography of Herbert W. Armstrong," *The Plain Truth*, June 1960, p. 32).

The fact that this new church organization was being formalized at the very same time that the radio program was being developed certainly influenced the selection of the group name. During the first two to three years, the format of the radio program was actually a fully-condensed church service, including music and an opening prayer. Therefore, it makes perfect sense that in the fall of 1933, the group would be named the Radio Church of God (*Autobiography of Herbert W. Armstrong*, 1967, p. 508).

BIRTH OF THE PLAIN TRUTH MAGAZINE

The new half-hour radio program on Sunday mornings was contracted to begin in the new calendar year, 1934. But in preparing for this debut, Mr. Armstrong felt compelled to address another

EARLY LIFE AND MINISTRY 1892–1934   73

priority at the same time. The end goal was not just to "be on the radio." He truly saw this radio program as *a tool* to accomplish something more profound. To him, it was always about proclaiming the true Gospel of Jesus Christ and providing a means for the called of God *to respond and to embrace that way of life.* He believed it himself and sought to live it. He wanted others to have the knowledge that God had shown to him, and likewise to have the blessings of that true way and the hope of a glorious future.

Therefore, the approaching debut of the new radio program inspired him to develop another significant program to work in concert with it. That new program was *The Plain Truth* magazine. Here is how Mr. Armstrong spoke of its origin:

> Not only did I set out with a will to produce the radio program, but I realized there must be follow-up if this new effort were to be resultful.
>
> Immediately the idea came of realizing, at last, the dream I had cherished since 1927—the publication of a magazine, to be called *The Plain Truth.* Back in 1927 I had made up an entire "dummy" of this proposed magazine. I had even written articles for it. . . .
>
> This ambition to publish *The Plain Truth* was the natural outgrowth of earlier business experience. Much of my 20 years of advertising experience had been spent in the class magazine field.
>
> Now, at last, I realized that this magazine was a "*must*" as a follow-up for the radio broadcast. . . .
>
> My idea for this magazine, from the start, had been to publish a magazine, *not* for church members, but for the general public—the unconverted and unchurched—an evangelistic-type publication to bring to the world God's TRUTH—making it PLAIN! ("The Autobiography of Herbert W. Armstrong," *The Plain Truth,* August 1960, p. 11)

An additional part of his strategy for follow-up was to continue those personal, local evangelistic meetings, to reinforce the teachings that would be proclaimed on radio and in print media:

> Also, I saw at once that the broadcasts should be followed up by continued public evangelistic services.
>
> Therefore, I wrote to the small number of members on the mailing list I had—perhaps 150—the news of the forthcoming THREE-POINT CAMPAIGN: (1) The half-hour Sunday radio program; (2) the new mimeographed magazine for interested listeners, *The Plain Truth*, and (3) personal public meetings ("The Autobiography of Herbert W. Armstrong," *The Plain Truth*, August 1960, p. 11).

The problem was, not only was there no immediate funding for the radio program, but neither was there funding for the new magazine. Yet Mr-s. Armstrong decided, with the support of the brethren, to step out in faith and launch this aggressive three-point campaign, trusting that God would provide the means for its success.

THE OFFICIAL LAUNCH

On the first Sunday of 1934 (January 7), *The World Tomorrow* broadcast went on the air for the first time. Here is Mr. Armstrong's account of the initial response to that broadcast, as well as the launching of the first issue of *The Plain Truth*:

> Just as the 15-minute morning devotional programs had brought an unexpected mail response, so did the half-hour regular program of our own. Only it now brought a larger response. I began with the first broadcast, that first Sunday in 1934, inviting listeners to write in for the new magazine, *The Plain Truth*.

At the same time I began work on producing Volume I and Number 1 of this magazine of my dreams. I did not even have a "scope" for hand-lettering the headlines. Neither did I have the regular mimeograph lettering guides for tracing, with the stylus, larger headlines. I was still living with the Fishers on their farm seven miles west of Eugene—my wife and children still at the Hall Street house in Salem. . . . That first issue of *The Plain Truth* was a pretty amateurish, home-made looking sort of thing. . . .

It was about November 1, 1933, that a few special offerings made it possible for us to purchase a very old, used, outdated Neostyle. It was a predecessor to the mimeograph. It was entirely hand operated. . . . We had also finally been able, before the first issue of *The Plain Truth*, to raise enough money to purchase a secondhand typewriter for $10.

And so finally *The Plain Truth*, home-made at Fishers' farm on the Neostyle, but containing priceless plain TRUTH, made its humble bow to the world February 1, 1934 ("The Autobiography of Herbert W. Armstrong," *The Plain Truth,* August 1960, p. 13).

This summarizes the early life and times of Mr-s. Herbert Armstrong, up through the initial launch of that very humble evangelistic work which would thereafter revolutionize the concept of Christianity in the twentieth century.

CHAPTER FIVE
FOUNDING AND GROWTH OF CHURCH AND COLLEGE 1934–1957

FAITH STRATEGIES BEGIN TO FORM

Through 1934 and 1935, Mr. Armstrong implemented and sustained his "three-point campaign" of radio broadcasts, monthly publishing of *The Plain Truth* magazine, and local evangelistic campaigns in the Eugene area. Committing in advance, financially, to pay for these programs well beyond his existing wherewithal certainly required an act of faith that God would provide the needed income. And the income always appeared right when required. It was all being operated on a shoestring budget, and Mr. and Mrs. Armstrong were the ones personally doing the lion's share of the manual work required to make it all happen, from the cleaning of local meeting halls to the physical production and mailing of mimeographed issues of the magazine. The hours were long and brutally taxing.

Yet, Mr. Armstrong was still hesitant to commit *very much more* to newer programs without "guarantees" of financial support. He describes that lesson regarding the first opportunity to expand the radio broadcast outside of Eugene, Oregon:

> But the point I wish to make is that, by the end of our first year on the air, CHRIST opened *another door*! He opened the door for us to go on station KXL, Portland, then only 100 watts.
>
> But at that time I was afraid to walk through that door—until *after* co-workers had PLEDGED enough money to pay for it. This very letter quoted above [a *Co-Worker Letter* dated December 20, 1934] went on to ask co-workers for those pledges—totalling only $50 per month, for the year

78   A PECULIAR TREASURE

1935. A coupon form of pledge was mimeographed at the bottom of the second page of the letter.

Our co-workers failed to pledge the needed $50 per month. And I failed to walk through the door Christ had opened. We had to wait almost two more years before God gave us another opportunity for His work to expand into Portland! Later other doors were opened, when I wanted definite pledges before walking through those doors. But definite pledges was not FAITH.

We had to learn, by experience, that when God opens doors for CHRIST'S GOSPEL, He expects us to start walking on through, IN FAITH, trusting HIM to supply our every NEED! ("The Autobiography of Herbert W. Armstrong," *The Plain Truth*, March 1961, p. 14)

Although the radio broadcasts and personal evangelistic campaigns continued through 1936, publishing of the magazine issues was interrupted. He simply did not have the time and resources to tend to all of those irons in the fire. Here is Mr. Armstrong's explanation of that:

Not only was the expansion of the broadcasting withheld two whole years, but *The Plain Truth was suspended from publication, also!* After I failed to TRUST GOD by going on KXL when He opened its door to us, we were allowed to print and send out only *two* more issues of *The Plain Truth*—March and July issues, 1935—AND THEN *The Plain Truth* WAS ENTIRELY SUSPENDED FOR TWO AND A HALF YEARS! . . . Not until January, 1938, did *The Plain Truth* appear again! ("The Autobiography of Herbert W. Armstrong," *The Plain Truth*, June 1961, p. 12)

This history is important because it reveals the thinking that Herbert Armstrong consistently used from that time forward concerning decisions about *bold expansions* of the work. What the world would consider as reckless disregard for fiscal prudence would

FOUNDING AND GROWTH OF CHURCH AND COLLEGE 1934–1957   79

be the *faith philosophy* that Herbert Armstrong would use to make many "audacious" strategic choices to walk through "new doors" in the ensuing years.

By the end of 1936, the *Radio Church of God* broadcast had indeed expanded and was then heard on KXL in Portland, and next on KSLM in Salem, through a networked transmission relay from the KORE broadcast in Eugene. Even though these were all small stations, by early 1937, Mr. Armstrong was reporting to his co-workers a listening audience approaching 50,000 every Sunday. By the end of that year, he was reporting over 100,000 listeners, based upon the mail responses they were receiving. At this time he was still using the "church service" format for the broadcasts, including music and a short prayer as a part of each program, more akin to the other ministers who were on the radio. This too would change dramatically as exposure grew.

During this same time Mr. Armstrong continued trying to work cooperatively with the other Sabbath-keeping groups in the area, but his success in pastoring expanding local congregations made possible by his radio broadcasts, seemed to have fostered jealousy among the other ministers. After it became apparent that their plots to undermine him would never cease, he finally broke with them and focused exclusively upon serving those who were coming into the church through his own personal ministry.

These continued to be what Mr. Armstrong called "the lean years." It was a very meager existence for his family. There were many times when it appeared there would be no funds to pay the bills, let alone the cost of continued broadcasts on the radio. *The Plain Truth* began to be published again in January 1938, but it was a continuing challenge from month to month to keep it all afloat. Citing a *Co-Worker Letter* from July 1938, Mr. Armstrong paraphrased:

> . . . only one in ten of those on *The Plain Truth* mailing list had ever sent a contribution of any kind toward the expenses of the work. And they had never been asked. The few contributors had become Co-Workers voluntarily, without

80 A PECULIAR TREASURE

solicitation. The other nine in ten had never received any solicitation for contributions ("The Autobiography of Herbert W. Armstrong," *The Plain Truth*, November 1961, p. 5).

He also stated that this same ratio of listeners to contributors would continue to apply (as of 1961) even as that work multiplied exponentially through the decades. But even though he never solicited contributions from his radio audience, the enterprise survived and grew, even if painfully, year after year:

> By April 5, 1939, a letter to Co-Workers found in an old file says: "At last, after many unavoidable delays, we are sending you *The Plain Truth*. This issue goes to about one thousand NEW READERS. It is still mimeographed, because we have not enough funds to print it, as we did two issues last year. It is a tremendous task, and nearly all the work is done by Mrs. Armstrong, our daughter Beverly who is office secretary, and myself."
>
> In spite of inside office, lack of light or ventilation, lack of desks, filing cabinets and office equipment, the work was GROWING! *The Plain Truth* circulation was growing. We were not able to get it out every month. There were seven issues in 1938. The June number was only the third during 1939. It was issued as often as there was enough money for paper, ink and postage. Yet already this little mimeographed "magazine" was being read by a few *thousand* people—and a hundred thousand or more were hearing the very Gospel Christ Himself preached every week—besides almost continuous evangelistic campaigns reaching hundreds ("The Autobiography of Herbert W. Armstrong," *The Plain Truth*, November 1961, p. 8).

NEXT BIG EXPANSION

The next big breakthrough occurred on September 17, 1940, when the *Radio Church of God* broadcast debuted in Seattle, Washington, on 1,000-watt station KRSC. The timing of world events with the war in Europe had provided an ideal opportunity for Herbert Armstrong to address those events in light of Bible prophecy, and people were responding:

> By mid-May, 1941, the weekly listening audience, over the three stations in Eugene and Portland, Oregon, and in Seattle, had grown to a quarter million people.
>
> That seemed a huge audience. Indeed, it *was* a huge audience. The work of God, having been started so very small was, as stated before, growing up.
>
> The circulation of *The Plain Truth* had gone up to 5,000 copies. . . . Beginning with the issue of August-September, 1940, *The Plain Truth* had "grown up" from a mimeographed paper to a 16-page printed magazine, bimonthly. By mid-May we were receiving between 200 and 300 letters from radio listeners every week, and mailing out 5,000 copies of *The Plain Truth* ("The Autobiography of Herbert W. Armstrong," *The Plain Truth*, January 1962, p. 11).

Even though this explosive new response to the radio program generated a sense of great satisfaction, it came with a huge burden of administration:

> Think of just the two of us—with at times the help of a girl who knew no shorthand and could not use a typewriter—handling and answering an average of 250 letters a week, beside all the other things Mrs. Armstrong and I had to do! Then having to call in a half dozen church brethren for volunteer help in addressing 5,000 copies of *The Plain Truth* BY HAND. And in those days we had to paste 1-cent stamps on

82 A PECULIAR TREASURE

every copy. Mrs. Armstrong had to cook paste of flour and water at home and bring it to the office to paste those wrappers ("The Autobiography of Herbert W. Armstrong," *The Plain Truth*, January 1962, p. 12).

A new office suite became available in Eugene, allowing for needed expansion. A secretary could now be hired. Little by little, an infrastructure began to be added to accommodate the growing enterprise.

SEEDS OF A NATIONAL WORK

It was also during this particular time in 1941 that Herbert Armstrong began to expand his horizons in considering what further work God may want him to do:

> The realization flashed to my mind with terrific impact that in WORLD WAR II—already then under way—America being then drawn closer to participation—that *I could see this "sword" of WAR coming* [Ezekiel 3:17–21; 33:1–19]! I looked around. NO ONE had ever sounded this warning! No one was then sounding it! I saw numerous prophecies showing how terribly God is going to *punish* America and the British Commonwealth people for our apostasy from Him. I saw our sins, individually and nationally, fast increasing!
>
> The conviction came. *IF* God opened doors for the MASS-PROCLAMATION of His Gospel, and of this warning, nationwide, I would walk through those doors and proclaim God's Message faithfully, as long as He gave me guidance, power, and the means.
>
> I had no illusions that I was chosen to be the "modern Ezekiel" to proclaim this message. But I did know that no one was sounding this alarm. . . .
>
> Of course I had been sounding this warning all along—but only in the Pacific Northwest. Now I began to see

FOUNDING AND GROWTH OF CHURCH AND COLLEGE 1934–1957 83

that God intended to send it to ALL ISRAEL. And He had revealed to me that that meant, today, the United States, the British Commonwealth, and the nations of northwestern Europe. The idea of *my* being used, personally, in reaching Britain and these other countries did not yet take sharp focus in my mind. But I *did*, now, for the first time, begin to *think actively and definitely* about this work expanding to the entire United States! ("The Autobiography of Herbert W. Armstrong," *The Plain Truth*, January 1962, p. 13)

The bombing of Pearl Harbor on December 7, 1941, provided the means for Herbert Armstrong to really begin to exploit a niche not being filled by anyone else on the radio:

A number of nationally famous news commentators and analysts gained the public spotlight—such men as Elmer Davis, H. V. Kaltenborn, Raymond Gram Swing—and some still in the public eye, Ed Murrow, Eric Severeid, and others—just to name a few.

But these men knew nothing of Biblical prophecy. Not knowing the real purpose being worked out here below, they did not grasp the true significance on the world of the future, of the news they were analyzing. They did not know where it was leading.

On the other hand, none of the ministers broadcasting religious programs had the newspaper and analytical background, nor, I may add, the true understanding of the prophecies, to connect that entire third of the Bible with the war events.

Putting the two together—factual knowledge and analysis of war events, with Biblical prophecies—put at my disposal a powerful interest-compelling message ("The Autobiography of Herbert W. Armstrong," *The Plain Truth*, January 1962, p. 39).

84 A PECULIAR TREASURE

Many of the higher wattage radio stations in larger market areas that Mr. Armstrong had contacted (including Chicago and Los Angeles) were not inclined toward additional religious programming. But they did seem receptive to Herbert Armstrong's program. As well, radio managers at stations already broadcasting the program began to suggest dropping the music, given that it was the hard-hitting news analysis that was actually driving the audience response:

> At first I was both reluctant and afraid to drop the music. So I experimented by reducing it. No harm resulted. There was no lessening in the response or expressed interest. I reduced it still more. Finally, it was eliminated altogether. We found, as radio station managers had recommended, that our program attracted and held a much larger interest when it started off with analysis of world events and the MEANING, as revealed in Biblical prophecy ("The Autobiography of Herbert W. Armstrong," *The Plain Truth*, January 1962, p. 39).

By the time Mr. Armstrong was negotiating the first expansion into the Los Angeles, California, market with KMTR radio in April 1942, he was prepared to make these significant changes:

> The time had come to drop the church-service type program altogether. Since the original broadcast name, Radio Church of God, did not invite a listening from non-churchgoers whom we wished primarily to reach, and since in the world's language the Message of the true Gospel—the KINGDOM OF GOD—is about tomorrow's world, I adopted the broadcast name, The WORLD TOMORROW!
>
> And so, mid-April, 1942, The WORLD TOMORROW went on the air in Hollywood ("The Autobiography of Herbert W. Armstrong," *The Plain Truth*, January 1962, pp. 39–40).

FOUNDING AND GROWTH OF CHURCH AND COLLEGE 1934–1957   85

Instead of having merely a single half-hour time slot each Sunday morning on KMTR, an opportunity opened for daily broadcasts at 5:30 P.M. The cost meant doubling the funds devoted to the whole work at that time. But rather than shying away out of fear, Herbert Armstrong applied the lesson he had learned in 1935 and made the commitment. Here was the result:

> But, miracle of miracles!—for once in our experience, the impact of this early evening DAILY broadcasting was as tremendous as the test of faith had been! Not once did I ask for contributions on the air, just as I had refused to do from the first broadcast in 1934. And the mailing address for free literature and *The* PLAIN TRUTH, offered on each program, was then Box 111, Eugene, Oregon.
>
> Not only was there an immediate tremendous increase in mail from listeners—there was a corresponding increase in tithes and offerings arriving in Eugene ("The Autobiography of Herbert W. Armstrong," *The Plain Truth*, February 1962, p. 12).

Due to the personal time commitment required, Mr. Armstrong was not capable of sustaining a nightly program in Hollywood for more than a few weeks. But the experience demonstrated the fruits that could be borne with such exposure. Likewise, pulling back to one day per week broadcasts allowed him finally to contract with WHO radio in Des Moines, Iowa:

> Station WHO was, at the time, probably the *very* MOST valuable single radio station we could have hoped to use. It was a 50,000-watt top-ranking station. It was one of *only eight*, of all radio stations in America, that still had an absolutely *exclusive* channel. . . .
>
> Of course, in 1941, this giant WHO was still completely beyond our reach. But by early 1942, with our income doubled, and with the very low rate offered by the manager of WHO, I felt ready to take this leap. . . .

86   A PECULIAR TREASURE

On Sunday night, August 30, 1942, for the first time in
my life I was speaking, from the studios of WHO, *to a
nationwide audience!* ("The Autobiography of Herbert W.
Armstrong," *The Plain Truth*, March 1962, pp. 19–20).

This was only the beginning of Herbert Armstrong's national
exposure as *The World Tomorrow* program began to be heard in
every state. Contracts with specific stations would come and go, but
increasingly that voice could be heard regularly from anywhere
across the continental USA.

ON THE THRESHOLD OF GREAT EXPANSION

Once *The World Tomorrow* radio broadcast began to be heard
nationwide in 1942, the whole focus of that little religious work
began to change. It was no longer just a local/regional outreach in
the Pacific Northwest, but now began to impact people nationwide.

From 1943 through most of 1945, new contracts with more
powerful radio stations were added, including XELO, a 100,000 watt
station in Juarez, Mexico, just across the border and covering the
entire USA with its transmission signal. The problem, however, was
that *The World Tomorrow* was typically being heard either very late
at night or very early in the morning, outside of the time that most
listeners would have tuned in. Only one station carried the
broadcast at 8 P.M., and then, only one night per week. By late 1945
that was about to change.

Mr. Armstrong considered 1945 a most pivotal year in history
affecting his work. It was a special moment in time which saw the
end of World War II, the simultaneous rise of the Soviet Union as a
communist geopolitical power, the birth of the United Nations as a
final attempt to solve man's problems, and the unexpected dawning
of the atomic era with the bombing of Hiroshima and Nagasaki,
Japan. These events cumulatively changed everything on the world
scene, and Herbert Armstrong was there with his unique brand of
radio program, showing how these troubling developments fit with

FOUNDING AND GROWTH OF CHURCH AND COLLEGE 1934–1957   87

last-day prophecies of the Bible. His was neither a traditional religious program nor a secular news program, but a combination of the two, and in that day it had no equal. In the decades since then, many others have tried to copy Mr. Armstrong's format, but without any of the impact that he enjoyed from being fresh and new. Critics would say he just happened to be in the right place at the right time to ride this unexpected *new wave* and to fill a developing niche market. He claimed, by contrast, that it was the Eternal God who had timed it all perfectly to achieve a *divine* purpose.

It was October 1945—just two months after the first atomic bomb was dropped—when *The World Tomorrow* expanded to an unprecedented six-night-per-week format:

> In 1944 we broke into an earlier time, 8 P.M. on XELO, with 100,000 watts of power—but still Sunday nights *only*. However, this prime listening time had greatly increased the number of listeners and the mail response.
>
> But now, at last, the Eternal God had opened the mighty door of super-power XELO at this prime 8 P.M. time, *six nights a week!*
>
> After this tremendous impact of *nightly* broadcasting got under way, the number of listeners to God's Truth increased faster than ever.
>
> Then, on the heels of this, GOD OPENED ANOTHER STILL BIGGER DOOR! Station XEG, with 150,000 watts, making it the most powerful voice reaching over the United States, opened its mighty doors—and at the prime listening time of 8 P.M., Central Standard Time, *and also six nights a week!* ("The Autobiography of Herbert W. Armstrong," *The Plain Truth*, October 1962, p. 16)

The after-effects of this new-listener response were significant. Thus, 1946 became the year requiring a *major expansion* of the infrastructure of that little church operation in Eugene to try to cope with the volume of letters flooding into the office. Requests for *The Plain Truth* magazine were skyrocketing, as well as for booklets like

88 A PECULIAR TREASURE

The United States and British Commonwealth in Prophecy. In order to afford to pay for these big, new radio contracts, Mr. Armstrong had often "robbed Peter to pay Paul" by cutting back on publishing. But now the demand for the printed material being advertized on the radio program made it mandatory to reinvest in that follow-up service. The scope was now beyond the capacity of any "mom-and-pop" outfit to manage.

Outgrowing Eugene, Oregon

With 75,000 issues of *The Plain Truth* now being printed, the capacity of local printers in rural Oregon was being taxed. The need also for expanded office facilities for a growing infrastructure led Mr. Armstrong to contemplate moving his headquarters. Also, prerecording multiple installments of *The World Tomorrow* broadcast to feed a six-night-per-week schedule on multiple stations across the country required the kind of studio equipment found in few cities. Because the real center for media and broadcasting was Hollywood, California, this was the area that became preeminent on his list of options. He did not want to be right in Hollywood and its culture, or even Beverly Hills, but he very much liked the neighboring community of Pasadena for its more conservative flavor.

At the very same time, the chronic, persistent lack of reliable shepherds to serve new local congregations was as troubling as ever before. What good was it for Herbert Armstrong to succeed in raising up a new local group through his evangelical efforts, if the man he left in charge of that group "flaked out" and destroyed the fellowship within six months' time? Something had to change:

> In Eugene, one of the four larger churches conducted a school for training ministers. It became headquarters for a new denomination. I had noticed that once *they* established a new small church group here and there, their little churches continued to hold together and grow. They had ministers

FOUNDING AND GROWTH OF CHURCH AND COLLEGE 1934–1957

available to pastor each new church raised up. They had a school for training ministers.

If necessity is the mother of invention, perhaps God created the necessity to get through my thick skull the realization that God wanted a college of His own, for the training of HIS ministers, as well as other trained personnel that soon would be required for His rapidly-growing Work.

And so it came about that, by the time of my flight to New York in late March, 1946 [to cover the first United Nations Security Council session], I was well aware of the need for a college. And I knew that college must be located in Pasadena, California ("The Autobiography of Herbert W. Armstrong," *The Plain Truth,* November 1962, p. 44).

AMBASSADOR COLLEGE IS CONCEIVED

After a nationwide baptizing tour by Mr. and Mrs. Armstrong in the summer of 1946, they returned home in the fall to focus upon finding a means to begin a college. The whole idea was quite audacious. How many would ever have dared to take the steps Herbert Armstrong had over the previous twelve years—generating a national radio broadcast and print program on a shoestring budget—let alone thereafter to have conceived starting his own college? He did not even have a higher educational degree himself. Who was he to start an institution of higher learning? Besides that, he had no available funds to invest in such a project. Everything coming in was being churned back into the Work to continue expanding the reach of that unique religious message. But he nevertheless went shopping for property in Pasadena, California, believing that if it was God's will, a way would open to turn it into a reality.

His initial concept of a college campus was simply a bare-bones facility to provide what was minimally necessary to meet basic needs. He looked at empty lots with the idea of building a facility. Many starts and stops occurred, but all efforts ran into severe obstacles.

90 A PECULIAR TREASURE

In November 1946 he stopped in to see a real estate broker whom he already knew, and from that time forward, everything changed:

> I was taken to a small mansion of some 18 rooms, on Grove Street just off of South Orange Grove Boulevard—Pasadena's "millionaire row" residence street. This was a 2¼ acre place known as the "McCormick estate" . . . .
>
> The property was on a hillside. It had been magnificently landscaped, although it appeared not to have been maintained in good condition for a few years. Beside the main building, there was a four-car garage with two servants' apartments. To the east of these buildings was a beautifully contoured slope to a balustrade, and then a six-foot drop of ornamental concrete retaining wall under the balustrade, dropping to a long, level space known as "the lower gardens." This space was headed by an ornate concrete tempietto, and ended at the other end with a large square pool and a classic pergola ("The Autobiography of Herbert W. Armstrong," *The Plain Truth*, December 1962, pp. 30–31).

The problem was, the retired lawyer who owned it wanted $100,000 cash for the property, quite out of the question for Herbert Armstrong. Eventually, miraculously, a lease-to-purchase arrangement was agreed upon, whereby the Armstrongs promised to pay $1,000 per month until July 1947 (ten months), only thereafter first taking possession of the property. Ultimately, the contract provided for the transfer of deed to be completed once twenty-five total months of payments had been made ($25,000). The lawyer never intended to honor the contract, thinking to take nine months of advance payments and then renege on his promise to turn over the property. However, by some clever maneuverings of Mr. Armstrong, they did indeed take possession of that property, and they did indeed obtain the deed as contracted. Audacious! In the name of the Radio Church of God, the Armstrongs now owned a mansion in Pasadena, California.

The Mission of Ambassador College

Once the contract was signed in the fall of 1946, immediate plans were made to open Ambassador College in the fall of 1947. Mr. Armstrong tapped his brother-in-law, Walter E. Dillon, to become President of Ambassador College. He held a Master's Degree in Education and was an experienced school principal. He had no foundation in religion, and that was just fine with Mr. Armstrong. In fact, it was preferable. The Armstrongs were not opening a religious seminary. It was conceived as a liberal arts college that would also include some religious courses. The initial advertisement spread featured in the January-February 1947 issue of *The Plain Truth* defined the purpose of this unique institution. Mr. Armstrong describes the purpose of that special magazine feature:

The center spread—pages 8 and 9—had a large 4-column picture showing a portion of the new campus. The article announcing the new college began on that page, with a 4-column headline: ". . . and *now* . . . OUR OWN NEW COLLEGE!"

The article explained that "an amazing new setup has come into our hands that is unique, and, we believe, without parallel! Prospective students learning of the unusual program are thrilled!"

Policies were announced. The article said: . . . "AMBASSADOR is to be a general liberal arts institution—not a Bible school, ministers' college, or theological seminary. It will fit students for all walks of life, offering a general and *practical* basic education. . . . There is no other college like AMBASSADOR." . . .

"But why should we establish and conduct a college in connection with this, God's Work?" the article continued. "The reasons are concrete and vital. . . . The work has grown to a scope where *called*, consecrated, properly educated and specially trained assistants, ministers and evangelists to follow up this work in the field, have become an imperative need." . . .

But why, then, was this not to be a Bible school, or theological seminary?

The article, continuing, explained that:

"Yet, the active ministry is *different* from every other profession in one very important respect. No man ever should enter it of his own volition. . . . A true minister of Jesus Christ must be specially *called* of God. And how may we *know* whether one is really called? Experience has shown human nature to be such that most who *think* that they are called are mistaken, and those who really are called invariably try to run from the calling! Jesus gave us the only test. 'By their fruits,' He said, 'ye shall KNOW.' But the fruits are worked out by experience, and that requires time. For that very reason, *our college cannot be a ministerial college*—though it *is* being designed so that, should we be fortunate enough to find one out of twenty really and truly called to the ministry, that one will have been prepared and properly trained. . . . These considerations led naturally to the policy of making AMBASSADOR a general liberal arts institution for all young men and women, regardless of future vocation, occupation or profession." ("The Autobiography of Herbert W. Armstrong," *The Plain Truth*, January 1963, p. 42)

Furthermore, how was Ambassador College to be different from other colleges?

The Biblical revelation provides man with the true *concept* through which to view and *explain* what he can observe. . . .

But the educational institutions of this world have rejected this FOUNDATION of knowledge. They have built an educational structure on a false foundation. They left God, and His revelation, out of their knowledge. They have built a complicated and false system composed of a perverted mixture of truth and error.

Ambassador College was to *correct* these ills and perversions in modern education. That was to be its basic policy.

The Board of Trustees of the Radio Church of God, of which I was Chairman, would set all policies until the college could be incorporated in its own name with its own Board of Trustees. Until that time, it would be operated as an activity of the Radio Church of God ("The Autobiography of Herbert W. Armstrong," *The Plain Truth*, May 1963, p. 26).

PREPARING FOR THE FIRST SCHOOL YEAR

Early 1947 saw the assembling of a new college faculty, including some retired professors and academics with prestigious degrees in history, languages, and music. None of them were members of the Radio Church of God or shared Mr. Armstrong's religious beliefs. He was serious about wanting Ambassador College to be a true liberal arts institution, with the caveat that *he alone* would teach the religious curriculum.

But a number of very serious problems emerged which put the new college much in jeopardy. Even though the Armstrongs were able to take possession of the property in July (a true accomplishment in and of itself), a building inspector then condemned the property as being unfit as a classroom because it did not meet current fire codes. The cost to improve the property to standards would be another $30,000, nearly one-third again the original purchase price of the property. How would they ever secure these funds, let alone have the work completed in time for opening that very fall term? On top of this, there were grumblings among members of the church in Oregon who Mr. Armstrong claimed resented his move to Southern California and his transition to a national focus away from prioritizing members in the Pacific Northwest. With all of these pressures coming to bear at the very same time in 1947, Mr. Armstrong describes being near despair ("The Autobiography of Herbert W. Armstrong," *The Plain Truth*, June 1963, p. 30). Many outsiders had already concluded that the idea of this new college was folly, speaking not in terms of "if," but "when" it would fold up. But he also describes his strong belief that God indeed was guiding it all. The fact that every obstacle was eventually overcome, even dramatically, was evidence to him that there was something going on here beyond what was visible to human beings.

COLLEGE OPENS WITH FOUR STUDENTS ONLY

Herbert Armstrong's audacious plan did indeed come to fruition, and Ambassador College did indeed open for business that fall. But the first class was very limited due to the construction delays of the summer:

> We had received some forty applications from prospective college students. But this reconstruction program had delayed the college opening. I had been compelled to notify all applicants that I would advise them when we finally were ready to open. . . .
>
> Ambassador College did finally swing open its big front door to students October 8, 1947. But by that time nearly all applicants had gone elsewhere. Besides our son Dick (Richard David), there was only Raymond C. Cole, who came down from Oregon where his family had been in the Church for years; Herman L. Hoeh, who came from Santa Rosa, California; and Miss Betty Bates from Oklahoma—four pioneer students—with a faculty of eight.
>
> Did ever a college start so small? Or with a ratio of two professors to each student? But the things of God, through human instruments, always start the *smallest*, and grow to become the BIGGEST! ("The Autobiography of Herbert W. Armstrong," *The Plain Truth*, June 1963, p. 30)

Opposition From Within

The main problem with hiring secular professors as college faculty was that their own religious views could not help but manifest in the course of performing their duties. Whether it was Far Eastern occultism, atheism, or Protestant Christian leanings, Mr. Armstrong faced challenges in maintaining control and preventing his vision of "God's College" from being hijacked in spirit before barely getting underway. This is how he described it:

> I was determined that the Ambassador policy was going to be inculcated thoroughly in faculty and students alike. Ambassador was to be God's college—not another rubber stamp of the educational institutions of this world! But, with a faculty trained in this world's scholarship, I found that it required determined dominance on my part, plus vigilance, to assure it ("The Autobiography of Herbert W. Armstrong," *The Plain Truth*, September 1963, p. 18).

Ironically, this would be *the very same circumstance* that would present itself in the 1970s, when worldly scholars attempted to take Mr. Armstrong's work in a divergent direction. However, his lack of "dominance plus vigilance" in those particular years (as he later admitted) would result in a very different outcome.

Because they became grossly overextended financially in taking on the overhead of the new college project in 1947, the Armstrongs fell behind in paying their bills for some of the major national radio contracts. They were forced to drop the six-night-per-week broadcast on station XEG through most of 1948. There was still significant national presence, but nowhere comparable to that which they had achieved previously. The cumulative effect of these pressures put Mr. Armstrong under great duress:

> Other bills were pressing. I was being hounded on every side for money by creditors. Many around me continued to

96 A PECULIAR TREASURE

harp about "when this thing folds up." But I was determined it was not going to fold up!

Two or three times, through those harassing months, I did give up and quit—at night after going to bed, trying to push the nightmare out of mind and relax into sleep. But always the next morning was *another day*—and I bounded back with renewed determination to *win through* to success! (p. 22)

In spite of the discouragement of having to scale back *The World Tomorrow* broadcasts—which Mr. Armstrong described as being "thrown off the air"—the established loyalty of existing radio listeners around the country held firm, even without those *nightly* programs in many areas. Tithes and offerings continued to pour in at near previous levels, proving that Mr. Armstrong's base of listeners included more than just fair-weather acolytes. This truly was something the religious media world had never seen before.

These perpetual financial crises also required Mr. Armstrong to cut in half the Ambassador College second-year curriculum. Half of his eight professors did not return for the second year, and classes were offered only three days per week. This action would make it impossible to complete a four-year program on schedule without additional efforts by the students (p. 45).

Several more financial crises arose from 1947–48, any one of which could have destroyed the college. Many times, the future of that college looked very bleak. Yet, time and again, income would dramatically appear just when needed, or else circumstances would open up to provide another temporary reprieve. It was not until January 1949 that the major financial crises ended and a little relief was finally realized ("The Autobiography of Herbert W. Armstrong," *The Plain Truth*, October 1963, p. 18).

Even so, during 1949, there were only three issues of *The Plain Truth* published, and Mr. Armstrong was still writing all of the articles himself ("The Autobiography of Herbert W. Armstrong," *The Plain Truth*, November 1963, p. 13).

FOUNDING AND GROWTH OF CHURCH AND COLLEGE 1934–1957   97

COLLEGE EXPANSION

Having weathered years of financial and personnel problems and having finally achieved a tiny moment of reprieve in early 1949, one would think it a chance to embrace the *status quo* for just a bit and seek to retrench. Not so with Herbert Armstrong.

A neighboring, dilapidated mansion adjoining the college property became available in May, and Mr. Armstrong could not pass up the opportunity to secure it. That very month, the 28-room Tudor-style building named "Mayfair" was added to the college campus. By the fall of 1949, it would become the first on-campus student dormitory. With this expansion, Mr. Armstrong felt that the college was finally beginning to come into its own.

Seven students participated in the second-year program during 1948–49, and then enrollment rose to twelve in the fall of 1949. The 1950–51 school year was the first one with a full, four-year program. That year saw a student body of twenty-two, including six women. Ambassador College was finally showing signs of "growing up."

An additional adjacent property was purchased in November 1950, and slowly the campus of Ambassador College began to take shape.

FIRST MINISTERIAL HELPER ASSIGNED

Recall that the fundamental purpose of Ambassador College was to train men who could be commissioned to help care for the brethren who were flocking into the Radio Church of God as a result of the successful radio broadcasts. Up until this time, Mr. Armstrong would lay the foundation for a local congregation, only to have that group decimated after he turned it over to a local representative. Suitable leaders needed to be trained to think and to behave as Mr. Armstrong would if he were doing the job himself.

But the first college graduation could not possibly occur until the spring of 1951 if a degree was considered to be absolutely essential. This would be the first time that any one of the first students might

98   A PECULIAR TREASURE

possibly be deployed as a minister. But Mr. Armstrong could not
wait that long. By early 1951, the churches in Oregon were once
again embroiled in problems as a result of poor local leadership.
Waiting even a few more months probably would have seen the
destruction of those congregations. The solution was to pull one of
the men out early and send him out to take control. Speaking of that
particular school year, Mr. Armstrong wrote:

> That school year Raymond Cole, one of the four pioneer
> students, was student-body president. However, the local
> churches I had left up in Oregon, at Eugene and Portland,
> these years without a Pastor, were in serious need of
> leadership. And so in February, 1951, we sent Mr. Cole to
> Oregon to pastor and revive the flock. This was the very first
> beginning of a ministry produced by Ambassador College.
> After three and a half years at Ambassador College, Mr. Cole
> was able to repair the situation in Oregon, and start building
> up again ("The Autobiography of Herbert W. Armstrong,"
> *The Plain Truth*, November 1963, p. 15).

Although Raymond Cole was "pulled green" for this assignment,
the success of his half-year shepherding of the Oregon churches
became the *very first fulfillment* of Mr. Armstrong's long-range
dream to cultivate a competent and devoted ministry to support his
work. The experiment was paying off.

The first graduation took place in the spring of 1951:

> Since we had operated on half-schedule in the 1948-49
> year, it had been made virtually impossible for students to
> graduate in four years. Mr. Cole returned to Pasadena in
> August, 1951, and graduated in 1952, along with our son
> Dick. However, by taking a heavier-than-normal load the last
> two years, both Herman Hoeh and Betty Bates graduated in
> June, 1951—completing their college work in four years (p.
> 15).

DELEGATION OF WRITING DUTIES

In addition to local pastors, Mr. Armstrong also needed help in producing the magazines:

A one-man ministry could not maintain several local churches, an expanding broadcasting work, editing and writing all the articles for a fast-growing magazine, teach four college classes, and act as executive head of a growing college, without something slipping backward somewhere.

But 1951 was the year that produced the first "fruits" of the new college.

In April of that year we began the first activity toward an enlarged PLAIN TRUTH. I was still unwilling to publish in *The* PLAIN TRUTH, articles written by students. Yet something had to be done. . . .

Twelve years before I had started a second magazine, called *The* GOOD NEWS. It was to have been a church membership organ, edited exclusively for baptized church members. *The* PLAIN TRUTH was to continue as the general magazine for as many of the general public as would request it. But at that time—February, 1939—I had been unable to continue publication of *The* GOOD NEWS beyond the first issue! The reason? Same reason—lack of funds, and inability of ONE MAN to do so much.

But now, twelve years later, I decided to bring *The* GOOD NEWS back to life. . . .

Consequently, in April, 1951, *The* GOOD NEWS was re-born!

Now, for the first time, our students began to make active contributions to the activities of this expanding Work! ("The Autobiography of Herbert W. Armstrong," *The Plain Truth*, January 1964, pp. 9–10)

Students began by writing and editing articles in *The Good News*, but by August 1952, Mr. Armstrong approved selected articles from other writers for *The Plain Truth* as well. Full sixteen-page issues of either one or the other magazine were now able to go out every month, and at the beginning of 1953 the number of radio stations carrying *The World Tomorrow* program was also rebounding.

Mr. Armstrong had turned one room of the main college building into a recording studio in 1948, and being able to make their own master recordings for the broadcast began to save as much money each month as the cost of the mortgage payment for the campus property. Students were also enlisted to learn to run the recording equipment, and Richard (Dick) Armstrong became the first radio studio operator ("The Autobiography of Herbert W. Armstrong," *The Plain Truth*, February 1964, p. 44). Over time, this formula for providing part-time work for students in "the Work" while completing their degrees on campus, would become a reliable means of training future full-time workers for a permanent, large-scale operation. In time, Mr. Armstrong would employ the very same philosophy—investing large initial sums to build upfront infrastructure in order to reduce long-range production costs—in other key areas, including publishing.

First Ministerial Ordinations

During this same period of time, the very first ordinations of new ministers were performed by Mr. Armstrong. Even though his evangelical work had been carried out for more than twenty years by this time, it was the first recorded instance of his exercising "authority" to induct *other servants* into the ministry of Jesus Christ:

On December 20, 1952, by authority of Jesus Christ, with fasting and prayer and laying on of hands of God's ministers, in congregation assembled in Pasadena, California, upon recommendation of the Board of Trustees of The Radio

Church of God, five of our young ministers were fully ordained.

They are Richard David Armstrong, Raymond Clifford Cole, Herman Louie Hoeh, Dr. C. Paul Meredith, and Roderick Carl Meredith—all graduates of Ambassador College, except Dr. C. Paul Meredith who already held the doctor's degree from Iowa State College, but who had completed the entire four years of Theological study at Ambassador College.

Upon recommendation of the Board of Trustees, two more of our young ministers, Marion Joel McNair and Raymond Franklin McNair, will be fully ordained following their graduation from the college January 30, 1953.

This ordination authorizes these ministers to perform all the duties and exercise all the powers of the clergy, and clothes them with all the AUTHORITY conferred by Jesus Christ upon His called and chosen ministers.

And so it is that God has sent to us here, caused to be thoroughly trained by education, by experience, and thoroughly fitted by conversion, consecration, and Holy Spirit-leading, SEVEN fine young ministers whom HE has called and chosen. They have studied hard and diligently for years. They are all experienced and competent. They have been tried and tested, and found faithful and loyal ("Seven Ministers Ordained," *The Good News*, February 1953, p. 2).

Remember that this ceremony of formal ordination was not *the very first time* that these men had begun to be used by Mr. Armstrong for official ministerial duties. We have seen already that Raymond Cole was sent to pastor the churches in Oregon for several months in early 1951 before this ordination took place later in December. Yet he was already preaching, baptizing, anointing for sickness, and officiating with many of those "powers of the clergy." A number of these men were also sent out on baptizing tours while still attending college, as well as writing articles for the church. Since this was all being done by delegation, it appears that Mr.

Armstrong used the example of Jesus in sending out His disciples with "power," even while *they* were still in training, not even yet having received the Holy Spirit, which would come only after Christ was resurrected (compare Luke 9:2–6 with Acts 2:1–4).

This example becomes important later in the story in comparing how Mr. Armstrong seemed to view the issue of ministerial authority early on, versus how that view changed over time as his ministry transitioned from a sole proprietorship to a more expansive, "corporate" structure. Once these new men began to be deployed, that Work was finally able to begin dealing more effectively with its growing pains and to serve a rapidly expanding membership. At the very same time, the introduction of these new men would see their personal influences begin to impact the doctrinal teachings more and more, as well as the "personality" of that church. The work that for the first twenty years had reflected Mr. Armstrong's "flavor" would begin changing to reflect the orientation of other men.

Mr. Armstrong's Institutional Philosophy

The March 1964 issue of *The Plain Truth* contains a revealing statement by Mr. Armstrong, defining the *overriding philosophy* regarding *monetary funding* of his work through Ambassador College, as contrasted with that of most other institutions of higher learning:

> . . . they [the Ambassador College institutions] rely solely on GOD ALMIGHTY, in living faith, as their sole source of financial support! Of course we are well aware that, if GOD sponsors and finances us, HE is going to insist upon directing our policies—just as human government, corporations, or foundations see to it that they pretty largely direct the policies of institutions *they* finance. We know well that if Ambassador Colleges depart from GOD'S ways and policies, God's financial sponsorship will stop forthwith.

But that's precisely the way we want it! And that is the real reason for the miraculous, almost incredible SUCCESS of these institutions! God Almighty will back financially—to an extent almost beyond human belief—any person or institution that will place himself or itself unreservedly and vigorously under His direction! ("The Autobiography of Herbert W. Armstrong," *The Plain Truth*, March 1964, pp. 17–18)

Eventually, when we begin to analyze in more detail the events of the early 1970s within the Worldwide Church of God and the basis upon which major changes began to be made "at the top," the significance of this *early philosophy* about trusting God in the face of financial threats will become more revelatory. But for now, back to the storyline.

EXPANDING INTO EUROPE

After the second-year commencement ceremony for graduates of Ambassador College in June 1952, Mr. Armstrong sent his newly-graduated son, Richard Armstrong, to Europe to investigate the potential of growth into England, France, and Germany. The result of this trip was the expansion of *The World Tomorrow* radio broadcast onto *Radio Luxembourg* on the first Thursday of January 1953. Mr. Armstrong would later mark this date as a significant turning point for the Work—the point at which God chose to *open the door* for the Gospel of Jesus Christ to be preached beyond the confines of North America. In order to support the growing number of listeners being attracted by that new program, Richard Armstrong became instrumental in laying the groundwork and then in opening an office for the church in London by early 1954.

Note at this point that of Mr. Armstrong's two sons, it was Richard as a young man who had shown the most earnest appreciation for his father's work in God's service. Garner Ted Armstrong, by contrast, had joined the Navy (in 1948) at age

104

eighteen without his father's knowledge or consent, and chose only much later to become part of his father's religious work ("The Autobiography of Herbert W. Armstrong," *The Plain Truth*, June 1964, p. 9). Much more will be chronicled concerning the eventual influence and pivotal role of Garner Ted Armstrong in that growing church, but for now it suffices to show that in the *early* 1950s, it was Richard—not Ted—who had made himself an invaluable resource to his father. Richard became a trusted instructor at Ambassador College during the 1953–1954 school year, but the need for leadership in the growing European work forced him back to London in May 1954.

After the groundwork laid by Richard, Mr. and Mrs. Armstrong finally made their own personal visit to Europe in August 1954, with Mr. Armstrong conducting personal appearances for new radio listeners in Belfast, Manchester, and London during September. Hundreds of attendees flocked to hear his message at each stop, and thus began expansion in earnest of that unique evangelistic movement into Europe, including the very first baptism for the Radio Church of God in England performed by Richard Armstrong ("The Autobiography of Herbert W. Armstrong," *The Plain Truth*, June 1964, pp. 12–14, 29). It would be the first of many to come.

TELEVISION BROADCASTS—A FALSE START

April 1955 saw the broadcast of *The World Tomorrow* program on televison for the very first time. The boom in television set production and the move away from radio by other major broadcasters caused Mr. Armstrong to conclude that television was the "new medium" required to remain relevant, that radio would soon become a dinosaur, and that failure to act might lead to a real loss in public exposure for his message. Investment in network radio broadcasting was therefore significantly reduced, and a huge investment of time and money was put into producing a television program instead. Initial results were promising:

FOUNDING AND GROWTH OF CHURCH AND COLLEGE 1934–1957

Our mail response was big, considering the number of stations—only 12. It was bigger than from similar radio broadcasts—but TV was so much more costly, we felt it *had* to bring a much heavier mail response, to justify its heavier cost. Actually, even with only twelve stations, *The* WORLD TOMORROW was being viewed by a million or more people—perhaps two or three million. We were delivering a dynamic Message in power to a *huge* audience, who were not only *hearing*—as you do on radio—but also *seeing*—for a full half-hour ("The Autobiography of Herbert W. Armstrong," *The Plain Truth*, April 1964, p. 44).

But in the end, the results were not really sustained and did not prove to be cost effective. The experiment with TV lasted only twenty-seven weeks. A once-per-week TV broadcast simply failed to produce the same result as a daily radio broadcast. Quite contrary to the expected trend, radio in the 1950s continued to thrive—people were buying more radios than ever before, and they were still tuning in to radio broadcasts much more than they were watching television. That would certainly change over the ensuing decades, but at this stage, radio proved still to be the sustaining bread-and-butter medium for Mr. Armstrong's message.

Through the 1950s, the broadcasts continued to bear fruit, *The Plain Truth* magazine continued to "grow up" and to expand in content and quality, and the Radio Church of God continued to multiply its membership. For the period from 1950 through 1954, Mr. Armstrong claimed an average annual growth rate of fifty-six percent (*The Good News*, June 19, 1978, p. 3). From 1955 through 1959, that rate of growth continued averaging almost thirty-five percent annually. This was a huge, sustained, cumulative increase, taking into consideration the multiplying effect of those numbers year after year.

Ambassador College continued to expand physically, with the acquisitions of adjacent campus properties such as the four-acre Hulett C. Merritt mansion in 1956—renamed Ambassador Hall—and the Lewis J. Merritt mansion—renamed Manor Del Mar ("The

106   A PECULIAR TREASURE

Autobiography of Herbert W. Armstrong," *The Plain Truth*, August 1967, pp. 18–19, 21–22). The college also continued to graduate the new men needed to take on the administrative tasks required to minister to an ever-growing membership. Although Mr. Armstrong did not choose to emphasize it in his autobiography, belief in keeping the annual Holy Days found in Leviticus 23 created continual logistical challenges—especially in accommodating the multiple thousands who gathered to keep the Feast of Tabernacles for a full eight days in the autumn.

TEXAS FESTIVAL SITE DEVELOPMENT

From the early 1930s, Mr. Armstrong had held the Feast of Tabernacles in Belknap Springs, Oregon, a small resort in the Cascade Mountains to the east of Eugene. This remained an annual festival site through 1951 (along with some keeping the Feast in Pasadena, California). But by the fall of 1951, attendance at Belknap Springs was reported at over one hundred fifty (*The Good News*, December 1951, p. 13). This site would be far too small in the future, and so by 1953 the annual festivals began to be hosted in Gladewater, Texas. Mr. Armstrong would eventually develop property in Gladewater for a major festival site, and later this would lead to a second campus for Ambassador College as well. Here is some of the history of that project in Mr. Armstrong's own words, from the April 17, 1952 *Co-Worker Letter*:

A year ago, only two or three days before Passover, I was prompted to get busy on long distance telephone and call up a limited number of Texas and Louisiana co-workers we had come to know personally that God had added to His Church. Gladewater seemed to be the most central location. I called up first Brother Roy Hammer at Gladewater. He and Mrs. Hammer said they would be delighted to have the Passover at their home. We sent Herman Hoeh (pronounced "Hay"), then one of our senior students, by plane to conduct the service. Only thirteen were able to make the trip to Gladewater on such short notice.

This spring a number of brethren, having heard of the service last year, wrote to ask if such a service would be held at Gladewater again this year. As the number of such requests increased, I had a general form-letter mimeographed after arranging with the Hammers to have the service once again in Gladewater. Several urged that Mrs. Armstrong and I would make the trip to Gladewater to conduct the service this year, so notices were sent out to that effect.

I had not realized how many kept writing in, wanting to attend this service, and we didn't expect more than part of them to really attend. Consequently we were not at all prepared for the conclave that poured in. Tuesday afternoon and evening cars began driving up in front of the Hammer residence with many different-colored license plates . . . As the people started pouring in at the Hammer home toward dusk, there was nothing to do but try to squeeze them all in the house and conduct the service as best we could. There were 85 adults who partook of the Passover, not counting children. We were packed in like sardines. . . .

On the Holy Day, Thursday [first High Day of Unleavened Bread], there were so many written questions turned in, and others asked orally during the service, that we never did get to a sermon. The entire time was taken up answering questions, and in a service of laying on hands for the receiving of the Holy Spirit on the eleven who were baptised during this conclave, and the blessing of infants and children, following the example of Jesus.

As it turned out, there was a huge and growing demand for a site where church members could keep the spring and fall festivals, and

108   A PECULIAR TREASURE

the site in East Texas became the strategic location where members who were now scattered across the entire country could gather. Mr. Armstrong continues:

> GLADEWATER, TEXAS, IS THE MOST CENTRALLY LOCATED PLACE, closest for the largest number. Now God always supplies every need, WHEN that need arises. During this festival, the son of Mr. and Mrs. Hammer, Buck Hammer, who owns a farm about seven miles west of Gladewater, offered to donate and deed over to us several acres of the most beautiful sloping, wooded land we ever saw, for this purpose. . . .

> We shall have to build a tabernacle—not a costly one, but one large enough,—with dining area for our festivals, and plan the kind of housing to be provided for all who come—perhaps well-planned but inexpensive cabins. However, we do not feel it wise to try to erect any buildings during the first year. For the festival next spring we will rent large tents, to provide a meeting place and dining facilities, and a large number of small tents which can be rented to each family. We will "rough it" our first year on the place next spring, and then try to have at least temporary buildings erected by the year following (*Co-Worker Letter*, April 17, 1952).

Thus began the development of a property that would serve the church well for many years. As the church continued to grow, this "Big Sandy" property in Gladewater would become the focal point of many Holy Day festival observances, including gatherings of more than ten thousand attendees by the late 1960s.

CHURCH GROWTH STATISTICS

To provide some perspective concerning the growth curve of the Radio Church of God through the 1950s, take a look at the statistics for attendance at the fall Feast of Tabernacles through that decade:

In 1953, approximately 1,000 attended for at least part of the fall festival in Gladewater (*The Good News*, November 1953, p. 1). In 1957, that number rose to 2,800. There were 4,000 attendees in 1958, 5,500 in 1959, and 7,000 in 1960 (*The Good News*, 11/57, p. 1; 12/58, p. 1; 11/59, p. 8; 11/60, p. 3). That trend would continue unabated through the 1960s as well. By 1960, there were also international feast sites, with 250 attendees in England, 475 in Africa (Rhodesia), 104 in Australia, and 444 in the Philippines. This tracking of annual festival attendance became an excellent barometer of the trending strength of the church as a whole—much more so than estimating broadcast listeners or mailing list recipients. The "real members" were ones who made the sacrifice to attend the Feasts.

CHAPTER SIX

KEY DEATHS, NEW MISSION, UNREST 1957–1974

GROWTH AND DELEGATION FOSTERS CULTURAL CHANGES

As mentioned previously, rapid expansion of the church required Mr. Armstrong to rely more heavily upon other men to begin writing articles and managing administrative duties. It is not surprising therefore that the 1950s witnessed a slow but persistent change in the culture of the church as a *governing structure* began to expand. By the late 1950s, there were an increasing number of articles in *The Good News* magazine addressing the topic of church government and the need for members to submit to ministerial authority. These articles were often penned by men such as Herman Hoeh and Roderick Meredith, two of the earliest ordained ministers who were wielding increasing authority within the church.

More detailed attention will be given in later chapters to these *changing leadership dynamics* through the 1950s, but for purposes of this brief introductory summary, take note of the fact that Mr. Armstrong came to believe that God would bless these *newly-ordained men* with the *same level of inspiration* in discovering new truth from the Bible as he himself had experienced during the first thirty years of his calling. That *single assumption* in his mind—that God would use other men equally—would become *pivotal* in shaping the eventual direction of that church in later decades. Whether it was actually true or not that God inspired these other men, accepting that God would bring "new truth" into the body through the *personal scholastic research of others* opened the way for many *new theories* to take root side-by-side with the doctrines of Herbert Armstrong, as they came to be taught to members of the church as "a package deal."

112   A PECULIAR TREASURE

Appointing a Vice President

The other critical decision made by Mr. Armstrong in the late 1950s was the appointment of his younger son, Garner Ted, as Vice President of the church and Ambassador College. Here is an expanded excerpt that will shed light on this pivotal decision:

However, by late 1957, the growth of the Work demanded more organization, and Garner Ted was made Vice-President of Ambassador College, and also Vice-President of the Radio Church of God (the incorporated name of the Work), on November 21, 1957.

Shortly afterward Roderick C. Meredith, who is second Vice-President, wrote an article on this nomination of Garner Ted to the Vice-Presidency.

I think our readers will find it interesting. So I include it here: . . .

Recently, Mr. Armstrong came to realize the need of someone who could be in *complete charge* of the Work during his absences on business trips or campaigns in God's service. . . .

Until very recently, Mr. Armstrong was hesitant about making such an important decision for two reasons. First, he had tried to work and cooperate with other ministers time and again in his early ministry. But *always* he was disappointed. These other men—*in nearly every case*—eventually turned to *lying,* to *stealing* God's tithe money, *adultery* or, they were just incompetent—and God bore no "fruit" through them.

So Mr. Armstrong learned the *hard way* that he must TEST and PROVE *any* man before placing him in an office in God's Church—not to speak of designating another man to have full authority to direct the entire Work in his absence!

Second, until the past few months there has been *no one* who was in any way qualified to take over the *many* and *varied* types of responsibilities that fall on the shoulders of the one in Mr. Armstrong's office.

The man in his position must be able to take over the broadcast and reach the world *effectively* with God's message. He must be able and competent to oversee the writing and editing of the magazine and booklets—and to do a considerable part of the writing himself. He must be able to *teach* and *instruct* in many ways, and he must have the executive know-how, and the *wisdom* and *balance* to guide the Work and Ambassador College in the sound policies it is now following.

This man must be able to be the *business executive* for the Work and College, and be able to command the respect of businessmen, engineers, architects, printers, advertising men, radio men, educators and a host of others. He must have a *sound mind* and a *balanced personality*. For wherever he is, he represents the *entire* Work and College! And he must have the *vision* to think BIG—to personally inspire and guide the Work around the *entire earth*, as God intends.

In addition to all these qualities, he must, of course, be thoroughly *yielded* and *consecrated* to God—totally SURRENDERED to His will. He must have the spiritual *love* and *compassion* to be a minister and help to all those he can personally reach, and these qualities must be the *motivating factor* in the exercise of all his gifts and in the administration of his high office in God's Work. And he must be a DRIVING FORCE—a *hard* WORKER—and show by his "fruits" that God is able to *use him* in effectively carrying out all the responsibilities and tasks that fall his lot. . . .

Mr. Armstrong recently made the official announcement that he was appointing Garner Ted Armstrong as the Vice-President both of the Radio Church of God and of Ambassador College. Thus, during any prolonged absence of his father, Mr. Ted Armstrong now has full authority to take complete charge and make any decisions necessary for the effective accomplishment of God's Work ("The Autobiography of Herbert W. Armstrong," *The Plain Truth*, September 1967, pp. 21, 31).

Within twenty years of the date of this announcement, Mr. Armstrong would come to regret this decision to put so much confidence in Ted. The eventual divide between father and son would become a most serious wound to the entire church. But back in 1957, Mr. Armstrong came to believe that Ted was his strongest asset. Even though his elder son, Richard, had shown much more loyalty and devotion to the church by his early personal choices, Ted's incredible *natural gifts* seemed to overshadow the manifested weaknesses in his personal character. Mr. Armstrong came to believe that his younger son was truly now "converted" and could fill his father's shoes if required.

RICHARD ARMSTRONG DIES

On July 23, 1958, Richard Armstrong was involved in a terrible car accident on the Pacific Coast Highway near San Luis Obispo, California. He was in the passenger seat as he and another minister were traveling north, conducting a visiting/baptizing tour. It was a head-on collision that impacted Richard's side of the car. He had multiple broken bones and internal injuries and died a week later on July 30. He was not yet thirty years of age, leaving a new wife and a two-month-old son (The Autobiography of Herbert W. Armstrong," *The Plain Truth*, October 1967, pp. 41–43). Compared with his more outgoing younger brother Ted, Richard had more quietly and steadily increased his contribution to his father's work through the 1950s. What would his influence have been upon that church as a whole had he lived through the 1960s and into the tumultuous decade of the '70s? Perhaps nothing would have been different. Perhaps everything would have been different. It is a question left only to speculation. Needless to say, the Armstrong family was devastated.

NEW COLLEGE CAMPUSES

Mr. Armstrong continued to "think big," and the growth of church membership in Europe and other countries around the globe led him to desire a branch of Ambassador College in the UK to facilitate training of ministers to serve new international congregations. Here are excerpts from his announcement to the church in June 1959:

> Also plans were made for establishing a second Ambassador College in Britain, beginning September next year, 1960. God opened to us one of England's fine, spacious country estates. . . . In this case, the estate has been subdivided into many smaller farms, and most of it sold, except for the fine big mansion, with its 8 acres of beautifully landscaped lawns, rose gardens etc., and a 2-acre plot containing brick housing units for the former employed staff, the fine brick stables, garages etc. These will make student housing, as also will servants' quarters in one large wing of the mansion. . . . We obtained it for less than we paid for any of our college buildings in Pasadena, tho this is larger than any of them, and even finer than any except Ambassador Hall. . . . This also provides adequate office space for our fast-expanding London office. Our London office manager told me the saving in office rent will more than pay for this fine property.
>
> Thus GOD has providentially opened to us a superb, magnificently landscaped 10-acre college campus, only five miles from the edge of London, walking distance from

116 A PECULIAR TREASURE

suburban train, with a fine, stately, 33-room college building, with ample classrooms, and offices and mailing rooms—and without putting any financial burden on our United States and world-wide work from Pasadena headquarters! (*Co-Worker Letter*, June 29, 1959)

This new campus in St. Albans would be named Bricket Wood. It would enhance the international presence of the Radio Church of God and act as an anchor for the development of churches across Europe.

In another letter from early 1963, Mr. Armstrong confirms his consistent strategy for managing the incredible growth of the church:

The Work CANNOT GROW unless the colleges continue to turn out an INCREASING number of graduates every year. This great Work now encompasses THE WHOLE WORLD. It now requires the full time work of HUNDREDS of trained men and women. It now reaches MILLIONS of people every week—our estimate is at least 22 million! (*Co-Worker Letter*, May 22, 1963)

Toward this end, *a third campus* of Ambassador College opened in Texas in 1964, on the grounds of the very property in Big Sandy that had been developed for observance of the annual festivals. An excerpt from a 1964 issue of *The Good News* provides background:

All of this time, the facilities in the East Texas woods were expanding to accommodate the Feast of Tabernacles. However, these facilities were *only* under use for *eight days* of the year.

When the need for a THIRD AMBASSADOR COLLEGE became so apparent that it could not be avoided, the obvious answer to the problem was to use the *already-existing facilities*—God had ALREADY PREPARED—in East Texas. . . .

With all of the last-minute activities, finally, dormitories were prepared; all the existing facilities were put into shape, personnel were hired, and the faculty moved in.

Sophomore, junior and senior students had been transferred over from the Pasadena Campus to set the pace and atmosphere in Big Sandy so that it would be *exactly the same* as the atmosphere in Pasadena and Bricket Wood—in fact, one student was sent from Bricket Wood so this atmosphere would also have its influence in Big Sandy. Six seniors, twenty-one juniors, and nineteen sophomores were joined by sixty-four freshman students and *Ambassador College was under way. . . .*

After exactly the same entrance examinations and entrance procedures, Ambassador College began with the full curriculum of classes on Tuesday morning, September 7, 1964 ("The THIRD Ambassador College!," *The Good News*, November 1964, pp. 21–23).

CONTINUED PHENOMENAL GROWTH

If it seemed that the incredible growth of the Radio Church of God through the 1950s could not be long sustained, more surprises were in store for the doubters. Again, just examine the records for attendance at the fall Feast of Tabernacles through much of the 1960s.

In 1961 a new festival site was opened in Squaw Valley, California, to help provide space for all attendees. This was a rented facility. Total attendance around the world that year (dominated by those gathering in Big Sandy and Squaw Valley) was 11,000 (*The Good News*, 9/61). In the fall of 1962 that number was 15,000—8,000 in Big Sandy alone and 5,000 in Squaw Valley (*The Good News*, 10/62). With a total of ten gathering sites around the world, the following three years reported 20,000, 25,000, and 31,000 attendees respectively (*The Good News*, 11/63; 10/64; 10–11/65). To handle this incredible influx, another new feast site

118 A PECULIAR TREASURE

was "rented" in Jekyll Island, Georgia, in 1964. The "meeting hall" was a giant circus tent erected on an open lot. This creative solution pointed out the lack of large convention facilities in many areas of the country at that time. Mr. Armstrong's solution was for the church to purchase land in strategic areas across North America and to erect large tabernacle buildings on-site. The first of these was opened for the Feast of 1968 in Mt. Pocono, Pennsylvania. Identical facilities opened in Lake of the Ozarks, Missouri, and Penticton, British Columbia, Canada, in 1969, and another in Wisconsin Dells, Wisconsin, in 1972. Total Feast attendance in 1970 included 70,000 people at twenty-two sites in twelve countries.

LOMA ARMSTRONG DIES

In early 1967, Mrs. Armstrong was stricken with a severe intestinal malady which left her in a perilous condition. After the initial three-week ordeal, she seemed to be improving somewhat, but then had a progressive downturn which ended in her death on April 15, 1967 (*Co-Worker Letter*, April 17, 1967). Here are the comments made by Mr. Armstrong to the church at that time:

> But I am deeply sorry to have to announce, at the same time, that my wife's critical illness has ended in the manner least expected—in her death just after midnight Saturday morning, April 15. . . .

> Thirty-four years ago, at this same time of year, when my father died having reached his 70th year, I had to learn that GOD'S PROMISES ARE ABSOLUTELY SECURE —but not always in the way we expect. . . .

> We did fully expect that God would heal her NOW. True, she was 75 1/2 years of age. . . .

God already had given my wife 5 1/2 years more of this life than He gave [King] David. She was just a few months older than I, though part of each year we were "the same age," as they are counted. Yet neither of us have felt or acted in any manner like "old folks," or "elderly" people. We never thought of her as being anywhere <u>near</u> seventy! (*Co-Worker Letter*, April 17, 1967)

What most forget today is that by 1967, both Mr. and Mrs. Armstrong had already lived "full lives." In their mid-seventies, most people would have long since retired from their life occupations. But interestingly, from the death of Mrs. Armstrong forward, the very *most significant* events in the history of Mr. Armstrong and the church would only then begin to unfold.

A New Commission?

Soon after Mrs. Armstrong's death, events began to take place that would lead Mr. Armstrong in a very different direction than could ever have been anticipated. That was the opportunity to meet in person with world leaders of many different countries. And based upon these spontaneous new opportunities, Mr. Armstrong came to believe that his commission from God was changing. Rather than just proclaiming the gospel to the masses through expanding media outlets around the world, it appeared to him now that God was opening *a new door* for him to take the gospel to *world leaders*. In 1971, Mr. Armstrong summarized this new philosophy to the church and looked retrospectively at how that transition had come to pass:

As I mentioned in my previous letter a month ago, the Work of necessity had to begin by reaching the grassroots—the masses of the common people—the RULED. We now are reaching more than <u>150 MILLION</u> of them. . . .

120   A PECULIAR TREASURE

But we have reached the point where it has now become necessary that we reach ALSO the RULERS—those in the very top echelons of POWER in the world. Because, whether we have realized it or not, this Work is the GREATEST, MOST EFFECTIVE activity on earth for WORLD PEACE! (*Co-Worker Letter*, May 28, 1971)

How did this opportunity open to him? The very first such contact seems to have resulted from trying to get *The World Tomorrow* radio program on a Jordanian radio station broadcasting from Jerusalem. This was in June 1967, soon after Mrs. Armstrong's death. The contract for radio time had been made with the Jordanian government (which at that time controlled the "old city" of Jerusalem), but before the first broadcast could be aired, the Israelis took over that portion of the city in the Six-Day War, resulting in Jordan losing control of this station. Negotiations with highly-placed representatives of King Hussein of Jordan led to Mr. Armstrong broadcasting from the city of Amman instead, with that broadcast signal reaching into Jerusalem. Mr. Armstrong would eventually meet with King Hussein in person (*Co-Worker Letter*, July 31, 1967).

A second opportunity to meet with people in high places came in February 1968, when King Leopold III of Belgium asked for a visit from Mr. Armstrong:

The wife of our office manager at Bonn, West Germany, happened to show a copy of the 1966 Ambassador College year book—"The ENVOY"—to an industrialist friend in Brussels. He was much impressed by the book, and the high character of Ambassador students, reflected in their photographs and action shots. This industrialist happened to be a personal friend of King Leopold of Belgium. He asked if he might show the ENVOY to the King. The King was quite impressed, and said he would like to meet the founder and Chancellor of this unique high-character educational institution (*Co-Worker Letter*, May 28, 1971).

The King of Belgium would become a personal friend to Mr. Armstrong, would visit Ambassador College a number of times in ensuing years, and would even travel with Mr. Armstrong on some of his future state visits.

A third event occurring in 1968 was the participation of Ambassador College in an archeological venture with Hebrew University to excavate the Temple Mount in Jerusalem. Mr. Armstrong summarized the project this way:

In September, 1968, Dr. Ernest Martin, Dean of the faculty at our English campus, and Dr. Herman L. Hoeh, Dean of Faculties at Pasadena, wanted Ambassador College to conduct an archeological project at a location in Israel, some miles north of Jerusalem. I was personally not interested in such a project. But I consented to their visiting Jerusalem to see whether permission could be granted from the government authorities.

Dr. Hoeh happened to be acquainted with Dr. Benjamin Mazar, archeologist, and former President of Hebrew University. He found Dr. Mazar at the time in charge of the most important "dig" so far undertaken, starting from the south wall of the Temple Mount. Three major United States universities had sought participation in this outstanding project. All had been rejected. But Professor Mazar offered a 50-50 joint participation to Ambassador College! . . .

I began to realize the scientific and educational value to Ambassador College. A luncheon was held in a private dining room in the Knesset—the government's capitol building. Present at the luncheon were five high-ranking officials of both the university and the government. And also, with me, were Dr. Hoeh, Mr. Charles F. Hunting, one of Ambassador's Vice Presidents in charge of finances for Britain, Europe and the Middle East, and Mr. Stanley R. Rader, our chief counsel (*Co-Worker Letter*, May 28, 1971).

122 A PECULIAR TREASURE

So from 1968 forward, Mr. Armstrong was suddenly catapulted into *the halls of power* around the world, and invitations to visit other heads of state would begin to multiply.

Take note, for a moment, of the fact that Mr. Stanley Rader was part of Mr. Armstrong's personal entourage in these early 1968 visits. He would likewise become a very formidable character in the church's history in the coming decade. Having first worked for Mr. Armstrong as an accountant and financial consultant in the late 1950s, even though he was not a church member, Mr. Rader would rise in influence to become the church's treasurer, chief legal counsel, and more importantly, a trusted confidant and traveling companion of Mr. Armstrong during this *new phase* of the Work.

SEEKING THE WORLD'S APPROVAL

Much more will be covered in chapter fifteen about this pivotal time period, but at this point in the storyline, note how 1968 marked a radical shift in Mr. Armstrong's approach to his religious mission, compared to his beginnings in the 1930s. Whereas the Radio Church of God had always celebrated its identity as being *contrary* to the world and its major institutions, now we see Mr. Armstrong beginning *to court* these very institutions and to attribute their flattering overtures toward him to God's special blessing. In the name of *opening doors* to proclaim the Gospel of Jesus Christ—a gospel very contrary to *every other religious work,* and one hated by most—Mr. Armstrong would begin to forge alliances with famous people and with worldly humanitarian institutions. Notice this in his description of the Jerusalem "dig" project:

> First, it is one of the most important scientific projects under way anywhere on earth today. It will mean great prestige and recognition of Ambassador College. If some wonder why we need recognition by the world, remember that we are commissioned to GO INTO THE WORLD TO PREACH THE GOSPEL. We have to deal with the world.

We have to obtain the use of the world's facilities—radio broadcast time on their radio facilities, television facilities, and publishing facilities when we buy large advertising space in the great mass-circulation magazines. This is increasing the readership of The PLAIN TRUTH by hundreds of thousands. Without favorable recognition and status in our "public image" we simply COULD NOT CARRY OUT CHRIST'S COMMISSION! (*Co-Worker Letter*, December 10, 1968)

What a drastic change in philosophy from the first thirty-five years of his ministry! When had he ever before needed personal visits with heads of state in order to secure access to radio broadcasting time and print media distribution? When previously had soliciting the "favorable recognition" of worldly institutions been required in order to proclaim the gospel and to build the church?

A decade later, in the June 19, 1978 issue of *The Good News*, Mr. Armstrong would publish to the church a summary of church growth statistics from 1950 through that present day. He showed in chart form that from 1950 through 1968, the church grew in membership by an average of 31.7 percent *annually*. But from 1969 through 1977, the church experienced an *average annual loss* in membership of 1.8 percent. Given that 1968 was the key year of this new *major pivot* in orientation toward seeking alliances with worldly institutions, what might that imply in the minds of those who believe (or once believed) God was the one who had been blessing Mr. Armstrong's efforts from the beginning? Mr. Armstrong himself had always asserted that God blesses us as we please Him.

WHAT'S IN A NAME?

It was also in 1968 that the name of the Radio Church of God was changed to the Worldwide Church of God. It is interesting that there is little to document how that name change was communicated to the church as a whole, but anecdotal accounts (to the extent they can be trusted) assert that Mr. Armstrong felt the church had outgrown the original name. No longer a single, small congregation in Eugene, Oregon, producing a local radio program, that church had grown over thirty-five years and claimed over 150,000 members, with offices and publishing operations around the world. And now, with the growing attention of world leaders, the church needed a name more befitting its blossoming new status. A document entitled, *1968 Certificate of Amendment of Articles of Incorporation of Radio Church of God*, confirms that the name change was approved in a meeting on January 5, 1968, and signed by Mr. Armstrong and the corporate Secretary, Mr. Albert J. Portune. The name change was filed with the state of California on June 18, 1968. The first use of the new name seems to have emerged in publications being produced by the church in very late 1968. It seems much more than coincidence that this name change was occurring in concert with a whole new view of the organization, its identity, and its mission before God.

Prophetic Expectation

By the late 1950s, thanks to certain prophetic speculations that had taken hold within the church, especially those advanced by Dr. Herman Hoeh, Mr. Armstrong and the whole church *believed sincerely* that the end of the age was at hand and that Jesus Christ would be returning to rule as King very soon. In fact, although never declaring it as an absolute fact, many writings of the ministry had primed the membership to believe that Jesus Christ would return in 1975. They were also schooled to believe that the faithful of God would be taken to a "place of safety" in 1972 to escape three and one-half years of great tribulation before that Second Coming. Mr. Armstrong's own view of his new commission before kings of this world was expressed in terms of "finishing the Work" in the run-up to 1972. Notice just one example:

"So there will be a Temple built on the spot of the old Temple in Jerusalem. The Jews will again be offering the daily sacrifices. This is shown not only by the fact that the type of Antiochus Epiphanes stopping the sacrifices in 168 B.C. indicates it — but also the prophecy of Daniel 12:11 which is a direct and specific prophecy of stopping the daily sacrifices 1290 days before Christ's coming, and the resurrection of the dead in Christ. . . ."

But be sure time is shorter than you supposed! Momentous prophecies are due for fulfillment, very rapidly, from now on! . . .

I will just say, now, that from those prophecies, it is possible that the taking away of the daily sacrifice in the Temple — the placing of the "abomination" there also — could take place early in 1972. This is indicated in Revelation 12:14 (another three-and-one-half-year period), by Rev. 3:10; and other facts of history and prophecy connected with Matthew 24:14 — as well as other prophecies in Daniel ("Personal from the Editor," *The Plain Truth*, June 1967, p. 5).

This is only a small excerpt that confirms the material that the whole church had been digesting for many years. Perhaps the most dominant example of this particular prophetic interpretation was found in Mr. Armstrong's 1956 article (turned into a very popular booklet), entitled, *1975 in Prophecy*. No, the article never drew a *firm conclusion* in "setting dates" for the return of Christ, but that was nonetheless *the effect* that it had upon many church members, especially given the title of the article. All eyes were focused upon 1972–1975, and that expectation continued unabated, even as the 1960s ended and the new decade of the 1970s began.

126   A PECULIAR TREASURE

TROUBLE ON THE HORIZON

Several critical factors were coalescing in the early 1970s to create *a perfect storm* within the Worldwide Church of God.

Firstly, as noted above, the greatest issue was the *membership expectation* of last-day prophecies beginning to unfold *in earnest* in 1972. They were awaiting Mr. Armstrong's signal that it was "time to flee." What would happen to the church if no such fulfillment manifested?

Secondly, there was a serious lack of cohesion within the ministry by this time, due to a difference in doctrinal interpretation among several factions which had emerged over the preceding decade. Several ministers, especially some who had sought higher degrees in worldly institutions, now brandished their credentials as "scholastic doctors" within the church, intent upon changing a number of long-held teachings of the church with which they disagreed. (Mr. Armstrong provides revealing insight into this controversy in his final writing to the church on June 24, 1985; *The Worldwide News*, pp. 2–3.) The irony was that, on the one hand, by the 1970s, Ambassador College was turning out many new graduates (including ministers) to serve the ever-growing needs of the church. But on the other hand, Ambassador College was turning out many new graduates (including ministers) who *did not* all share the original orientation of their founder, Mr. Herbert Armstrong—an orientation that had been *the core of that church* from the beginning. Many of Mr. Armstrong's teachings were now under fire from within. These "doctors of the law" claimed he had never been a true "Bible scholar." He was "an amateur" and needed their *superior skills* to help "fix" doctrinal errors long held in the church. Until this time, Mr. Armstrong had rejected the majority of these pressures from within. He *pushed back* very hard against this liberal faction in the ministry, asserting often that God had *revealed* these doctrines to him and therefore he *refused to change them*! He would point to the monumental growth and success of that enterprise under his direction as proof that God had led him into the Truth. But now, with an end to that phenomenal growth pattern, would his strong defense endure?

Thirdly, Garner Ted Armstrong had assumed an ever-increasing role throughout the 1960s, becoming "the public face" of that church by the end of the decade. *His* was now *the voice* of *The World Tomorrow* radio broadcast, not his father's. *His* was now *the face* in the new TV programs. At the very time the Radio Church of God began to reach more people around the world than ever before, it was Garner Ted—not his father—who was branded as *the spokesman* for that empire. But this charismatic spokesman had some personal problems which could not help but become public in due time. And inconveniently, the timing of those personal revelations would manifest publicly in the early 1970s.

Garner Ted Suspended

In the fall of 1971, Mr. Armstrong had no choice but to suspend his son from ministerial duties. The earliest announcements emphasized that it was due to stress and exhaustion from too many duties. But by the spring of 1972, given that the media was digging deep for specific details, Mr. Armstrong finally wrote the following to the whole church:

> I hope you will realize that this is the most difficult and painful announcement that I have ever had to make in a Co-Worker letter.

> Last autumn [1971] I was dismayed to learn that my son had been so overcome with personal, emotional problems, that it led to conduct inconsistent with the high standard of the Work of the Church of God and the scriptural qualifications for a minister of Jesus Christ, and rendered him incapable of carrying on the duties of a minister, and of his responsibilities of Executive Vice President.

128   A PECULIAR TREASURE

The Board of Directors of Worldwide Church of God, and
the Board of Trustees of Ambassador College, grieved as we
were, had no choice but to remove Garner Ted Armstrong
from his office and his responsibilities. Mr. Albert J. Portune
was made ACTING Executive Vice President of both
corporations, and Mr. Garner Ted Armstrong was granted a
leave of absence, hoping that full repentance and overcoming
of his personal, emotional problems would allow
reinstatement without a long delay, and for the protection of
the Work, no public announcement was made (*Co-Worker
Letter*, April 25, 1972).

Garner Ted's disappearance during the months he was put on
"sabbatic leave" created a vacuum, publicly, for the church. All at
once, the charismatic spokesman and "face" of the church was gone,
and without any credible explanation. By the spring of 1972, the
impact of lower financial contributions was being felt, and it
appeared that the absence of Garner Ted on radio and TV was a key
factor. The May 1972 issue of the *Ministerial Bulletin* (a publication
sent to all Worldwide Church of God ministers from Headquarters)
included a letter from Roderick Meredith (in charge of Church
Administration). It is revealing:

As many of you know, the general income for the Work,
for the building fund and even for the spring Holy Day
offerings is down considerably this spring. In addition, the
numbers of new Co-Workers, numbers of visit requests and
numbers of new prospective members are also down on a
percentage basis. There are <u>several</u> factors which contribute
to this picture . . . One is the "1972 syndrome" [meaning the
failed prophetic speculations of the ministry]. In spite of all
our statements or wishes to the contrary, a lot of our
brethren HAVE let this affect them—even <u>before</u> most of
them realized there was a really serious problem with Mr.
Ted Armstrong. Because they think we were dogmatic on
this point in the past, many are distrusting the Church a little

more in general and are retrogressing spiritually and, at the same time, obviously, in their support for the Work. . . .

The second internal area we need to concentrate on has been called the "G.T.A. syndrome." Because of the uncertainty of Mr. Garner Ted Armstrong's real status for a while, many brethren and Co-Workers became discouraged or "uneasy." Some began cutting down on or withholding their tithes and offerings—a few even sending us anonymous letters to this effect.

There is nothing like a significant drop in income to get the attention of any corporate empire like the WCG had become. A number of the very ministers who had first objected fiercely to allowing Garner Ted to continue as a minister—deeming him unfit—now clamored to bring him back. And a loving father, who was eager to see his son restored to good graces within "the Work," was easily convinced to accept Garner Ted's claims of heartfelt repentance. Here is an excerpt from Mr. Armstrong's letter to the church about the reinstatement of his son:

Messrs. Portune, Antion and Dart—all Vice Presidents, Mr. Stanley Rader and I, are returning to Pasadena from a momentous meeting with my son Garner Ted Armstrong. I had spent the better part of two days with him last week, and I knew then that with God's help, and countless hours of submissive, prevailing prayer on his part, coupled with the prayers of thousands for him, his problems have now been overcome. There is no question in our minds that God is calling him back now, with plans for the greatest lunge forward this Work of God has ever taken. He is like a <u>NEW</u> Garner Ted Armstrong, and we believe God will now use him with far greater power in getting out Christ's Gospel to the world than ever before. We know God has forgiven, and filled him—and us—with a completely new dedication for the

130   A PECULIAR TREASURE

finishing of the Work for this age (*Co-Worker Letter*, May 31, 1972).

But had that prodigal son really turned over a new leaf? Time would tell.

Solving the "1972 Syndrome"

So now they had solved the "G.T.A. syndrome" by bringing him back. But what about the "1972 syndrome" which was still suppressing income and causing disaffection among the base of church members? It was not possible to force world events to coincide with unwise prophetic speculations of the past. What could be done to soothe members who were discouraged and even depressed because Jesus Christ was not truly coming to usher in His Kingdom right away?

The *nagging problem* now plaguing the church was the burden of "difficult doctrines" which members were required to practice, most especially the teaching on divorce and remarriage. Mr. Armstrong had taught from the beginning of his ministry that marriage was *bound for life*, and, that there was *no option for remarriage* while an original mate was still alive. The huge influx of new members who had joined the church in preceding decades included some who were divorced, and in many cases, these had remarried and had children of these second marriages. Much more will be detailed later about this doctrinal issue, but at this point in the storyline, note simply that there were many members who had acquiesced to this "hard teaching" and were remaining celibate—even separating from second marriages—in order to avoid committing adultery before God and missing out on God's special protections in *the last days*. As long as there was hope that this requirement to endure *physical deprivation* of companionship would end soon—because Jesus was returning by 1975—many were willing to "tough it out." But when 1972 came and went, with no fulfillment of these great, biblical last-day events, many of these celibate members became restless. If Jesus Christ did not return in the next decade, or even *in their entire lifetimes*, would they be willing to remain single and celibate? The answer for many was, "no." The ministry became fearful that there would be a *mass exodus* of members. What could be done?

THE 1972 DOCTRINAL COMMITTEE

The solution was to find a way to justify *relaxing* these "burdensome" doctrines and to make it easier for people to remain members in good standing. How could these members be given what they wanted, humanly, while remaining loyal to the church and keeping those tithes and offerings coming? It would be very difficult to announce a *radical new change* concerning the marriage doctrine—to begin to permit divorcees to remarry—without offending many "conservatives" within the church who believed the original teaching came from God Himself. Mr. Herbert Armstrong had always asserted that God *had revealed* that Truth to him. If the current doctrine was actually in error and needed correction, it would undermine *the very legitimacy* of Mr. Armstrong's ministry. But that is exactly what would occur with the creation of a new doctrinal committee to "re-prove" all of the church's former teachings, one by one. And eventually the leader of that committee would be none other than his son, Garner Ted Armstrong. The liberal scholars in the church finally had their opening. In the name of *growing in grace and knowledge* (2 Peter 3:18), they would challenge *every former doctrine* of the church, one by one. In hindsight, Mr. Armstrong would write of that time:

> But soon a few would-be scholars had established themselves into a "Doctrinal Team." What started as an honest effort to find and establish real TRUTH in due time turned into a group of "would-be scholars" not appointed by me, seeking to destroy the true doctrines of the Church.

132   A PECULIAR TREASURE

This brought controversy into the Church. These self-professed "scholars," influenced by teaching in universities in which they were enrolling for higher degrees, were becoming more and more liberal. They wanted to skirt as close as possible to the precipice of secularism, falling off the cliff into Satan's world (*The Worldwide News–Special Edition*, June 24, 1985).

The goal was to change the marriage doctrine. But how to go about it? It would be better to sponsor a change in a "lesser doctrine" first, especially if there was one *inherently* hard to understand anyway, and one that many of the church members would not care that much about. Once *the precedent* for changing doctrine was established, it would be easier thereafter to make changes to more important doctrines. It would be a classic "priming of the pump."

THE PENTECOST DOCTRINE

The Doctrinal Committee decided to tackle the issue of Pentecost early on. The annual Holy Day of Pentecost had been kept on a Monday within the Radio Church of God since 1937. Why so, when the Jews *did not* keep Pentecost on Monday, and when *no other major religious group* emphasized a Monday either? Mr. Herbert Armstrong had gone to *great lengths* over many years to justify a Monday Pentecost, even though the biblical texts providing instruction for counting (especially Leviticus 23:15–16) are confusing at best. There had been several ministers under Mr. Armstrong who had questioned a Monday Pentecost from the 1950s, arguing instead for a Sunday observance. Those arguments had been crushed time and again by the weight of Mr. Armstrong's claim of inspiration from God.

Was the true Church founded on a Sunday in A.D. 33 as the *Catholic and a few Protestant churches* claim?

REMEMBER, if any church which claims apostolic authority has erred in the traditional date of its founding, *how can we believe that its other traditions are true?* ("Was the New Testament Church Founded on Sunday?," *The Good News*, May 1959, p. 5)

Other "scholars" in the ministry were not convinced. They knew they had *no way* to effect a change as long as Mr. Armstrong was so adamant. But after the prophetic failures of 1972, Mr. Armstrong's technical biblical scholarship became suspect, and the liberals had their opening. It took until early 1974 for that first major change to be accomplished, but indeed, Mr. Armstrong *finally acquiesced* to the committee scholars, and the announcement was made to the whole church:

> We did not have, at that time, access to all of the scholarly research that we have today. . . .

> According to the facts available to me and that small parent church at that time—back in 1927 to 1933—Pentecost was put on a Monday.

> But now, consider: Why did God use me in founding Ambassador College? Simply to provide an educated ministry for His Church? Ambassador College has indeed provided an educated ministry. It has developed a scholarly research team. Today at the Pasadena Headquarters it has provided me—and the Church—with many facilities I did not have in 1927.

> And that team of scholarly researchers—delving into every possible phase of this subject in depth—has now indeed brought me new facts—new evidence (Personal letter to the church from Mr. Armstrong, February 11, 1974).

Now, no doctrine of the church was immune to re-review. If Mr. Armstrong was wrong on Pentecost, what else might he have erred in teaching to the church over the first forty years?

CHAPTER SEVEN
TURMOIL, ATTEMPTED RESTORATION, DEATH 1974–1986

THE HOUSE OF GOD

In 1974, the Doctrinal Committee was dismantling core teachings of the church. At the same time, the most aggressive physical building project ever conceived by Mr. Armstrong—the Ambassador Auditorium—was nearing completion. It was built on the Pasadena college campus to serve not only as a venue for college functions and local church services, but to be made available for secular concerts and fine arts performances. The idea for this grand structure formulated in Mr. Armstrong's mind in the early 1960s, and architectural plans and funding arrangements were already being developed by the mid-1960s (*Co-Worker Letter*, February 28, 1964). Although Mr. Armstrong made sure to affirm that this was not in any way a "holy temple," he did indeed envision this building as bearing similarities in quality and grandeur to Solomon's Temple, and as a *signature edifice* to proclaim the identity of the true Work of God on earth.

After many delays, groundbreaking was finally accomplished on January 14, 1972. It took over two years to complete the project, and when it was finished, it bore a commemorative plaque with the inscription, "TO THE HONOR AND GLORY OF THE GREAT GOD." Mr. Armstrong wrote to the church:

> This magnificent new Auditorium will be dedicated to the Honor and Glory of the GREAT GOD on May 6th, with some 600 ordained ministers of the Worldwide Church of God, from all parts of the world, in attendance (*Co-Worker Letter*, April 28, 1974).

REDEFINING MARRIAGE—A PRECEDENT

Immediately on the heels of the Pentecost change in February 1974 was the announcement of a *redefining* of what it means in God's eyes to be "married." In May 1974, the "liberal ministers" once again prevailed in securing Mr. Armstrong's approval for their long-sought change, and for the first time allowed hundreds and even thousands of members to remarry, who until that time had been told that to do so would be adultery. Mr. Herbert Armstrong approved that change—making the announcement on May 6, 1974, to an assembly of ministers in the new Ambassador Auditorium. Is it not ironic that the dedication ceremony of this building to The Great God was accompanied by a monumental change in doctrinal teaching which would upend the very idea that God had ever "led" Mr. Armstrong in any *unique* way over the past forty years? Until that time, Herbert Armstrong had vociferously opposed the idea of any amendment. It was his son, Garner Ted Armstrong, and a cadre of other ministers, who had lobbied for years for this change. When Mr. Armstrong finally approved it, he claimed authority as an apostle of Jesus Christ to do so. But from which direction had the inspiration really come—from on High, or from his mortal underlings?

Would this *relaxation* of the marriage doctrine solve the problem of *member discontent* resulting from the failure of ministerial prognostications about the return of Jesus Christ? Only time would tell. Mr. Armstrong confirmed the long-reaching tentacles of those past disappointments, which had still not dissipated even by 1976:

> Before 1972 many of you made great sacrifices for the precious WORK OF THE LIVING GOD. I TOLD YOU, time and again, I was NOT setting dates—there was no ASSURANCE our Work would be over by January, 1972. Yet some DID set the date, and when the Work was NOT finished in January, 1972, some said, "Well, MY LORD HAS DELAYED HIS COMING. I've been sacrificing to support the

Work. NOW I'm going to SPEND THAT MONEY ON MY OWN SELF ENJOYMENT. Christ may not come for another thousand years!" (*Co-Worker Letter*, August 19, 1976)

The membership numbers did finally stabilize again. But what those 1974 doctrinal changes *did* accomplish *for certain* was to make *every other doctrine* of the church suspect. If the marriage doctrine could have been so wrong, what else had Mr. Armstrong gotten wrong? Through the remainder of the decade, many more changes were made to church teachings, some by formal proclamation, but many more by *quiet adjustment* in ministerial practice and in private counseling. In short, many of the doctrines that formerly had made members of the Worldwide Church of God seem so "outside of the mainstream" were now being modified to make it *easier to coexist* with the world. If Jesus Christ was not really coming "soon," then the people would have to have a respite from some of those "hard teachings" that made them such oddballs in their local communities and which threatened to drive future members (and tithe contributions) away.

Recall that since 1968, the *primary commission* of the church had been amended *to begin cultivating relationships with world leaders* as a means of proclaiming the gospel. The church budgetary expenses for Mr. Armstrong to move in such grand circles could not be funded without loyal, tithe-paying church members, and therefore, relaxing *hard doctrines* served the "greater good" of keeping those members loyal, and thereby preserving "the Work" abroad.

The AICF

In June 1975, Mr. Armstrong announced to church members the creation of a new legal entity to augment his work overseas. The Ambassador International Cultural Foundation (AICF) would be a secular organization and would have its own magazine. Mr. Armstrong described it this way to the church at large:

138   A PECULIAR TREASURE

Now about the new magazine. Some weeks ago I authorized the formation of a new FOUNDATION—named the Ambassador International Cultural Foundation. It is non-profit, dedicated to serving humanity worldwide. It has become a necessary adjunct to this new worldwide dimension of getting Christ's TRUE Gospel to the nations through heads of government. . . .

This new Foundation is giving us great added prestige, credibility, and favor. It is something NO ONE can CRITICIZE. It doesn't sound "religious." Already it has met with GREAT AND FAVORABLE RESPONSE.

And on the heels of this, the TREMENDOUS ANNOUNCEMENT of a new magazine! Under the auspices of the new Foundation, I have just authorized the publication of a NEW MAGAZINE that will go before KINGS! Bi-monthly! It will be the very highest quality magazine in every respect. It will contain in easy-to-understand language articles on the very PURPOSE for human life upon earth, the AWESOME human potential, HOW world PEACE will soon come! It will carry the GOSPEL MESSAGE in the same PLAIN and UNDERSTANDABLE LANGUAGE I use personally in speaking with world leaders, heads of government, and their top officials. It will reveal what science cannot, what religion has not, what education doesn't teach. It will have a larger size page, fully-illustrated, in full-color (*Co-Worker Letter*, June 5, 1975).

What was not published to the members were some *additional comments* made by Mr. Armstrong to the ministers of the Worldwide Church of God specifically, in an issue of *The Bulletin* (a publication sent only to the ministry):

Now about the Foundation and the NEW MAGAZINE.

One thing has been a serious handicap, and caused me and my touring team no little embarrassment. We have had to say that we represent either Ambassador College, or Worldwide Church of God.

I am regarded as an Ambassador for WORLD PEACE. But if I represent a CHURCH, immediately that shouts to them "RELIGION!" and that sparks prejudice and competitive religious prejudice. If I try to get away from appearing to be a religious crusader by representing Ambassador College, they ask, "where is this college? How many students do you have?" A college even with two campuses, having enrollments of only some 500 to 700 sounds pretty small, compared to the universities all over the world each with from 5,000 to 68,000 students.

Christ said we must be "wise as serpents, and harmless as doves." Some weeks ago I authorized the forming and incorporating of a new FOUNDATION, named "The Ambassador International Cultural Foundation." It is non-profit, dedicated to serving humanity worldwide. . . .

Already we are finding that this new Foundation is giving great added prestige, credibility and favor. It is something NOBODY CAN CRITICIZE! It carries no RELIGIOUS connotation! (*The Bulletin*, June 3, 1975, pp. 293–294)

Again, compare this approach to God's Work with that of the previous forty years. Was it truly God's will that the spokesman for Jesus Christ be "acceptable" to the nations, so as not to offend non-Christians? If so, it was certainly a departure from his early ministry. Was the gospel truly being proclaimed through partnering with world leaders and secular humanitarian organizations that were attempting to solve the world's problems through *their own physical devices*? If you are aiding someone *trying to solve problems without God's help*, does that action really "open the door" to allow you to

140 A PECULIAR TREASURE

convince them of the need for the return of Jesus Christ as Savior? This was the philosophy that was increasing through the 1970s in the Worldwide Church of God, and the Ambassador International Cultural Foundation seemed to be the epitome of that new strategy.

The AICF actually seems to have been the brainchild of Stanley Rader, who was increasing his influence greatly within the WCG during this very time. Concerning his visit in August 1976 with the Prime Minister of Israel, Yitzhak Rabin, Mr. Armstrong wrote:

> My appointment with the Prime Minister was at noon Monday. Ambassador Ravid (also formerly Ambassador to Guinea) went along with us. As you know, I am nearly always accompanied on such visits with Mr. Stanley R. Rader, our chief legal counsel, and now also Vice President for Financial Affairs, and Executive Vice President of the Ambassador International Cultural Foundation (AICF). This time Mrs. Rader also accompanied us (*Co-Worker Letter*, August 19, 1976).

MR. ARMSTRONG MARRIES AGAIN

In 1977, at the age of eighty-four, Mr. Armstrong announced to the church his marriage to thirty-eight-year-old Ramona Martin, who had a fifteen-year-old son from a previous marriage. She had been in the church since 1962, becoming one of Mr. Stanley Rader's secretarial assistants in 1974, and thereafter working more closely with Mr. Armstrong as well (*The Worldwide News*, April 25, 1977). Here are some excerpts from the letter Mr. Armstrong wrote to the whole church the day following his marriage:

> Since her death [Loma Armstrong], God miraculously has opened to me doors (Rev. 3:8) to kings, emperors, presidents and prime ministers, so that Christ's message may be taken into nations whose doors were closed to this message. At this stage no one but myself can do this. And I could not endure

TURMOIL, ATTEMPTED RESTORATION, DEATH 1974–1986   141

the grueling worldwide travel had not God blessed me with youthful vigor, vitality, and energy (Isa. 40:28–31) enabling me to carry on more vigorously than one in a hundred half my calendar age. This almost constant travel (last year 300 out of 365 days) and loneliness has reawakened me to the serious need God recognized when He said, "It is not good that a man should be alone." . . .

Of course no one could take the place of my beloved wife of fifty years. But the Work of God must go on, finishing the GREAT COMMISSION God committed to me, in this new and MOST IMPORTANT phase of the entire Work. And God now has graciously provided the wife to be constantly at my side—a woman truly led by God's Holy Spirit. We have given the matter much time, to be sure it has grown into true love and like-minded rapport, as well as definitely sure it is God's will.

This is to announce my marriage to Ramona Martin, in an informal and simple ceremony, attended only by our respective families on Sunday, April 17th, Garner Ted Armstrong officiating (*Co-Worker Letter*, April 18, 1977).

In spite of Mr. Armstrong's heartfelt belief at the time that God was behind his new marriage, that turns out not to have been so. The couple were separated in 1982, and after the legal filing of divorce made headlines in local newspapers, Mr. Armstrong wrote the following to the church:

But in my letter to you April 18, 1977, I said the loneliness had reminded me how God said, "It is not good that a man should be alone," and I felt God had, after 10 years, provided me with a wife to be constantly at my side and give the help and companionship needed for God's Work.

142 A PECULIAR TREASURE

But with deepest regret I have to say to you now, Mrs. Ramona Armstrong has refused to be at my side here in Pasadena headquarters or in further travel, but has insisted on living separately in Tucson. It has been determined by events, facts and fruits that I am not spiritually bound by God and only by man's law of this world.

Circumstances now render it ill-advised that I condone the continuation of the legal marriage, both from the Church point of view and of my own. It was my hope and effort to resolve the matter, and with the least publicity possible, for the benefit of the Church, for her and for myself. All attempts to do so have failed. It has therefore become necessary that I accede to the advice of Church legal counsel and file the necessary legal proceedings. I assure you every effort has been made, at cost of heavy stress on me personally, to avoid this.

God HATES divorce. So do I. I have gone to every effort to prevent this. It would be inappropriate at this time that I state all the facts, but if necessary and proper later, I will reveal more. . . .

This determination SHOULD NOT BE USED AS A PRECEDENT TO ENCOURAGE OR JUSTIFY OTHER DIVORCES IN THE CHURCH (*Co-Worker Letter,* April 21, 1982).

For the first forty years of his ministry Mr. Armstrong had championed the *inviolability* of marriage, but then compromised in 1974 to permit divorce within the church, followed next by his own marriage to a divorcee and then subsequent divorce. Sadly, all of this provided *great fodder* for critics of the Worldwide Church of God, and Mr. Armstrong in particular.

A Near-Death Experience

In August 1977, four months after his new marriage, Mr. Armstrong suffered a serious health episode which nearly ended his life. Here is how he described the event to the church leadership seven months later:

> First, I want to say a few words about my illness. Last August I was scripturally dead. The doctor called it heart failure. . . . But the nurse who was in charge has told me that she came in and saw that my face was ashen white, and immediately she took my pulse and there wasn't any.
> So the blood was not circulating, not to show even one point on the blood-pressure instrument.
> So then they started working over me, and I think Ted anointed me. My wife's sister was there. . . . She and the nurse used mouth resuscitation and heart massage until they got me breathing.
> The nurse's estimate from the time she had noticed this until I began taking the first breath was at least thirty seconds. She said it was a minute and a half, though, that it was touch and go, because I'd lapse back and quit breathing. And after about a minute and a half I was breathing enough on my own, and I've continued all right since, and I hope the rest of the life that God wants for me on earth (Excerpts from *Address to the 1978 Ministerial Conference*, March 1978).

Mr. Armstrong would refer back to this near-death event many times in subsequent years, viewing it as a turning point in God's work through him. Treating it as *a wake-up call*, his physical recovery seemed to coincide with a drive to initiate a spiritual recovery for the entire church. Putting up with liberal elements within the church leadership that had been slowly but persistently watering down doctrines was finally becoming *too much*.

144   A PECULIAR TREASURE

The Systematic Theological Project (STP)

We have already documented the disagreements that existed between Mr. Armstrong and his son concerning doctrines of the church and his son's personal behavior (chapter six). After suspending Garner Ted Armstrong in 1971 but then reinstating him into the church in 1972 and further elevating him to Vice President at the same moment, the hope was that father and son would be able to work together cooperatively thereafter. But the same old differences about church doctrine and administration persisted, and it all finally came to a head in early 1978.

There was much written by Mr. Armstrong and others at the time these volatile events were unfolding. Rather than reciting some of the more emotional statements recorded in the moment, the following excerpt from June 1985—just months before Mr. Armstrong's death—seems to document how he viewed those 1978 events after eight years of reflection:

It had become custom to hold an annual ministerial conference of ministers at Pasadena headquarters. In the 1974 to 1977 conferences, these meetings had been marred by controversies over doctrinal issues.

Just before the January, 1978, conference I was determined to prevent doctrinal controversy. I was also due to leave on another 'round-the-world trip. I had decided to postpone the trip until after the conference in order to keep controversy out of the conference. But the one to be left in charge in my absence urged me to remain for the opening morning session, so that I could open the conference, and keep my departure at 12 noon, and he gave me his word no doctrines would be discussed in the conference, only administrative matters.

I agreed to this. I opened the conference, left immediately for the airport and had lunch on the plane. I was going first to Japan, then across the north pole to

TURMOIL, ATTEMPTED RESTORATION, DEATH 1974–1986

Europe, and into western Africa before returning to Pasadena.

I had not gotten very far out over the Pacific Ocean that afternoon, until in the afternoon session of the conference a voluminous printed work called "Systematic Theology Project," or "STP" for short, was distributed to the ministry with specific instructions that this was a definite outline of basic Church doctrines, and no minister was to preach anything contrary to this treatise.

I knew absolutely nothing of this STP, or that it had been in preparation. It had been carefully concealed from me. It was a flagrant violation of the promise made to induce me to leave so this doctrinal change in Church teaching could be given to all ministers without my knowledge. I knew nothing of this STP, in spite of claims made by others, until a copy was brought to me by some loyal ministers in late April or early May of 1978 when I then notified every minister in the world to return his copy immediately and ignore all its liberal doctrines and teachings.

It has come to my attention that some of the liberals, no longer members of God's Church, have claimed that I did know of this infamous STP project. That is positively NOT TRUE. A few papers on one or two subjects, which were not liberal, had been brought to me in Tucson, Ariz., but no clear mention was made of the preparations under way for producing this STP project. None of the liberalized teachings in the STP were shown to me or approved by me at any time.

Some of these liberal ministers who worked on and produced the STP and the one who was in charge of executive administration in my absence were disfellowshipped and others left the Church (*The Worldwide News—Special Edition*, June 24, 1985).

146 A PECULIAR TREASURE

GARNER TED ARMSTRONG EXPELLED

The "one who was in charge of executive administration," and finally expelled by Mr. Armstrong in 1978, was none other than Garner Ted Armstrong, his beloved son. No matter how many sacrifices (compromises) had been made to try to keep father and son together, in the end, their stark difference in approach to both doctrine and administration made mutual cooperation impossible. Garner Ted Armstrong immediately set up a new church organization to compete with his father, and although it never even remotely succeeded on the scale of his father's work, it did become a persistent thorn in his side, as members of the Worldwide Church of God now had "an alternative" place to fellowship with an "Armstrong figurehead," if they ever became disgruntled with any aspect of the parent organization. There was never to be a public reconciliation between father and son.

CONTRACTION OF AMBASSADOR COLLEGE

After so many years of growth and expansion, the tumultuous 1970s likewise took its toll upon Ambassador College. In 1974 the Bricket Wood campus in England was closed, followed three years later by the Big Sandy campus in 1977. As Chancellor of Ambassador College, Garner Ted Armstrong had worked very hard to secure accreditation for the four-year liberal arts program. Mr. Armstrong later condemned this pursuit as a symptom of the liberalizing ills within the ministry:

It was then that the matter of obtaining accreditation from the organized accreditation societies of secular education became a problem. The liberals at Pasadena wanted accreditation. They did not want to be accredited as a Bible college, but as a full competing college or university. As such the college would fall under the rules of the secular accrediting society, which would more or less determine policy and curricula.

Finally this effort on the part of the liberals increased the enrollment of the college from the approximate 500 limit that I had set to about 1,400 and going up. It was no longer God's college. I had realized the danger of a student body in excess of 500 students, in residence on campus, and had set that as a definite college policy. But during those years when I was absent from Pasadena headquarters most of the time, changes were being gradually made in college policies as well as Church doctrines (*The Worldwide News—Special Edition*, June 24, 1985).

Therefore, with the ouster of Garner Ted Armstrong in 1978, the one remaining campus of Ambassador College in Pasadena would be closed temporarily, and then reopened with a renewed mission and spiritual emphasis. Mr. Armstrong wanted immediately to expunge the administrative philosophy of his son from that most-beloved institution:

From its founding I had made the slogan of the college, "Recapture True Values." The college started with the highest moral and spiritual values. It was God's college. A high moral and spiritual conduct had been vigorously taught and maintained. There was much teaching against "necking," and any sort of lovemaking among students. "Going steady" toward marriage was forbidden until the end of the first semester of the senior year. Smoking and the use of drugs were positively prohibited.

But as the liberal element gained control of the campus administration during those years of my long absences from Pasadena, the high standard of student conduct was more and more liberalized through lack of discipline or enforcement. The college was coming to be more like other college campuses.

148   A PECULIAR TREASURE

At this juncture let me jump ahead of the sequence of events a bit to say that, after sufficient recovery from my heart failure in August of 1977, I found it necessary in 1978 to close the college at Pasadena completely (the colleges in Bricket Wood, England, and at Big Sandy had then already been closed) and to start Ambassador College in Pasadena all over again with one freshman class only, except for a few in proper attitude and character who were retained to allow them to complete their studies until graduation (*The Worldwide News—Special Edition*, June 24, 1985).

This aggressive revamping of Ambassador College would become one of the strongest proofs of Mr. Armstrong's intent to fight back against the liberalism that he felt had permeated the church for so many years.

Legal Attack Against the WCG

In the aftermath of the separation of father and son, early 1979 brought on a legal challenge to the Worldwide Church of God that threatened the very existence of the organization. Much has been written about this aggressive action by the State of California to take control of the church, but again, let Mr. Armstrong relate his personal view of these events:

At the time of the Feast of Tabernacles that fall, 1978, at a Festival held by one of these split-off liberals and a few who followed, in their own Feast of Tabernacles, a conspiracy was hatched to attack and destroy the Church by the legal process of a class action lawsuit. Some six or seven liberals, former members, signed the suit against the Church. This resulted in an ex parte order by a judge. Secretly without prior notice, deputies on order of the Attorney General's office swooped down on the Church on the morning of Jan. 3, 1979. The ex parte order had been signed by a judge late the day before.

TURMOIL, ATTEMPTED RESTORATION, DEATH 1974–1986   149

A very severe struggle for the existence and life of the Church ensued. Some months later the State dropped the case, and still later an appellate court judge issued a declaration from the bench that the lawsuit was groundless and should never have been filed. Even to this day some newspaper comments mention the false charges accusing me of misuse of millions of dollars of Church funds, but they never mention our vindication of these false charges (*The Worldwide News–Special Edition*, June 24, 1985).

STANLEY RADER TAKES CENTER STAGE

The individual who rose to public prominence in helping to defend the WCG against this legal attack was none other than Stanley Rader, Treasurer and Chief Counsel for the church. It was he who became the face of the church through all of the ensuing legal proceedings, as well as in addressing church members and students at Ambassador College to provide updates through all of the months of contention. Mr. Armstrong himself had fled to his home in Tucson, Arizona, to avoid the personal reach of officials of the State of California who were seeking to subpoena him. He would not return to his home on the grounds of the California campus until the lawsuit was resolved in the church's favor in early 1981. (The author happened to have been present as a student of Ambassador College in Pasadena during this very time, and is speaking from firsthand knowledge.) Stanley Rader was hailed as a hero, further cementing Mr. Armstrong's loyalty to him and providing insulation against his detractors. Although Mr. Rader had only chosen to become baptized as a member in 1975 (some twenty years after his first exposure to the church), Mr. Armstrong further ordained him as a minister of the church—and at the very highest level, as an Evangelist—on September 27, 1979, in the midst of his aggressive legal defense of the church. Here, from the church announcement of his ordination to the ministry, is a succinct summary of Mr. Rader's background:

PASADENA — Before the 1979 Feast of Tabernacles, Worldwide Church of God Pastor General Herbert W. Armstrong ordained three men to the rank of evangelist Sept. 27 at his home in Tucson, Ariz. . . .

Stanley Rader, 49, was appointed one of eight members of the Worldwide Church of God board of directors by Mr. Armstrong in January and is also the Church treasurer and general counsel to Mr. Armstrong. His first contact with the Church came when Mr. Armstrong hired him as a tax adviser to the Work in 1956.

In 1962 Mr. Rader graduated from the University of Southern California's Law School with the highest grade average in its history. He served on USC's faculty until 1965, during which time he also taught accounting at Ambassador College.

A personal aide and traveling companion to Mr. Armstrong since 1968, Mr. Rader has been responsible for setting up many of Mr. Armstrong's meetings with heads of state and leaders of the educational and business community around the world. Most recently Mr. Rader spent two months making arrangements for Mr. Armstrong's visit with leaders of the People's Republic of China.

Mr. Rader, who was baptized by Mr. Armstrong in Hong Kong in 1975, is also the executive vice president of the Ambassador International Cultural Foundation, the humanitarian arm of the Church that promotes Mr. Armstrong's trips abroad, and through which they are conducted (*The Worldwide News*, October 29, 1979, p. 1).

So, a man who *seemed* to have no personal conviction in the *religious teachings* of Herbert Armstrong during his first twenty years of association with the church finally becomes baptized in 1975, and then, contrary to all of Mr. Armstrong's previous policies against ordaining "a novice" to the ministry (1 Timothy 3:6), Stanley Rader is ordained within four years, not to an introductory level of the ministry, but to the very highest rank.

Was Mr. Rader truly devoted to his new role as a spiritual shepherd of God's flock? Another long-time teaching of Mr. Armstrong was that true ministers never retire from serving God's people. Yet, after Mr. Rader's successful legal defense of the church, he retired from both his organizational and ecclesiastical responsibilities in 1981, never apparently serving the church publicly again. Furthermore, Mr. Armstrong revealed that it had been Mr. Rader's intention to resign from his executive service to the church just prior to the actions of the State of California in early 1979. He stayed on only to see the church through the difficult legal battle:

> Mr. Rader had expressed a desire to retire from his official Church executive position prior to the Jan. 3, 1979, state invasion. He and I had agreed to his retirement from this executive position very shortly before Jan. 3, 1979, to take effect very soon after the beginning of the year in 1979. When the State attack was launched Jan. 3, it became necessary for him to stay on. . . .
>
> I feel this Church would be derelict in its appreciation if it does not make suitable acknowledgment for such service, rendered two years after Mr. Rader had planned to retire from active executive duty.
>
> For the past five months or so he has said publically, in the public press, and before our own congregations, that it is his desire to return to private law practice, and has made public statements of intent to resign as treasurer and board member of the Church by July 1. Now he has asked that this date be moved up to March 1.
>
> To show our appreciation, it is my judgment as Pastor General of this Church, that we should express our gratitude and heartfelt appreciation by a special bonus of $250,000, net to him (*The Worldwide News—Special Edition*, March 6, 1981, p. 9).

In today's figures, that bonus would be worth well over $600,000, and was on top of his very lucrative, contracted salary.

152   A PECULIAR TREASURE

It was quite a retirement gift for a newly-ordained "spiritual shepherd" of God's church.

THE "BACK ON TRACK" YEARS

In the aftermath of his son's ouster from the church in 1978, Mr. Armstrong began to define a new mission to try to *undo the damage* that had been done by liberal leaders within the organization during the preceding decade. Most often in writing to the membership, he described this effort as putting the church "*back on track.*" It was a phrase used over and over again, and one that was quickly parroted by the laity to show support for their founder's efforts.

Less than two years ago, God brought me back from death. Recently I asked myself <u>WHY</u> did God bring me back? <u>HOW</u> has God used me these 22 months? The answer is: PUTTING GOD'S CHURCH BACK ON THE TRACK!

Brethren, we've got to FACE IT! God's Church—and Ambassador College—had been shockingly derailed—SECULARIZED! The whole WORK had become the work of MAN! My son Garner Ted had taken to himself authority never given to him. He took advantage of the fact I was in other parts of the world, carrying Christ's Gospel Message into other countries, to assume authority to CHANGE DOCTRINES, and to CHANGE POLICIES. I had denied him BOTH! Much of it was done SECRETLY! Top-ranking ministers were warned of being fired if they told me what was going on.

Many of the basic BIBLE TRUTHS God had revealed to me as the very FOUNDATIONAL BELIEF OF THIS CHURCH were BEING CHANGED! It was no longer <u>GOD'S</u> College or <u>GOD'S</u> Church! It was becoming precisely what my son is now trying to build—"GARNER TED

ARMSTRONG'S CHURCH"! He was surrounded by a small group of secular self-professed "intellectuals." . . .

Jesus Christ is the HEAD of this Church and entire Work.

HOW has He used me, since bringing me back from total heart failure and death? Recently I asked myself this question. Although Christ has made me His Apostle to carry HIS GOSPEL around the world, He has used me since my recovery primarily in SETTING HIS CHURCH AND HIS COLLEGE BACK ON GOD'S TRACK! GREAT PROGRESS HAS BEEN MADE! But the job is not yet complete (*Co-Worker Letter*, July 24, 1979).

For the past two years I have been laboring very hard to be Christ's servant and apostle in SETTING GOD'S CHURCH BACK ON THE TRACK. The entire Church had been derailed. A <u>LIBERAL</u> spirit from Satan had been injected into some in high positions under me at Headquarters in Pasadena. Instead of wholeheartedly OBEYING Christ through HIS WORD, THE BIBLE, there was creeping in, during years when I was in other parts of the world up to 300 out of the 365 days in the year, a LIBERAL spirit of SATAN.

Those leaders to whom I had delegated the responsibility of ADMINISTERING the POLICIES and DOCTRINES Christ had set in God's Church through His apostle, went way BEYOND the authority given them. They started CHANGING POLICIES and watering down God's TRUTH, changing DOCTRINES, compromising—seeing HOW CLOSE they could go—and lead the Brethren in going—to the ways of SATAN! They wanted to be more LIBERAL—more like THIS WORLD OF SATAN. . . .

154   A PECULIAR TREASURE

But for two years Jesus Christ has been using me and those loyally still with and under me to SET BACK ON GOD'S TRACK God's Church.

AND THE CHURCH IS MOSTLY BACK ON THAT TRACK NOW (*Co-Worker Letter*, September 15, 1980).

How did Mr. Armstrong define what he considered to be "off track" and requiring correction? Notice (from above) that he listed, specifically, *doctrines, policies*, and *Bible truths*!

Satan has attacked this Work this year and also me personally as never before. But Jesus Christ, as He promised, has not left nor forsaken His Work or me, or us in it. We have been getting His Church and Work back on the track—HIS track—this year. I know He is pleased, because He has blessed this WORK this year as NEVER BEFORE!

Let us now get whatever remains to be put back on the track, and PUSH AHEAD AS NEVER BEFORE THIS COMING YEAR (*Co-Worker Letter*, December 27, 1981).

Notice that Mr. Armstrong seemed always to speak of "back on track" as a *progressive effort*, one making great strides, but not yet fully accomplished. How fully must a train's wheels be *on the tracks* in order for it to be sound again? What was never emphasized in the analogy is that a train even ninety percent *on track* is still ten percent *off track*, and thereby quite unstable. However, the *"back on track"* phrase would continue to dominate until his death, but always in a qualifying way, as not having yet been fully achieved:

On behalf of Jesus Christ, Head of God's Church and his work, I THANK YOU with all my heart for your faithfulness and liberality. And what a year it was! The Church and work made great strides in itself getting "back on God's track," and in GIVING and proclaiming Christ's last Gospel message to a dying world in confusion (*Co-Worker Letter*, January 11, 1984).

Now a recap of what has happened to the Church and its work.

God had blessed His Church with an unprecedented approximate increase of 30 percent per year for 35 years. As these liberals began gaining more and more control God removed His blessing. I have often said that God blesses us as we please Him. During these liberal years in the 1970s, the income virtually stagnated. In 1974 the Church experienced a 1.6 percent decrease in income under 1973, the first negative growth in the Church's history. It fell another 4.8 percent the following year.

Since God brought me back from total heart failure, and directed me in removing these liberals, and putting the Church back on track, He has restored His blessings. Income for the Church this year will run two times the dollar volume of 1978. Income growth is allowing the Church to get the Gospel of the Kingdom of God to the world as a witness as never before. These physical blessings are matched by new spiritual growth and new truth added to His Church (*The Worldwide News–Special Edition*, June 24, 1985).

WHICH DOCTRINES, POLICIES, AND BIBLE TRUTHS?

"*Back on track*" began to be applied to almost every aspect of church activity, including emphasis upon increasing the evangelical outreach work, as well as overcoming personal spiritual laxity. But Mr. Armstrong originally applied it to *doctrine, policies*, and *Bible truths* that had been corrupted by liberal elements. To gauge how many of those items had been fully restored by 1985—*put back* as they were before liberal ministers changed revealed Truths—what did Mr. Armstrong include on that list to be fixed? From the same letter to the church in June 1985, here is what he wrote concerning *specific doctrinal controversies* in the early 1970s:

> I quote now from a memorandum by Leroy Neff, the current treasurer, who was on the first Doctrinal Research Committee [from 1972] and wrote concerning others on the committee. I am quoting this to give an example of the direction some of the liberals on the doctrinal committee were taking.
>
> 1. Any marriage where the people are unconverted, or did not fully know what they were getting into, was not a valid marriage.
>
> 2. Polygamy was tacitly approved by God in Old Testament times, so multiple marriages or divorces in modern times might just be a form of polygamy by having wives sequentially rather than concurrently.
>
> 3. God divorced ancient Israel and then both parties were free to remarry.
>
> 4. The ministry should be able to loose marriages that God had joined.
>
> These liberals wanted complete freedom in the Church for divorce and remarriage at will. Other questions raised by the liberals were complete freedom for any type marriage, some more and some less freedom from tithing, doing away with or modifying Church teachings on healing by direct prayer as in James 5:14, complete freedom for women in facial makeup, and even the approval of celebrating birthdays (never approved in the Bible) and even of voting in elections as part of the world.
>
> On the Pasadena campus more and more friction developed between the liberals and those loyal ministers and members who held to the biblical truths God had placed in His Church. It was a sort of cold war of nerves.
>
> It had become custom to hold an annual ministerial conference of ministers at Pasadena headquarters. In the 1974 to 1977 conferences, these meetings had been marred by

controversies over doctrinal issues (*The Worldwide News–Special Edition*, June 24, 1985).

How many of those liberal ideas actually became approved doctrines during the 1970s? Well, polygamy (item #2) was never approved, but every other numbered point (1, 3, & 4) was approved (even reluctantly) by Mr. Armstrong in 1974! Yes, it was never his idea, but *he certainly signed off on those changes* (in spite of emphasizing that they were done without his knowledge). The same is true concerning a change in *the doctrine of divine healing*, when church members in the mid-1970s were advised it was no longer wrong to use the full gamut of modern medicine that had previously been prohibited as an act of faithlessness. The use of makeup was approved at that time as well. The doctrine on tithing had only been modified in a small way, again, with Mr. Armstrong's sign-off, but changed it certainly was! There was never an announced acceptance of the celebration of birthdays, or a change to allow voting. So then, of all the doctrines and policies that Mr. Armstrong listed (and these were by no means all that were actually changed), which ones of them had gone "off track" and needed to be put "*back on track*"? Apparently, it would imply a need to restore the original teachings on *marriage, tithing, modern medicine,* and *makeup*! (Remember that the first major doctrine changed through liberal lobbying was the Holy Day of Pentecost when it was moved from Monday to Sunday in 1974. In that June 1985 article, Mr. Armstrong did not reference that Pentecost change, but it certainly had been the *number one target* of those liberals seeking to change church doctrine, as has already been documented.)

Given that Mr. Armstrong was very sincere in his commitment to doing God's will, how is it possible that he could have approved changes to doctrines that he would later claim to be abominations? That same June 1985 article to the church is very revealing:

A primary reason for the contentions and slowing down in the growth of the Church during the liberal years is the fact that, in our desire to hold rebellious and liberal ministers and members within our fellowship, we did not rigidly obey the command of Romans 16:17: "Now I beseech you, brethren, mark them which cause divisions and offences contrary to the doctrine which ye have learned; and avoid them." Also in I Corinthians 5:11: "But now I have written unto you not to keep company, if any man that is called a brother be a fornicator, or covetous, or an idolater, or a railer, or a drunkard, or an extortioner; with such an one no not to eat" (*The Worldwide News–Special Edition*, June 24, 1985).

So here is an admission that these liberals could have been *pulled up short* early on (especially his own son), but since they were not, that is why the church got "off track."

WHICH DOCTRINES WERE ACTUALLY RESTORED?

If, by 1985, Mr. Armstrong felt that the church was *mostly "back on track,"* which of these *particular doctrines* he listed had been *restored* within the church in order to make that reformation evident?

What about the marriage doctrine? The new liberalized marriage doctrine was *never restored* to the original! The same "new" *liberal change* in 1974 to permit divorce and remarriage was *still being practiced in 1985*, just as much or even more so than it was in 1974. What about tithing? Those "small" changes in defining "titheable increase" were likewise never restored to the original definition. What about the use of modern medicine? Once again, the relaxation in doctrine of the 1970s was *never again restored* to that which Mr. Armstrong originally taught to the whole church. Well then, what about women's makeup?

Finally, yes, we have a doctrine that Mr. Armstrong *made sure* to restore to his original teaching! In fact, earlier, in 1981, he emphasized that the issue of women's makeup was *the very root cause* of all of those problems in the church:

FOR THREE YEARS the living Christ has been working to put His Church back on the track! But how did the people of the living God get off track? . . .

But, as Satan maneuvered to start ALL HUMANITY off the track in the garden of Eden, so in these latter days, he maneuvered to use the women of God's Church to start the END-TIME Church off the track. And the whole Church was deceived! . . .

Jesus Christ through me has been GETTING US ALL BACK ON THE TRACK, ready for His return to earth as the KING OF KINGS, and Lord of lords. The Church, as HIS BRIDE to be spiritually MARRIED to Him, is to rise to meet Him in the air as He descends. Women of the Church, do you think Jesus Christ will say to me, "SEND A PROCLAMATION TO ALL WOMEN IN THE CHURCH TO PREPARE FOR MY COMING. TELL THEM TO GO TO THEIR DRESSING TABLES, PLUCK OUT THEIR EYEBROWS, PAINT IN NEW ONES HIGHER ON THEIR FOREHEADS, AND USE COSMETICS TO MAKE UP THEIR FACES TO MEET ME IN THE AIR"?

No, dear people, I don't think He will have me make such a proclamation. But rather: Wash the dirt off your faces! CLEAN UP your faces!" . . .

Satan used human reason and make-up and WOMEN to START the ball of LIBERALISM AWAY FROM GOD and TOWARD SIN to rolling in the Church beginning October, 1974 (Herbert W. Armstrong, "How Subtly Satan used MAKE-UP to Start the Church Off the Track," *Pastor General's Report*, November 2, 1981; *The Worldwide News*, November 16, 1981).

Compare his very strong emphasis upon *one particular point* within the first three years after his son's 1978 departure—women's makeup—with that which he wrote a few years later, in 1985, near the end of his life. By 1985, he was *no longer* claiming that it was women in the church and makeup in particular that had started the problem, but instead, *liberal scholars* who were clamoring for *many changes in doctrine*, of which makeup was only a relatively minor issue.

160   A PECULIAR TREASURE

The point is this: When Mr. Armstrong told members in the early 1980s that *corrupting the makeup doctrine* had been *the major issue* that took the church "off the track," restoring *that one doctrine* to the original teaching became the *best evidence* that the church was now "mostly" *back on track* again. It was a change in doctrine that was *dramatic in its effect* upon the membership, and was easily demonstrated by the fact that women who were previously wearing makeup to church services during the 1970s now came to church without it. It seemed to be a very bold move to "restore" past conservatism.

But again, what about all of those other doctrinal changes that Mr. Armstrong cited in 1985 as having been sponsored by liberals in the early 1970s, like the definition of marriage, the teaching on modern medicine, and redefining tithing? And what about the Pentecost change that had really started it all off? Absolutely *none of those teachings* were ever restored! But to the church in the early 1980s, that single reformation on women's makeup made everyone feel that they were finally back in the good graces of God again. They were "mostly" *back on track.*

MYSTERY OF THE AGES

Perhaps the most lasting legacy produced by Herbert Armstrong in his final years was the release of a new book in August 1985, entitled, *Mystery of the Ages.* Here is what Mr. Armstrong wrote to the church about his last published work:

We of God's true church do keep God's commandments. But the churches of this world say the commandments were done away. Therefore their eyes, even though they do not realize it, are blinded to the truth as revealed in the Bible. That is why the churches of "traditional Christianity" do not and cannot understand the Bible.

This new book MYSTERY OF THE AGES does put the many "pieces of the jigsaw puzzle" properly together. Because the world has been unable to do this, the Bible and the things in the Bible have certainly been a mystery. . . .

This new book MYSTERY OF THE AGES unveils all these mysteries. It puts the many different parts of the "jigsaw puzzle" together. It is, in fact, a synopsis of the entire Bible. It is my prayer that you will read it along with your Bible—that it will make your Bible come alive and understandable. And with God's Holy Spirit dwelling in you, I feel sure that it will. I am now in my 94th year and I feel that this book is the most valuable gift I could possibly give to you. This book is a partial expression of my thanks and gratitude to you for being a co-laborer with me and with Jesus Christ. With all my heart, I do appreciate and thank God for your part with me in the wonderful work in these closing days (*Co-Worker Letter*, September 12, 1985).

In reality, *Mystery of the Ages* did not really reveal anything "new" to church members that had not already been published by Herbert Armstrong many years before. The very same interpretation of the Bible can be found in his 1950s and 1960s publications, as in, for instance, *The Wonderful World Tomorrow—What It Will Be Like*, as well as many articles in *The Plain Truth* and *The Good News* magazines (later turned into booklets). All of these early writings described the same foundational understanding of the Bible in opposition to what is taught in the churches of the world. *Mystery of the Ages* was therefore a very good *repackaging* of what some would call "Armstrong theology." It took the very same teachings that had made his work unique through much of the twentieth century and re-formatted them into a single volume, with a very clever and attractive messaging theme. If one wanted to know how Herbert Armstrong and the Worldwide Church of God differed from all other churches, simply read *Mystery of the Ages* and it would all unfold right there in one succinct storyline. The genius was in the

162 A PECULIAR TREASURE

organization and simplicity of the work. And even today, more than thirty years after its introduction, used copies of *Mystery of the Ages* are still having an impact upon certain individuals who pick it up for the first time. Amazingly, it really did turn out to be one of Herbert Armstrong's most significant final legacies.

SUCCESSION

Mr. Armstrong's health was such that by mid-1985 he seemed seriously to be considering the likelihood that he might not last much longer. That too is reflected in the same article we have been quoting:

> A final personal word. In a few days I will be 93 years of age. For some years now, there have been some, like vultures, waiting for me to die. They would like to come back and take over the leadership of the Church in my stead. I have been deeply concerned about this, but in no sense worried. This is the Church of God, not of any man. Jesus Christ is the living Head of this Church. I am not.
>
> And Jesus Christ will never receive any of those who have gone out to draw a following after themselves to come back and lead God's Church into Satan's liberalism. It would be no longer God's Church, even as Ambassador College was no longer God's college, and Christ had to start it all over again through me with one freshman class.
>
> When I have, even rarely, mentioned my concern in this category, the response of members has always been the belief that God will keep me alive. I hope that He will, and I do try to take every care of my health and physical condition, but whether God keeps me alive 10 more years, or only 10 more minutes is entirely in God's hands. Brethren, put your faith in Christ and the living God and not in me. If Christ should remove me, He will direct the Advisory Council of Elders to select one of them to continue leading you until the coming

TURMOIL, ATTEMPTED RESTORATION, DEATH 1974–1986

of Jesus Christ in power and in glory. Pray that God will keep YOU in His Church until He replaces this evil world and brings the wonderful, peaceful and blessed Kingdom of God (*The Worldwide News–Special Edition*, June 24, 1985).

Again, it appears that he was adamantly against his son, Garner Ted Armstrong—or any other minister who had departed—making a comeback within the Worldwide Church of God after his death. And although he had published his confidence in the church's Advisory Council of Elders to appoint his successor, in the closing days before his death, he *apparently* changed his mind and decided to appoint his own successor:

This is my first letter to you in 1986, and could very well be my last. Now in my 94th year I am in a very physically weakened state enduring severe pain and with virtually no strength whatsoever. I briefly described my condition in last month's co-worker letter to you, and now it has worsened. It may be that the Work God has given me to do is complete, but not the Work of God's Church, which will be faithfully doing God's Work till Christ, the True Head of this Church, returns.

After much counsel and prayer over the past months God has led me in announcing a decision last week to appoint Mr. Joseph W. Tkach, director of Church Administration, to the office of Deputy Pastor General, to assist me while I am in a weakened state, and should God choose to take my life, to place himself totally in Christ's hands to lead God's Church under Christ, succeeding me as Pastor General, in the difficult times ahead. Christ will lead in the decision about which men will continue the telecast (*Co-Worker Letter*, January 10, 1986).

And indeed, it would be Mr. Joseph W. Tkach who would assume that position after the death of Herbert Armstrong.

Death and Burial

The Worldwide News carried the church announcement of the death of Herbert Armstrong:

Family and Church members, dignitaries and representatives of national governments paid their last respects to Herbert W. Armstrong, 93, at Mountain View Cemetery in Altadena, Calif., Jan. 19. About 4,700 were in attendance.

Mr. Armstrong, apostle and pastor general of the Worldwide Church of God, editor in chief of the Church's publications and founder of Ambassador College and the Ambassador Foundation, died at 5:59 a.m., Jan. 16, while resting in the bedroom chair of his late wife, Loma. . . .

Mr. Armstrong's burial plot lies between his mother, Eva Wright Armstrong (1866-1961), and his wife, Loma Dillon Armstrong (1891-1967). Mr. Armstrong's son Richard (1928-1958), who died in an auto accident, is buried on the other side of Mrs. Loma Armstrong (*The Worldwide News*, January 27, 1986, pp. 1, 12).

That same article also reported on some of the comments made by the new Pastor General, Joseph Tkach:

In a Jan. 16 co-worker letter Mr. Tkach said, "I am deeply saddened to have to inform you that Herbert W. Armstrong's illness has ended in the manner least expected by all of us.". . .

In the letter Mr. Tkach told brethren: "The greatest tribute we can give Mr. Armstrong is to *do the Work* we've been called to . . . Let us *carry on* in FAITH. There is much yet to do!"

The same day, in a letter to the ministry, Mr. Tkach wrote: "God mercifully granted us what Mr. Armstrong considered several additional years of his leadership, to *turn the Church around* from the liberalized path it had strayed onto in the middle seventies. God used him powerfully to get the Church *back on track."*

"I am personally deeply sobered and humbled by the responsibilities God has placed on my shoulders," Mr. Tkach said (*The Worldwide News*, January 27, 1986, p. 1).

Thus completes a summary of key events in the life of Herbert Armstrong from 1892 to 1986. In spite of some unavoidable expounding along the way, this is still merely a succinct chronicle of those events it is most necessary to document as a beginning point in analyzing *the real value* of Herbert Armstrong's work and achievements.

What is the true and lasting legacy of Herbert and Loma Armstrong? Was it merely an empire built by a very determined and very lucky salesman? Is there anything of value that survived the relatively short twentieth-century lives of the individuals themselves? Is it possible that it really did emanate from a purposeful God who used them to confirm real Bible Truth? That is what a deeper, detailed analysis will seek to determine.

CHAPTER EIGHT
THE AFTERMATH 1986–1997

After the death of Herbert Armstrong in 1986, what happened next?

This is the period of time that most interests those who were members of the Worldwide Church of God at some time during the 1980s–90s. It covers the most traumatic events in that church's history for many, because many assumed that *God's Work* would move forward and continue to reflect the tenets of Herbert Armstrong, even under the stewardship of a new Pastor General. How wrong they were.

Many other writers have already documented the blow-by-blow events that occurred after Mr. Joseph Tkach took the reins as Pastor General of the Worldwide Church of God in 1986. In short, he and his son, Joseph Tkach, Jr., used the ensuing decade to dismantle most of what Herbert Armstrong had built since the 1930s. For those who remained loyal members of the church through the 1980s and respected the legacy of Mr. Armstrong, it was traumatic to see every teaching that had set that church apart destroyed one by one. A number of ministers who did not agree with the changes eventually separated and started their own groups, later writing in detail about their own experiences and rationales, and lamenting the treachery they witnessed in the actions of the new Pastor General. Anyone who cares to delve into the weeds of that story can find ample documentation by the ones who lived through it.

But this particular work postulates (as you will see in the chapters to come) that the *seeds of destruction* of the Worldwide Church of God were already planted long before Mr. Armstrong died. All of those who became "shocked" in the 1990s at how easy it was to *change every doctrine* of the church after 1986 were simply never clued in to the insidious weaknesses which had been imbedded decades before. In other words, long before Mr. Armstrong died, doctrinal changes that he himself approved—and was never able to rescind—*set the precedent* for Pastors General to make *any and all changes they chose to*, and at will. If you want a church that does not change its teachings, then *do not ever begin to change its teachings!* And *if you do* start changing major doctrinal teachings, do not then be surprised if a successor follows the same example and changes even more. If God inspired your doctrine, it is divine. If not, then none of it matters anyway.

Mr. Armstrong had always touted his willingness to change when shown that he was wrong, but up until the 1960s, that concept was always applied to rooting out *past Protestant practices* that he had inadvertently brought into the church from his upbringing, before he was shown by God what was *the real truth* of the matter. But once he claimed that *God had shown him* a new cardinal principle *by revelation* through his Bible study, that principle was thereafter cited as a doctrine *put into the Church by Jesus Christ.* If his claim is true that Jesus Christ put many of those doctrines into the Radio Church of God originally, then how can they later be overturned through "better" human scholarship? Either Jesus Christ gave it as a divine gift, or else He did not. "Growing in grace and knowledge" can never mean *casting out what Christ revealed* as being holy. That whole line of reasoning is nonsense. And yet that is exactly the concept that became institutionalized during the 1970s in the WCG, twenty years before the Tkaches capitalized upon that same notion and used it to totally "transform" the church.

If *doctrinal change* to a church is like an iceberg piercing the hull of a giant ocean liner, then the Worldwide Church of God was *already* like the sinking Titanic beginning way back in the early 1970s. By the early 1990s, the ship had already been taking on water for almost twenty years, even though the *"back on track"* years made it appear "topside" that everything was still OK. When it finally broke apart and sank in the 1990s, the passengers (WCG members) who loved that ship were shocked and disillusioned. They had been told the ship was seaworthy all along. When the waters finally

THE AFTERMATH 1986–1997 169

started covering their ankles, ministers started jumping ship, becoming captains of their own lifeboats, and offering *safe havens* for those who sought to hold onto some portion of Mr. Armstrong's legacy.

So all of those holding to the idea that everything was *just grand* until Mr. Armstrong died, are like those rearranging deck chairs on a great sinking ship, denying that water is flooding in below decks. There are many who have written their accounts of this time period, from the perspective of ones believing that the first real damage to the WCG occurred after 1986. But if it is true that the *proverbial iceberg* actually struck twenty years earlier, then we prefer to spend more of our time on those events. Let the others parse every nuance of the *final death throes* of the 1990s, which they believe was so *new and totally unexpected.* Here you will see instead the evidence of why *it was not new at all*, and why it should have been anything but unexpected.

However, to provide a necessary summary of events of the 1980s–90s for the record, here it is. Even as Part II of this work has tried to allow Mr. Armstrong to tell *his own story*—rather than to give prominence to his detractors—so will we document the aftermath of his death from the words of the succeeding Pastor General, because all we really need to know is found in his own account.

IN HIS OWN WORDS

In 1997, Joseph Tkach, Jr. wrote a book entitled, *Transformed by Truth*. It tells the story of the actions of he and his father as they led the Worldwide Church of God after 1986. The citation on the back cover tells it all:

For nearly seventy years the Worldwide Church of God, founded by Herbert W. Armstrong, preached a "different gospel." Then, in December 1994, eight years after Armstrong's death, the church publicly renounced its

170   A PECULIAR TREASURE

unorthodox teachings, embracing historic Christianity. What
happened? Toward the end of his life, Armstrong himself
expressed the first doubts. Soon falsehood after falsehood
fell away and the plain truth prevailed. In this fast-paced
narrative, Joseph Tkach, son of Armstrong's handpicked
successor and head of the church, tells this remarkable
account of the transforming power of the Gospel.

First, it is interesting that Mr. Tkach would make it sound as if
Mr. Armstrong formed a *deathbed doubt* about the doctrinal basis
upon which the entire church had been founded since the 1930s.
Really? Quite unlikely. It is always easy to put words into the mouth
of someone who is now dead and can no longer speak for himself.
The last writings of Herbert Armstrong tell quite a different story, as
we have already seen.

From Mr. Tkach's *Transformed by Truth*, here is an abbreviated
history of key events after 1986:

- Joseph Tkach, Sr. begins to pull foundational church literature
  from circulation from 1986 to 1994, including *Mystery of the
  Ages* and *The United States and Britain in Prophecy.*
- Joseph Tkach, Sr. preaches his "Christmas Eve sermon" in
  December 1994, finally "coming clean" about his plan to
  repudiate the need for God's people to keep the seventh-day
  Sabbath or to tithe, and approving Christmas observance and
  other Protestant doctrines as well. This single sermon removed
  any doubt about the real agenda for the future.
- Influential ministers begin to defect and establish competing
  churches from as early as 1989, but especially after the Christmas
  Eve sermon in 1994.
- The resulting *massive hemorrhage* of members and tithe money
  forces the Worldwide Church of God to terminate many
  employees and begin selling property and assets.

THE AFTERMATH 1986–1997   171

- Ambassador College achieves accreditation in 1994, becoming Ambassador University, but then is forced to close altogether in 1997 for lack of funds.
- Joseph Tkach, Sr. dies of cancer in September 1995, and his son, Joseph, Jr. takes over as Pastor General.
- Joseph Tkach, Jr. never considers that he has made a mistake, but sees his actions and those of his father as courageous, necessary steps to bring the church out of doctrinal error and into the true light of Jesus Christ.

Providing specifics about the membership and financial losses, Mr. Tkach writes:

The Worldwide Church of God reached its peak attendance in 1988—two years after Mr. Armstrong's death—with 126,800 members and 150,000 in attendance. Those figures stayed relatively stable until 1992, when a slight dip was noted. By 1994 church attendance had slipped to 109,600 . . . and then came the Christmas Eve sermon. In the year following that milestone message, attendance plummeted to 66,400 members, and by the time of this writing it had leveled off at around 58,000.

Our membership losses have resulted in a corresponding drop in income. Receipts worldwide in 1990 amounted to more than $211 million. By 1994, the year immediately preceding "The Sermon," income stood at about $164.6 million. The following year income dropped to $103.4 million. In this past year our receipts totaled about $68.5 million. We expect a national income of $38 million in 1997 (*Transformed by Truth*, pp. 71–72).

It is interesting that Mr. Tkach claims there was never any "blueprint" they were following in order to transform the church. He claims that he and his father were merely following God's lead, step by step. They did not know where it would lead. The following citation is very interesting:

172   A PECULIAR TREASURE

Early on, there were some astute members who saw that the first two or three changes we made required that other changes would soon have to be made. They accurately predicted most of the corrections we announced in the following three or four years. Yet at the time we saw none of this. These people would make their predictions, and we would reply: "That's silly. Why are you saying we're going to change things that have been integral to our identity as a denomination?" We steadfastly denied we were even thinking about such changes, for the simple reason that we weren't considering any such thing. But as time went on and we answered more questions, we ended up making some of the very changes our critics had predicted. It looked as if they had more credibility than we did; I freely admit it appeared as though we really did have some sort of hidden agenda, that we weren't telling the whole story (*Transformed by Truth*, p. 84).

Mr. Tkach ends his account with the following announcement:

As I conclude these words in early May 1997, we have just received a press release from the National Association of Evangelicals. Its first two sentences read: "The Board of Directors of the National Association of Evangelicals (NAE) has voted overwhelmingly to accept the Worldwide Church of God (WCG), headquartered in Pasadena, California, into membership. The application process included examination of doctrinal changes which have taken place in the once-controversial denomination" (*Transformed by Truth*, p. 200).

After 1997, this newly *transformed* church would continue to root out every possible vestige of Herbert Armstrong's teachings, and Mr. Tkach and his staff would continue to apologize to the world—and especially to the Protestant establishment—for ever having believed Herbert Armstrong's interpretation of Scripture.

By 2009, it was finally time to abandon the moniker, *Worldwide Church of God,* and to adopt a new name that would truly demonstrate how far removed they had become from their past history. Thus, Mr. Tkach announced their new name: *Grace Communion International.* To this day, they are still running from their religious roots and seeking to be accepted among the traditional Christian denominations.

PART III

"ARMSTRONGISM" EXAMINED WITH RESPECT TO THE ANTAGONISTS

CHAPTER NINE
SOURCES OF INSPIRATION

Herbert Armstrong's detractors provide a wealth of information that is very helpful in testing the evidence. Among those who have concluded emphatically that he *was not* led or inspired by God with his controversial teachings, how do they prove it? If correct, one would think our very best source of proof would come from those particular leaders of the Worldwide Church of God who *became compelled* to lead their members in repudiation of most of Mr. Armstrong's teachings after his death. They claim to have done so *in conscience*, believing sincerely that Herbert Armstrong was wrong, and that is why they became willing to put the entire church through an excruciating transition to reject the foundation of his most beloved teachings. Yes, let us begin with their take on their own founder's legacy.

Recall that it was Joseph Tkach, Sr. who succeeded Mr. Armstrong as Pastor General after his death in early 1986, initiating the *transition*. When Mr. Tkach died in 1995, his son, Joseph, Jr., took up the reins and carried forward his father's grand vision. As referenced in chapter eight, Joseph Tkach, Jr. wrote a detailed account about his own thinking during those tumultuous years in his 1997 book, *Transformed by Truth*. The subtitle of the book says it all: "*The Worldwide Church of God rejects the teachings of founder Herbert W. Armstrong and embraces historic Christianity.*" What is his reason for concluding that Mr. Armstrong's doctrines were not only empty, but dangerous? Upon what premise was this analysis based? You need to weigh it.

In chapter seven entitled, "What We Believed," Mr. Tkach begins a detailed survey of Mr. Armstrong's most prominent teachings. The first and most important point he makes is that Herbert Armstrong did not really originate any of his own teachings, but borrowed them

178   A PECULIAR TREASURE

all in one way or another from other religious teachers, especially
Protestants!

> Mr. Armstrong was nothing in his theological approach
> if not eclectic. He borrowed and adapted most of his
> "unique" teachings from others. Often when we try to tell
> some of our people that Mr. Armstrong borrowed much of
> his teaching from outside sources, we meet heavy resistance.
> So we sometimes respond with the following: "Allow us to
> lay out a challenge aimed at combating the idea that these
> doctrines were specially revealed to Herbert Armstrong. We
> want to show that they really did not pour directly from the
> Godhead into his mind. Here's our challenge: You know the
> distinctive teachings of Herbert Armstrong; now you name
> the teaching and we'll tell you where it came from. We'll
> show you what preceded Herbert Armstrong and
> demonstrate that the teaching was *not* specially revealed to
> him and it *wasn't* restored from the first century"
> (*Transformed by Truth*, p. 88).

Before addressing some of the specific examples of these "copied"
doctrines, let us first examine the root of Mr. Tkach's thesis. It
presumes that in order to justify rejecting the theology of
mainstream Christianity (which Mr. Armstrong certainly did), any
"true apostle" claiming divine inspiration from God, 1) must
proclaim only concepts that are *totally original* and have *never been*
"*discovered*" by any past religionist, and 2) must have received that
inspiration by means of direct "speaking" from God, like Moses
receiving the Law by God's direct dictation to him upon Mt. Sinai.
The inference is that if there were no "*Sinai dictation session,*" and
what was received was not *totally unheard of previously* by
mankind, it could not have been attributed to any special work of
God. There is also a third inference in the quote above: that Herbert
Armstrong *believed* points one and two to be true and predicated his

Sources of Inspiration

own legitimacy as an instrument of God upon their validity. But are those assertions accurate?

From Where Did His Understanding Derive?

Did Herbert Armstrong ever claim that God poured divine truth into his head in one or more secret, secluded meetings with Jesus Christ? Not that we can find. In fact, he seemed to have published many statements over the years describing openly the means by which he gained his understanding of God's Truth, and it was not through the equivalent of a *Sinai dictation*. There is no doubt, however, that he claimed to have been *uniquely and miraculously inspired* by God.

First, notice that he claimed *the work itself* was the purposeful endeavor of God, not man:

> Yes, we *CAN KNOW*, if willing to know, whether we are right or wrong. It is not a matter of superior intellect, but of SUBMISSION TO GOD.
>
> But the conclusion of the whole question is this: I did not start this work of my own accord at all. It is the very last thing I would have wanted, in my days of carnality, to do. IT IS GOD'S DOING!
>
> By circumstances, God forced me to submission. The living CHRIST so manipulated events and the force of circumstance that He literally PLUNGED me into His Work. It is not my work—it is THE VERY WORK OF GOD.
>
> And *THIS* can be easily proved, to those willing to know the TRUTH! ("Personal from the Editor," *The Plain Truth*, December 1963, p. 41)

Notice next that he also claimed to have been called and commissioned *uniquely* as a representative of Jesus Christ to confirm God's Truth with authority:

180 A PECULIAR TREASURE

It was in this UNIQUE manner that I was brought to discover THE MISSING DIMENSION IN EDUCATION —the truth as to WHY humanity was put on this earth—the true PURPOSE of human life—the CAUSE of all the world's unhappiness, unsolvable problems and evils—the difference between the TRUE VALUES and the false—THE WAY that can be the ONLY *CAUSE* of PEACE between nations, groups and individuals—the only CAUSE of true success in life with happiness, peace, prosperity and abundance.

No, I know of no one who was thrust into the Ministry of Jesus Christ, untaught by MAN, but by the living Christ through His written Word, in the manner in which I was. I didn't realize it yet, but I was being brought into His Ministry by the living Christ in a manner UTTERLY UNIQUE, and totally unlike any other of which I know! (*Autobiography of Herbert W. Armstrong*, Vol. 1, 1986, pp. 318–319)

Mr. Armstrong compared his special calling to that of the Apostle Paul. Notice his statement in the November 29, 1954, *Co-worker Letter,* which he repeated many times over the years:

And so I say to you, as the Apostle Paul said to those at Galatia: I certify you, brethren, that the GOSPEL which is preached of me is not after man, for I neither received it of man, neither was I taught it but BY THE REVELATION OF JESUS CHRIST. . . . When it pleased God, who . . . called me by His grace, to reveal His Son in me that I might preach Him to the world; immediately I conferred not with flesh and blood—neither went I to any sect or denomination or human theologian, but I went directly to the WORD of GOD, on my knees, corrected, reproved, and instructed in God's righteousness and TRUTH.

So, like the Apostle Paul, Herbert Armstrong claimed to have been chosen and inspired by God in those things that he taught. But

SOURCES OF INSPIRATION 181

did he ever claim that this *revelation process* took place in *the very same way* as God taught the Apostle Paul?

The Apostle Paul, telling us under God's inspiration of how he came to KNOW God's Truth, said: "But I certify you, brethren, that the gospel which was preached of me is *not after man.* For I neither received it of man, neither was I taught it, but by the revelation of Jesus Christ." He received it, as he implies, from an appearance of the living Christ, in person, even after His resurrection and ascension.

I, too, received Christ's Gospel NOT from MAN. I, too, certify that the Gospel I have taught and proclaimed is *not after man.* I entered no theological seminary, where I would have received a particular denominational teaching and set of doctrines and practices. I was *not* taught by MAN. But I was taught, as was Paul, by the revelation of Jesus Christ—Paul from the living Christ *in person*—who is the Word of God in *person*—but I from the *written Word of God* —which is the SAME revelation, now set in print ("Personal from the Editor," *Tomorrow's World*, February 1972, p. 3).

This is precisely what Herbert Armstrong claimed *consistently* over all of the years of his ministry—that God did indeed reveal through him *real Truth* which the world's religions had never understood, but he claimed that *the process* by which God performed that miraculous revelation occurred as he sought understanding through *his study of the Bible.* Do not confuse this with the idea that anyone who chooses can sit down with a Bible and "figure out" the truth. Millions attempt to do exactly that, but they all arrive at very contradictory conclusions. Since the one true God cannot be the source of so many disjointed theories, all of these "Bible scholars" cannot therefore be legitimate. Mr. Armstrong never claimed that the way in which God worked with him was also open to everyone else to copy. He did indeed claim to have been a *specially chosen* instrument through whom God made special revelations known, which were hidden from others. But we find no evidence that he ever claimed to have received that revelation in some supernatural setting.

Neither did he claim to have received that body of knowledge all at one time. In fact, from the beginning he readily emphasized that God taught him *one doctrine at a time* over a protracted period of years.

> In these beginning years of my ministry I went along with many of these religious practices—and even some doctrines—commonly accepted by the evangelical denominations, and which I later had to UN-learn. I had to learn one doctrine, and one truth, at a time ("The Autobiography of Herbert W. Armstrong," *The Plain Truth*, November 1959, p. 9).

In a separate chapter we will address in detail this crucial topic of "admitting error," and show how the original meaning of "correcting error" had subtly changed by the 1960s. In the earliest years, Mr. Armstrong cited his willingness to "admit error when proven wrong" as another proof of the true Church, but back then, his purpose was the progressive expulsion of more and more *falsehoods of past Protestant tradition.* At some point, this principle morphed into an instrument used—especially after the 1960s—to begin dismantling key doctrines of the church which previously had been ascribed as God's *special revelation.* But at this point, it is sufficient to note that Mr. Armstrong did indeed claim a unique calling by God to be a minister of Jesus Christ, as well as being an instrument through whom real Truth was revealed.

Recall that Mr. Tkach implied in his book the notion that if Mr. Armstrong did not have a *Sinai revelation experience,* and if he did not receive special knowledge in one session—like having truth "pour directly from the Godhead into his mind"—we are asked to discount his entire legitimacy. He further asserts that he and his father were the ones who first helped to enlighten members of the Worldwide

SOURCES OF INSPIRATION 183

Church of God to these facts, even though members were thoroughly taught the history of Mr. Armstrong's calling, commission, and source of inspiration over decades of his writings. How exactly should any member of the church have ever believed Mr. Armstrong received his knowledge in the very same way that Moses or the Apostle Paul had been inspired? We find no record of any such claim.

ALL DOCTRINES COPIED?

What about Mr. Tkach's claim that Mr. Armstrong had never really offered any "new truths," but merely doctrines that had been copied from other religionists, especially Protestants? Here again is what he wrote:

> . . . Here's our challenge: You know the distinctive teachings of Herbert Armstrong; now you name the teaching and we'll tell you where it came from. We'll show you what preceded Herbert Armstrong and demonstrate that the teaching was *not* specially revealed to him and it *wasn't* restored from the first century" (*Transformed by Truth*, p. 88).

Mr. Tkach then describes the results of his challenge to church members:

> When someone takes us up on this challenge, almost always the first doctrine to be mentioned is *the Sabbath.* "Sorry!" I say. "The Seventh-day Baptists had that first, long before Mr. Armstrong." You should see the looks on people's faces as we start naming the origins of one doctrine after another (*Transformed by Truth*, p. 88).

But again I ask, when did Herbert Armstrong ever claim he was the first to teach that the seventh-day Sabbath should be kept by

Christians? Did not he write very specifically and repeatedly about his first experience in 1926 with proving the Sabbath? All members of the church became well versed in the story of Mrs. Armstrong becoming convinced by a neighbor that Saturday was the true Sabbath, and Mr. Armstrong's vehement opposition to this notion. Here is one of many references that he made over the years:

> It was then that a Bible-believing woman, neighbor of my parents in Salem, Oregon, convinced my wife that the Bible enforced observance of the seventh-day Sabbath in this New Testament time of grace! The facts of my outraged reaction at this "religious fanaticism" have been published many times.
>
> I was unable to talk, reason, argue, cajole, or threaten her out of her newfound conviction. I was literally angered into my first STUDY of the Bible—to *prove* to her that "all these churches couldn't be wrong"—and that the Bible commanded and enforced the observance of Sunday, in this New Testament period ("Personal from the Editor," *The Plain Truth*, September 1964, p. 2).

How did that neighbor woman already know about the Sabbath in 1926? She was a member of a seventh-day church whose history was well established. Small as that movement was compared to Sunday-keeping churches, there was nothing new about Sabbath-keeping Christians. And yes, Mr. Tkach is correct that the Seventh-day Baptists were certainly part of that history.

Why then does Mr. Tkach imply that Mr. Armstrong had taught that he himself had originated Sabbath-keeping? How could any Worldwide Church of God member ever become *shocked and disillusioned* to "discover" this fact for the first time in the 1990s? There is no way any member of that church should ever have imagined that Herbert Armstrong was the first to teach Christians to keep the Sabbath. He never claimed it!

SOURCES OF INSPIRATION   185

Again, the implication seems to be that if Mr. Armstrong was not the originator of a particular religious concept, he was not an inspired servant of God, and the doctrine must not be true either. But how does the validity of the seventh-day Sabbath rest upon Herbert Armstrong? Either the Bible certifies the validity of the Sabbath, or it does not. And many (though a very small percentage of all claimed Christians) over the centuries have recognized that the Sabbath was instituted for all of mankind from the beginning of Creation. Herbert Armstrong was admittedly a latecomer to that knowledge. But he certainly became the most effective minister in the twentieth century to spread that "old knowledge" and to convince many thousands to begin keeping it.

REVELATION THROUGH TECHNICAL STUDY

We have already seen that Mr. Armstrong claimed to have been inspired by God to begin understanding Bible truths as he engaged in an intensive personal study program. He did not claim this was a *carte blanche* method available to anyone else seeking to understand real truth, but stated that *he himself* had been *chosen by God* and blessed with special understanding which had eluded all other scholars. Notice how he describes that study process in more detail. Here is how he related that very first study to disprove the Sabbath:

> I sought, wrote for, and obtained at the public library every book or booklet possible purporting to refute seventh-day Sabbath observance. I searched every nook and cranny of the New Testament to find the sanctification, making holy, or command to observe Sunday. It was like hunting for the needle in the haystack—the needle that isn't there! ("Personal from the Editor," *The Plain Truth*, September 1964, p. 2)

186   A PECULIAR TREASURE

So Mr. Armstrong admits that he sought out scholarly books by every author he could find on the topic that he was studying. Here are some further references:

> After much careful research, involving study of evolution—the writings of Darwin, Huxley, Haeckel, the earlier Lamarck, plus Spencer, Vogt, Chamberlain and other modern geologists and evolutionists—as well as a careful study of Genesis and other parts of the Bible—of all the scientific facts bearing on the subject I could find—I became SURE! I had PROVED that God *IS*!
>
> Next I entered an intensive study to determine whether the Bible can be PROVED to be the inspired Word of God—the revelation of knowledge from the Creator of mankind. By many infallible proofs, this was PROVED! ("Personal from the Editor," *Tomorrow's World*, February 1972, p. 2)

These kinds of statements were so commonly repeated by Mr. Armstrong over the years that members certainly should have understood it was his *systematic practice* to gather as many scholarly works as possible in his search to verify real truth. And his consistent claim was that God led him *during these intensive studies* to pick out sound principles vs. the weak and unsubstantiated. His methodology had never been to lock himself in an empty room, waiting for God to bestow upon his mind *new and unique knowledge* from on high.

This brings us to the next challenge offered by Mr. Tkach. What other prominent teachings of Herbert Armstrong does he attempt to discredit, and why?

> How about *the nature of man*? Sorry—the evangelist Charles Finney heavily influenced our former ideas on that. In fact, after Mr. Armstrong's death when my dad moved into his predecessor's office and cleaned out his desk, guess what book he

found there explaining the nature of man? You guessed it—a work by Charles Finney (*Transformed by Truth*, p. 88).

First, the main principle that Herbert Armstrong and Charles Finney shared somewhat in common was a belief that man has an obligation to try to obey godly principles, as opposed to the most common Protestant idea that "Adam's fall" made it impossible to do so, and that even to try is a denial of grace. Finney taught that man has a choice, and that God would not have given him choice if there was no way for him to succeed in doing right. This is about as close a correlation as can be found between the two men's teachings. What is certain is that Charles Finney, although considered heretical by many mainstream Christians, was still an evangelical Protestant who rejected the seventh-day Sabbath and almost every other principle embraced by Herbert Armstrong. It is also certain that Charles Finney did not truly concur with the Radio Church of God teaching about the nature of man, which was well documented in the original *Ambassador College Correspondence Course* from the 1960s.

But does the fact that Herbert Armstrong read Charles Finney's works prove he copied from him, and even if so, that Mr. Armstrong's teaching on man's nature is erroneous? Again, the truth should either stand or fall based upon God's revelation in the Bible. Either the evidence is there or it is not, regardless of who may have "first" gleaned some aspect of that truth. Since Mr. Armstrong made it very clear from the beginning that he was willing to embrace *bona fide principles* that could be substantiated as *truth*, regardless of the original source, how would that weaken the veracity of one of his teachings, to discover that another human being understood that same principle before Herbert Armstrong did?

MANY NUGGETS OF TRUTH IN THE WORLD

What Mr. Tkach seems to ignore is another cardinal principle taught by Herbert Armstrong over the years: that there are many *nuggets of truth* to be found *even among deceived peoples of this world.* The key is to recognize, not that all points of truth are *totally unknown,* but that man has never been able to *assemble them together* into the "big picture" necessary to solve his problems. Mr. Armstrong taught that Satan is the great deceiver of mankind by means of mixing truth with error. If Satan offered only pure falsehoods, it would never serve his purpose. His speciality is in *perverting* the Truth of God! What makes deception so "deceptive" is the use of *a lot of truth* with just enough error to make the whole product corrupt and worthless to mankind.

If this assessment of man's knowledge within the world is true, what would that then mean to us? It would mean that the completed picture of God's *true Way of Life* does not include *exclusively* elements that are *totally foreign* to the scholars of this world! It is very likely that Satan has inspired some of those true principles to be understood as wrappings for his lies, like mixing bitter medicine within something that is sweet. It is easier to disguise the lie when enshrined within a basically sound principle.

What Truly Made His Work Distinctive?

In essence, what Herbert Armstrong claimed to have accomplished was not *figuring out all unique principles* that had never been discovered by any other man before, but to have been *miraculously led by God* to test each principle and to *correctly verify* which precepts had merit and which did not! Again, this orientation to searching out truth by examining the arguments of human scholars *one doctrine at a time* is *exactly what he did,* and what he *admitted* in his writings he had done over many years.

If that is true, why then should we become disillusioned to find that he had a library full of religious and scientific writings by this world's elites? And to the extent that one of those scholars understood a particular nugget of real truth, how does it discredit Mr. Armstrong that he identified that particular valuable principle out of myriad falsehoods and added it to the body of his own teachings? He claimed that this was the very process that God used to help him assemble the *full tapestry* of God's revealed Way of Life.

After building the case to discredit Mr. Armstrong's claims, Mr. Tkach finally goes on to acknowledge that he never claimed any *Sinai revelations*:

> When he said something had been revealed to him, he did not mean that God had poured the new understanding directly into his waiting mind. No, whatever the new teaching happened to be, it usually came through a more human channel (*Transformed by Truth*, p. 90).

However, he provides this admission by relating an uncorroborated anecdote suggesting that Mr. Armstrong's definition of "revelation" was *accidentally discovered* by a particular close acquaintance. The implication remains that laymembers of the church were basically duped into believing that he had received a sudden inspiration of all truth, similar to Paul being struck down on the road to Damascus, and upon being finally enlightened, church members became highly disillusioned. You must decide whether that version of history seems to have any substance.

What you are going to find as we continue forward with this analysis is this: What made Herbert Armstrong's work verifiably *unique* was not that every single element of his teaching *in itself* was revolutionary. As Mr. Tkach correctly points out, that is not really so. Yet who can deny that Herbert Armstrong's overall work was absolutely distinctive? The very fact that his detractors refer to it as *Armstrongism* confirms the point. If the total body of doctrine that Herbert Armstrong professed was really nothing special, why are Joseph Tkach and others even talking and writing about it? Why are you taking the time to read about it now? If his work was merely copied from other men, how did his legacy become so unusually distinctive?

What you will discover is that *the body of doctrines* that Herbert Armstrong assembled was absolutely distinctive and unmatched by any other man. The only real question is, was that body of doctrine professed by Herbert Armstrong a manifestation of the true Jesus Christ, or was it not?

CHAPTER TEN
UNIQUE SALVATION DOCTRINE

In the previous chapter, we found that Mr. Armstrong never claimed to have received God's inspiration in the very same way that Moses or the Apostle Paul did, but he consistently explained that revelation process *openly* to the whole church from the very beginning. He also never claimed to have been the first man to have understood many individual principles, but unashamedly discussed his study of *many* religious and secular authors in his quest for real truth. On what basis, then, should any of the church membership ever have become *shocked and disillusioned* to discover that Mr. Armstrong was not the originator of Sabbath-keeping (for example) in the twentieth century? We find no evidence that he ever claimed to be such an author.

What further evidence can we glean from the historical account provided by Mr. Tkach to prove his point? As one who felt sincerely that Mr. Armstrong was not inspired by God in what he taught, we should be able to put his rationale to the test.

NOTHING NEW, EXCEPT . . .

In the very same chapter in which he threw down the gauntlet to claim that *not one* of Herbert Armstrong's teachings was original—but rather borrowed from other religionists—Mr. Tkach then begins to list "Seven Key Doctrinal Emphases" which made the Worldwide Church of God stand out from all other churches. Here is how he prefaced that itemized list:

For those who may not be familiar with what the Worldwide Church of God formerly taught, allow me to briefly sketch out seven areas of doctrine that, taken together, set us apart from

192 A PECULIAR TREASURE

all other organizations, denominations, and churches. Our former doctrinal distinctives cannot be limited to the following, but in my opinion what follows represents the chief teachings that defined us as a group and distinguished us from all others (*Transformed by Truth*, p. 91).

Notice, he seems to concede that the *collective body* of doctrine—"taken together"—was indeed distinctive. So in spite of feeling that Mr. Armstrong was not inspired by God to come to understand any specific *unique* truths, he does, after all, acknowledge that *the package* of doctrinal teachings was indeed unique among this world's religions. But his admission does not stop there. Concerning his assessment of one of those seven points in particular, entitled, "What Is Salvation?" (p. 94), he summarizes Mr. Armstrong's teaching as follows:

We used to teach that no one was "born again" until the final resurrection. We said that those who believed in the death and resurrection of Jesus and who committed themselves to obeying the law were "begotten" (which we understood to mean "conceived") sons of God and would be "born again" at the time of the resurrection. Until then, a believer was only conceived, not born. Therefore, no one was "saved" in their earthly life; they had to await the return of Jesus Christ for that. At the resurrection the believer would be raised up and finally be born again.

What follows this summary, however, is quite stunning. Mr. Tkach concedes:

This was one of the few doctrines taught by Mr. Armstrong that has no known precedent; it appears to be unique to him (p. 94).

UNIQUE SALVATION DOCTRINE   193

So much for the initial challenge on page 88—"now you name the teaching and we'll tell you where it came from." By page 94, Mr. Tkach seems to have negated his own premise. And this is not an inconsequential teaching. The belief concerning what salvation is all about and how it is achieved is a *defining signature* for any and every religion.

SALVATION TEACHING AND BEING "BORN AGAIN"

This particular doctrine of begotten vs. born again was not included in our earlier list of five simple identifiers of the true Church of God, but it certainly could have been. It is another example of a key part of God's plan for mankind which is not understood at all by others professing to be Christians. How is it that Herbert Armstrong seems to have been the only one who recognized such simple and prolific statements in the Bible about the salvation process? The interchange between Jesus and Nicodemus makes it very simple to discern that being "born" involves being in *the form of Spirit*, not flesh:

> Jesus answered, Verily, verily, I say unto thee, Except a man be born of water and of the Spirit, he cannot enter into the kingdom of God. That which is born of the flesh is flesh; and *that which is born of the Spirit is spirit*. Marvel not that I said unto thee, Ye must be *born again*. The wind bloweth where it listeth, and thou hearest the sound thereof, but canst not tell whence it cometh, and whither it goeth: *so is every one that is born of the Spirit* (John 3:5–8) [emphasis mine].

How simple is that! Jesus Christ defined very specifically that the "born again" state does not exist in a flesh body, but requires a *Spirit body* which then has the same capacity to move like the wind, invisibly but powerfully. But perhaps that interpretation twists the Scripture? Or might it actually be confirmed in other Bible passages as well?

> Whosoever is born of God doth not commit sin; for his seed
> remaineth in him: and he cannot sin, because he is born of
> God (1 John 3:9).

One who is truly "born again" does not commit sin. Not because the law has been done away, making it *impossible* to sin, but because that individual has been born into the spirit realm—now having *inherent* life—possessing full power and perfect control to obey the law. Anyone in the flesh, no matter how spiritually mature, has no such perfect control, and therefore continues to sin. Any flesh being claiming he is not still a sinner is only proving he is not a true Christian.

> If we say that we have no sin, we deceive ourselves, and the
> truth is not in us. If we confess our sins, he is faithful and
> just to forgive us our sins, and to cleanse us from all
> unrighteousness (1 John 1:8–9).

As we have already seen in earlier chapters, one of the hallmarks of the true Church is acknowledgment that God's spiritual Law is still in force—not done away. Anyone claiming *it is done away* is unavoidably claiming he is *not committing sin*. Where there is no sin, there is no law, because sin is the transgression of the law (1 John 3:4). So the only one who is totally sinless is one who has already been perfected and given an eternal, spiritual body.

But if we are not yet "born again," what are we at this time? Mr. Armstrong's teaching made it abundantly clear. We are *begotten* of the Spirit, even as human life begins with begettal in the womb, requiring time to mature before finally being born. And what is the responsibility of one of those priceless, begotten children of God in order to grow spiritually toward that ultimate maturity?

> We know that whosoever is born of God sinneth not; but he
> that is begotten of God *keepeth himself*, and that wicked one
> toucheth him not (1 John 5:18) [emphasis mine].

UNIQUE SALVATION DOCTRINE   195

"Keepeth himself" how?

If ye love me, *keep my commandments*. And I will pray the
Father, and he shall give you another Comforter, that he may
abide with you for ever; Even the Spirit of truth; whom the
world cannot receive, because it seeth him not, neither
knoweth him: but ye know him; for he dwelleth with you,
and shall be in you (John 14:15–17) [emphasis mine].

A begotten child of God has received only *an earnest*—a down
payment—of God's Holy Spirit.

In whom ye also trusted, after that ye heard the word of
truth, the gospel of your salvation: in whom also after that ye
believed, ye were *sealed with that holy Spirit of promise*,
Which is *the earnest of our inheritance* until the redemption
of the purchased possession, unto the praise of his glory
(Ephesians 1:13–14) [emphasis mine].

Receiving the Holy Spirit through baptism is only a *down
payment* of that Spirit, infusing in us *a begettal* of new spiritual life.
But birth—being born again—is the ultimate *transformation* when
the flesh body dies, being replaced by a new spiritual body. And in
the meantime, the work of a true Christian is to be *an overcomer*,
learning to walk more and more over time as Christ Himself walked.

Wherefore we labour, that, whether present or absent, we
may be accepted of him. For we must all appear before the
judgment seat of Christ; that every one may receive the
things done in his body, *according to that he hath done*,
whether it be good or bad (2 Corinthians 5:9–10) [emphasis
mine].

There will indeed be a Judgment, and we will each be judged
upon what we did with our calling during that gestational period we

were given for growth, following our spiritual conception. The repetition of these basic principles is prolific throughout the New Testament. Why, then, did *no other religion* pick up on that thread of simple truth? Mr. Tkach says that only Herbert Armstrong taught it.

The alternative that most believe—including Mr. Tkach—is that one becomes a Christian by making *a verbal profession*, "I accept Jesus Christ as my Savior." Then he is automatically "born again." Having been "born," the law does not apply, and he is no longer capable of committing sin. No matter what he does for the rest of his life, his salvation is "guaranteed," being already "born," or completed. Too bad that such a notion is simply inconsistent with everything recorded in the Bible. What is the simple truth about what is truly required for salvation?

> And he said unto me, It is done. I am Alpha and Omega, the beginning and the end. I will give unto him that is athirst of the fountain of the water of life freely. *He that overcometh shall inherit all things; and I will be his God, and he shall be my son.* But the fearful, and unbelieving, and the abominable, and murderers, and whoremongers, and sorcerers, and idolaters, and all liars, shall have their part in the lake which burneth with fire and brimstone: which is the second death (Revelation 21:6–8) [emphasis mine].

Can it be any more plain? Salvation will not be granted to anyone based upon a *profession with his mouth*. It is all about what he *does* to show honor to God's Law (respect for the Ten Commandments), which is what it means to be an "overcomer." Mr. Joseph Tkach changed his mind and came to believe he is already born again, just like the majority of religious movements claiming to be Christian. It is interesting that on this particular critical issue affecting our very hope of salvation, he acknowledges that Herbert Armstrong offered a teaching found in no other church in the twentieth century. But

UNIQUE SALVATION DOCTRINE 197

what is the real truth about God's standard for human salvation? You must weigh the evidence and decide for yourself.

ANOTHER UNIQUE TEACHING

Closely related to this teaching about *when and how* salvation is achieved is another doctrine taught by Herbert Armstrong that has no parallel in any other religion. That is the teaching about the *ultimate hope* to be realized by those who do indeed become "born again." What will those spiritual children actually be doing for all eternity? We know that they will have new spiritual—immortal—bodies, but what will their status be in that Kingdom of God? Will they become angels, disembodied spirits, or something else?

Herbert Armstrong taught that the hope of the saved is to become *full members of the God Family*, sharing all of the power and glory possessed now by God the Father and Jesus Christ; literally becoming "God, as God is." It is a teaching that makes most so-called Christians cringe: denouncing it as blasphemous while they sniff the air for the damnation of hell fire, like lightning, to strike down its adherents. How utterly audacious to believe that human beings will actually become God! Yet that is exactly what Herbert Armstrong taught, and that which the Worldwide Church of God promoted during all of those decades of incredible growth. Here is one example to confirm that consistent teaching, still evident even soon before he died:

The divine family is God. There is one God—the one family, consisting of more than one Person. . . . God then purposed *to reproduce himself*, through humans, made in his image and likeness . . . with the possibility of being born into the divine family begotten by God the Father. . . . And *that is why God put man on the earth!* (*Mystery of the Ages*, 1985, p. 78).

Mr. Tkach acknowledges this history under item number two on his list of seven key doctrinal emphases of the former church:

> We taught that God was literally reproducing Himself through mankind. Our destiny was not to remain merely human, but to become God—born again as members of God's family. Just as human children are fully human, so (we thought) God's children will be fully God (*Transformed by Truth*, p. 94).

He fails, however, to acknowledge that this is another teaching of Herbert Armstrong that was *absolutely unique* among today's religions. You will find no other church that taught this God-Family doctrine. There was no one from whom Herbert Armstrong could copy. It simply did not exist. The very closest teaching one can find may be that of the Mormons or the Eastern Orthodox Church. In each case, these groups espouse a form of *apotheosis*—the eventual deification of humans. But their ideas are hardly similar to that of Mr. Armstrong because their entire concept of the natures of "God" and man is very different. There is absolutely no precedent we know of for teaching that man was created in the image of God because God is re-creating Himself and expanding His own Family. It is yet another key reason that "Armstrongism" is so distinct within the religious world, in spite of claims that every teaching was merely "copied."

But is there any biblical substance for belief in the God-Family plan? If there is, why would no other religious movement have stumbled upon it, even in part? Let us see.

God did indeed create man in His very own image (Genesis 1:26). No other creatures hold that distinction. Yes, some of the angelic host do appear with certain attributes like unto men (Ezekiel 1:5–10), but usually combined with the features of animals like lions, birds, oxen, etc. Most Christian religions believe the hope of the saved is to become angels, sitting on clouds and playing harps. Yet the Bible refutes that utterly! The angels were created by God to be

UNIQUE SALVATION DOCTRINE   199

the servants of God, like the butlers and maids in the royal household.

Notice first that Jesus Christ did not become an angel at His resurrection. He became *the Son of God*, an honor that was never offered to any being in *the angel class* of creature:

> Being made so much *better than the angels*, as he hath by inheritance obtained a more excellent name than they. For unto which of the angels said he at any time, Thou art my Son, this day have I begotten thee? And again, I will be to him a Father, and he shall be to me a Son? And again, when he bringeth in the firstbegotten into the world, he saith, And let all the angels of God worship him. And of the angels he saith, Who maketh his angels spirits, and his ministers a flame of fire. But unto the Son he saith, *Thy throne, O God*, is for ever and ever: a sceptre of righteousness is the sceptre of thy kingdom (Hebrews 1:4–8) [emphasis mine].

This makes it very plain that Jesus Christ was high above the angels, resurrected to sit on a throne, and like His Father, *called God*! But what does that have to do with the future of resurrected human beings? Most accept that Christ is God, but reject that man will follow the same path. Yet Jesus Christ is called *the firstbegotten* (v. 6 above), not *the only* begotten. If there is a first, it is because there will be others to follow. And is not that exactly what the called of God are told to do, to follow Him? "He that saith he abideth in him ought himself also so to walk, even as he walked" (1 John 2:6). But where is the evidence that God is going to reward "the saved" of men with a resurrection to glory as Jesus Christ received?

> The Spirit itself beareth witness with our spirit, that we are *the children of God*: And if children, then heirs; *heirs of God, and joint-heirs with Christ*; if so be that we suffer with him, that we may *be also glorified together* (Romans 8:16–17) [emphasis mine].

Human beings are consistently called the children of God. Most try to dismiss this as a doting sentiment of the Father, like the pet owner who fawns over her little dog and calls it "my baby." But that is not the way God behaves or thinks. He is never frivolous with names and titles, and when He calls someone His own *child*, it deserves serious consideration. Those children are also called heirs, and not just some token, second-rate heirs, but *joint heirs with Christ*! No angel was ever offered such a future, only human beings. What does it mean to be joint heirs with Jesus Christ? The Bible makes that very plain as well. Concerning Christ and those who will follow Him, we are told:

> And they sung a new song, saying, Thou art worthy to take the book, and to open the seals thereof: for thou wast slain, and hast redeemed us to God by thy blood out of every kindred, and tongue, and people, and nation; And hast made us unto our God *kings and priests: and we shall reign on the earth* (Revelation 5:9–10) [emphasis mine].

Jesus Christ, as the Son of God, is going to rule. Those who follow in His footsteps—the perfected children of God—will likewise be glorified.

> That they all may be one; as thou, Father, art in me, and I in thee, that they also may be one in us: that the world may believe that thou hast sent me. And *the glory which thou gavest me I have given them*; that they may be one, even as we are one: I in them, and thou in me, *that they may be made perfect in one*; and that the world may know that thou hast sent me, and hast loved them, as thou hast loved me (John 17:21–23) [emphasis mine].

Made perfect in one, how? By being born into the very God Family and sharing with the Father and with Jesus Christ all of the glory, honor, and privileges of royal children, including offices as

Kings and Priests. This is a future offered to no other creature—angel or otherwise—a theme that is replete throughout the Bible.

Do the words of the Holy Scripture really make that such a far-out concept? The Bible repeatedly calls the saved, children, heirs, joint heirs, kings, and priests. Why would Herbert Armstrong be the only religious leader to pick up on this theme and form a salvational doctrine around it? You can choose to dismiss it as blasphemy if you will, but to say there is no biblical substantiation for the concept would be absurd. The texts listed above are only a very brief example. But once again, you must choose what you believe to be true, based upon the evidence or lack thereof.

What is absolutely true, however, is that the idea that Herbert Armstrong copied all of his teachings from other religionists is very easy to disprove. It would appear that Mr. Tkach had a strong personal reason for wanting to believe there was nothing unique, perhaps to make it easier to dismiss his predecessor's credibility and to convince others of the same. But again, the very history of that church organization and its *clearly unique doctrines* in the twentieth century make that an indefensible position.

Next, we finally will address what Mr. Tkach called "the central plank" of that church's doctrine—the teaching about modern Israel in prophecy.

CHAPTER ELEVEN
ANGLO-ISRAELISM

Finally, we want to address a teaching that Mr. Tkach considered the capstone of all, calling it "the central plank" of doctrines within the Worldwide Church of God—Anglo-Israelism. What is Anglo (British)-Israelism, and what was its true significance within the body of doctrinal teachings of Herbert Armstrong? How and why has it been repudiated by so many in the world today, and is there any basis for thinking it might actually have some merit?

ANGLO-ISRAELISM DEFINED

In general, Anglo-Israelism involves the belief that those identified as the Jewish people today do not represent *the entire house* of modern Israel, but only a small remnant, at most, of three tribes—Judah, Levi, and Benjamin. It asserts that the northern kingdom of Israel—which God called *distinctly* the *House of Israel* after its separation from the southern *kingdom of Judah* after the death of King Solomon—was later taken into captivity by the Assyrians and transported out of the Promised Land, becoming *lost in identity* as Israelites, but nonetheless producing descendants of those original *Ten Tribes* who have come forward to this very day. It asserts further that those Israelitish descendants eventually migrated away from Assyrian control in the east, settling in northwestern Europe and in the British Isles, from which also North America became the primary target of settlement. These Anglo-Saxon/British/American peoples are believed, therefore, to have legitimate claim as *bona fide* descendants of Abraham, Isaac, and Jacob, equal to that of the descendants of the House of Judah—today called *the Jews*.

There are many different religious and political groups that profess varying versions of this belief, all having their own particular agendas at heart. Many are simply attracted to the idea of being the physical descendants of "God's chosen people" as an exercise in human vanity. Who would not like to discover that he actually descended from a very prestigious line of forebears chronicled in the Bible? Others take it a step further and claim that the Jews today are imposters, using the concept of Anglo-Israelism to justify persecution toward them. Others who are part of the "Christian Identity" movement take it even further and use their claim of being the "true Israelites" to justify wholesale racial hatred toward "all others" and to engage in anti-government activities to resist their own "Egyptian oppression" in the name of God. Many of today's most right-wing, anti-government, racist extremists lay claim to the idea of non-Jewish Israelites as a core belief. Above all, the very concept of *a modern discovery* of the *lost Ten Tribes* not only taps a romantic yearning in many for mystery and drama, but also provides a classic foundation to promote almost anything one chooses, including many very self-serving and dangerous ideas. Today, there are many peoples of varying races who lay claim to being the "true descendants" of Israel, making the whole issue appear to be quite a circus.

Mainstream "Christian" churches by and large despise the tenets of Anglo-Israelism, not only because of the troubling fruits in so many groups that profess them, but also because it challenges many of their own assertions about God's Law—the Ten Commandments. Many of them profess that they believe any *true Israelite* is required to "keep the law" today. But since they despise the idea of being "under the law," they will run from any proposal that remotely *hints* they might be subject to it. Their strongest argument for being *exempt* is that they are "Gentiles," and thereby automatically free from obligation (more on this point later). This strategy is simple and circumvents the messier debates about whether or not the New Covenant does away with the Ten Commandments. But if it somehow became plausible that *a whole lot of other people* turned out to be *bona fide* Israelites today, that simple argument would fall flat. Since they have no intention of ever being "under the law," they also have no intention of accepting that anyone but a very small group of "professing Jews" are actually Israelites today. So mainstream Christians have many reasons to despise Anglo-Israelism and deny it even a cursory consideration.

EARLY INFLUENCE IN CHURCH HISTORY

Herbert Armstrong was not the first to advocate belief in British Israelism, but he certainly became best known for promoting it in the twentieth century. Although there may have been underground movements for centuries suggesting the connection of modern Britons with the Israelites, it was not until the 1800s that the concept began to be popularized more openly. Then in 1902, a man named J. H. Allen wrote a definitive book entitled, *Judah's Sceptre and Joseph's Birthright*, giving more substance to the theory than ever before. It was this work that influenced many—likely including Herbert Armstrong—to examine its merits. The end result was Mr. Armstrong's most popular book, entitled, *The United States and Britain in Prophecy*, with nearly six million copies mailed out during his fifty-year ministry. It would be an understatement to say that from very early in his search to find the truth of the Bible in the 1920s, British-Israelism played a role. But why was that so, and what was his particular motivation for embracing such a provocative concept? Was he seeking to justify persecution of the Jews, racial intolerance, or rebellion against our human governments? Or perhaps was it merely an "attention getter" he felt would help make *his brand* of religion more distinctive? We shall soon see. The written evidence is enlightening.

Joseph Tkach called belief in Anglo-Israelism the central plank of the church:

206   A PECULIAR TREASURE

Why do I call this theory the central plank? It affected nearly everything we did. Its influence was both pervasive and powerful.

One of the strongest reasons Mr. Armstrong taught Sabbath-keeping so forcefully was that he regarded it as *the* sign that the United States was one of the ten lost tribes of Israel. As long as Americans worshiped on Sunday rather than on the Sabbath, they would forget their true heritage as Israelites—and would be in grave danger of divine judgment. . . .

Our whole commission was to tell people to start keeping the Sabbath; then they would recover their identity and then they would be ready for the Lord's imminent Second Coming.

Without British-Israelism, much of the reason for a passionate proclamation of the Sabbath is taken away (*Transformed by Truth*, p. 121).

When the Worldwide Church of God finally rejected this belief in the 1990s, how does he describe the result?

A few years ago when we realized this theory was unbiblical and actually served to cloud the real gospel, we stopped preaching and teaching it. Thus the central plank cracked. Yet none of us foresaw the effect this would have on our theology as a whole. To a large degree, most of us did not realize (any better than a few of our members still do) how central Anglo-Israelism was to our entire system. When this plank finally cracked, it created a snap heard 'round our theological world (*Transformed by Truth*, p. 122).

How then do we summarize Mr. Tkach's interpretation of the effect of British-Israelism upon the Worldwide Church of God? It is unbiblical, it contradicts the true Gospel message of Christ, it was the central plank in the entire body of church doctrine, and disproving it also proves that Sabbath-keeping is unnecessary. Are these conclusions sound? Let us put each of them to the test.

Is It Unbiblical?

How can we test whether the whole idea of Anglo-Israelism might be unbiblical, or not? First, are the historical events claimed in the theory really contrary to what the Bible shows? Is it true (biblical) that the nation of Israel became divided into two kingdoms after the death of Solomon? Yes (1 Kings 12:19–20). Is it true that those first called the "Jews" did not encompass the majority of Israelite descendants, but specifically those of the House of Judah only? Yes (2 Kings 16:1–6). Is it true that the particular kingdom called "the house of Israel," made up of the northern ten tribes (including the two sub-tribes of Joseph—Ephraim and Manasseh), was taken into captivity by the Assyrians, and never recorded in the Bible as having returned to the Promised Land? Yes (2 Kings 17:18, 22–24). Is it true that the particular kingdom called "the house of Judah" included only three tribes, Judah, Levi, and Benjamin, and that this house went into a separate—Babylonian—captivity more than one hundred thirty years after the northern kingdom had already been removed? Yes (Ezra 1:5). Does this text also record only the return of the Babylonian captives, not the Assyrian captives? Yes.

Those who challenge this history seek to use texts like Nehemiah 11:20 to "prove" that *all* of the tribes were represented among those who came back from Babylon: "And the residue of Israel, of the priests, and the Levites, were in all the cities of Judah, every one in his inheritance." But this does not say that this residue included families of all the original tribes. The emphasis is upon the tribe of Levi, containing the priests, and the inheritance that they reclaimed was only in *the southern kingdom* of Judah. The genealogy of the families returning from Babylonian captivity is recorded in both Ezra and Nehemiah, and not one family of any of the tribes of the northern kingdom—the House of Israel—is recorded.

Therefore, what is "biblical" is this: The majority of the nation of Israel *did indeed* lose their land and became transported slaves, never returning to their original inheritance. They lost their language and their very identity as Israelites. The only ones to retain their national identity and the Hebrew language were a remnant of the southern kingdom of Judah, a small fraction of the original nation of Israel. This is what the Bible records.

The only question remaining is, what actually happened to those *Ten Tribes* that disappeared under the curse of God for their idolatry, never to return to the Promised Land? There are three dominant possibilities: 1) They died out completely, leaving no descendants at all. 2) They did not die out completely, but their few children were so intermingled with other peoples and races that the Israelite bloodline was effectively diluted and/or extinguished. 3) The captives did indeed maintain cohesive bonds and perpetuated a bloodline that remained dominantly "Israelitish," even though they lost the knowledge of who they were.

Which of these theories, if any, might be true? Mr. Joseph Tkach says the whole theory is unbiblical. He cannot mean that the history of the *Assyrian captivity* of the *House of Israel*, separate and apart from the *Babylonian captivity* of the *House of Judah*, is unbiblical. That would be foolish. What he seems to base his assertion upon is the uncertainty about what happened *after* they became "lost." How could anyone "connect the dots" to prove that any modern-day nation(s) is descended from a captive nation that became lost by God's design thousands of years ago as a curse upon them? That is indeed a valid question. We cannot look to Bible history to tell us. God chose not to record specifically what happened to them. Yet many have attempted to do so through speculation, convoluted assembly of "facts," and emphasis upon folklore. There is no true "evidence" in any of this, and that is what Mr. Tkach seems to emphasize:

> When you start carefully reading Anglo-Israelite literature, you begin to notice how it generally depends on folklore, legends, quasi-historical genealogies, and dubious etymologies. None of these sources proves an Israelite origin for the peoples of northwestern Europe. Rarely, if ever, are

ANGLO-ISRAELISM

the disciplines of archeology, sociology, anthropology, linguistics, or historiography applied to Anglo-Israelism. Anglo-Israelism can operate only outside the sciences. And its handling of the biblical data is no better. To make many of its conclusions plausible, it must ignore large portions of Scripture which would immediately puncture it with holes the size of football fields (*Transformed by Truth*, p. 131).

He never tells us exactly what these texts are from the Bible which would make it plain that the idea of God preserving modern descendants of ten lost tribes is unbiblical. Again, his greater emphasis seems be a lack of "scientific proof" that it actually happened. But if it were God's express will to *blot out* this historical link and to intervene *to prevent* man from discovering this proof through his own scientific methods, how then would archeology, anthropology, and historiography preempt such a God? After all, we are not dealing with a human endeavor here, but the work of an invisible Creator who is carrying out a very definite plan upon this earth. And it happens to be a God who shows much disdain for the sciences of man and the products of his own academia.

For it is written, I will destroy the wisdom of the wise, and will bring to nothing the understanding of the prudent. Where is the wise? where is the scribe? where is the disputer of this world? hath not God made foolish the wisdom of this world? For after that in the wisdom of God the world by wisdom knew not God, it pleased God by the foolishness of preaching to save them that believe (1 Corinthians 1:19–21).

If the only principles we accept as truth must be confirmed through man's scientific applications, then *Christianity itself* fails that test most miserably. How do archeology, anthropology, and historiography confirm that Jesus Christ was the literal Son of God, that man has the hope of eternal life after death, and that the Bible is the uncorrupted Word of that God, preserved from antiquity?

210 A PECULIAR TREASURE

There are no "scientific proofs" for any of those beliefs. But for those who accept those principles in faith, is there anything else we can do—as Christians, not as godless scientists—to test the viability of the claim that modern Israelites are still extant today? Yes indeed.

GOD NEVER RENEGES

The best evidence to support Anglo-Israelism is not an attempt to "connect the dots" by tracing their descendent migrations through history. It is to analyze God's promises. God never lies, and God made very specific promises concerning things He would do for the descendants of Abraham. Here is a very succinct summary of key promises.

To Abraham, God made an unconditional promise after he proved his faith in willingly offering his own son, Isaac, for sacrifice:

> . . . By myself have I sworn, saith the LORD, for because thou hast done this thing, and hast not withheld thy son, thine only son: That in blessing I will bless thee, and in multiplying *I will multiply thy seed as the stars of the heaven*, and as the sand which is upon the sea shore; and *thy seed shall possess the gate of his enemies*; And in thy seed shall all the nations of the earth be blessed; because thou hast obeyed my voice (Genesis 22:16–18) [emphasis mine].

All Christians recognize the spiritual aspects of these promises, ultimately fulfilled in the Messiah—Jesus Christ—as the one "Seed," and His never-ending Kingdom to come. But Anglo-Israelism claims the promises were two-fold—both physical and spiritual—one promise of "race" (great national blessings among the nations of men) and the second, that of "grace" (Jesus Christ as Savior of all). Might that be true, or it is simply a twisting of the Scripture? Notice how greater details are given by God when He reconfirms this same covenant with Abraham's son, Isaac:

Anglo-Israelism

Sojourn in this land, and I will be with thee, and will bless thee; for unto thee, and unto thy seed, *I will give all these countries*, and I will perform the oath which I sware unto Abraham thy father; And I will make thy seed to multiply as the stars of heaven, and *will give unto thy seed all these countries*; and in thy seed shall all the nations of the earth be blessed (Genesis 26:3–4) [emphasis mine].

Perhaps this promise still refers only to Jesus Christ becoming King of all "countries" in the future? But notice how God inspired Isaac to bespeak the birthright promise upon Jacob:

Therefore God give thee of the dew of heaven, and *the fatness of the earth*, and plenty of *corn and wine*: *Let people serve thee, and nations bow down to thee*: be lord over thy brethren, and let thy mother's sons bow down to thee: cursed be every one that curseth thee, and blessed be he that blesseth thee (Genesis 27:28–29) [emphasis mine].

Well, it still may just be a restatement of the promise of Jesus Christ to come. But there is more. When God reconfirmed the covenant directly with Jacob, this is what He said:

And, behold, the LORD stood above it, and said, I am the LORD God of Abraham thy father, and the God of Isaac: the land whereon thou liest, to thee will I give it, and to thy seed; And *thy seed shall be as the dust of the earth*, and *thou shalt spread abroad to the west, and to the east, and to the north, and to the south*: and in thee and in thy seed shall all the families of the earth be blessed. And, behold, *I am with thee, and will keep thee in all places whither thou goest*, and will bring thee again into this land; for I will not leave thee, until I have done that which I have spoken to thee of (Genesis 28:13–15) [emphasis mine].

One can still attempt to say this applies only to the spiritual return of Jesus Christ, but it is getting a little harder for that to seem credible. It begins to sound like God perhaps was making a physical promise of wealth, prosperity, and world influence to a physical people. If it is only about Christ, then why do they first *go out* under Christ, and then have to *come back* into the Promised Land later? Is not Christ bringing the Promised Land—the Millennium—with Him when He *first arrives* on earth? Is Christ going to scatter Israel during the Millennium, and then gather them together again later on? That simply does not match any other prophecy. The scattering happens *before* Christ's return—as punishment for their idolatry—and then the *gathering back* into their original homeland occurs immediately with the return of Christ to become King. Here is a further promise made by God to Jacob.

> And God said unto him, Thy name is Jacob: thy name shall not be called any more Jacob, but Israel shall be thy name: and he called his name Israel. And God said unto him, I am God Almighty: be fruitful and multiply; *a nation and a company of nations shall be of thee, and kings shall come out of thy loins*; And the land which I gave Abraham and Isaac, to thee I will give it, and to thy seed after thee will I give the land (Genesis 35:10–12) [emphasis mine].

If this promise is speaking only of the *spiritual gifts* to be given by Christ after His return, then it would appear God is being partial, singling out the descendants of Jacob (now called Israel) for that reward to the exclusion of others. Yet we know that Christ is coming to offer that salvation to all mankind, not just to physical Israelites, let alone to one tribe only. Might this mean that there really is a dual aspect to God's promise—one physical, for a temporary time, and the other spiritual, related to salvation to come later?

ANGLO-ISRAELISM   213

BIRTHRIGHT VS. SCEPTRE PROMISES

We find also that God made promises and recorded additional prophecies concerning what would happen to these peoples. There were *birthright promises*, and separate promises of kingship—*sceptre promises*.

Now the sons of Reuben the firstborn of Israel, (for he was the firstborn; but, forasmuch as he defiled his father's bed, *his birthright was given unto the sons of Joseph* the son of Israel: and the genealogy is not to be reckoned after the birthright. For *Judah prevailed above his brethren*, and of him came the chief ruler; but the birthright was Joseph's (1 Chronicles 5:1–2) [emphasis mine].

And when Joseph saw that his father laid his right hand upon the head of Ephraim, it displeased him: and he held up his father's hand, to remove it from Ephraim's head unto Manasseh's head. And Joseph said unto his father, Not so, my father: for this is the firstborn; put thy right hand upon his head. And his father refused, and said, I know it, my son, I know it: *he also shall become a people, and he also shall be great*: but truly his younger brother shall be greater than he, and *his seed shall become a multitude of nations*. And he blessed them that day, saying, In thee shall Israel bless, saying, God make thee as Ephraim and as Manasseh: and he set Ephraim before Manasseh (Genesis 48:17–20) [emphasis mine.

What J. H. Allen (and later, Herbert Armstrong) pointed out is that these two distinct promises were not given to the same peoples. The birthright promises were given specifically to Joseph, the son of Jacob (Israel), who became preeminent among all his sons. Joseph was not the firstborn, but then neither had Jacob been the firstborn. Yet it was God's will to give Jacob and Joseph the rewards of the firstborn over that of their older brothers. So Joseph received *the double portion as a firstborn*, which went to his two sons, Ephraim and Manasseh (now making a total of thirteen tribes, not just twelve). Judah received the rulership—the promise of God to wield the authority of the throne. Joseph's sons would never have that kingship, but neither would Judah's sons have the birthright promises. Contained in this biblical fact of distinction is the key to the whole theory of Anglo-Israelism.

God gave specific prophecies concerning the physical descendants of Israel, all of which would apply in *the last days*: "And Jacob called unto his sons, and said, Gather yourselves together, that I may tell you that which shall befall you *in the last days*" (Genesis 49:1) [emphasis mine]. *The last days* typically refers to that time *leading up to* the arrival of Christ, not the time of His actual Kingdom.

God's prophecy for Ephraim and Manasseh *in the last days* is even more specific by far than we have yet seen, and helps confirm that what God had in mind was more than just a spiritual promise of the ultimate Kingdom under Jesus Christ:

> Joseph is a fruitful bough, even a fruitful bough by a well; whose branches run over the wall: The archers have sorely grieved him, and shot at him, and hated him: But his bow abode in strength, and the arms of his hands were made strong by the hands of the mighty God of Jacob; (from thence is the shepherd, the stone of Israel:) Even by the God of thy father, who shall help thee; and by the Almighty, who shall bless thee with blessings of heaven above, blessings of the deep that lieth under, blessings of the breasts, and of the womb: The blessings of thy father have prevailed above the blessings of my progenitors unto the utmost bound of the everlasting hills: they shall be on the head of Joseph, and on the crown of the head of him that was separate from his brethren (Genesis 49:22–26).

ANGLO-ISRAELISM   215

This promise of greatness was never given to Judah. It was Ephraim and Manasseh whose descendants carried that birthright promise into the House of Israel—the northern kingdom of Ten Tribes—separate and apart from the House of Judah. And yet, during the biblically-recorded history of those Ten Tribes—even until their ultimate disappearance into captivity—*no such greatness was ever manifested.* Did God lie?

God also made specific promises to Judah. The *sceptre promise* of rulership over Israel was assured in the hands of a descendant of Judah. Here is God's prophecy concerning Judah *in the last days*:

> Judah, thou art he whom thy brethren shall praise: thy hand shall be in the neck of thine enemies; thy father's children shall bow down before thee. Judah is a lion's whelp: from the prey, my son, thou art gone up: he stooped down, he couched as a lion, and as an old lion; who shall rouse him up? *The sceptre shall not depart from Judah, nor a lawgiver from between his feet, until Shiloh come*; and unto him shall the gathering of the people be (Genesis 49:8–10) [emphasis mine].

This confirms that this *last-day* prophecy is talking about the time *prior to* the return of Christ, because it occurs *until Shiloh* (the Millennium) *comes*! If that is true of the Judah prophecy, so it is true of the Joseph prophecy. God later confirmed this very same promise to King David:

> And when thy days be fulfilled, and thou shalt sleep with thy fathers, I will set up thy seed after thee, which shall proceed out of thy bowels, and I will establish his kingdom. He shall build an house for my name, and *I will stablish the throne of his kingdom for ever.* I will be his father, and he shall be my son. If he commit iniquity, I will chasten him with the rod of men, and with the stripes of the children of men: But *my mercy shall not depart away from him*, as I took it from

Saul, whom I put away before thee. And thine house and thy kingdom shall be established for ever before thee: *thy throne shall be established for ever.* According to all these words, and according to all this vision, so did Nathan speak unto David (2 Samuel 7:12–17) [emphasis mine].

This cannot be spiritualized away, applying only to Jesus Christ. Jesus Christ is certainly the final descendant of David who will sit upon that throne for eternity, but this promise of God begins with the physical son of David—Solomon—and applies all through time till the return of Christ. Christ has never and will never commit sin. Yet this prophecy states, "if he commit iniquity . . ." Therefore the promise of a perpetual kingship without end applies to a *human dynasty*, not just a spiritual one.

I have made a covenant with my chosen, I have sworn unto David my servant, Thy seed will I establish for ever, and build up thy throne to all generations (Psalm 89:3–4).

The rest of the theory of Anglo-Israelism seeks to demonstrate from God's prophecies that David's royal line would cease to rule over the House of Judah (which was certainly fulfilled through the Babylonian captivity), but would nonetheless be preserved and transferred to rule over the descendants of the House of Israel, wherever they would be planted by God after their migrations.

For thus saith the LORD; David shall never want a man *to sit upon the throne of the house of Israel* (Jeremiah 33:17) [emphasis mine].

Did God fulfill His promises concerning the future of the nation of Israel—His peculiar treasure? Many have read these biblical promises of great national wealth and power to be wielded by the descendants of Abraham, Isaac, and Jacob in the last days and have

ANGLO-ISRAELISM   217

become discouraged by the fact that the modern Jews today have never manifested its fulfillment.

What most have forgotten is that when analyzing the history of the Worldwide Church of God and the teachings of Herbert Armstrong, this is really the key which makes the question most relevant. If God is true and the Bible is His divinely-inspired Word, then the promises of God must always be sure. Those who reject Anglo-Israelism still have a serious dilemma. They become hard-pressed to explain how God followed through on all that He has prophesied.

What then have we learned about this proposition thus far? The basis of the theory is very credible from the Bible.

IS THE GOSPEL OF JESUS CHRIST UNDERMINED?

Does belief that there are modern-day descendants of the lost Ten Tribes of Israel playing a major role in world affairs today actually undercut or contradict the Gospel of Jesus Christ? That all depends upon what you consider to be the Gospel of Jesus Christ. If you have embraced a Protestant, Sunday-keeping, grace-without-obedience orientation to Christianity, then British-Israelism definitely gets in the way. If you believe "the gospel" is a message *about* the person of Jesus Christ—with the idea that He did it all so that we have to do *virtually nothing* to be saved—then Anglo-Israelism is certainly an annoying thorn. But if you understand that the true Gospel of Jesus Christ is *the proclamation that He Himself brought*—to reveal the good news of the coming Kingdom of God—then the role of Israel, both physical and spiritual, ceases to be an inconvenient annoyance, and instead offers a key to understanding God's Master Plan of salvation.

We have already provided a description of the key components of God's saving work with mankind. That program to offer salvation to all humanity begins with His particular work with Israel—His *peculiar treasure*. But as we have proved, singling out Israel was not an act of bias or racism on God's part. His work through Israel is the

218   A PECULIAR TREASURE

means by which *the entire world* will one day be blessed. And in reality, the physical nation of Israel has actually been the tool God has used to show us *how not* to do things. Their example consistently has been one of failure. They never truly received the great blessings God promised originally because they could never actually follow through and do what God required of them. That history of failure was written as a lesson to all of those who would be offered *true salvation* through the ministry of Jesus Christ. But that salvation process still requires becoming a spiritual Israelite!

> For in Christ Jesus neither circumcision availeth any thing, nor uncircumcision, but a new creature. And as many as walk according to this rule, peace be on them, and mercy, and upon *the Israel of God* (Galatians 6:15–16) [emphasis mine].

Paul was writing the above to a *Gentile church* in Galatia, and yet he called them "the Israel of God." Jesus Christ made plain that the *true Israelites* are not the ones who have a physical pedigree, but those who actually *respect God's Law* and act in faith to obey it, even as did Abraham:

> They answered and said unto him, Abraham is our father. Jesus saith unto them, If ye were Abraham's children, ye would do the works of Abraham. But now ye seek to kill me, a man that hath told you the truth, which I have heard of God: this did not Abraham (John 8:39–40).

The Apostle Paul confirms the very same principle. It is not about who are your physical ancestors, but *what you do* to show honor and respect to God:

> For circumcision verily profiteth, if thou keep the law: but if thou be a breaker of the law, thy circumcision is made uncircumcision. Therefore if the uncircumcision [physical

ANGLO-ISRAELISM 219

Gentiles] keep the righteousness of the law, shall not his uncircumcision be counted for circumcision [a member of Israel]? And shall not uncircumcision which is by nature, if it fulfil the law, judge thee, who by the letter and circumcision dost transgress the law? For he is not a Jew, which is one outwardly; neither is that circumcision, which is outward in the flesh: But he is a Jew, which is one inwardly; and circumcision is that of the heart, in the spirit, and not in the letter; whose praise is not of men, but of God (Romans 2:25–29).

So the true message of the Gospel of Christ is not that Israel ceases to be important, but a clarification of *who* truly represents God's favorites—His peculiar treasure. Salvation is still based upon being part of Israel, because the Church of God is *spiritual Israel*:

Ye worship ye know not what: we know what we worship: for *salvation is of the Jews.* But the hour cometh, and now is, when the true worshippers shall worship the Father in spirit and in truth: for the Father seeketh such to worship him. God is a Spirit: and they that worship him must worship him in spirit and in truth (John 4:22–24) [emphasis mine].

With that principle in mind, how then does it make sense that Anglo-Israelism undermines this spiritual Truth of Christ's Gospel message? It only does so for those groups that have warped and twisted the concept to justify partiality, selfishness, and racism. But is that what Herbert Armstrong was doing by embracing the belief?

Recall that Mr. Tkach went to great lengths to confirm that Anglo-Israelism was *the central plank* of the entire church built under Herbert Armstrong. And by attacking that single plank, he asserts that the whole ideology of the church comes crashing down with it and is proven to be without substance. But is that true?

220   A PECULIAR TREASURE

What is the real history of that concept within the Radio Church of God, and what was its true relevance?

ORIGIN OF BRISTISH-ISRAELISM IN THE CHURCH

Remember that Herbert Armstrong began his road to conversion by questioning *everything*, and firstly, the very existence of God. Step by step, he put every assumption and theory to the test in seeking to distinguish real truth from mythology. He studied evolution to see if it had any merit. He found that it did not. He proved to himself that there really is a Master Architect who created and sustains this universe, and he ultimately came to believe that the Bible is the inspired—holy—writing of that very Creator God. So how then did British-Israelism come to play any part?

As we have already noted, the entire Bible centers around God's work with and through His *peculiar treasure*—Israel. Those books are filled not only with the historical exploits of the ancient Israelites, but also many prophecies concerning their future. Other nations are chronicled in the Bible *only insofar* as they interface with or have some impact upon Israel. Herbert Armstrong recognized this fact. He was highly interested in those prophecies of the last days upon this earth before the return of Jesus Christ. He correctly identified Israel as the *continuing central character* in the play. While the majority viewed the Israelites as characters who made their exit from the stage during the second act, Mr. Armstrong understood that Israel was still very much the "leading lady" in that drama, and she would be just as prominent in the *Final Act* as she had been in the earlier scenes.

So why then did Herbert Armstrong embrace British-Israelism? It was not a desire to substantiate racism or any other arrogant claim of being "the chosen ones" by birth. All of these others who have co-opted the concept seek to prove they have some "inherent right" to God's favor by birth. They do exactly what the Jews of Christ's day did—they use a *physical pedigree* to substantiate themselves carnally. It is nothing but human arrogance. But that was not the

ANGLO-ISRAELISM

orientation of Herbert Armstrong, and that is easily proved. Here is the official statement of the Radio Church of God's doctrinal position as published in the 1948 *Fundamentals of Belief*:

> We believe the PROMISES were made to Abraham and his "seed," Christ, and that the Covenants (including the New Covenant), and the promises pertain alone to ISRAEL. That our white, English-speaking peoples of today are enjoying the national phases of the promises—that of MATERIAL blessings—called the "Birthright," which was handed down thru the sons of Joseph, Ephraim and Manasseh, whose descendants we are; but that the "Scepter"—the promise of kings, and the SPIRITUAL phase of the promises, including Christ and salvation thru Him—was given to and shall not depart from Judah of whom are the race we know today as the Jews. We believe eternal life is God's gift resting upon the promises made to Abraham and his "seed," Christ, designating this earth (made new), not heaven, as our eternal home and reward. That salvation is thru Christ alone, and not inherited thru the Birthright (right of birth) and that salvation is freely open to Gentiles, who, thru Christ, become Abraham's children and are adopted into the family of Israel and become heirs according to the promises.

This statement confirms there was no claim that physical descendants of Israel have any "inside track" to salvation. Quite the opposite, only those who become *spiritual Israelites* through conversion—and from *any and all* of the races of humanity—have real hope of salvation.

Why then does it matter whether or not modern-day descendants of Israel still carry the birthright promises of Abraham, if those physical blessings do not grant salvation? The answer has everything to do with the credibility of God and His assurances.

GOD'S CREDIBILITY AT STAKE

Recall that we have already examined God's specific promises to Abraham, Isaac, and Jacob, and those long-range prophecies in which God said that the descendants of Israel would hold great sway in world affairs *in the last days*, before the return of Christ (Genesis 35:10–12; 49:8–10, 22–26). Yet, if you believe that the only remaining descendants of Israel are those identified as the Jewish people today, you have a serious problem. This is the basis of the challenge first posed by J. H. Allen.

> Is it any wonder that skepticism is rampant, both in the church and out of it, since the common error of Christendom is to regard the Jews as the whole house of Israel? Is it any wonder that Tom Paine lost his soul while following the beaten path of this fallacy? For he did give the Bible up as a myth, and boldly states in his writings that he was led into infidelity because he saw that the Jews did not and never could verify the promises concerning Israel. . . . In 1898 B. Fay Mills, the one-time Spirit-filled evangelist, said, "In the fourth place, the prophecies of the Old Testament (to Israel) have not been realized. "Today," he says, "the Bible is no more inspired than the Koran" (*Judah's Sceptre and Joseph's Birthright*, pp. 77, 340).

It appears that Herbert Armstrong became compelled by this very pointed challenge of disheartened religious scholars, American patriots, and snide agnostics, all of whom had lost faith in God's promises:

> This promise never has been fulfilled in the Jews. It cannot be "spiritualized" away by interpreting it as being inherited only through Christ. It could not pertain to the Church, for there is but ONE true Church acknowledged in the Bible, and it is not a nation, or a group of nations, but ONE

Church of called-out individuals scattered through ALL nations. Yet this amazing promise MUST stand fulfilled, unless we are to deny the Bible and God's sacred Word!

Here is the enigma of the ages! Is this a divine promise unkept? Thomas Paine and Robert Ingersoll [a nineteenth century agnostic orator] lost faith in God and rejected the Bible because they believed these tremendous national promises were never fulfilled.

The very fate of the Bible as the revealed Word of God — the evidence of the existence of God — hangs on the answer to this momentous question. The Jewish people did not fulfill these promises. They do not refer to the Church. The world with its great church leaders does not know of any such fulfillment. Did God fail? Or has He made good this colossal promise unknown to the world? (*The United States and British Commonwealth in Prophecy*, 1967, p. 32)

Herein lies the *real reason* that Anglo-Israelism became part of the doctrine of the Radio Church of God. Herbert Armstrong did not shy away from any philosophical challenge. He wanted to know the real truth, and if this question of God's promises made to Israelite descendants could not be answered, then it would indeed make the Bible no more inspired than the Koran.

Did he find evidence of the fulfillment of those promises in our day? Mr. Armstrong found that the assertions of J. H. Allen did indeed have merit. The only manifestation in our modern world of a migratory people rising up with power, might, and prestige as *a nation and company of nations* is the United States of America and the British Commonwealth.

But what about Joseph Tkach's assertion that the whole theory depends upon "folklore, legends, quasi-historical genealogies, and dubious etymologies"? That only addresses attempts to produce *bona fide* historical "evidence" to link those ancient Lost Tribes, through murky history, to *a particular people* of this present day. It is true that such evidence is at best questionable. But again, if God is the One who specifically scattered them—intervening supernaturally *to cause them to become lost in identity*—how then is Anglo-Israelism discredited solely because man's documented history is sketchy? "I said, I would scatter them into corners, I would make the remembrance of them to cease from among men" (Deuteronomy 32:26). Therefore, if the recorded history were *not* sketchy, would that not imply that God failed to do what He claimed—that He would hide them from view?

Regardless, the issue is actually a red herring. It does not address at all the more important question; if not the USA and Great Britain, then *who else* could be the fulfillment of God's birthright promises to Joseph? You see, it is not enough just to pick apart evidence supporting a particular theory. Recall that the very basis for Herbert Armstrong's taking up the issue was *to defend the credibility of the Bible as God's inspired Word*. So, if you do not believe there is sufficient evidence to "prove" that modern Anglos are that fulfillment, you are still left to prove *how God has not lied*! The challenge of Thomas Paine, Robert Ingersoll, and B. Fay Mills is still outstanding. Joseph Tkach has never answered their challenge. Herbert Armstrong did.

It is not the intent of this piece to examine detailed elements proving that the USA and Great Britain match historically all that God said He would do in the last days to certify the birthright promises of Abraham to a modern people. That can be gleaned by reading directly from Mr. Allen's and Mr. Armstrong's books. But, suffice it to say, you will be hard-pressed to identify any other nations that even remotely fit those specific prophecies better than do the British and Americans. As a matter of fact, apart from a calculated orchestration on God's part, it is hard to see how those particular peoples could so closely have come to embody those very prophecies by coincidence. With or without the ability to "connect the dots" sufficiently through the genealogies of ancient history, what we see *before our very eyes* today is *a startling fulfillment* of all that God said He would perform. Mr. Armstrong summarized it this way:

ANGLO-ISRAELISM   225

Between them the British and American peoples had acquired more than two thirds — almost three fourths — of all the cultivated physical resources and wealth of the world! All other nations, combined, possessed barely more than a fourth! Britannia RULED THE WAVES — and the world's commerce was carried on by water! The sun never set on British possessions!

NOW THINK!

Could the British and American peoples be ignored in prophecies of world conditions that fill a third of the entire Bible — when some 90 percent of all those prophecies pertain to national and international world happenings of *our time, now*? (*The United States and British Commonwealth in Prophecy*, p. 9–10)

And that leads us directly to the next very important reason that Anglo-Israelism became so important within the Worldwide Church of God.

RELEVANCE OF THAT KNOWLEDGE

Besides showing evidence that God did indeed keep His promises to Abraham, Isaac, and Jacob, Herbert Armstrong claimed that this knowledge had even more far-reaching application. Identifying who are those modern descendants of Israel today provides the basis for applying long-range Bible prophecies concerning the last days to our present time. He called that knowledge the "master key":

This very eye-opening, astounding IDENTITY is the strongest PROOF of the inspiration and authority of the Holy Bible! It is, at the same time, the *strongest proof* of the very existence of THE LIVING GOD!

An exciting, pulsating, vital *third* of all the Bible is devoted to PROPHECY! And approximately 90 percent of all prophecy pertains to OUR TIME, now, in this latter half of the twentieth century!

It is a WARNING to us — to our English-speaking peoples — of immediate and life-and-death import!

The prophecies *come alive* once their doors are opened by this now-discovered MASTER KEY! (*The United States and British Commonwealth in Prophecy*, p. 4)

And what was the overriding message he claimed had been recorded by God for those end-time descendants of Israel? Was it a big *pat on the back*, confirming *their rights* as the favorites of God? Was it a message to justify racism—the assertion that white, English-speaking peoples have reason to look down their noses at all others? Was it a message encouraging Americans and Britons to sit back and enjoy the fruits of their inherent favor with God because they deserve it? This is precisely what most radical groups preach, that have co-opted Anglo-Israelism as a tool to moralize their hatred and personal arrogance. But that is not how Herbert Armstrong used that knowledge.

On the contrary, Mr. Armstrong's real thrust with British-Israelism was another unique doctrine taught by no other religionist. Oh yes, J. H. Allen understood the *underlying principles* of the separate houses of the Israelites and the difference between the birthright and sceptre promises. But even Mr. Joseph Tkach acknowledges that Mr. Armstrong's take was unique indeed:

Previous Anglo-Israelites emphasized God's blessings to Israel. Nobody said anything about the curses.

Herbert Armstrong noticed the curses (*Transformed by Truth*, p. 127).

Yes, indeed. Herbert Armstrong actually used British-Israelism as a vehicle to carry *a warning* to the nations—not a pat on the back. We have already seen that he never claimed physical Israelites have any inside track to spiritual salvation. Neither did he encourage smugness among those he believed were literal descendants of the lost Ten Tribes. Quite the contrary, he emphasized that because they are *apostate* Israelites—not showing proper respect at all for God—they are soon to reap the very fruits of their rebellion and hardness of heart.

But if they were promised riches and power nationally—and that is exactly what they are enjoying—why would any of them worry about the future? Is not God duty-bound to keep them "on top" in perpetuity? Hardly. And that is the greatest key of all.

Mr. Armstrong makes the point that God was "duty-bound" to bless the modern descendants of Israel—whether they were "good people" or not—because His promise to Abraham was unconditional. However, God never promised that those children would *retain* their blessings forever. No, to the contrary, He made it plain that the day would come when those rebellious children would have all of their wealth, might, and influence taken away from them. Even as God had intervened supernaturally to elevate them above all peoples upon the earth in the last days, so would He at some point bring them low, breaking their pride and humbling them before the world. This is the essence of the events prophesied to occur before the Second Coming of Jesus Christ. It is not just a generalized work to deal with all humanity as if they are in one big pot, but a *targeted work* to humble specific nations at the hands of others. And unless you know the identity of *the major players* in this drama, you will lack the keys to recognize what is transpiring on the world stage. This was the unique interpretation that Herbert Armstrong offered, and the reason that Anglo-Israelism became such an important doctrine of the church:

> The Birthright, once we received it, was stupendous, AWESOME! — unequaled among nations or empires!
>
> But *what have our peoples done* with that awesome blessing?
>
> They were still ISRAELITES, even though they themselves knew it not!

228   A PECULIAR TREASURE

They were still rebellious, "stiff-necked," stubborn!

Once the British peoples, and the Americans — the "lost" Israelites now supposing they are Gentiles — found themselves basking in the pleasant sunshine of such wealth and power, they were less willing than their ancient forefathers to yield to their GOD and HIS WAYS. They felt no NEED of Him, now! It seems few ever turn to God until they find themselves in desperate need or trouble.

But after God had withheld the Birthright 2520 years, and then, when our peoples deserved *nothing* from God, He has *suddenly* bestowed on us national blessings unparalleled in history — the unconditional PROMISE to Abraham had been KEPT! *No longer* is God obligated by His Promise to *continue* our undeserving peoples in world prestige, dominance, wealth and greatness. Once we had been *given* such unrivalled position, it was up to us whether we should keep it. . . .

After the national Birthright had been withheld 2520 years, and *then* bestowed — *after* God *gave* our peoples that national POWER, and has now, because of our national rebellion against His Laws *broken* the pride of our power — *after* He shall have punished us with unprecedented DROUGHT and epidemics of disease in its wake — then IF the British and Americans still continue in their evil ways — still refuse to repent and turn to their God, then: " . . . I will bring seven times more PLAGUES upon you according to your sins," says GOD (*The United States and British Commonwealth in Prophecy*, pp. 181, 189).

WAS BRITISH-ISRAELISM "THE CENTRAL PLANK"?

If, therefore, that teaching was so important to the church, as we have seen that it was, is Mr. Tkach correct in his assessment? We are asked to believe that British-Israelism was "the central plank" of the Worldwide Church of God, meaning the foundational principle upon

ANGLO-ISRAELISM

which all other doctrines were dependent, including the seventh-day Sabbath. But is that true?

We have just established why that doctrine is a "major key" to understanding what the Bible says *has already happened* and *will happen* in the future. But does that make it the central plank of all doctrine? Not at all. If anything, the true *central plank* of "Armstrongism" is defined by all that we have examined concerning what makes his beliefs truly *different* from all other churches. This includes his teaching about the nature of God, the nature of man, the reason for man's very existence, and the real plan being carried out for the salvation of humanity. As we previously documented, this "take" upon the Gospel of Jesus Christ was *absolutely unique* from any other religion. And that interpretation of the gospel was truly the heart and soul of the church. Anglo-Israelism is merely *a single piece of the greater puzzle* which adds dimension in explaining *how* God is bringing His great purpose to fruition. But even without that special knowledge to allow us to interpret current events in this world, the basis of our opportunities and responsibilities in God's salvation plan is still intact. If we did not understand how God has fulfilled His promise to Abraham, the faithful—those believing in the veracity of God's character—would still act in faith to confirm God's honor. But being able to see *the reality* of God's fulfillment of His promise to modern-day Israel is simply an additional blessing that allows us to answer the naysayers like Thomas Paine, Robert Ingersoll, and any others who might assert that God is either a liar, or non-existent.

DOES THE SABBATH HANG UPON BRITISH-ISRAELISM?

Is it really true that in discrediting Anglo-Israelism, the validity of the seventh-day Sabbath is simultaneously undermined? We are told that Mr. Armstrong concentrated his warning message to the USA, Britain, and the northwestern democracies of Europe because—believing that they are the literal descendants of Israel—they are obligated above all other peoples on earth to keep the Sabbath. But if they in fact are not the descendants of Israel, then they do not need to worry about the Sabbath.

The problem with this theory is that it once again presumes the validity of the Protestant—law-done-away—version of Christianity. If you believe that God only mandates the keeping of the seventh-day Sabbath for physical Israelites, then proving that none but those recognized today as Jews are actually Israelites is an excellent way to nullify Sabbath-keeping for the rest of us. But that is not what Herbert Armstrong taught. Regardless of your views about British-Israelism, the issue of the Sabbath is totally separate. The Radio Church of God professed that God made the Sabbath for *all mankind*, regardless of race, creed, or national origin. So proving that white, English-speaking peoples are not actually the progeny of Israel would hardly nullify the teaching that we should all be keeping the Sabbath. It would merely discredit the prophetic assumptions made about what the immediate future holds for those physical nations. Claiming that Anglo-Israelism was the central plank, and that discrediting it likewise destroys any basis for Sabbath-keeping, simply does not hold water. It defies simple logic. The reason that Mr. Tkach makes the claim, however, is fairly clear. If your true objective is to discredit the Sabbath, why not try to tie it to a teaching that seems more radical and hard to substantiate. By attaching the Sabbath to Anglo-Israelism as a "straw man," then destroying that straw man brings down the Sabbath along with it in one easy and convenient stroke.

As emphasized throughout, you must decide for yourself which assertions, if any, have merit. But an honest assessment of the historical facts about what Herbert Armstrong actually taught shows that it was not so flimsy as his detractors would have you believe. There is a reason that thousands responded to his message and that the church grew by leaps and bounds from the 1930s through the 1960s. And there is also a reason *The United States and British Commonwealth in Prophecy* was the most requested book in the history of that church. That work gave context to the Bible for our time and made world events come alive with relevance for the future.

If it is true that God is still dealing dramatically with those *physical* descendants of Israel, then much of what transpires in the future will center around His fulfilling very specific promises of blessings and cursings for their behaviors. But most importantly, the true Israel of God—those called to be part of the Body of Jesus Christ, His *peculiar treasure*—will at the same time receive either blessings or cursings based upon their response to, or rejection of, His divinely-revealed Truth.

PART IV

IF IT WAS GOD'S *PECULIAR TREASURE*,
WHAT WENT WRONG?

CHAPTER TWELVE
TRANSFORMATION OF CHURCH PERSONALITY

We have already provided a summary of many parts of the story, explaining "what happened." The chronology of key events is well documented. But *why* did many events take place over time to *transform* the underlying philosophy of Mr. Armstrong's work through those years? What were *the hidden forces* at play that influenced the focus and direction of that organization over time?

ORGANIZATIONAL PERSONALITY

No matter what kind of enterprise it may be, every organization has a unique personality, even as does every individual. In this regard, *personality* refers to characteristics that influence our perception of one's character. Sometimes personalities are manufactured by design. But in most cases a personality emerges spontaneously over time without any conscious, calculated agenda. An individual becomes "known" for certain traits, and his image derives from the *perceptions* that others have about him. The same is true of organizations. Whether it is planned or accidental, calculated or not, every business, fraternity, club, charity or church also acquires a distinctive personality. Many different—even contradicting—labels may be attached to an organization, based upon divergent perceptions about that group. It is all very subjective. That is why many seek to generate their own identities with aggressive programs to foster positive perceptions and to create goodwill. Much of the marketing industry exists specifically to create positive identities in the minds of the masses, to generate good feelings about a company and its products. The business of politics is all about crafting an identity that will generate confidence and popularity, leading to votes. But whether we try to or not, we all

236   A PECULIAR TREASURE

generate an identity of some kind which can be described as a personality. It is part of the "footprint" we each leave in this world.

The work of Herbert Armstrong certainly had its own personality as well, but not one that remained constant over time. Setting aside the polarizing opinions about the "footprint" left by that work—either good or bad—what were some early and later characteristics of that organization, and how did the personality of the Radio Church of God *transform* over time?

EARLY *PERSONALITY* OF THE RADIO CHURCH OF GOD

One of the earliest hallmarks of the evangelistic effort that ultimately became the Radio Church of God was *humility*. Firstly, its origin with a handful of members in rural Oregon certainly bespeaks a very humble beginning. But it was also "humble" with regard to the *leadership style* manifested by Mr. Armstrong while the church was being served single-handedly by him and his wife, Loma. Many stories from those earliest years paint a picture of a man whose personal philosophy about conducting that work was incredibly meek. Not so with the content of his messages as he stood before assemblies to preach. Those sermons were anything but meek or mild. It was his authoritative, thundering assertion about Bible truths that electrified his audiences. And yet, at the very same time, his manner when dealing with individuals one-on-one was often much more self-deprecating.

The *Autobiography of Herbert W. Armstrong* is the best single source for detail about those early years, but admittedly, trusting Mr. Armstrong's own accounts might not be considered very objective for proving his virtue of humility. Regardless, accepting those accounts at face value provides a fascinating contrast between his early leadership style vs. that which would be ascribed to the Worldwide Church of God decades later. The *transformation of organizational personality* is what we want to examine.

Recall that Mr. Armstrong emphasized often how God had dealt with his youthful vanity and arrogance by bringing him low over a

TRANSFORMATION OF CHURCH PERSONALITY   237

number of years. By the time he began to preach (if his own
testimony is at all trustworthy), he had come to recognize his own
unworthiness. There may be no better means to verify a man's *sense
of self* than to note how he reacts to criticism, especially a public
challenge. One particular anecdote will demonstrate this point about
Mr. Armstrong, although there are many such examples that could
be cited from his writings. Here is his account of a 1933 incident:

> In this neighborhood, near the school house, lived an
> elderly "Bible scholar" with quite a reputation in the
> community. His name was Belshaw. He owned the most
> extensive theological library in the district—probably the only
> one. The neighbors regarded him as something of a Bible
> authority.
>
> Mr. and Mrs. Fisher had warned me of one of his habits
> which was traditional in that neighborhood. In Eugene,
> adjoining the University of Oregon campus, is a theological
> seminary. Frequently advanced students were sent to one of
> these country school houses to hold a short series of
> meetings as part of their training. It was Mr. Belshaw's
> custom to attend one of the first two meetings, and to put the
> speaker on the spot by heckling him with a trick question.
>
> It was Mr. Belshaw's contention that these young men did
> not really have a thorough knowledge of the Bible. He was
> sure that he did. He was adept at asking questions the
> answer to which he was pretty sure the young preacher, or
> preacher-to-be, did not know. If he could tangle the speaker
> up and expose his ignorance, the neighbors would have a
> good laugh—and then fail to attend any further meetings.
>
> "If Mr. Belshaw can trap you with a trick question, no one
> will attend your meetings after that," warned Mr. Fisher, "He
> nearly always has a question these young men can't answer.
> But if you can answer him, or turn the tables on him, the
> news will spread all over the neighborhood and the
> attendance will increase."

238   A PECULIAR TREASURE

Mr. Belshaw had not put in an appearance the first night. Apparently he had decided to first see whether I had a good crowd. But the second night, he was one of the 19 present.

He interrupted my sermon.

"Mr. Armstrong," he called out, "may I ask you a question?"

"Yes Sir, Mr. Belshaw," I replied, "you may" ("The Autobiography of Herbert W. Armstrong," *The Plain Truth*, May 1960, p. 12).

The point is not to reprint the whole story of Mr. Belshaw's tricky technical question about salvation and how Mr. Armstrong replied to win the point based upon his effective use of Scripture. The point is the manner in which he chose to handle a disrespectful confrontation which he knew in advance was coming. The purpose of that evangelical work under Mr. Armstrong was not the idolization of a preacher, but the spreading of a unique take on the gospel about the Kingdom of God. Mr. Armstrong did not seem to focus on himself, but on the message he wanted to share. He could have barred the man from attending "his meeting," or he could have refused the question as being impolite or disrespectful. All of that was true. And many other men—concerned most about their personal dignity—would have bristled with indignation at the effrontery of such behavior.

But the *personality* Mr. Armstrong manifested during those early years was one of humble confidence, with a focus upon the spiritual work, willing to cooperate with others who shared that goal and not making himself the object of vain adulation. This same meek approach is reflected in many of his accounts about confrontations with those who sought to undermine him in some way, including the story of his giving up a very small salary to another minister to create peace for the overall good of the brethren (*The Autobiography of Herbert W. Armstrong, The Plain Truth*, June 1960). And that style of leadership became the earliest *personality* of the Radio Church of God as well. After all, with Herbert Armstrong as the single driving force at that time, it only makes sense that the early church would be a close reflection of his own sense of values and style. His personal managerial style became synonymous with the personality of the church. But the truth is, it simply did not remain that way over time.

THE LATTER PERSONALITY

Fast-forward forty years to see the transformed *personality* of the Worldwide Church of God in the mid-1970s. It was anything but humble. By that time, the church had hundreds of ministers and administrative staff on several continents, three college campuses, worldwide recognition from prolific media exposure, and a Pastor General spending much of his time overseas in high-profile meetings with world leaders and dignitaries. Quite a contrast to that insignificant, humble, one-man ministry of the 1930s. Along with the money, influence, and public visibility came a definite change in the *character* of that physical church body. That difference was reflected in the way the church was perceived by members and non-members alike, and also by the way the organization functioned internally.

In all fairness, it would be impossible for any organization that had grown so aggressively over a relatively short period of time to have remained the same. It is ridiculous to expect that a multimillion-dollar international enterprise with over 100,000 members and millions of media subscribers would resemble in any way the original shoestring assembly of farm families led by a poor preacher and his wife in the 1930s. The common denominator they still shared is that Herbert Armstrong was at the helm—the CEO, if you will—throughout all of those decades of growth. But the transition from a mom-and-pop operation to an international corporate enterprise made it impossible for things to remain the same. Sometimes a very astute small business owner might find a way to preserve his company's original personality, even after that business has grown substantially. But most often, monumental growth begets a total rewriting of organizational character.

240 A PECULIAR TREASURE

The *fundamental mission* of Herbert Armstrong never changed through all of those years. No matter how much the characteristics of that physical church changed over time, he was resolutely committed to what he called "The Great Commission," taking the *real truth* of the Bible to the world. His writings show a consistent and dogged determination to resist any attempt to modify that focus or to retool the basic drive of his work. But success can be a two-edged sword. As his work was increasingly successful in reaching and influencing more and more people around the world to respond to that message and to join the church, the challenges of managing such a gargantuan enterprise and keeping it focused upon his own values and principles became ever more difficult.

Culture vs. Personality

If *personality* defines the face that an organization presents to its customers and to outsiders, *culture* defines the environment that exists internally. By the 1970s, the culture of the Worldwide Church of God as a corporate entity included the full range of human "problems" found in any large, hierarchical organization. In any collective endeavor there will be many personal agendas which threaten to detract from the true organizational mission. But while well-managed groups find ways to *neutralize* this inevitable tendency and to create a *positive culture* that fosters unity and common purpose, the Worldwide Church of God instead developed a *toxic climate* of factionalism which ultimately tore it apart from the inside out. A snapshot of that organization in the mid-1970s shows a leadership team at war with itself, including several high-profile players under Mr. Armstrong vying for dominance. Everything the church previously held dear had been called into question by that time, from its most fundamental doctrinal theology to its philosophy about church governance and leadership.

Did these internal political maneuverings bleed over and affect the "customers" of the church—its members and co-workers? Absolutely. Members in smaller, more outlying areas may have been better insulated against these influences for a time. But when major rifts in ideology saw dozens of ministers defect in 1974, followed by the ultimate expulsion of Garner Ted Armstrong in 1978, no member was left unaffected.

The Tail Wags the Dog

What is true from documented history is that Herbert Armstrong lost control of the physical organization he had started with his wife in 1933. He acknowledged that fact himself to the whole church in the wake of the internal turmoil of the 1970s. Here are just a couple of excerpts to verify it from Mr. Armstrong's own point of view:

> This brought controversy into the Church. These self-professed "scholars," influenced by teaching in universities in which they were enrolling for higher degrees, were becoming more and more liberal. They wanted to skirt as close as possible to the precipice of secularism, falling off the cliff into Satan's world.
>
> These were the years when my commission required that I be absent from Pasadena, and traveling overseas to almost all parts of the world as many as 300 of the 365 days of the year. This liberal group, small at first, came to be in executive positions at Pasadena, surrounding and influencing the one responsible for day-to-day administration at headquarters during my absence. Much of what they did was carefully kept from me.
>
> Those of higher rank, but subject to the one in day-to-day executive administration at Pasadena, who were steadfastly loyal to the Church and its true teachings, were suppressed or gradually removed from Pasadena and sent "into the field," pastoring single churches in other locations. So much of what was going on in Pasadena was kept from me that I did not realize the direction the Church was actually traveling into controversy, liberalism and either Protestantism or total

secularism (*The Worldwide News—Special Edition*, June 24, 1985; *Recent History of the Philadelphia Era of the Worldwide Church of God*).

Brethren, we've got to FACE IT! God's Church -- and Ambassador College -- had been shockingly derailed -- SECULARIZED! The whole WORK had become the work of MAN! My son Garner Ted had taken to himself authority never given to him. He took advantage of the fact I was in other parts of the world, carrying Christ's Gospel Message into other countries, to assume authority to CHANGE DOCTRINES, and to CHANGE POLICIES. I had denied him BOTH! Much of it was done SECRETLY! Top-ranking ministers were warned of being fired if they told me what was going on.

Many of the basic BIBLE TRUTHS God had revealed to me as the very FOUNDATIONAL BELIEF OF THIS CHURCH were BEING CHANGED! It was no longer GOD'S College or GOD'S Church! It was becoming precisely what my son is now trying to build -- "GARNER TED ARMSTRONG'S CHURCH"! He was surrounded by a small group of secular self-professed "intellectuals" (*Co-Worker Letter*, July 24, 1979).

Mr. Armstrong speaks of the problems as having begun in the early 1970s, with the surge in liberal influence among *scholarly* leaders. Yet, what has never been well-documented are the *many earlier events* that actually *fostered* the environment which would ultimately *produce* these later results. It is always easier to see something in hindsight. Criticism is not intended here, but simply an objective examination of critical events that opened the door for what Mr. Armstrong admitted later was *the loss of control* over his own work. In the business world, it would never suffice for a CEO to blame his underlings for the fact that his company *ran off the rails*.

The real culprit might be one or more executives in the chain of command, but the individual at the top is still accountable for oversight.

Likewise, there are a number of actions (or lack of actions) over many years that paved the way for that church organization to "get out of hand." An obvious weakness was the love of a father for a son, and the desire for that son to be a prominent leader of the church, in spite of the fact that the son did not truly share his father's values and beliefs. But deeper than that, there were other more subtle elements at play from decades before the 1970s that coalesced to produce the results.

DELEGATION HAS INHERENT RISK

Over time, as that work grew, Mr. Armstrong's sole focus could not remain upon preaching and writing. That seems to be where Mr. Armstrong truly excelled. But the fruit of his successful labors meant that hundreds—and ultimately thousands—of new members began pouring in, and that meant a formal structure had to be created to serve that growing church body. The need for organizational management expertise therefore increased in importance. No longer could he and Mrs. Armstrong single-handedly do everything, like printing *The Plain Truth* magazine by hand on a mimeograph machine while also conducting the spiritual work to preach and to support member families.

And once Mr. Armstrong began to enlist the help of others to manage critical responsibilities—especially after graduates from the new Ambassador College began to be deployed as "minister helpers" in the early 1950s—he faced the very same problems as do all small-scale proprietors when their businesses grow beyond their personal abilities to manage single-handedly. Once you are forced to begin delegating key responsibilities to others, there is less personal control to assure that the work is done exactly the way you would do it yourself. Some individuals are both good entrepreneurs *and* good large-scale managers, but that is not often the case. Many very successful small-scale businesses have failed once they grew too large for the original proprietor to manage on his own, because he simply did not have the ability to translate his small-scale success into a large-scale operating environment.

Every individual has his own ideas about what to do and how to do it. Without very careful oversight and explicit programs from the top to keep an organization precisely focused upon its founder's philosophy and values, it is inevitable that the underlings will eventually exert personalized influence that will affect the culture of the enterprise. If those key helpers truly share the founder's values, looser oversight might still work out fine. But if not, conflict and disappointing results are inevitable. An old management axiom is, "You get what you *inspect*, not what you *expect*." Merely *assuming* that your management team understands and *supports* your vision and is pulling in the same direction—rather than *ensuring* it through close oversight—invites unexpected surprises.

Examples of Progressive Organizational Drift

What are some examples of very early changes that took place within the Radio Church of God as that organization grew over time? The more significant and profound changes that occurred in later years were preceded by more subtle, philosophical detours along the way.

One of the early issues that set Herbert Armstrong in opposition to many of the leaders of the Church of God, Seventh Day in the 1930s was a dispute over how much of a role the doctrine against eating pork should play as a condition for baptizing new members. The other local leaders considered abstinence from pork-eating to be a key indicator of one's spiritual commitment to the truth. They asked the question as a test, and failing to give the correct answer meant no baptism. Mr. Armstrong did not agree. When he was challenged by these ministers about baptizing before confirming the acceptance of "not eating pork," this is how he replied:

TRANSFORMATION OF CHURCH PERSONALITY   245

In Matthew 28:19–20, God's order is, 1) Go and preach the Gospel (compare with Mark's version, same words of Jesus, Mark 16:15), 2) baptizing those who REPENT and BELIEVE; then, after that, 3) teach them to observe the COMMANDMENTS. Since people cannot fully comprehend the truth of the Commandments and the teaching of the Bible until AFTER they receive the Holy Spirit, and since there is no promise God will give the Holy Spirit until after baptism, therefore I baptized them after repentance and faith, just as the Bible instructs—and *then*, after laying on hands with prayer for their receiving of the Holy Spirit (Acts 8:12, 14–17; Acts 19:5–6; I Tim. 4:14; II Tim. 1:6, etc.), I taught them God's Commandments, and not to eat unclean meats, etc. Every convert I had ever baptized had obeyed all these truths as soon as I taught them. They were submissive, teachable, yielded to God, hungry for His truth. The KNOWLEDGE of the Lord is something to teach *converted* people whose minds are opened by God's Spirit. We must continually GROW in this knowledge ("The Autobiography of Herbert W. Armstrong," *The Plain Truth*, June 1960, p. 13).

So during the early years of the Radio Church of God, Mr. Armstrong did not use the litmus test of pork avoidance—or other particular doctrines of the church—as a reason to refuse baptism. He looked for other indications that the individual was truly called by God and serious-minded about accepting that call.

Yet, fast-forward thirty years, and by the early 1960s, similar *litmus test items* were absolutely being demanded by ministers under Mr. Armstrong before they would baptize new members. Besides eating unclean meats, abstinence from smoking tobacco became a prominent test question. By the late 1960s, it had become increasingly difficult for any new contact to be "approved" to even attend church services, let alone become baptized. Can you imagine Mr. Armstrong treating those early farm families in Eugene, Oregon, that way? After the church became large and prestigious, people virtually had to beg and plead to finally receive an "invitation" to attend Sabbath service. And if one was still smoking, he was often rejected outright until he quit the habit. Never mind that Mr. Armstrong's *fundamental premise* included that one called of God requires the active power of the Holy Spirit to really overcome and make spiritual progress. Over those ensuing decades, many weaknesses which Mr. Armstrong believed would be overcome by the sincere initiate *after baptism*, were now required to be achieved *before* ever being considered for baptism.

This change does not appear to have occurred because Mr. Armstrong made an *executive decision* to repudiate his former philosophy and to begin accepting the old Church of God, Seventh Day ideology. If that were so, then he would have needed to admit that he was foolish and wrong-minded ever to have made the stand that he did back in the 1930s. It is not apparent that he ever made such an about-face or believed that his original approach was wrong. Then why was his own church imposing similar "conditions" upon new members thirty years later, if he had come to believe strongly that it was an unwise and faulty policy? This is very likely an example of *organizational drift*—a slow change in philosophy that occurs obliquely over time from the cumulative influence of other key individuals in an enterprise.

Whereas the original *personality* of the Radio Church of God was of a humble, inviting group, in which those with the potential of valuing the Truth of God were encouraged to participate in spite of their current weaknesses, the personality of the later Worldwide Church of God presented the image of *an exclusive club* whose entrance required *jumping through many hoops* to prove one's "worthiness." Again, the point is not to debate which orientation is superior, but to emphasize the fact that a significant and far-reaching *change* occurred away from Mr. Armstrong's original philosophy, in spite of the fact that he was the undisputed leader during all of those years.

Another example of this inadvertent change in philosophy due to the subtle and progressive influence of underlings is the role of the

TRANSFORMATION OF CHURCH PERSONALITY   247

ministry in relation to the laity. There is much more we will cover on
the details of evolving church government, but for now, simply
compare the original belief Mr. Armstrong expressed in the early
years with that which was promoted by his subordinates years later.
Another of his stories from the 1930s is revealing:

> The quotation "God helps them that help themselves" is
> not found in the Bible, as many believe, but it is a saying of
> Benjamin Franklin. Yet it does express a Scriptural principle.
> Long ago I learned that I cannot carry others into the
> Kingdom of God on my shoulders, or drag them in. I can
> only point the way, proclaim the truth, give counsel and
> advice, aid in many material ways, and pray for others. I can
> give aid and help—but each must stand on his own feet
> before God, and by strong motivation yield to allow God to
> transform him and mould him into God's own holy character.
> God does it by the power of His Holy Spirit. But we also have
> our part in denying ourselves, in overcoming, and in DOING!
> It is the DOERS, not those who hear only, who shall be
> justified through Christ's blood and enter finally into His
> Kingdom (Rom. 2:13). ("The Autobiography of Herbert W.
> Armstrong, "*The Plain Truth*, September 1960, p. 8)

Here he expressed an important philosophy concerning the
limits of ministerial authority due to *the impossibility* of any third
party being able to generate character development in someone else.
Yet by the early 1960s, that concept seems to have been forgotten.
Notice the contrasting ideology being taught to the church:

> Does the Church also have power to intervene in your
> private life, in your home, if you are going contrary to the
> general practice and teaching of this Church? . . .
> God has given us a responsibility for your sake to
> intervene on special occasions in your personal life—in

matters of adultery, drunkenness, utter lazyness, etc. It isn't a question of our wills, it is for your sakes.

The great requirement is that you learn to submit to the government of God. After you have recognized that this *is* God's Church, that we are fulfilling that commission which God has commanded, you are to submit to God's government in the Church ("How Far Does Church Government Extend Into Your Life?" by Herman L. Hoeh, *The Good News*, January 1961, p. 12).

This "intervention" was not just limited to blatantly bad behavior that might affect the whole church. Local ministers slowly began to *insert themselves*, unsolicited, into individual and family matters, justifying this intrusion in order to "get the church ready" for the return of Christ and to "make the church clean." They were going to investigate and find out where *hidden sin* might lie and "help" members to overcome and grow spiritually.

Notice that, ironically, the Herman Hoeh article was written to the church only three months after Mr. Armstrong published the chapter of his autobiography detailing the need to exercise *wise ministerial restraint.* How is it that he himself is still espousing one philosophy while his underlings are promulgating an ideology that opens the door for contradiction? Contradiction is exactly what occurred in subsequent years as the ministry became more and more aggressive in asserting not only the rights of ministers to intercede in the personal affairs of members, but a zealotry to do so. Where was the hand of the Pastor General to reinforce his earlier *acquired wisdom* and to teach the growing corps of new minister helpers how to think about their duties? It is another example of *the tail wagging the dog.*

Lest someone feel incensed that Mr. Armstrong's management ability is being impugned unfairly, recall that we have already seen evidence from his own hand that control of that church had already been wrested from him by the early 1970s. The question is not *whether he failed* to maintain a strong executive hand on the corporate church, but *when and why did he lose control?*

An interesting aspect of the history of the Radio Church of God is how and why much of Herbert Armstrong's *original personality and philosophy* failed to become instilled in that larger body over time as it became more expansive. To that end, we will examine other events that transpired in the early Ambassador College days, as well as a biographical sketch of some of the early ministers who left their indelible mark upon that work.

Recognizing the philosophical tug-of-war that took place at the top—that prevented Mr. Armstrong's original personality and organizational principles from being instilled in that larger body—is integral to understanding many later events that occurred within the Radio Church of God.

But it was not solely these dynamics at the leadership level that generated organizational chaos in the 1970s. There were also significant pressures from "the bottom up" that became a real catalyst for radical change within that church. No one else has seemed to notice these forces, let alone analyze them thoughtfully. In the next chapter, we will do precisely that.

CHAPTER THIRTEEN
MOTIVES FOR MEMBERSHIP

Most of those who spend time dissecting the history of the Worldwide Church of God focus almost exclusively upon Mr. Armstrong himself, or upon other influential leaders within that organization. But what about the members who made up that expansive body? From the earliest years, did the laity itself have attributes that influenced some of the critical outcomes manifested much later? When we analyze the history of *the membership* in that church during the twentieth century, we identify additional pieces to the puzzle which help augment our understanding of the multidimensional forces producing the final outcomes.

Who were these people who responded to that original work, and what were their motivations for joining such an unusual and nonconformist religious movement? Although many interesting characteristics could be highlighted, let us focus upon five major categories that seem to encompass the majority of members by attribute. Many of these could apply to other churches as well, but they certainly apply to that particular body we are analyzing.

THE FEARFUL

From the beginning, a major aspect of Mr. Armstrong's *World Tomorrow* radio broadcasts and articles in *The Plain Truth* magazine was a focus upon biblical prophecies highlighting terrifying events to occur on this earth before the return of Jesus Christ to usher in His Millennial reign of peace. Here is just one example—an excerpt from page 14 of the 1956 edition of his book entitled, *1975 in Prophecy*:

Yes, WAKE UP! America and Britain! You have grown calloused and indifferent to world revolution, world wars and cold wars and the threat of hydrogen-bomb war.

You Americans and British! You smug, proud, stiff-necked complacent people! You enjoy a prosperity God never lavished on any other people—you heedlessly permit yourselves to become soft and decadent, setting your foolish hearts on a lush, push-button, prosperity of leisure. You ignore that entire prophetic THIRD of GOD'S WORD, warning you of impending disaster and offering you divine protection from it!

Will any one of you who now read this warning awaken to the *stern reality*?

GOD ALMIGHTY now reveals, in time to prevent it, that *one third* of all our people *will soon die* of starvation and disease—that our day of reckoning is upon us!—that we are to be stripped of our wealth and prosperity on which we set our hearts—that a *second third* of our people—of *your personal* friends, relatives, acquaintances—will be killed by the awesome hydrogen-bomb invasion—that our proud United States and British Commonwealth are now destined to be suddenly *crushed in defeat!*—that the remaining third left alive are to be carried as captives, scattered over the land of our enemies and their allies AS ABJECT SLAVES!—and that even millions of *them* shall then be tortured inhumanly in organized *religious* persecution, until their breath expires in martyrdom!

Jesus Christ said, "Ye shall be HATED of ALL NATIONS ... Then shall they deliver you up to be afflicted, and shall KILL YOU."

Do you foolishly and carelessly assume He meant somebody else? Our booklet "U.S. and Britain in PROPHECY" *proves* He meant US. We are *the* nations that are HATED by all other nations today—or hadn't you realized that alarming *fact*?

Jesus Christ meant US—and His words are as certain and sure as the rising and setting of the sun!

Luke's inspired account of Jesus' words makes it even more specific: "For these be the days of vengeance, that all things which are written may be fulfilled" -- that is, when the prophetic things of your Bible come to their CLIMAX, and all prophecies are suddenly and rapidly fulfilled at this END-TIME! "And they"—speaking of *our nations*, "shall fall by the edge of the sword, and shall be led away captive into all nations." (Luke 21:22, 24). This prophecy refers only *typically* to the Jewish captivity of 70 A.D. It refers primarily to *OUR* future.

Jeremiah was inspired by the Almighty to picture this invasion, defeat and captivity and to explain WHY it's coming!

The anticipated timing of these prophetic fulfillments was not realized, but the Bible is specific nonetheless that such cataclysmic events will indeed occur on this earth before Christ's return. Mr. Armstrong's focus upon these facts from a biblical perspective certainly got the attention of many of his listeners. And many of the people who responded and later became members of the Radio Church of God were ones who took these warnings very seriously.

When God saved Paul and Silas miraculously from incarceration in Thyatira by loosening their shackles and opening the doors of the prison (Acts 16:25–27), the Roman jailor would have killed himself at that moment had Paul not restrained him. The man was terrified by the experience.

Then he called for a light, and sprang in, and came trembling, and fell down before Paul and Silas, And brought them out, and said, Sirs, what must I do to be saved? And they said, Believe on the Lord Jesus Christ, and thou shalt be saved, and thy house (Acts 16:29–31).

In a similar way, many whom God called in our time were shaken by world events and fear of what the future might hold for them. They, too, responded by imploring, "What must we do to be saved?" Mr. Armstrong confirmed what was required to become pleasing to God and to receive His favor, including protection from those terrifying events to come. The answer was to begin keeping God's commandments!

If ye love me, keep my commandments. And I will pray the Father, and he shall give you another Comforter, that he may abide with you for ever; Even the Spirit of truth; whom the world cannot receive, because it seeth him not, neither knoweth him: but ye know him; for he dwelleth with you, and shall be in you (John 14:15–17).

Because thou hast kept the word of my patience, I also will keep thee from the hour of temptation, which shall come upon all the world, to try them that dwell upon the earth (Revelation 3:10).

So, out of fear, many began to keep the weekly Sabbath day, the annual Holy Days, and all of the other commandments which were demonstrated to be part of the spiritual Law of God. They may never have really come *to appreciate* those laws, but they became willing to embrace them if that is what it took to secure their place under God's protective wing (Deuteronomy 32:10–12). This is the first major category of members who responded to the Radio Church of God.

The Followers

The famous French novelist and playwright, Alexandre Dumas, gave us this axiom: "Nothing succeeds like success." Many successful enterprises seem to generate special—invisible—momentum over time by attracting followers from the sidelines who become swept up in the movement. Everyone loves a winner and to be associated with the excitement of a curious new enterprise. As unorthodox as the work of Herbert Armstrong was within the religious world, once enough pioneer members had responded to provide a viable base, and once that organization had grown sufficiently through the 1950s, the Radio Church of God began to achieve more of an "acceptance," if for no other reason than it was undeniably successful and growing with huge momentum. The average annual growth in membership continued at the absurd rate of *thirty percent per year* all the way until 1968. Amazing!

During the 1960s and beyond, the constituency of "average" new members changed. No longer did one have to be willing to become a complete and total laughing stock in the world, as did many of those earlier responders who joined in the 1930s or 40s. By the 1960s, the media exposure from radio and magazine distribution—not to mention those huge conventions (Feast of Tabernacles) held each fall all over North America, with thousands of members descending upon communities and spending so much money—lent a more respectable (and accepted) image for the church. The positive reputation of Ambassador College did as well. After all, they thought, even though they hold weird beliefs, if they are that big and still growing—and with that much money—they must have something going for them. New members were now able to join without nearly the degree of stigma which had been associated with membership in earlier decades.

As well, there are always those who naturally seem to gravitate to "new" religious movements, and now there was another option to consider among the other major denominations.

God's church has always existed in a mixed multitude. When Israel received miraculous favor from God, who gave them freedom from Egyptian slavery and made of them a new nation, more than just the true descendants of Abraham formed the huge army of the Exodus. "And a mixed multitude went up also with them; and flocks, and herds, even very much cattle" (Exodus 12:38). Yes, Israel attracted attention from many others who recognized their success and their undeniable momentum, and so sought to share in the blessings. If all had continued to go well for them, and if that initial momentum had been sustained without challenge or interruption, it is possible that these "fair-weather followers" might have continued happily and productively within the congregation. But since that was not God's will to allow, it was only a matter of time before many who had ridden the early waves of success would become disenchanted once Israel fell on hard times. "And the mixed multitude that was among them fell a lusting: and the children of Israel also wept again, and said, Who shall give us flesh to eat?" (Numbers 11:4).

These fair-weather *followers* constituted a second and growing category of church member during the history of the Radio Church of God.

THE INFLUENCED

Another major category of member, which became more significant in later years, included those who grew up as children within the church, or else those who joined primarily because someone they loved was a devoted member.

The more time that passed since the beginning of Mr. Armstrong's work, the more children there were who were raised to maturity being taught those doctrines of the church. While the earliest decades were dominated by members who had chosen that way of life for themselves as adults, the demographics changed over time as more and more attendees included second and third generation participants. Many of those children did not choose to continue in their "parents' religion" once they matured, but then again, many others *did* choose to stay with the church to one degree or another. Yet, among those who stayed for a time, how many of them were truly convicted in that way of life vs. just continuing what was familiar to them from their childhood? This category of member included those who did not necessarily make *major* changes in their lives to begin keeping God's commandments. They just kept doing what they had been taught to do by someone else.

Additionally, it would be nice to think that in every case in which a husband and wife (for example) both became baptized members, each of them was truly acting according to very strong personal faith before God. But that is often not the case. It has nothing to do with a lack of honesty, necessarily. A husband may truly believe at the time that he is responding according to his own personal convictions. But even though he may not recognize it in himself, he may actually be responding more so to create peace in his home and to please his wife who has become a devoted member. If one does not already have strong religious convictions of his own, why not adopt those that will make his family life more harmonious? Has this really been an historic factor in choice of church membership? Of course it has! Even if it is not evident at a given moment, many have looked back later and admitted that they were not really convicted personally in the doctrines of the church as much as they were trying to accommodate a converted loved one.

Whether it involves husbands and wives, children, siblings, or even close friends, this collective category became another significant demographic of membership within the church begun under Mr. Herbert Armstrong.

THE OPPORTUNISTS

Akin to *the followers* in some ways, there are others who may join a church for yet *different* reasons. Unlike *the followers*, who may just get caught up in an emotional response and become swept along by the swift-moving current of a popular movement, *the opportunist* calculates his membership for very definite reasons. This is the individual who sees a particular advantage in being a member which has nothing to do with agreement with the group's doctrine, and in essence feigns belief to gain acceptance. This does not mean the opportunist necessarily has any evil intents. It simply means his fellowship with the group really is not rooted in a true concern for what that group stands for doctrinally.

The motives for such affiliation can be as diverse as there are human minds to dream them. An individual may simply seek inclusion in a social network which church membership provides, regardless of which group it is or what it teaches. If he likes the people and builds some strong friendships, that may be enough to make him want to stay. Or, he may crave something else that a church assembly provides, like an audience for the display of his personal talents, like singing or playing an instrument, group activity organization, sports participation, cooking, charity outreach, etc. Perhaps church affiliation is the best opportunity he has to develop and to exercise those kinds of interests. In each of these examples, we are not talking about an insidious agenda to undermine or to harm the church in any way. It simply addresses the reality that some people join and remain in a church fellowship for reasons that have nothing to do with strong agreement with doctrine. And the larger and more prominent a particular church becomes over time, the more attractive it will likewise become to many who may have these kinds of *innocent*, howbeit *ulterior*, motives.

The opportunist can also include those who have quite nefarious intentions which are detrimental to the body. This no doubt affects all secular groups and churches of this world as well to some extent, but it is especially a consideration for the true Church of God, wherever that Body may exist. Why? Wherever that Church resides, it is always the primary target of Satan the Devil (Luke 22:31; 1 Peter 5:8). There is no group he desires to destroy more than the one that Christ has built, and so the probability of having some of these negative influences is always greater than it would be in the world.

> Another parable put he forth unto them, saying, The kingdom of heaven is likened unto a man which sowed good seed in his field: But while men slept, his enemy came and sowed tares among the wheat, and went his way. . . . The field is the world; the good seed are the children of the kingdom; but the tares are the children of the wicked one; The enemy that sowed them is the devil (Matthew 13:24–25, 38–39).

Were there individuals from all four of these categories—the *fearful*, the *followers*, those *influenced by others*, and the *opportunists*—who attached themselves to the Radio Church of God over those years in which it grew so phenomenally? Yes indeed.

THE TRUE BELIEVERS

The fifth and *most significant* category of member in that church included those who came to value the actual doctrines of the Radio Church of God and who counted them as a gift from God rather than as a burdensome obligation. It does not mean that they may not have come in originally for a different reason. They initially may have been among the fearful, the followers, the influenced, or even the opportunists. But the difference is, that over time—as they learned more of God's Truth and began to practice it in their lives—they became compelled by the legitimacy of those principles and *proved* the intrinsic value of those doctrines by living them. This is exactly what Christ admonishes His called children to do. "Prove [by real application] all things; hold fast that which is good" (1 Thessalonians 5:21). Once you have proven *through exercise* that a commanded principle actually leads to blessings rather than cursings—meaning you confirm that it "is good"—who can later convince you it is not so? What is proven is proven. How did such a transition to real belief come for many?

There were many aspects of church doctrine that Mr. Armstrong never chose to emphasize on *The World Tomorrow* radio program in the early years. An example of that is the annual Holy Days. He most definitely put a spotlight upon the seventh-day Sabbath, but he never really taught about the *annual* Sabbaths on the air (the same is true in his autobiography). That was one part of the doctrine that new contacts would learn after they requested more information from the church. The radio broadcast messages focused upon more basic topics which would really get people's attention and draw them to the program—Sunday vs. the Sabbath, Christmas as pagan, the resurrection not on Sunday, man not an immortal soul, man not promised heaven, the Ten Commandments not done away, the modern descendants of Israel, prophecy of last-day tribulation, etc. What then does this imply?

Regardless of which issue may have initially attracted a listener to Mr. Armstrong's message, if he continued to pursue the deeper layers of that way of life, he eventually faced the requirement of significant changes which were never anticipated at the outset. Example (my own father's true story):

A man hears Herbert Armstrong on the radio for the first time in 1958. The program that day is confirming the identity of modern Israel, which this man already happens to understand. The man is attracted because this preacher acknowledges a truth that other preachers will not, which seems to give Mr. Armstrong some unique credibility. So he listens to more programs to see what else this unusual man might say. He hears Mr. Armstrong claim that Christmas is pagan, and then challenges his audience to prove it from the encyclopedia. The listener did not expect that. But guess what? He looks it up and discovers he was right! Christmas really was never Christian at all. That is something new to him. Then he learns there is no basis for worship on Sunday. What? Really? And because he was challenged by Mr. Armstrong to prove it for himself, he does so. He learns further that the true Gospel of Jesus Christ is not a message *about* Christ, but *the very message* Christ Himself taught—the Good News of the coming Kingdom of God. With one issue after another, this man becomes convicted of truths he did not know before but which are very clear from the Bible. This knowledge will now require major changes in his personal practices as he begins to worship God correctly.

This man does not know about the Holy Days yet. In fact, even when two ministers come through his local area on a baptizing tour in late 1959 (there was no local minister or congregation in his area yet), they baptize him without requiring him to have that knowledge. He only finds out about the annual Holy Days a few weeks later from church letters. He thinks, what? Keep these other strange "Jewish" days? What have I gotten myself into? But he studies that too, and attends the Feast, and embraces those doctrines as well. After all, it

MOTIVES FOR MEMBERSHIP

261

is all part of the "total package" which Mr. Armstrong has been preaching with such authority. So many of those doctrines are ones that *no other church* is teaching in that way, and yet they are *right there* in the Bible! It all fits together. Even if some teachings have less "black and white" support in Scripture by comparison to many others, they are still not contradictory at all, and in fact complement everything else which *can be proven* very easily.

Over the years, he gains a real respect for all of those teachings he first thought were so "strange." He originally was introduced to them one at a time. There were many changes that had to take place in his thinking, but looking back, he can say that he really *proved* the value of those doctrines by actually *living them*, and seeing the *bona fide* blessing of God come as a result of that obedience.

> . . . prove me now herewith, saith the LORD of hosts, if I will not open you the windows of heaven, and pour you out a blessing, that there shall not be room enough to receive it (Malachi 3:10).

My father's story is only one among thousands from those who became *true believers* at one time or another. Maybe the first thing that "hooked" one of these individuals was a fear about coming national tribulation. Maybe she already had a family member in the church which caused her to "give it a try" also. Maybe he was just curious about this new denomination which seemed unusual and exciting at the time. Maybe she saw an opportunity to help herself in some personal way by joining. Regardless of the initial motivation, those *who stayed* because they discovered there was *real substance* within the body of belief that Mr. Armstrong was preaching became *convicted in mind and heart*.

Whether or not they were each simply brainwashed by a clever cult leader—that is not the point at hand. We are cataloging the different *major categories* of those individuals who became members of the Radio Church of God. The *true believers*—regardless of what path they each trod to arrive there—became the foundation of that peculiar but dynamically-growing religious movement.

So, interestingly, the fearful, the followers, the influenced, and even the opportunists, all had the chance to become *true believers*. But what about the ones who never did so?

The Unconvinced

What about the ones who joined for whatever reason, but who never really came to love the doctrine for its own sake—the ones who merely *tolerated* those teachings as a way of preserving their rights of membership in the physical organization?

What percentage of the entire membership ultimately divided between the *true believers* and *the unconvinced*? No one really knows for sure. And how did this *mixed multitude* behave once serious trials began to affect that church as a whole in later years? Most of what we know is derived by observing the personal choices members made when those difficulties emerged. Choices under pressure are always most telling.

What should be easily discerned by common sense is that any member of the Radio Church of God who did not really value *the doctrine* was primed to give it up if the circumstances were right. Those who were only "putting up with" those *hard and inconvenient* dos and don'ts were the first to celebrate when the ministry began to change them in order to be less restrictive.

Which say to the seers, See not; and to the prophets, Prophesy not unto us right things, speak unto us smooth things, prophesy deceits (Isaiah 30:10).

For of this sort are they which creep into houses, and lead captive silly women laden with sins, led away with divers lusts (2 Timothy 3:6).

MOTIVES FOR MEMBERSHIP

This statement by Paul is not meant to be condescending to women, but it addresses a natural vulnerability in an impressionable young woman who might be "led on" by a clever and persuasive young rake. She is vulnerable because she wants to be convinced it is OK to do what she wants to do anyway. When a persuasive suitor comes along, she becomes putty in his hands. This is the analogy God chose to use to describe the mental orientation of *many* of His called children—both male and female—who were seduced later on by ministers who told them what they wanted to hear. Because they had never become *truly convicted* that the laws of God were good and profitable for them, they were itching for an excuse to renounce them without feeling they were "disobeying."

The actions of the ministry—those leading that body—set into motion that prophesied departure from Truth. But such changes could never have been effected if a significant portion of the membership was not already primed and eager for "relief." There is no doubt, however, that God holds ministers accountable for the destruction and scattering of the flock.

> Woe be unto the pastors that destroy and scatter the sheep of my pasture! saith the LORD. Therefore thus saith the LORD God of Israel against the pastors that feed my people; Ye have scattered my flock, and driven them away, and have not visited them: behold, I will visit upon you the evil of your doings, saith the LORD (Jeremiah 23:1–2).

This, however, does not exonerate *the members* of that body from their own accountability before God.

> If thou sayest, Behold, we knew it not; doth not he that pondereth the heart consider it? and he that keepeth thy soul, doth not he know it? and shall not he render to every man according to his works? (Proverbs 24:12).

The catalysts that ultimately produced major upheaval within the Worldwide Church of God included dynamics that derived from both minister and laymember alike. It was the culmination of significant attitudes within *both groups* that sparked the perfect storm of events which generated the results witnessed over the last forty years. There is no way to understand *the full story* of that church during the twentieth century unless the orientation of the laity is considered along with that of the ministry. The transitional make-up of that body and the reasons for member participation had everything to do with what happened in the end.

With deep-seated discontent brewing among ministers and laymembers alike, this emerging powder keg needed merely the right match to set off an explosion. What would such a match turn out to be? In the next chapter we will find out that answer.

CHAPTER FOURTEEN
THE PROPHECY DEBACLE

If it is possible that Herbert Armstrong was indeed used by God to reveal biblical truths concerning the real meaning of salvation for mankind, how then do we explain the failures that occurred with his prophetic speculations?

As already shown, the "hook" of connecting biblical prophecies to current events was a huge factor in attracting people to the Radio Church of God. Many were strongly affected by prognostications that we were living "in the last days," and that many of the Bible's long-range prophecies would be fulfilled "in our time." But the failure of apocalyptic events to climax as expected in the 1970s led to the "1972 Syndrome," as many members became discouraged and restless, clamoring for changes. Many simply gave up their belief altogether and walked away. If then God was truly involved, how do we account for these realities? How is it possible that Herbert Armstrong was not *a false prophet*?

HERBERT ARMSTRONG NOT A PROPHET

For all of Mr. Armstrong's focus upon and expounding of Bible prophecies, he never actually claimed to be a "prophet." Is that surprising? And what exactly would that mean anyhow? Let him define it himself:

> Thousands know that I, personally, have been called and chosen for a very definite commission in God's service. But I have definitely NOT been called to be a PROPHET — except as that word, Biblically used, does sometimes refer to a minister or speaker — one who proclaims the Gospel of Jesus Christ.

Emphatically I am NOT a prophet, in the sense of one to whom God speaks specially and directly, revealing personally a future event to happen or new truth, or new and special instruction direct from God — separate from, and apart from what is contained in the Bible. And I never have claimed to be.

There is no such human prophet living today! ("Personal from the Editor," *Tomorrow's World*, February 1972, p. 1)

This statement had to be written to the whole church in 1972 because, in spite of never having claimed to be one given *divine insight* into future details, the church had indeed come to attribute such powers to Mr. Armstrong. If it seems that this is merely a legalistic parsing of words, that is exactly how many in the church may well have viewed it also. Regardless, the reality was that expectations of church members had been elevated to anticipate the return of Jesus Christ by the mid-1970s. When it became clear in 1972 that this would not happen, a lot of backpedaling had to be done. But unlike other churches that have leaders claiming to have received *divine insight* through *dreams or visions* to declare the who, what, where, and when of events that will take place in the future, Herbert Armstrong never did that. His statement to the church was accurate. But he also acknowledged why he was being forced to make such a clarification in early 1972:

It has never been our intention to SET DATES! Time after time, I have said — Garner Ted Armstrong has said — our literature has stated — "WE DO NOT SET DATES!"

Yet, in our human zeal and enthusiasm for getting this greatest mission on earth done, we have a few times come close to it or appeared to — and that we deeply regret ("Personal from the Editor," *Tomorrow's World*, February 1972, p. 30).

THE PROPHECY DEBACLE   267

Here is an example of one such *zealous speculation* concerning future events:

> While I EMPHASIZE, we cannot set dates, yet I am prepared to say now, for the first time, the second coming of Christ COULD happen during this coming decade, which we enter later this very week. Don't under any circumstances take that as setting a date -- but we are now far closer to the END OF THIS WORLD -- and the beginning of the happy and peaceful WORLD TOMORROW than people realize! TIME IS SHORT! (*Co-Worker Letter*, December 29, 1969)

This is not the kind of wording that would be used by a cult leader claiming to have received *inspiration from on high* about specific dates for future events. It admits to being a speculation. But that does not change the fact that such wording caused members to get their hopes up nonetheless. It is no different than a daddy promising to "try" to take his child to the zoo on the morrow. It is not an absolute commitment, but the child's disappointment is no less severe if that outing fails to materialize.

It is also true that Mr. Armstrong's underlings were often *less constrained* in their prognostic assertions than was he. Evangelist Roderick Meredith is a good example. Notice some of his quotes from the 1950s and 60s:

> After 1965, we are destined to run into increasing trouble with the Gentile nations. America and Britain will begin to suffer from *trade embargoes* imposed by the brown and oriental races. . . .
>
> We will begin to experience the pangs of *starvation* and the *scarcity* of goods! (*The Plain Truth*, August 1957, p. 6)

> You might as well wake up and FACE FACTS! The world you live in won't be here 15 years from now! (*The Plain Truth*, December 1963, p. 7)

268 A PECULIAR TREASURE

Frankly, literally *dozens* of prophesied events indicate that this final *revival* of the Roman Empire in Europe—and its bestial PERSECUTION of multitudes of Bible-believing Christians—will take place within *the next seven to ten years of* YOUR LIFE! (*The Plain Truth*, February 1965, p. 48.)

Many—not just a few—of Mr. Armstrong's helpers made such unreserved statements over the years, in writings and in sermons, and 1972 is when those ill-advised chickens came home to roost.

Interestingly, Mr. Armstrong previously had already identified these *expectations* as a problem within the church. He was not happy with the prospect of people being members for the wrong reason:

Reports indicate that many have "come in" to God's Church in this manner: They have come to really SEE and KNOW that this is, truly, GOD'S Church. They know there is terrible WORLD TROUBLE just ahead. They have heard how God's Church is to be taken to a PLACE OF SAFETY. . . . So these people come in, selfishly, for a sort of spiritual and physical SECURITY -- to assure PROTECTION when the Great Tribulation bursts upon the world! But they are NOT themselves "on fire for GOD!" They are spiritual DRONES! And God will not give them protection! (*Co-Worker Letter*, March 2, 1967, pp. 6–7)

If Herbert Armstrong did not claim to possess special divine insight into times, places, and dates for future fulfillment, it confirms that in that sense he was not claiming to be a prophet. And if he was not a prophet, the fact that he disappointed the church with failed personal speculations likewise would not constitute being *a false prophet*. But again, that is not how it felt to many of his disappointed followers.

THE PROPHECY DEBACLE   269

THE ORIGINAL PURPOSE OF PROPHECY EMPHASIS

What was the real purpose—the intent—of Mr. Armstrong in seeking to be specific about Bible prophecy in light of current world events? Why was he doing it? Was it to make people think he was a prophet like Isaiah or Jeremiah? If not, then why did he focus so much upon those long-range prophecies in the Scriptures? The answer is found in his own writings, for those who desire to understand.

1. He sought to confirm that the promises of God from antiquity have indeed come true. He leveraged evidence of *past fulfillments* of God's *prophetic promises* to substantiate the very validity of the Bible. Key in this was proving that God indeed fulfilled His promises to the physical descendants of Abraham:

> This promise never has been fulfilled in the Jews. It cannot be "spiritualized" away by interpreting it as being inherited only through Christ. It could not pertain to the Church, for there is but ONE true Church acknowledged in the Bible, and it is not a nation, or a group of nations, but ONE Church of called-out individuals scattered through ALL nations. Yet this amazing promise MUST stand fulfilled, unless we are to deny the Bible and God's sacred Word!
>
> Here is the enigma of the ages! Is this a divine promise unkept? Thomas Paine and Robert Ingersoll [a nineteenth-century agnostic orator] lost faith in God and rejected the Bible because they believed these tremendous national promises were never fulfilled.
>
> The very fate of the Bible as the revealed Word of God — the evidence of the existence of God — hangs on the answer to this momentous question. The Jewish people did not fulfill these promises. They do not refer to the Church. The world with its great church leaders does not know of any such fulfillment. Did God fail? Or has He made good this colossal

270 A PECULIAR TREASURE

promise unknown to the world? (*The United States and British Commonwealth in Prophecy*, 1967, p. 32)

2. He sought to prove that the Bible, though ancient, is a living book, speaking of events transpiring *in our very time*, not just about things that are past:

> Prophecy is the proof of *divine revelation*! If One, in the Bible, speaking and claiming to be God, can make prophecies and tell what is going to happen in the future to nations, to cities, to empires, then if it actually happens *in every case*, and without a miss, you'll know *that* was a real God speaking.
>
> But, if it were some person writing this, some *human mortal* writing in ignorance, groping in superstition, making great boasts, and claiming that he could foretell what was going to happen to proud cities, to nations, to great empires, and then it never happens, you know that *that* man was merely writing make-believe *out of his own imagination*.
>
> Yes, prophecy is the proof of God, the *proof* of the divine revelation of the Bible. Prophecy is a taunting challenge that the skeptic *dares not accept*! (*The Proof of the Bible*; HWA, 1958, p. 4)

So this confirms the second significant reason that Bible prophecy was a major part of his emphasis. It offered hope that there really are solutions for man's troubles, no matter how ominous are the events transpiring on the world stage. It was a key aspect of preaching the Gospel of the Kingdom of God.

3. He sought to convince people that time was short, that a sense of urgency was imperative, and that they needed to act immediately to prepare their own lives for the end.

Conclusion: Mussolini is the head of the Beast of Revelation 17, raising up the modern Roman empire. Last admonition:

"Stop and think! WHY should Hitler, Mussolini, Stalin, the rulers of Japan, wish to plunge the world into war? WHY? You cannot answer. They do not know. They are YIELDING to impulses and suggestions. God help us to pray! We need His protection" (*The Plain Truth*, February 1938, "How Demons Are Plunging the World Into War," p. 3).

This was an assertion that man has an invisible enemy who is seeking to destroy. Hitler and Mussolini were not final pieces of the puzzle, but it certainly holds true that they were motivated by *the very same enemy* who has been influencing many world events since the Garden of Eden. The manifestation of these same wicked devices on the world scene in 1938 was just as relevant to people of that day as similar manifestations might be to us today. The rise of dictators in the 1930s was not a proof that the *end of the age* was imminent (even if that is what was anticipated), but the admonition for God's people to take these forces seriously and *to become spiritually converted in heart and mind* was not a vain exercise.

4. To teach that Christ told us *to watch*. Mr. Armstrong taught that we must care about current events in light of Bible prophecy because God said so, and also to avoid becoming deceived.

Jesus Christ *thunders* to those of us living in the *end time*, "Watch ye therefore, and pray always, that ye may be accounted worthy to escape all these things that shall come to pass, and to stand before the Son of man" (Luke 21:36). (*Tomorrow's World*, September 1971, "Are You Watching?" p. 40)

5. To offer the means to "save our skins" from terrible tribulation to come upon the earth.

2520 years from the year of the fall of Babylon ends in 1982. Seven years before that encompass 3 ½ years of tribulation, plus the final trumpet period before Christ takes over. Admonition: Get urgent so you can be spared from tribulation! (*The Plain Truth*, June 1953, by Herman Hoeh, "What Are the Times of the Gentiles?")

So based upon these very specific reasons given for emphasizing long-range biblical prophecy, we have documentation for *why and how* it *originally* became so important within the church. It was never about trying to prove that Herbert Armstrong had some special gift as a soothsayer, but a tool to help God's people establish and preserve a foundation of personal faith in the midst of difficult times.

MILK DOCTRINES VS. STRONG MEAT

In hindsight, how much should this *Bible prophecy emphasis* have captivated the more experienced, committed members of the Radio Church of God? Sadly, the original purposes for studying prophecy (listed above) seem to have been forgotten quickly by minister and laymember alike. Think about it. Once someone responded to Mr. Armstrong's radio broadcast, had "proved" that the things he was preaching were absolutely supported in the Bible, and also had proved by those prophecies that the Bible was truly relevant for people today, should that *novice-level understanding* have continued to be the dominant focus? Put another way, if much of the *stated purpose* of studying prophecy is to confirm that *the Bible is true, that God fulfills His promises*, and that *we live in the end times*, once those truths were *proven* by them, should they have continued to be such a fixation?

Recall that in Mr. Armstrong's own early quest to prove the Bible (when he was still an infant in his own understanding), he studied evolution vs. Creationism, concluding eventually that evolution is a sham. Was that study an end in itself, or merely *a stepping stone* to

THE PROPHECY DEBACLE

more important truths? What if he had stopped there, focusing forevermore upon the technicalities of Creation science vs. evolutionary theory, hashing and rehashing that very basic aspect? But he did not do that. Proving that God is real and that the Bible is true is only *a baseline* for going on to uncover *the more important aspects* of who and what God really is, what man really is, and what is the true purpose of all of this existence. Once he proved the basics, he went on to build upon that foundation. It is even as the Apostle Paul explained:

> For when for the time ye ought to be teachers, ye have need that one teach you again which be the first principles of the oracles of God; and are become such as have need of milk, and not of strong meat. For every one that useth milk is unskilful in the word of righteousness: for he is a babe. But strong meat belongeth to them that are of full age, even those who by reason of use have their senses exercised to discern both good and evil (Hebrews 5:12–14).

Proving that God is real and that the Bible is true are examples of "milk doctrines." It is merely the *basic foundation* needed before going on to learn what God really requires of us for salvation.

What does that have to do with studying prophecy? Most of the *stated reasons* for pointing *World Tomorrow* radio listeners to long-range prophecy was to help them come to have confidence that God is real, that the Bible is true, and that the Scripture is meaningful for people today. It is the very most basic, rudimentary, foundational instruction! It is all part of the "milk doctrines."

PROPHECY BECOMES A DRUG

Yet, ministers and members of the church became captivated by those long-range Bible prophecies well beyond just proving belief in God and the Bible. Why? They became convinced that long-range prophecies which *were not yet fulfilled* could be "figured out" in

274   A PECULIAR TREASURE

advance, like a puzzle to be deciphered. Recall that this was one of those *legitimized reasons* previously listed (Point #5 above) for studying prophecy—to allow them to be in the right place at the right time when bad things happened, presuming that they could "save their skins" by having advanced knowledge of what was coming.

Many ministers spent their time trying to come up with clever theories that would link Bible prophecies to modern-day nations and individuals on the world scene, not to bolster their own faith in God, but in the hope of becoming known in the church as a "discoverer of new truth." The favorite sermons for many members became those speculating upon the who, what, when, and where of the future, rather than those sermons explaining how to become a better Christian. The word *prophecy* itself became synonymous with *speculation* on *who* in the news today might do *what* in the future. Many members who had been encouraged by Mr. Armstrong to study the Bible in order to grow closer to God, instead used their "study time" as "puzzle solving time." Rather than to use the Bible as a two-edged sword of introspection—to help show where personal faults lay (Hebrews 4:12) and thereafter doing the hard work to break bad habits—it was much more attractive to *study prophecy*. After all, it was private time used to read the Bible, right? So God must be pleased.

UNDERSTANDABLE BUT DANGEROUS

It is very understandable that people discovering value in God's Master Plan for salvation would become fascinated by what He says in the Bible is coming next. Jesus Christ's disciples were excited and intrigued by His prophecies, and His words made them eager to gain even greater enlightenment.

And as he sat upon the mount of Olives, the disciples came unto him privately, saying, Tell us, when shall these things be? and what shall be the sign of thy coming, and of the end of the world? (Matthew 24:3)

THE PROPHECY DEBACLE

275

The prophet Daniel likewise had a keen desire to understand more specifics about those final days which God had shown to him in part. "And I heard, but I understood not: then said I, O my Lord, what shall be the end of these things?" (Daniel 12:8)

Curiosity about last-day prophetic fulfillment is common to all peoples whom God has called. And is it any wonder? After all, once one is called to understand the glorious plan by which God is bringing salvation to the world, once one becomes convinced that Jesus Christ is returning to become King over this earth, and once one comes to love and cherish the hope of that Kingdom, how could one not take an interest in the details of how God will bring these awesome events to pass? It is very natural that God's children should long to know more about when and how these monumental events will unfold, especially those who believe they are living in the very era of their eventual fulfillment.

But herein lies the problem. We easily become obsessed with finding out details of future events, not just out of innocent curiosity, but as part of a plan to protect ourselves from the terrible persecutions that are certain to accompany these culminating days. If we truly believe that there will be tribulation upon this earth on a scale never before experienced by humankind (Matthew 24:21), which of us would not have an interest in knowing enough of the specifics so that we can maneuver ourselves out of harm's way? Can any of us honestly say that possessing such knowledge would not be very appealing? If Daniel and the Twelve Apostles had a keen desire to know these things, who among us can honestly claim to be indifferent to those same tantalizing details?

Why is it a problem to have a strong desire to know the specifics of future prophetic fulfillment? It is because such desires easily lead to obsession and work counter to the *faith* God requires each one of us to manifest. God said plainly, "the just shall live by faith" (Habakkuk 2:4; Romans 1:17; Galatians 3:11; Hebrews 10:38). Faith is the evidence of things *not seen* (Hebrews 11:1). It means that we believe and act upon the promises of God, even when those promises are not yet manifested for us to see. It means that we are willing to trust God implicitly for our protection, not demanding to be "tipped-off" in advance in order to have confidence.

Yet nearly a third of the Bible is prophecy, and the Bible was recorded for the Church. Does that not imply God wants His people to spend a lot of time reading and examining prophecy? That was exactly the rationale of many in the WCG who became obsessed with analyzing long-range prophecies for the purpose of ferreting out new tidbits of enlightenment. But such justification totally misses the point of *why* God put those long-range prophecies in the Bible to begin with. Most assume automatically they were recorded as a puzzle for us to "figure out." This is justified by pointing out that God said these secrets would be made known at the time of the end: "And he said, Go thy way, Daniel: for the words are closed up and sealed till the time of the end" (Daniel 12:9). Well, many reason, this is now the time of the end, so that means God is now making it possible for the true church to solve the great mysteries that the patriarchs never understood, including who, what, where, when, and how all these final events will take place. All we have to do is keep digging and theorizing enough, and we will eventually put all the pieces together. And that is exactly what many of the ministers under Mr. Armstrong believed was true.

The True Purpose of Long-range Prophecy

But is that really true? The true purpose for those long-range prophecies in the Bible is not what most have ever considered, and in part, because of those mistakes made in the WCG, a much better understanding has since emerged for us, if we will learn from that past.

Here is the secret: God did not intend even for the last-day Church—*His peculiar treasure*—to figure out the specific details of events to come. As already shown, God said the just shall live by faith, not by having the answers to the tests in advance. Why then were those prophecies recorded? First, they were given so that we would have a *general idea* of the events that would occur before the

THE PROPHECY DEBACLE

277

return of Christ. This is why Christ gave a synoptic blueprint in Matthew 24. The events leading to the return of Christ are said to be so intense, so alarming, so provocative, and so overwhelming, that without some forewarning, many of God's people would give up and believe it impossible for this whole story to have any happy ending. Notice how Christ reveals His true intent and purpose by the admonitions He makes to the hearers:

> And Jesus answered and said unto them, Take heed that no man deceive you (Matthew 24:4).

> And ye shall hear of wars and rumours of wars: *see that ye be not troubled*: for all these things must come to pass, but the end is not yet (v. 6) [emphasis mine].

> But he that shall endure unto the end, the same shall be saved (v. 13).

The backdrop for *all of His statements* about last-day events is the admonition not to allow *anything we might experience* to shake our confidence. Why did He give the details that He did about the terrifying events to come? To comfort the elect and to prepare them in mind for the fact that horrendous things necessarily will befall them, so that *when they actually transpire*, they will be steeled to endure and not to faint! It was the same reason Christ told His disciples ahead of time that one of them would betray Him. Why did He speak that prophecy at that particular moment? Was He putting a puzzle before them to challenge them to figure out the traitor's identity in advance, so that the one who guessed that it was Judas could be recognized as being something special? Of course not! Christ clarified His purpose very distinctly:

> I speak not of you all: I know whom I have chosen: but that the scripture may be fulfilled, He that eateth bread with me hath lifted up his heel against me. Now I tell you before it

come, *that, when it is come to pass, ye may believe that I am he* (John 13:18–19) [emphasis mine].

Why was this prophecy recorded in advance? So that His followers would not lose faith in Jesus as being the Christ once they found out He had picked a traitor to be one of His disciples! If someone claimed to be the Son of God but then picked a confidant who manifested defective character, would that not make a normal person question His judgment? If He is truly the Son of God, why did He not know the real heart of Judas? Jesus headed off that potential doubt by telling them *in advance* that the betrayal would take place, so that *when it occurred*, they would still believe and not doubt Him.

Notice the timing. When were those disciples going to understand the full prophecy about Judas? When did it matter for them to understand? *After* it was fulfilled! Yes, Jesus did tell John privately that the traitor would be the one to whom He gave the sop (John 13:25–26), but this was not so that John could publish it to the others in advance. The final betrayal was happening even as He was speaking. The real value of Jesus' prophecy concerning Judas was for the church in the time of the aftermath. John was selected by God to record this event in his gospel account. It was not just a game of hide and seek. It all had purpose.

Which brings us to the second major purpose for long-range prophecies: They were recorded by God in advance, so that after they come to pass, *God*—and not any man—will receive the credit for having known the end from the beginning. Why were all of those Old Testament prophecies recorded concerning the Messiah who would be slaughtered as a sacrificial Lamb? Was it a puzzle given to allow the Jews to figure out how to spot the true Christ in advance? Of course not. No one in Israel ever figured out beforehand from Scripture that the Messiah would first come to die, and only later come as a conquering King. They had the Scriptures in their possession for all those centuries—and knew them backwards and forwards—and yet *not one of them* ever put the pieces together. The

THE PROPHECY DEBACLE

concept of a *First* and then only later a *Second* Coming was anathema to them, in spite of the fact it had been clearly recorded by Moses, Isaiah, and many other prophets of old for thousands of years. And no one in those days leading to His first arrival was allowed to put those pieces together and proclaim it to the world. No, God intentionally kept that nugget of truth hidden. For how long? Until Jesus Himself revealed the meaning to His disciples *after it was already in the process of being fulfilled!*

> From that time forth began Jesus to shew unto his disciples, how that he must go unto Jerusalem, and suffer many things of the elders and chief priests and scribes, and be killed, and be raised again the third day (Matthew 16:21).

Even then, Peter and the other disciples still did not understand, because it was never in their thinking that the Messiah would need to be killed (v. 22). Only after His actual death and resurrection did all these things really sink in. And then, afterwards—only afterwards—did all those prophecies of old make sense. Given that God allowed *no man* to "figure out" the truth about the Messiah's death before it came to pass, who received the glory when it actually transpired—after Jesus had fulfilled dozens of long-range prophecies? Not a single man, but God only. Long-range prophecies were recorded in the Bible and brought down through time so that *when they come to pass* just as God said they would, mankind will know that a purposeful God has truly been orchestrating *a divine Master Plan* through all the ages.

Such a testament gives all honor and glory to God, and never allows any man to share the stage with Him. What would happen if God allowed someone to ferret out one of these secret meanings in detail in advance? Once it came to pass, that man would be jumping up and down saying, "See, I told you that is how it was going to happen! I knew it all along. That proves I was something special in God's church!" But this God of the Bible is a jealous God, and He does not intend to share His glory with any man. No, when all of these last-day prophecies actually come to pass and match precisely what was foretold, God is going to make sure that *He alone* receives the awesome recognition for that fulfillment. That is why no one else will be allowed to have the details in advance. They were not recorded for that purpose. By reading those prophecies, God's church today—wherever it is—can be comforted by understanding the *general blueprint* by which God is working; and when they literally see those things begin to occur, rather than becoming fearful—having their faith destroyed—they can instead be fortified, knowing that it is all happening according to a Master Designer's plan.

The leadership of the Radio Church of God did not understand this principle of *the real purpose* of long-range prophecy. Because of that, serious mistakes were made in allowing church members to hope that Mr. Armstrong and others would tell them, "when shall these things be? and what shall be the sign of [His] coming, and of the end of the world?" Well-meaning but ill-advised speculations destroyed the confidence of many, and it was a key reason for the eventual fracturing and later implosion of that organized body.

But is that fact proof that Herbert Armstrong was a "false prophet"? Or is it possible that God was indeed working through and inspiring him concerning matters of real substance? Was there a difference?

Recall from chapter two that wherever you find God's *peculiar treasure*, it will be a body that first receives *divinely-revealed doctrine*, but then departs from it *en masse*. That has always been so! The only real question is, what factors would cause *God's true church* to lose faith and to abandon its foundation of Truth? God said it would happen. What would be the cause?

Doctrine Is Not Prophecy!

Another key that Worldwide Church of God members did not possess was understanding the difference between *doctrine* and *prophecy*. Most still today do not understand that distinction! Yet it provides many of the answers we are seeking.

Doctrine includes the definition of right vs. wrong, an understanding of facts concerning the physical and the spiritual realms, and a general understanding of God's plan in dealing with humanity. Doctrine includes everything His called people need in order to know what pleases Him and what displeases Him, how to worship Him properly, and what to eschew in order to avoid His displeasure. It also includes an understanding of who and what God is, who and what man is, and the general blueprint for understanding the Master Plan that God is using from beginning to end. All of this comprises a succinct definition of *doctrine*.

Separate and apart from this is *prophecy*. Members of the Worldwide Church of God were never told there was a difference. To them, dabbling in prophecy was part of "the doctrine" of the church. So when many speculations failed, they counted it as evidence of "false doctrine." But that is not true!

Prophecy is about God recording advanced details of events to come, and for particular reason. We have already discussed the purpose of *long-range* prophecy. It was recorded by God so that His people will not be shaken when they experience severe tribulation, and also to attest *in advance* that God is carrying out a very purposeful plan *exactly as He has predetermined.* When events transpire that *exactly match* what God prophesied in advance, it is proof that a Master Architect is at work.

Short-range prophecy is something we have not yet addressed. What is the difference? *Short-range prophecies* are given to substantiate both God *and the prophet representing Him.* Such prophecies are understood quickly, due to the limited time period that they involve. Examples include Moses testifying in advance to Pharaoh what God was about to do (Exodus 12–13), Macaiah testifying to Ahab what God was about to do (1 Kings 22:14–38), and Jeremiah facing off against Hananiah to prove which one of them was authorized to speak in God's name (Jeremiah 28:5–17). In these cases, God used *prophecy* to prove that a servant had been given a special commission by God to achieve a particular purpose. That purpose is always *to communicate a vital message to a target audience*, not to elevate the prophet for his own vanity.

Regardless, whether we are talking about *short-range* or *long-range* prophecy, we are talking about God communicating/recording special messages for particular purposes at particular times. But this is all *totally separate* from doctrine—the revealed knowledge of right vs. wrong for *all of humanity* that applies *at all times*, in every age.

Why is this distinction important? The proof that we are seeking in identifying God's *peculiar treasure* will be found in examining *the doctrine*, even as outlined in chapter one. That is our true yardstick. And as documented in chapter two, wherever that true church is found, it will be a physical body prophesied to go astray in time. What would cause it to do exactly what God said would occur? If the true church (physically) always holds fast to God's Truth, makes good decisions administratively, and avoids all errors in judgment (like in dealing with prophetic speculation), then there would be no causation for disappointment and resultant apostasy. Yet that apostasy was prophesied by God, so there likewise has to be a cause in the form of *mistakes made*!

Why is it not possible that the *unwise handling of prophecy* could have been one of those causative factors that God foresaw? If that is perhaps true, then it would help to preserve the possibility that Herbert Armstrong's work was indeed inspired by God, doctrinally, in spite of the errors prophetically and administratively.

Is that just grasping at straws? Is it an attempt to justify the legitimacy of Mr. Armstrong's work at any cost? As always, you must be the judge. But for those of you who continue to find value in the unique *doctrinal teachings* of Herbert Armstrong—explanations from the Bible that make more sense than those of any other religion out there—then just maybe this clarification about prophecy (its history within the Worldwide Church of God and its proper role in the greater scheme of things) will be of benefit.

CHAPTER FIFTEEN
1968 IN PROPHECY

In Part II, we covered the importance of Mrs. Loma Armstrong *in particular* in the overall work and ministry of her husband. Very few today recognize how critical *he always claimed that she had been* in the success of his ministry.

With that fact now well established, is it true that the church got stronger, not weaker, after Mrs. Armstrong died in April 1967? Was there really no dangerous vacuum that ensued? As Mr. Armstrong *expected* to occur, did her death become a "wake-up call" to the whole church, marking a *positive turning point* for ministers and laity to finish God's work with renewed *unity of purpose*? Or did it become something else instead?

The summary of the events of the 1960s and early 1970s cited key events that began to transpire in the late 1960s. But it is worth asking if perhaps the death of Loma Armstrong was *a catalyst* for some of those key events that followed. Here is a restating of those events with that particular question in mind.

1975 ... OR 1968?

One of the booklets written by Herbert Armstrong—first published as an article in 1956 and creating a real stir concerning expected catastrophic future events—was entitled *1975 in Prophecy.* It highlighted Bible prophecies of great tribulation to befall human beings before the return of Jesus Christ, and it speculated upon the possibility that many of those events might coalesce by the mid-1970s. Because of such writings, the eyes of most church members became focused like laser beams upon the 1970s, waiting to see what God would do.

But what if the very most critical events affecting that church had already transpired before the 1970s even began, occurring with little fanfare or recognition? What if the stage had already been set (unknowingly) for prophesied tribulation *within that church*, and what if the very seeds of that institution's own destruction had already been planted? What if the truly most decisive turning point occurred in 1968, not in 1975?

What were these key events, and what did they have to do with the death of Loma Armstrong in early 1967?

A CORPORATE NAME CHANGE

Perhaps this is merely a superficial consideration with little real significance, but changing the name of the Radio Church of God to the Worldwide Church of God in 1968 *did* have relevance, even if only a symbolic one. Large corporations make changes to their names for reason. In most cases, if they are not trying to communicate something important through this action, they would not bother to do it. It is expensive and tedious for any large organization to change its legal name. In many cases, a name change signals a desire to change *the public image* of the enterprise.

One of the first *observable changes* that took place after Loma Armstrong's death was a change in the name of the church. Oddly, in this case, unlike the kind of fanfare that typically accompanies such organizational rebranding, renaming the Radio Church of God to the *Worldwide Church of God* was introduced to its members with very little hype. Is that because this change was not being made with current members (customers) in mind, but perhaps in order to affect the impression among outsiders?

As noted previously, a document entitled, *1968 Certificate of Amendment of Articles of Incorporation of Radio Church of God*, confirms that the name change was approved in a meeting on January 5, 1968, and signed by Mr. Armstrong and corporate Secretary, Mr. Albert J. Portune. Anecdotal accounts assert that Mr. Armstrong felt that the church had outgrown the original name. It was no longer just a "radio church." The church needed a name that reflected the fact that it had now "grown up" into a *worldwide* operation.

After that change, did the church still hold its same philosophy and mission, or did this *seemingly symbolic change* actually portend more significant organizational shifts to come?

A WHOLE NEW COMMISSION

Recall that 1967/1968 was the time period when Herbert Armstrong was thrust accidentally into personal contact with several world leaders for the first time.

The first was a meeting with King Hussein of Jordan in the summer of 1967, soon after Mrs. Armstrong's death (*Co-Worker Letter*, July 31, 1967). The second was a meeting with King Leopold III of Belgium in February 1968, which would bloom into a long-standing personal friendship. The third event occurred in September of 1968, with Mr. Armstrong's meeting with five high-ranking Israeli government and university officials in the Knesset (*Co-Worker Letter*, May 28, 1971).

How did he interpret these unexpected opportunities? Did he view them merely as tangential occurrences in the course of executing his long-standing strategy for spreading the gospel? No, these new interactions with renowned men caused Mr. Armstrong to conclude that God was now opening "a new door" for his Work *through* visits with world rulers.

GIANT doors have been opening before me, one after another, with invitations for personal conferences with heads of state -- presidents, kings, prime ministers -- and many others in high offices of POWER, in many countries around the world. The remarkable thing is that I did not seek or initiate these meetings -- not once! I was invited. . . .

Even though the time has come, in this great Commission, when it is necessary for me to have these personal meetings, there is absolutely NO WAY I could have taken it into my own hands and accomplished it. It <u>had</u> <u>to</u> <u>come</u> like a continuous chain of MIRACULOUS occurrences. And <u>it</u> <u>is</u> <u>having</u> <u>TREMENDOUS</u> <u>SIGNIFICANCE</u> <u>to</u> <u>the</u> <u>finishing</u> <u>of</u> <u>this</u> <u>most</u> <u>important</u> <u>Commission</u> <u>on</u> <u>earth</u> <u>in</u> <u>1900</u> <u>years</u>!

Of course you've been reading, in The PLAIN TRUTH, of some of these meetings with the world's rulers. And many more such articles and reports are coming in future issues. Then later, I will take you into my confidence and give you the exciting facts of the incredible circumstances, <u>and</u> <u>the</u> <u>surprising</u> <u>providential</u> <u>manner</u> in which these giant doors have opened before me, one after the other in time order.

These very important meetings <u>have suddenly catapulted</u> <u>the</u> <u>entire</u> <u>Work</u> <u>up</u> <u>onto</u> <u>a</u> <u>new</u> <u>and</u> <u>higher</u> <u>plateau</u>! The Work has moved suddenly into a TOTALLY NEW PHASE! These providential new developments signal the warning to YOU and to me that we do not have much time left to get done THE MOST IMPORTANT JOB ON EARTH IN 1900 YEARS! We have now been moved into <u>the</u> <u>last</u> <u>and</u> <u>final</u> <u>phase</u> of the Work for this Age! (*Co-Worker Letter*, April 12, 1971)

This *last and final phase*—expected by him at that time to lead directly to *the end of the age* spoken of by Jesus Christ—occurred more than fifty years ago as of this writing. With that in mind, what do we conclude today—in hindsight—about Mr. Armstrong's *heartfelt conviction* that God was leading him to finish *the final phase* of God's work *through meeting with world leaders*? If the world did not end when he expected it to (in the 1970s), and it did not even end in the 1980s before he died, and it *still has not ended* even today, something about his conclusion back in 1968 could not have been correct!

The fact is, since the prophesied *consummation of the age* (end of the world) did not occur, then whatever Mr. Armstrong was doing while meeting with heads of state from 1968 through the mid-1980s *was not* God's final warning to the world! It simply cannot be. Yet there are many former members and ministers of the Worldwide Church of God today who will not face that fact. Herbert Armstrong believed sincerely that God would use him to "finish the Work." Certain ministers under him boldly proclaimed to the laity that if Herbert Armstrong died before the return of Christ, it was never the true Church of God. Is it any wonder that so many became disillusioned when these prophetic speculations failed? And many of those prognostications were predicated upon the belief that Herbert Armstrong's "open door to visit kings" was testament to his commission at the very end of the age.

Perhaps "visiting kings" was still an endeavor ordained of God, but if so, it was not so that Herbert Armstrong could fulfill an *Elijah commission* to prepare the way for *the imminent return* of Jesus Christ. Even as John the Baptist performed his commission to prepare the way for *the first coming* of Christ (Matthew 17:11–13; Luke 1:17)—and did so *immediately preceding and leading into* the beginning of Christ's first ministry on earth—the Bible shows that *a last-day Elijah* will perform his commission by giving a warning *just prior to and leading into* the *Second Coming of Christ* (Malachi 3:1; 4:5–6). What value is an urgent, "last-minute" warning that comes more than fifty years before the prophesied event? That simply does not add up. And all of these individuals out there today trying to "carry on" that *particular* commission of Herbert Armstrong are fooling themselves.

What Were the Fruits?

Herbert Armstrong always pointed to "the fruits" of any endeavor to substantiate it as having divine inspiration. When challenged by those who claimed he was a fraud, he would point to "the fruits" of the Radio Church of God as evidence of God's guiding hand. He would point to the reach of his radio broadcast and print publications around the world, and he would point to the growth of the church, year after year. In all of these "evidences," he did indeed have justification for claiming that he was a legitimate minister of Jesus Christ, called by God for a commission to go to the world with power to proclaim the real Truth of God. Why and how did he manifest legitimacy in this? Because he accomplished so much in that regard! The fruits of that physical church were evident! Many still claimed he was just lucky, or diabolically clever, but a great religious empire was built under him nonetheless. He claimed it was the divine intervention of God that made all of that possible. And if that is not true, then some other evidence would have to be brought forth to substantiate it. You certainly cannot "prove" he was not legitimate by showing that he was an utter failure. He was not! The size and eventual reach of that church was unmistakable. *It did indeed bear fruit!*

But what about this "new commission" that began in 1968? What about this *brand new* attempt to fulfill God's will by beginning to go to *the rulers* of this world?

> As I mentioned in my previous letter a month ago, the Work of necessity had to begin by reaching the grassroots -- the masses of the common people -- the RULED. We now are reaching more than 150 MILLION of them. . . .

> But we have reached the point where it has now become necessary that we reach ALSO the RULERS -- those in the very top echelons of POWER in the world. Because, whether we have realized it or not, this Work is the GREATEST, MOST EFFECTIVE activity on earth for WORLD PEACE! (*Co-Worker Letter*, May 28, 1971)

How was Herbert Armstrong's *Work* to be a catalyst for world peace? Initially, it was because he felt it was a new platform to *warn national rulers about the imminent return of Jesus Christ*, with

God's Kingdom finally bringing *peace* to the world. But sadly, as it became evident that Jesus Christ was not returning within months (or even years), rather than to reassess the value of devoting so much time to meeting with heads of state to "warn them," the concept of "bringing world peace" quickly morphed into a program to *join with nations and worldly institutions* to try to make *this current world* a better place. But this new concept was a total departure from the church doctrine that Herbert Armstrong had championed for over forty years! Until 1968, the thrust of the message was a true warning:

> Cry aloud, spare not, lift up thy voice like a trumpet, and shew my people their transgression, and the house of Jacob their sins (Isaiah 58:1).

Herbert Armstrong thundered with authority that the whole world was suffering because of sin—the rejection of God's divine Law. But once it became possible for Mr. Armstrong to spend significant amounts of his personal time in high-level, diplomatic settings around the world, that fiery proclamation of the need to repent was replaced by a soft, appeasing message about "an unseen hand" that was coming to solve the world's problems.

What was the evidence—the fruits—that this kind of *new commission* was ever intended by God? How would you measure it? If proof of having a divine commission *to raise up a church* is given by producing a large, worldwide organization (which Herbert Armstrong actually accomplished), what would be the proof that one was sent by God to speak to kings? Is the very fact that you are *permitted to speak to kings* evidence that God is the One who is blessing it as a new commission?

No, Mr. Armstrong clearly stated the "why" of his wanting to meet with world rulers. Mere *opportunity to rub shoulders with powerful people* is not a reason to do it, and certainly it is not *evidence* of God's involvement! The "why" was to *complete a new commission* (an Elijah commission) *to warn the world* just prior to the appearance of Jesus Christ! If that was the "why" of its being done, then what should we be able to observe retroactively as *the fruits* of that endeavor? Was there ever any evidence that such a commission was given by God?

From 1968 to the mid-1980s, did those national leaders receive a bone-chilling warning about the imminent return of Christ, with His *new government* soon to dethrone those current kings, presidents, and prime ministers? Did Mr. Armstrong speak to them the way Elijah spoke to King Ahab, or as John the Baptist spoke to King Herod? Was the entire world warned with mighty signs and miracles about their national sins and the need for repentance? Has there even yet been the kind of "witness" comparable to that which God prophesied would occur before the arrival of His Son? No such warning message was ever proclaimed by Mr. Armstrong to kings, and we have still not seen the fulfillment of that prophecy of a true *warning Work.* Instead, with Mr. Armstrong's visits to heads-of-state, diplomacy was the order of the day, including the giving of expensive gifts, and only a *very veiled message* about Jesus Christ—often without even using His name! Is that really what we saw from Elijah and from John the Baptist? Is that truly the way we think God is going to make final preparation for Christ's return?

So again, in evaluating Mr. Armstrong's *very strong and sincere belief* in 1968 that God had tasked him with *a brand new commission,* do the fruits actually bear this out? The nations were not warned as God promised He will do, and Jesus Christ did not return in the years following the conclusion of those international state visits. According to Mr. Armstrong's own standard of proof, this aspect of his work does not pass muster.

Besides warning the world before Christ's imminent return, visiting heads-of-state was also expected to "open doors" to allow the Worldwide Church of God more access to preach the gospel to these leaders' peoples. But God had already opened doors for radio broadcasts and print publications in most of these areas, even without visiting their national leaders (like King Leopold of Belgium). But what about the bonds he forged with leaders in

1968 IN PROPHECY
291

countries like Japan, especially? The hope was that this personal rapport with the Japanese Prime Minister and other officials would "open the door" for eventual church congregations in Japan. But that never happened! There were a whole lot of state banquets and formal meetings with dignitaries across Asia, but those contacts never produced congregations! The one country in that region where the church flourished was the Philippines (a Catholic country), and that work had been accomplished beginning in the early 1960s, long before visiting world leaders became a goal. And in every other country where the church had been previously *shut out* from operating (like most of the Buddhist nations), even after years of hobnobbing with Buddhist dignitaries, the church mostly was still *shut out* from forming congregations there! So once again, what were the real fruits? The claim was made repeatedly that this activity would "open doors." But the Gospel of Jesus Christ was *never really preached* there, and the church did not gain *any significant foothold* because of those meetings. No fruits!

A COMMISSION . . . OR A TEST?

Therefore, if it is true that *God was opening a new door* in 1968 to allow Mr. Armstrong access to many rulers of this world, then at a minimum, God's purpose *was not* what he thought it was. But if God *was* indeed involved, what might His purpose have been instead?

Might it have been *a test*, and not a commission at all? Might it have been *a temptation* permitted by God, similar to the one documented previously (in the mid-1940s), when Mr. Armstrong was offered a lot more money to give up religion and to become a secular radio announcer instead? Recall what he wrote about Mrs. Armstrong's reaction to that offer?

In all this, Mrs. Armstrong was my faithful partner and helper. She even "scolded" me (she wasn't really serious) for telling her of that offer (*Co-Worker Letter*, September 1, 1968).

In like manner, what if it was never God's will at all for Mr. Armstrong to begin seeking meetings with world leaders? What if this was another temptation that threatened to sidetrack him from his *real commission* in God's service? What if this was just another way that his old weakness of vanity was being tested?

> The opening of my eyes to the TRUTH brought me to the crossroads of my life. To accept it meant to throw in my lot with a class of humble and unpretentious people I had always looked upon as inferior. It meant being cut off from the high and the mighty and the wealthy of this world, to which I had aspired. It meant the final crushing of VANITY. It meant a total *change of life*! (*The Plain Truth*, April 1959, p. 6)

Yet, here, beginning in 1967/68, Herbert Armstrong was being offered a chance to move into those very lofty circles of "the high and the mighty and the wealthy of this world" which he had always craved! But this time, he would not have to abandon his service to God in order to gain that prestige. By concluding that God was the One *sending him*, he could hence have *the very best of both worlds*! However, when faced with temptation this time, he did not have Loma Armstrong at his side to temper his natural attraction to a very tantalizing opportunity.

If this is not a credible assessment of what happened, then someone needs to show how those world visits actually fulfilled *any spiritual purpose of God*!

Unintended Fruits

The fruits hoped for were never realized in pursuing this "new commission" to visit kings. But there were indeed other fruits borne. What were they?

Once Mr. Armstrong began devoting the majority of his personal time to state visits around the world, it became impossible for him to "mind the store" back home. He was forced to delegate much more to other men in running church operations. After the final expulsion of his son, Garner Ted Armstrong, from the church in 1978, recall how Mr. Armstrong assessed the reason for such serious problems through the 1970s:

> For the past two years I have been laboring very hard to be Christ's servant and apostle in SETTING GOD'S CHURCH BACK ON THE TRACK. The entire Church had been derailed. A <u>LIBERAL</u> spirit from Satan had been injected into some in high positions under me at Headquarters in Pasadena. Instead of wholeheartedly OBEYING Christ through HIS WORD, THE BIBLE, there was creeping in, during years when I was in other parts of the world up to 300 out of the 365 days in the year, a LIBERAL spirit of SATAN.

> Those leaders to whom I had delegated the responsibility of ADMINISTERING the POLICIES and DOCTRINES Christ had set in God's Church through His apostle, went way BEYOND the authority given them. They started CHANGING POLICIES and watering down God's TRUTH, changing DOCTRINES, compromising -- seeing HOW CLOSE they could go -- and lead the Brethren in going -- to the ways of SATAN! They wanted to be more LIBERAL -- more like THIS WORLD OF SATAN. . . .

> But for two years Jesus Christ has been using me and those loyally still with and under me to SET BACK ON GOD'S TRACK God's Church (*Co-Worker Letter*, September 15, 1980).

Herbert Armstrong had been the one-and-only CEO of the Worldwide Church of God through that entire time. If he was at the helm, how did that church go so far away from what he deemed important? His answer, above, was that he was away from home for 300 out of 365 days per year. The inference is that had he *not been away* so much, he might have *prevented* this liberal cancer from ever taking hold.

And why was he away so much of the year? Because since 1968, he had been fulfilling that "new commission" to *warn rulers* of the *imminent arrival* of Jesus Christ.

So the very *unintended consequences* of latching onto this *new commission* in 1968 was *the implosion of his life's work* through the 1970s, as other men dismantled and restructured the Worldwide Church of God in his absence.

And once again, what was the *spiritual payoff* for all of those meetings with world rulers over the ensuing decade? Nothing! The only real fruit was a time of upheaval and tribulation for members of the Worldwide Church of God.

For all of this, we still have not answered the question: If God was behind Herbert Armstrong in the raising up of that church, why did He allow him to take such a wrong turn in 1968? Herbert Armstrong was well-meaning. He loved God and wanted to fulfill that calling in His service. So if that church was being led by God, why did God not prevent such a devastating mistake?

Recall that the true Church of God was prophesied to apostatize (depart from revealed Truth). How would such a rejection of God ever take place among His chosen people? Something would have to start the dominos falling. Having Mr. Armstrong distracted from active leadership of the church—by traveling so often overseas—would surely provide an excellent opening, allowing others to fill the void back home. But which doctrine of the church would be the first domino to be "tipped" by the liberals—and why? And how would such a "small change" turn out to be "the shot heard 'round the world"? That will become plain in the next chapter.

CHAPTER SIXTEEN
THE PENTECOST PRECEDENT

Why did a change in the doctrine of Pentecost in 1974 (covered in chapter six) become so significant to the Worldwide Church of God? After all, it seemed like such a small change at the time—really just an inconsequential *adjustment*. Why should it even matter whether that particular Holy Day is observed on a Monday or on a Sunday? To many church members in 1974 it *did not* matter, and that very fact subtly set the stage for a cascading chain of unexpected events which would reverberate through that organization over the next twenty years.

To those who disregard Herbert Armstrong's work as having any divine inspiration from God, the 1974 Pentecost change is *still* highly relevant, historically. Forget (for the moment) that we may be talking about God's true Church—His *peculiar treasure*. Anyone who wants to understand how the Worldwide Church of God ultimately became a Protestant, Sunday-keeping, "born-again" group by the mid-1990s *must* look at 1974 for context. The historical dynamics were quite amazing, whether you believe God was involved or not. However, very few have really recognized this fact, especially among those who still believe that Mr. Armstrong was a legitimate servant of God. Most of the remnant groups today—which emerged from that parent body in the 1990s in order to preserve "traditional Armstrong teachings"—*still* do not get it. Yet the history is right there in black and white for anyone to see. Without the change in Pentecost in 1974, later changes to repudiate the seventh-day Sabbath, the doctrines on the nature of God, the nature of man, and the hope of human salvation *could never have been made*! Most people focus upon the late 1980s (after Mr. Armstrong's death) as the most *transforming period* in that church's history. They fail to recognize that, truly, the most pivotal event affecting that church's future was a seemingly innocuous decision to change the counting rule for the day of Pentecost twenty years beforehand. The ultimate dismantling of that church in the 1990s was only the final act in a play whose storyline unfolded slowly over two decades. What is the proof?

A FORTY-YEAR PRECEDENT

What is true is that before 1974, major doctrines of the Worldwide Church of God had always been *certified as true* by claiming God's divine guidance. Technical explanations of Hebrew and Greek words—as well as a good dose of historical exposition—were always part of "the evidence," but in the end, the supreme reason any contentious doctrine was resolved in a particular way related to *God's divine inspiration.* How did they know they had the Truth? Not because their technical scholastic process was better than any other church, but because *God picked them* to be His peculiar treasure, and with that special calling came the gift of *miraculous understanding.* Why miraculous? Because the very best capabilities of natural human wisdom can still never lead to real Truth. If that is not so, all of these brilliant minds upon this earth would agree on the meanings of the Bible. But *they do not.* There are as many contradictory conclusions about "Bible truths" as there are men with prestigious degrees to write papers and lead symposiums. Experts are everywhere, but virtually *none of them* are in agreement. So much for the ability of human intellect and the scientific method to lead to indisputable spiritual Truth. In the end, whose interpretation will we trust? Which "expert" opinion will prevail? In every religious organization, *someone* makes that call. Within the Radio Church of God, Herbert Armstrong held that authority, and he made those decisions claiming *God's divine guidance* for legitimacy. In doing so he raised up a religious movement that thumbed its nose at every sacred cow of mainstream Christianity. He was unapologetic, insisting he had the backing of God for everything he was teaching,

THE PENTECOST PRECEDENT

even though the collective body of this world's Bible "experts" opposed him. Here are two examples of his intrepid independence and claim of divine inspiration in opposition to the world's scholars:

> And so I say to you, as the Apostle Paul said to those at Galatia: I certify you, brethren, that the GOSPEL which is preached of me is not after man, for I neither received it of man, neither was I taught it but BY THE REVELATION OF JESUS CHRIST. . . . When it pleased God, who . . . called me by His grace, to reveal His Son in me that I might preach Him to the world; immediately I conferred not with flesh and blood—neither went I to any sect or denomination or human theologian, but I went directly to the WORD of GOD, on my knees, corrected, reproved, and instructed in God's righteousness and TRUTH! (*Co-worker Letter*, Herbert W. Armstrong; November 29, 1954)

> This world rejects God's TRUTH—God's WAY of life. It follows the way that leads to curses. . . . Instead of the true spiritual waters of life that would satisfy, they try to quench their thirst on excessive strong drink that brings spiritual drunkenness.
> And, truly, they are SPIRITUALLY DRUNK! Their spiritual eyes are so blurred and out of focus by the false spiritual wine of pagan myths, superstitious religions, atheistic concepts, and vain philosophies, that TRUTH is completely blurred to their sight—they are UNABLE to grasp it! (*The Plain Truth*, "Heart to Heart Talk With the Editor," August 1961, p. 25)

The Radio Church of God was founded as a reactionary religious movement, asserting its disdain for traditional ecclesiastical dogma and the foolishness of this world's lofty, howbeit *blinded*, "experts." Those who came into the church in those early years were *escaping* their past indoctrinations of "nominal churchianity"—*casting off* the bonds of "accepted" Bible scholarship—having found it miserably unsatisfying and totally lacking in substance. Here is an example of that *culture of disdain* for traditional religious conformity as it was expressed on the topic of Pentecost:

> The New Testament Church was not founded on Sunday. But it did start on the annual Sabbath day called "Pentecost" or "Feast of Firstfruits." Also called the "Feast of Weeks." . . .
>
> It is of very grave importance that we figure the right day. This day, and this only, is made HOLY by the Eternal Creator (*Pagan Holidays—or God's Holy Days—Which?*, 1957, 1970, pp. 29, 31, Herbert W. Armstrong).

> Almighty God is *not the author of confusion*! (I Cor. 14:33.) He has placed specific offices in His True Church today to determine just such things as how to count Pentecost (Eph. 4:11-13). Pentecost ALWAYS FALLS ON A *MONDAY*, there is *NO OTHER DAY ACCEPTABLE* IN GOD'S SIGHT! (*Ambassador College Correspondence Course*, Lesson 35, 1965, p. 7)

This claim of divine inspiration is certainly no proof to anyone who doubts Herbert Armstrong's ecclesiastical legitimacy. But among those who *did* believe it was the work of God—not of man—the final claim of authority for *any doctrinal teaching* was that God *actively guided* Mr. Armstrong through the forest of religious confusion to confirm *miraculously* the correct answers to doctrinal questions. Members were taught that the true Church of God is founded upon a Rock—a sure foundation—which is Jesus Christ Himself. Therefore, it is accurate to say that during the first forty years of that work—from 1934 until 1974—the culture of the church was permeated with the idea that God *guided* His church into all Truth from the beginning: "Howbeit when [it], the Spirit of truth, is come, [it] will guide you into all truth" (John 16:13). This is exactly what Mr. Armstrong claimed had happened, and he continued to make that very bold and provocative claim, even through 1973:

> God has led his church and has not let His church be deceiving so many people all through these years . . . and I say that by the authority of Jesus Christ (Transcript of Bible study, Pasadena, CA, Herbert W. Armstrong, April 17, 1973).

THE 1974 CHANGE IN PRECEDENT

Yet, less than a year after making this statement about God leading His Church into Truth, he approved a change in the date for Pentecost, citing new availability of *better technical scholarship* from worldly religious "experts," thereby destroying a forty-year precedent! Here is what he wrote in April 1974 in the 79-page "Pentecost Study Material," distributed primarily to the ministers:

> It is the fact that one of the translators of the RSV, who is Chairman of the Revision Committee now revising the RSV, said not only that [that is, that the Hebrew *mi* or *min* should never be translated "from" but "beginning on"], but that he will strongly recommend the revision will so translate it, that caused me to CHANGE the Pentecost from Monday to Sunday (A Simplified Note from Herbert W. Armstrong, para. 4).

Compare this *very new precedent* with his previous claims of *divine guidance* for all such decisions. For the first time, as it related to a *major teaching* of the church, Mr. Armstrong no longer claimed that God had guided him through *divine revelation* to resolve a sticky doctrinal point. Instead, the entire authority for changing Pentecost from Monday to Sunday hinged upon *improved understanding* of Bible passages through the wise counsel of *more knowledgeable experts* in the world. Regardless of whether you believe this approach makes more sense or not, what is significant is that 1974 marked the first time that such a device was employed to repudiate a prominent, long-held teaching within the Worldwide Church of God. It ushered in a brand new era—akin to opening Pandora's Box—that would *transform* that influential religious organization within twenty years.

Gone, hence, was the claim that God was at the helm from the beginning, steering attentively, and preventing the natural weaknesses of His human crew from precipitating gross navigational errors. Now was introduced a brand new paradigm: The church was told that God never really prevented major doctrinal error from becoming imbedded in those foundational teachings. Jesus Christ was, in essence, a distracted skipper who let his inexperienced first mate—Herbert Armstrong—navigate a loose and wandering course, getting it right sometimes by chance, but winding up off target just as often.

Most compelling was Mr. Armstrong's own change in writing and speaking, as evidenced in his statements to those prominent church ministers who gathered for the dedication ceremony of the new Ambassador Auditorium in May 1974:

> Now how God would let His own Church go several [thirty-five or so] years in error may be a little difficult for some to believe. But the more important thing is your attitude (Ambassador College Auditorium dedication ceremony, May 6, 1974, p. 62, reel 2).

Having taught for nearly forty years that the human scholars of this world—none of which ever advocated a Monday Pentecost—were wrong, and that only the true church possessed this precious truth, now the church was told that human scholars were actually our best source for *real wisdom*, and we should not dwell upon the fact God had let His true church get it wrong all that time. A *good attitude* was now our best ally.

THE PENTECOST PRECEDENT   301

With that change, a host of doctrinal publications had to be rewritten. Here are some of those former writings which were immediately edited or discontinued:

> Yes, Jesus founded His church on the day of Pentecost—not before then! . . .
> Was the true church founded on a Sunday in A.D. 33 as the *Catholic and a few other churches claim*? REMEMBER, if any church which claims apostolic authority has erred in the traditional date of its founding, *how can we* believe that its other traditions are true? . . .
> *Pentecost in 31 A.D., the exact day upon which the true church was founded by Jesus Christ, was June 18. This day was a* MONDAY. . .
> God's true church—the church that Jesus built—has been observing the *true* day of Pentecost to this day. That is why it has not forgotten the right year in which it was founded. All other churches have resulted from apostacies and have accepted pagan doctrines. They have forgotten the right year and the right day. They are not the churches that Jesus promised to build and *which He promised to guide into all truth*! Only the *true* church which has kept the *true* day of Pentecost could remember when Jesus founded his church (*The Good News*, "Which Is the True Church?," Herman Hoeh, May 1953, pp. 9–10).

> The Day of Pentecost or Firstfruits is a *sign*. It identifies those who have God's Holy Spirit, those who are God's elect, those who will be resurrected when Jesus Christ returns to this earth!
> The Day of Pentecost identifies God's ONLY TRUE CHURCH! Only God's true Church keeps the day of Pentecost at the right time in the right way—with the understanding of God's plan. THAT IS BECAUSE ONLY GOD'S TRUE CHURCH RECEIVED HIS HOLY SPIRIT AND WAS FOUNDED BY JESUS CHRIST ON THE

DAY OF PENTECOST IN 31 A.D.! (*Ambassador College Correspondence Course*, Lesson 35, 1965, p. 16)

THE AFTERMATH OF THAT CHANGE

Why was the 1974 change in Pentecost so significant in the resulting history of the Worldwide Church of God? Because it marked the beginning of a whole new philosophy for determining what that church would accept as doctrine. But could not the Pentecost decision simply stand alone as an exception? Could not all of the other doctrines just continue to be confirmed as they were beforehand without impact?

Impossible! Why? Because for the first time, like it or not, every single doctrinal position now came into question. How could they not? If confidence in those original teachings had always rested in the belief that God *miraculously guided* Mr. Armstrong to "get it right"—even in spite of his human limitations—the "necessary" change in Pentecost after four decades proved that, in reality, "the king has no clothes!" If Mr. Armstrong could be so wrong about Pentecost, what else might he also have gotten wrong? *Nothing* now could be taken for granted. *Everything* was suddenly subject to question. And so it *was* questioned—all of it.

One by one, every single doctrine of the church was "reexamined" by a committee of the "best scholars" of the church. Here is that *doctrinal committee* described by Mr. Armstrong in his letter to the church on February 11, 1974, announcing the Pentecost change:

> In a former letter, I told you we had called a special team of Ambassador College's most scholarly researchers to reexamine all evidence on setting the day for Pentecost . . .

> A committee of our best researchers and scholars at Pasadena Headquarters was appointed to reexamine for me this subject in depth. . . .

The Pentecost Precedent

303

> To assist Mr. Armstrong, we contacted world-famous translators—scholars who actually rendered the Hebrew. . . .

> We did not have, at that time [in early years], access to all of the scholarly research that we have today. . . .

> Ambassador College has indeed provided an educated ministry. It has developed a scholarly research team (pp. 3, 7, 5, and 6 respectively).

Having now "gotten their feet wet" by correcting the "long-held error" on Pentecost, *what else* needed to be reexamined for veracity, just in case Mr. Armstrong erroneously assumed God had guided him into truth on *those doctrines* also? Do you see how this one change set a new precedent that necessarily called *everything* into question? And what was the result of that *progressive* reevaluation?

Before he died in January 1986, Mr. Armstrong seemed, first of all, to *acknowledge* that this philosophical change *actually did occur* in the 1970s. Then secondly, he seemed to concede in retrospect that it was a mistake to begin pandering to the scholars of the world. From *The Worldwide News—Special Edition,* June 24, 1985, in his very last article to the church, entitled, *Recent History of the Philadelphia Era of the Worldwide Church of God,* he stated:

> A small few Ambassador graduates who had become ministers in the Church were somewhat scholarly inclined, especially one who had a specific problem. He suffered from an inferiority complex. Because some of our graduates at the time were enrolling in outside universities for higher degrees, a few came to conceive that a "scholar" was in the loftiest position of humanity.

> If this inferiority sufferer could feel in his own mind that he was a scholar he would feel elevated above other people and therefore delivered from feelings of inferiority. He began to question some of the established doctrines of the Church

of God, such as counting the day of Pentecost, divorce and remarriage, tithing and others.

Soon he was entering into what he considered a scholarly research to DISprove some of the Church's basic teachings. Gradually one or two others, then even more, joined in a self-appointed "scholarly research" to DISprove plain biblical truths.

It became evident that those attending other universities came to consider Ambassador College as inferior and substandard intellectually and academically because of our belief in God. Secularism and the anti-God approach of evolution seemed to them far superior to the revealed knowledge of God.

Mr. Armstrong never advocated returning to a Monday Pentecost before he died, at least not publicly. Even if he had wanted to, it would have been virtually impossible by that time to take that organization back. But it surely appears that he came to regret the entire movement that surfaced in the early 1970s to elevate those worldly scholars.

The unnamed man whom Mr. Armstrong highlighted in the quote above was Dr. Ernest Martin, one of the very first ministers of the church to resign during that era, in January 1974. Dr. Martin soon repudiated much of what he had once accepted, believed, and taught as a minister under Mr. Armstrong. He had been an early advocate of a Sunday Pentecost—writing a technical paper on the subject as early as 1961. He was only one of many ministers who apparently harbored contrary ideas about church doctrines, but ideas which they kept under wraps for years. After the change in Pentecost was finally achieved in February 1974, the table was set for a feast of controversy concerning *all* of these previously suppressed agendas. All of a sudden, it was open season on the teachings of the church.

The final result of that act in 1974 was manifested after Mr. Armstrong died in 1986. His successor, as Pastor General, used the

THE PENTECOST PRECEDENT
305

very same arguments about *growing in grace and knowledge* through the "reevaluation" of long-held doctrines as a means to repudiate the rest of those teachings that had separated the Worldwide Church of God from mainstream Christianity, including the seventh-day Sabbath, the nature of God, and man's very purpose for being created. The entire body of church doctrine was completely gutted. But those who believe that the culprit was the new Pastor General fail to recognize the real history. None of those later changes that dismantled fundamental doctrine could ever have been foisted upon the membership if not for the precedent of 1974. Even as Mr. Armstrong later regretted it and fought a losing battle against liberalism through the 1970s and 1980s because of it, so did his successor use that same precedent to dismantle the church altogether. The tools had already been handed to him.

Remember what Mr. Armstrong was quoted earlier as saying in 1961 concerning the so-called wise of this world and its scholars?

> And, truly, they are SPIRITUALLY DRUNK! Their spiritual eyes are so blurred and out of focus by the false spiritual wine of pagan myths, superstitious religions, atheistic concepts, and vain philosophies, that TRUTH is completely blurred to their sight—they are UNABLE to grasp it! (*The Plain Truth*, "Heart to Heart Talk With the Editor," August 1961, p. 25)

What was not given to you earlier is the sentence Mr. Armstrong wrote *immediately following* that statement, concerning the grave accountability of those *who do see*. Here is what he said:

> But, if God has opened *our* eyes—set them in sharp, clear focus—permitted us to comprehend, through His precious Spirit, what the world is not able, yet, to see, we need to remember this is DANGEROUS KNOWLEDGE—for God will hold us accountable for what we do with it! (*The Plain Truth*, "Heart to Heart Talk With the Editor," August 1961)

306 A PECULIAR TREASURE

What did the Worldwide Church of God do with that charge they once believed God had given to them through the gift of divinely revealed Truth? In the end, they decided those teachings were really not of God, had never been of God, and that they had all been deceived to ever think that they were true. Thanks to turning to the real scholars of this world for truth beginning in 1974, they eventually repudiated everything Herbert Armstrong ever taught. This was the *real gift* that "better scholarship" brought to that organization.

What if Christ Was the Foundation?

If Herbert Armstrong was just another man who found a clever way to make a name for himself through religion, then it really does not matter what eventually occurred in that organization. But what if that body of believers keeping those unique and controversial doctrines *really was* the true Church of God in this age—God's peculiar treasure? What then would be true about that pivotal change in Pentecost in 1974?

Wherever the true Church exists, it is a Body founded upon Christ Himself as the foundation, not upon any man.

> Therefore thus saith the Lord GOD, Behold, I lay in Zion for a foundation a stone, a tried stone, a precious corner stone, a sure foundation (Isaiah 28:16).

> Now therefore ye are no more strangers and foreigners, but fellowcitizens with the saints, and of the household of God; And are built upon the foundation of the apostles and prophets, *Jesus Christ himself being the chief corner stone* (Ephesians 2:19–20) [emphasis mine].

In all times that God performed a work through chosen servants, whether with ancient Israel or the New Testament Church, it was established from the beginning upon a sure foundation, and then

THE PENTECOST PRECEDENT

307

those servants were commanded to hold fast and refuse to depart. They were specially called, and they received the Truth—not through better access to human scholars—but by the miracle of divine revelation.

> But ye are a chosen generation, a royal priesthood, an holy nation, a peculiar people; that ye should shew forth the praises of him who hath called you out of darkness into his marvellous light: Which in time past were not a people, but are now the people of God: which had not obtained mercy, but now have obtained mercy (1 Peter 2:9–10).

The world would view these special ones as fools, and only the truly called would have a chance of showing real respect for Jesus Christ. All of the others would show disdain and contempt for His revealed teachings:

> Unto you therefore which believe he is precious: but unto them which be disobedient, the stone which the builders disallowed, the same is made the head of the corner, And a stone of stumbling, and a rock of offence, even to them which stumble at the word, being disobedient: whereunto also they were appointed (1 Peter 2:7–8).

Given what the Bible tells us about all of these dynamics, and the fact that the true Church of God would indeed reject its spiritual foundation—Jesus Christ—what would it mean then if the Worldwide Church of God really did turn out to be God's inspired work in the twentieth century? It would mean that the change in Pentecost in 1974 from Monday to Sunday was not the minor or trivial "adjustment" so many thought it to be.

JESUS CHRIST REJECTED BY ISRAEL

If God did indeed use Herbert Armstrong as an instrument to deliver inspired truths to the true Church in this era of time, then what that man taught did not come out of his own thoughts or through his own acquired wisdom. Though absolutely fallible humanly—and definitely no accomplished Bible scholar—it must have been God inspiring him every step of the way and making sure that the true foundation of that Body was sound—Jesus Christ, the Word of Truth. If Jesus Christ is the One who guided and inspired Mr. Armstrong to confirm a Monday Pentecost for so many years—even against the ridicule of every other religious body in the world—then rejecting a Monday Pentecost was no mere "adjustment." That act was a slap in the face of the Revelator who gave it to the Church through divine inspiration.

And is it not interesting that—according to Mr. Armstrong's teaching—the Day of Pentecost pictures the gift of the Holy Spirit to the true Church: those who are the firstfruits of God's work with mankind? According to that teaching, God took a people who by nature could achieve nothing of themselves and freely gave to them knowledge and power to confound the whole world:

> The LORD did not set his love upon you, nor choose you, because ye were more in number than any people; for ye were the fewest of all people: But because the LORD loved you, and because he would keep the oath which he had sworn unto your fathers, hath the LORD brought you out with a mighty hand, and redeemed you out of the house of bondmen, from the hand of Pharaoh king of Egypt (Deuteronomy 7:7–8).

> For ye see your calling, brethren, how that not many wise men after the flesh, not many mighty, not many noble, are called: But God hath chosen the foolish things of the world to confound the wise; and God hath chosen the weak things of the world to confound the things which are mighty; And

THE PENTECOST PRECEDENT   309

base things of the world, and things which are despised, hath
God chosen, yea, and things which are not, to bring to nought
things that are: That no flesh should glory in his presence (1
Corinthians 1:26–29).

The whole point of God's Work with man was to use a very small
body of believers as a forerunner, toward the ultimate end of offering
salvation to the whole world. That true Church would receive its
power from God, not from man, and its teachings would be the gift
of Jesus Christ, their foundation. Pentecost embodies *the whole idea*
of that small true Church as the firstfruits of God's Work, and the
Holy Spirit as *the singular element* given to set it apart. God gave
that Spirit for the very first time on the Day of Pentecost (Acts
2:1–21), the day the New Testament Church was founded. And if Mr.
Armstrong was correct in saying that only the true Church keeps the
correct day—Monday—and that Monday Pentecost is a *special sign*
that sets that true Church apart from the deceived, what did the
change to Sunday in 1974, based upon "better knowledge" from
worldly scholars, signify in the eyes of God? If that work was truly
the work of Jesus Christ from the beginning, then that very change
epitomized the prophesied rejection of the true Cornerstone by those
who should have known better.

Judah hath dealt treacherously, and an abomination is
committed in Israel and in Jerusalem; for Judah hath
profaned the holiness of the LORD which he loved, and hath
married the daughter of a strange god. The LORD will cut off
the man that doeth this, the master and the scholar, out of
the tabernacles of Jacob, and him that offereth an offering
unto the LORD of hosts (Malachi 2:11–12).

The Book of Malachi is a prophetic book written to confirm what
would happen very soon before the return of Jesus Christ. It was not
written for ancient Israel, but for those who would become *spiritual*
Israelites (of all nations and races) through begettal of the Holy

310   A PECULIAR TREASURE

Spirit (1 Corinthians 10:11)! And what did this Malachi prophecy say would lie at *the root* of Israel's departure from God—an act that would cause God to reject them and to withdraw His special inspiration and protection?

> And now, O ye priests, this commandment is for you. If ye will not hear, and if ye will not lay it to heart, to give glory unto my name, saith the LORD of hosts, I will even send a curse upon you, and I will curse your blessings: yea, I have cursed them already, because ye do not lay it to heart. Behold, I will corrupt your seed, and spread dung upon your faces, even the dung of your *solemn feasts*; and *one* shall take you away with it (Malachi 2:1–3) [emphasis mine].

What does this passage tell us? God's own people—the true Israel—would follow their leaders—the priests—into commission of an abomination. Why would God become so unhappy with them? Because those leaders would stop giving glory to Him, and begin giving it instead to men! How would they perpetrate this act of gross disrespect toward God? The last portion of verse three tells us that *one particular solemn feast* would be at the heart of their provocation: "and one [feast] shall take you away with it."

Which commanded feast of God would spiritual Israel profane, and how would this act become such a stench in the nostrils of God? Whatever the answer is, something they would do to corrupt *a particular feast* of God would give glory to man, and no longer to God. What could it be?

If you come to believe that the Worldwide Church of God was the manifestation of God's true Work in this time, and that Herbert Armstrong was the legitimate instrument of God to do that Work, and if you come to believe that God withdrew His protection from that body *at some point*, allowing that church to be destroyed by the mid-1990s, what will you conclude became the catalyst that set these events into motion and ultimately fulfilled this very prophecy of Malachi 2?

THE PENTECOST PRECEDENT   311

Might it not have been the change in Pentecost from Monday to Sunday in 1974? After all, did not that change meet the criteria for an act of disrespect toward Jesus Christ, *if He had indeed revealed a Monday Pentecost through Mr. Armstrong*? If Monday was the correct day all along, what did God think about His chosen ministry changing it to Sunday after nearly forty years, based upon "better scholarship" from deceived human theologians of this world? Is it just possible that God foretold that it would be *Pentecost*—the annual feast representing the miraculous gift of God's Spirit to the Church—that they would corrupt, making it more than just a simple "adjustment"? Is it possible that this change would signify *a whole new precedent* in rejecting Jesus Christ as the true foundation of that work, as they thereafter turned to the wisdom of men for their source of knowledge? You be the judge. But it is a possibility that most former members of that church will still not countenance today, even though they advance *every other explanation* for why the church organization they loved as God's true Work ultimately ended in such confusion.

Again, regardless of whether you believe Herbert Armstrong was inspired by Jesus Christ to do a unique work in God's name—or not—no one else has documented the profound effect that the 1974 Pentecost change had upon that church over the ensuing twenty years. It was indeed a turning point. Without the change to a Sunday Pentecost based upon *more credible human scholarship*, there could have been no effective argument for the rejection of the weekly Sabbath in 1994, based upon the expertise of "real Bible experts." The first change begat the last, and all of those changes that occurred in between.

Those continuing to believe that Pentecost is a commanded festival of God to the true Church in this age need to weigh seriously how God wishes us to keep it. Does the day upon which you keep it reflect your thankfulness for the revelation of Truth through *a divine gift of God*, or does your choice of day and manner of practice espouse reverence for the prowess of men? How does God view what

you are doing? Never underestimate the importance of the correct
day. After all, Mr. Armstrong said:

It is of very grave importance that we figure the right day.
This day, and this only, is made HOLY by the Eternal Creator.

CHAPTER SEVENTEEN
A TALE OF TWO STUDENTS

Now, it is time to highlight two particular individuals from that early church history who personified—ultimately—two very opposing ideologies. It is the tug-of-war between these two divergent ideologies that would later destroy the Worldwide Church of God as we know it today. Some very strong similarities, and yet even more significant differences, in these two particular individuals will serve to explain the dynamics of the organizational drift which eventually manifested, and the very different responses that each of these men had toward it. Those two men were Herman L. Hoeh and Raymond C. Cole, two of the very first four students enrolled in Ambassador College for its inaugural year in 1947.

Special Note: Most of the quotations used herein from Mr. Armstrong's autobiography cannot be found in the "book" version (Volume II) assembled by the WCG in 1986/1987. By that time there was a clear intent to expunge Raymond Cole's name from that history as much as possible, as well as to eliminate statements that, in hindsight, might not reflect well upon Herman Hoeh. To get the true words of Mr. Armstrong *unedited*, you must go back to the original "The Autobiography of Herbert W. Armstrong" published serially in *The Plain Truth* from 1957 to 1968.

THE PURPOSE OF AMBASSADOR COLLEGE

Recall that Ambassador College was conceived by Herbert Armstrong to be a liberal arts institution, not specifically a "Bible school." Here is how he described the purpose of that new college when recruiting students for the first time in the January-February 1947 issue of *The Plain Truth* p. 9:

But why should *we* establish and conduct a college in connection with this, God's work?

The reasons are concrete and vital. . . .

[T]he work has grown to a scope where *called*, consecrated, properly educated and specially trained assistants, ministers and evangelists to follow up this work in the field have become an imparative [sic] need.

The time has come when we must lay definite PLANS for carrying the true Gospel of the Kingdom of God into *all nations*, in *many languages!* . . .

Yet, the active ministry is *different* from every other profession in one very important respect. No man ever should enter it of his own volition . . . A true minister of Jesus Christ must be specially *called* of GOD. And how can we *know* whether one is really called? Experience has shown human nature to be such that most who *think* they are called are mistaken, and those who really are called invariably try to run from the calling! Jesus gave us the only test—"By their *fruits*," He said, "ye shall KNOW."

But "the fruits" are worked out by experience, and that requires time. For this very reason our college *cannot be a ministerial college*—though it *is* being designed so that, should we be fortunate enough to find one out of twenty really and truly called to the ministry, that one will have been prepared and properly trained.

So the plan was to use the new college as a pool from which future ordained helpers would be recruited, but never guaranteeing a ministerial commission to anyone merely by virtue of enrollment or graduation. In reality, most of those initial male enrollees went on to become ministers (and many of the female students became ministers' wives), but over time, as the college grew, Mr. Armstrong's vision of ordaining only selected, hand-picked men from the larger pool of graduates became a reality.

A TALE OF TWO STUDENTS
315

Who was it, then, that responded to this initial advertising campaign and was accepted as part of the inaugural class in the fall of 1947?

THE STUDENT BODY OF 1947

While some forty students had applied for the fall of 1947, because of delays in getting the campus prepared and the buildings approved for occupancy, most of those applicants went elsewhere by the time Mr. Armstrong finally contacted them to say it would actually open as scheduled. The only ones left by then were Mr. Armstrong's eldest son, Richard, a young woman named Betty Bates, Herman Hoeh, and Raymond Cole.

Let Mr. Armstrong introduce those first four students:

Ambassador College did finally swing open its big front door to students October 8, 1947. But by that time nearly all applicants had gone elsewhere. Besides our son Dick (Richard David), there was only Raymond C. Cole, who came down from Oregon where his family had been in the Church for years; Herman L. Hoeh, who came from Santa Rosa, California; and Miss Betty Bates from Oklahoma—four pioneer students—with a faculty of eight ("The Autobiography of Herbert W. Armstrong," *The Plain Truth*, June 1963, p. 30).

Richard Armstrong became an ordained minister and key instrument in the work of his father, yet died from injuries in a tragic car accident in 1958, thus limiting his long-term influence upon the Radio Church of God. After graduation in 1951, Betty Bates became a college employee and instructor for women students for about seven years under Mr. Armstrong before finally focusing instead upon her own family. Only Herman Hoeh and Raymond Cole—from that very first year—would become long-term, ordained evangelists whose influence would reach into the tumultuous years of the 1970s.

WHAT THEY SHARED IN COMMON

The young Herman Hoeh and Raymond Cole actually had much in common. In spite of the fact that they were two years apart in age (Raymond, the older), and one was rather tall (Herman) while the other rather short in stature, they were both hard workers, came from strong families, and were both regarded as being very mild and unassuming in personality. They were each driven to achieve, but both gained reputations over time for being outgoing and considerate to others, and for "quiet" acts of benevolence toward those in need.

Although Herman Hoeh gained the more prominent reputation for being "brainy" (as Betty Bates was reported to have called him), he and Raymond Cole were both very scholarly-minded, and each was very *professorial* in his thinking and speaking style. In time, both would be known as very good speakers, but neither of them had the natural, "entertaining style" of Mr. Armstrong (or later, his son, Garner Ted Armstrong), although both would aspire to emulate it. A Herman Hoeh sermon on some point of history, the calendar, e.g., could be excruciating for one not inclined to meaty scholarship, and Raymond Cole could exhaust one trying to take notes, citing voluminous scriptural references to document his point. Both men loved knowledge, read avidly, and *studied* for a hobby. Raymond Cole's vocabulary was incredibly extensive because, from his youth, he loved to study the dictionary *for fun*. Mr. Armstrong had to teach both of these young men to try to speak on the level of their audience, given that it was something that came naturally to *neither* of them.

While Herman Hoeh first heard Mr. Armstrong on the radio in his native California, Raymond Cole was raised by parents who had migrated to Oregon from Oklahoma in 1936, in part, to learn more from this unusual radio preacher. So, in this, the two men differed. Raymond was taught at the feet of Mr. Armstrong from age eleven, and of parents who came from a tradition of Sabbath-keeping. Herman Hoeh was breaking new ground from his upbringing by

A Tale of Two Students

responding to this unique teaching. Yet both of these men showed an early and determined commitment to that way of life—and also to the man through whom they had first learned it.

Another quote from Mr. Armstrong gives more detail about that very first year at Ambassador College:

> We had no facilities for housing students. Our own son, Richard David (Dick), lived with us in our new home (new to us, that is). Betty Bates had rented a room out in the east end of Pasadena, some five miles from the college. She used the city bus service for transportation. The other two students, Raymond Cole and Herman Hoeh, rented a room together some 2½ miles from the college. They used less expensive transportation—shoe-leather. They managed to prepare their own food, somehow, in their room.
>
> Those pioneer students had to "rough it" in a way I am sure our students of today do not realize. They certainly did not live in luxury. We did manage to employ these pioneer students for part-time work, at $40 per month. But they had to pay $31.50 room-rent—per *each*! In order to have enough to eat, they often picked lamb's-quarter—in place of spinach—where it grew along certain sparsely settled streets and in vacant lots, then prepared it after returning home from school.
>
> Herman Hoeh received weekly packages of food from his parents to help out. Raymond Cole sometimes had a meal with his sister, who was employed in our office. And, many times, they simply went hungry. They were more hungry for an education than for physical food.
>
> Yet they never mentioned any of this, and I have only learned of it myself very recently.
>
> They heard talk from others about "when this thing folds up." But there was no thought of the college "folding up" in their minds—even as there wasn't in mine. They had faith. They were there for a *purpose!* It was a mighty serious

purpose! It was the one goal of their lives, and they concentrated on it and worked at it with all their energies! That is why these men, all three, became top-ranking ministers in the greatest activity on earth today!

The part-time work these pioneer students did was janitor work ("The Autobiography of Herbert W. Armstrong," *The Plain Truth*, July 1963, pp. 13–14).

Not mentioned by Mr. Armstrong was the fact that before Herman Hoeh and Raymond Cole were employed eventually by Mr. Armstrong part-time doing landscaping and janitorial work on campus (funds being very limited at first), they each supplemented their meager living by "setting pins" in a local bowling alley. These two men roomed together, studied together, went to church together, worked together, and suffered deprivation together, all for the mutual love they had for what they were being offered through Ambassador College.

These two men also shared something else in common. In spite of the fact that they would each take very different paths once the troubles within the Worldwide Church of God emerged in the early 1970s, they each maintained a personal respect and regard for Mr. Armstrong till their dying days. While others became quick to criticize and to denigrate because of painful experiences over the years, neither Herman Hoeh nor Raymond Cole subscribed to that orientation nor gave in to such feelings of offense.

The Differences

For all of the early similarities which would dominate most appraisals, Herman Hoeh and Raymond Cole actually differed in ways that would become more and more pronounced as the years unfolded.

First, in spite of being mild in demeanor and personal expression, Herman Hoeh was very motivated to make a splash as a writer, and to bring his scholarly abilities to the fore. He had ideas,

A Tale of Two Students

and he yearned for those ideas to become part of that visible work which was growing under Mr. Armstrong. Again, let Mr. Armstrong provide that perspective:

But 1951 was the year that produced the first "fruits" of the new college.

In April of that year we began the first activity toward an enlarged PLAIN TRUTH. I was still unwilling to publish in *The* PLAIN TRUTH, articles written by students. Yet something had to be done.

Herman Hoeh had submitted a few articles for *The* PLAIN TRUTH, but none had been used. They were not written in what I termed "Plain Truth STYLE." Yet young Mr. Hoeh did not give up. Every month or so another manuscript was handed to me. . . .

I mentioned, a while back, that Herman Hoeh had turned in to me a number of articles, before any were published. Shortly before we began the GOOD NEWS, in April, 1951, I began to realize that Mr. Hoeh showed considerable promise as a writer and editor. Even though I never published them, he persisted in writing articles. But they simply were not written in what I called PLAIN TRUTH *style*.

So one day—it must have been February or March, in 1951, I stopped him beside my car, parked between the Library and the Administration buildings. Possibly he was handing me another manuscript just as I was about to leave in my car.

"Herman," I said, "I have only a few moments' time—but let's see if I can explain to you the PLAIN TRUTH *style* of writing." . . .

I probably did not devote more than five or ten minutes to the explanation. But that alert and scholarly mind of Herman Hoeh's grasped immediately the style. He began to examine a number of my articles from a new angle. He captured the method. He began to write in *The* PLAIN TRUTH style! ("The Autobiography of Herbert W. Armstrong," *The Plain Truth*, January 1964, pp. 9, 11–12)

Raymond Cole, by contrast, presented no such inclination to pursue a particular personal, predetermined role, but left that to Mr. Armstrong's judgment. He, too, would eventually contribute some few articles to *The Good News* and *The Plain Truth* magazines, but very few over the ensuing years. Instead, Raymond Cole's long-term role would be defined by filling *immediate necessities* of the growing church. Another statement by Mr. Armstrong concerning events in autumn, 1950, will help capture this early trend:

> That school year Raymond Cole, one of the four pioneer students, was student-body president. However, the local churches I had left up in Oregon, at Eugene and Portland, these years without a Pastor, were in serious need of leadership. And so in February, 1951, we sent Mr. Cole to Oregon to pastor and revive the flock. This was the very first beginning of a ministry produced by Ambassador College. After three and a half years at Ambassador College, Mr. Cole was able to repair the situation in Oregon, and start building up again.
>
> Since we had operated on half-schedule in the 1948-49 year, it had been made virtually impossible for students to graduate in four years. Mr. Cole returned to Pasadena in August, 1951, and graduated in 1952, along with our son Dick. However, by taking a heavier-than-normal load the last two years, both Herman Hoeh and Betty Bates graduated in June, 1951—completing their college work in four years ("The Autobiography of Herbert W. Armstrong," *The Plain Truth*, November 1963, p. 15).

Raymond Cole provides more details about this church crisis of 1951, which required attention outside of Ambassador College. It actually involved a serious dispute about one of the Radio Church of God's fundamental doctrines concerning observance of the Holy Day

A TALE OF TWO STUDENTS   321

of Pentecost. In the year 1999, two years before his death, Raymond Cole wrote this:

> Although the subject of Pentecost had become sensitive and divisive even in the 1940s the intensity of the subject was growing in the latter '40s and was also geographically spreading. Unrest had developed in as diverse areas as San Antonio, Texas; Wichita, Kansas; Portland, Oregon; Seattle, Washington; as well as Eugene, Oregon. Satan was intensely at work. He hated the real truth about Pentecost. An alarming effort was made to destroy the fledgling church before trained and loyal ministers could be sent to the growing number of areas across the United States where the Truth was taking root. For a number of reasons, I was chosen by Mr. Armstrong, even before ordination, to go out to these troubled areas and quell the unrest about Pentecost. These defensive measures took me to Portland, Oregon for a year—prior to graduation. My matriculation from college was postponed for one year (*An Open Letter From Raymond C. Cole*, December 1999).

At this point, it is important to remember that Raymond Cole was the individual entrusted by Mr. Armstrong, even though he was only twenty-five years old and not officially "ordained," to tackle this serious threat to the church and to quell the unrest. It was a very distinct assignment from that which was given to Herman Hoeh:

> Consequently, in April, 1951, *The* GOOD NEWS was re-born!
> Now, for the first time, our students began to make active contributions to the activities of this expanding Work!
> That same year, Herman Hoeh—our "straight-A" student—began to remove some of the teaching load from my shoulders, by assisting in the teaching of the Bible courses.
> Also, for several months during 1951, Raymond Cole acted as Pastor of the church at Portland, giving it a spiritual

"shot in the arm" ("The Autobiography of Herbert W. Armstrong," *The Plain Truth*, January 1964, p. 10).

FUTURE ROLES ARE SET

What is described here is the beginning of two very distinct roles that these young men would begin to fill within the church over ensuing years. Both men became *Evangelists*—a level "second in command" under Mr. Armstrong. But Herman Hoeh became immediately involved in teaching at Ambassador College and writing for the church publications. He would be the first to complete a Ph.D. in theology at Ambassador College, would become known as the "church scholar," and would emerge as one of the most visible and popular personalities within the Radio Church of God. His scholarly *backing* would be counted upon to give "legitimacy" to Herbert Armstrong's doctrinal teachings over time.

Raymond Cole, by contrast, would be used much more *in the background* of that great work, continuing to be assigned by Mr. Armstrong to handle *immediate and challenging needs* of an organization adding *thirty percent* to its membership on average *each year* through all of the 1950s and most of the 1960s. It is one thing to have a successful radio and print operation that is generating great response. It is quite another to successfully *manage* the influx of those new members and actually provide an effective structure for their care and nurture. Raymond Cole would spend most of his career with the sheep—in "field operations"—as a Regional Director in various areas of the country, away from "Headquarters" in Pasadena. His *name* would be recognized by many, but he would be largely "unknown" by most personally, except for those with whom he had worked and served directly. (In fact, his younger brother, Wayne Cole, would become better known to the church in time, being assigned ultimately to more visible roles, as was Herman Hoeh.)

In addition, because of the practical building skills he had learned from his father as a youth, Raymond Cole would also be assigned by Mr. Armstrong to a monumental, long-term

A Tale of Two Students

construction project for the church: to develop large-scale, church-owned convention properties and facilities to accommodate the exploding attendance each year at the annual fall Feast of Tabernacles assemblies. It became impractical and unwieldy for even the most sophisticated commercial convention operators in the largest cities to accommodate over ten thousand attendees in multiple sites around North America for eight days each year. So even as Mr. Armstrong chose to take advantage of economies of scale to start his own college, his own printing press (the Ambassador College Press becoming one of the largest on the West Coast during the 1960s), so, too, he met this daunting challenge of convention planning by buying property across the United States and Canada and building his own self-contained infrastructure. The scholarly-minded Raymond Cole would probably never have predicted the direction of his activities to help the church through those dramatic years. But even as Herman Hoeh devoted his all to fulfill his visible and more "glamourous" role, so Raymond Cole willingly gave his all to his own calling—in perhaps the more obscure, but equally critical role—in the background of that unique and incredible work.

The stage had been set; the individual players had become icons in their respective roles through two decades of incredible growth and organizational success. But the early 1970s would see the beginning of serious cracks in that institutional armor, and no one would be left unaffected. The divergent choices made by Herman Hoeh and Raymond Cole during those very volatile years would mirror the very same tug-of-war faced by every other member—sooner or later—and the outcome of those choices would reveal a previously hidden, deep-seated ideology concerning Herbert Armstrong and his work.

1972–1974—The Foundation Cracks

Between 1972 and 1974, the first major rift would occur to divide Herman Hoeh and Raymond Cole between two competing and starkly contrasting philosophical camps. Until that time, the two men had been united in their mutual support and defense of Herbert Armstrong and his rulings as Pastor General of the Worldwide Church of God. There had certainly been threats to the church in previous decades, but those had always been relatively minor by comparison. Members would leave, and even some ministers would choose to separate. But since the church was growing at an average rate of thirty percent each year (through 1968), any potential repercussions from defections were always mitigated by the greater influx of new members. For many years that church had *real momentum*. And sustained momentum is a wonderful balm to mask organizational weaknesses.

But by the early 1970s, that momentum had petered out. Notice Mr. Armstrong's admission in 1972:

> Yesterday the Budget Committee met to set the budget for the coming year, 1973. God's Work is a GROWING Work. It is geared to a pattern of CONTINUAL GROWTH. We cannot go on to successfully COMPLETE the Great Commission the living Christ is carrying on through us, UNLESS we do have a real healthy INCREASE in income year by year. For 35 years that increase was approximately 30% year by year. The increase is far short of that this year -- has been for three or four years (*Co-Worker Letter*, November 2, 1972).

Why such a reverse by 1972? Remember that the church had been conditioned by the ministry *for years* to expect that the very last-day prophecies of the Bible concerning the Second Coming of Jesus Christ "might possibly" be fulfilled between 1972 and 1975. When that time period arrived and it became apparent that events in the world did not make those prognostications realistic, a great part of the church became very disappointed, and even worse, restless. Restless, because many members had been conforming to certain doctrines of the church that were very difficult to bear, especially the prohibition against marriage for one who was previously divorced. As long as they believed that Jesus Christ would return "soon," they tolerated this burden as a necessary sacrifice in order to be spared prophesied cataclysmic tribulation and the loss of ultimate salvation. But once any real hope of a "quick end" to their physical toil in this world had been dashed, a sudden *priority shift* emerged to make their current lives "more bearable" within the church. If time was going on after all, many demanded the right to marry whom they chose. The great new growth in membership ended, and the wider undercurrents of unrest became most ominous to a ministry now facing the fruits of the disappointment they themselves had engendered through ill-advised prognostications about "the last days."

The sudden reality of this loss of new growth caused the whole ministry to sit up and take notice. Why had the momentum ceased? Where would the church go from here? What would happen if this was not just a temporary setback? What if total membership actually started to shrink? As Mr. Armstrong stated, the budget of the church for decades was "geared" toward having, not just modest annual growth, but *significant* growth in contributions to fund an expanding work. The idea of stagnation, let alone contraction, was appalling.

Calls for change became loud and persistent. Something must be done, but what? Highly-placed ministers, especially Mr. Armstrong's own son, Garner Ted Armstrong, began to champion the relaxation of certain "hard-line" doctrines of the church to calm the restlessness of the laity. Suffice it to say here that the battle lines became drawn between two camps within the ministry: one defending the long-held doctrines of the church, and the other advocating a progressive "recalibration" of teachings to make it more palatable for members to remain loyal, preserving their goodwill (a.k.a. financial support). Many of these "liberal" ministers had secretly harbored contrary views about some of Mr. Armstrong's doctrines for years (and admitted so years later in their personal writings). But these "positions" could never gain any traction during the 1960s because Mr. Armstrong was *adamant* in defending his original teachings, including the teaching condemning divorce and remarriage in the church. So those with progressive doctrinal views had to "lay low" and bide their time. The crisis of the early 1970s provided the opportunity they had been waiting for. Before he died in 1986, Mr. Armstrong wrote retrospectively about that volatile time period, and this is how he assessed *the root cause* of the decline in church growth:

> Now a recap of what has happened to the Church and its work.
>
> God had blessed His Church with an unprecedented approximate increase of 30 percent per year for 35 years. As these liberals began gaining more and more control God removed His blessing. I have often said that God blesses us as we please Him. During these liberal years in the 1970s, the income virtually stagnated. In 1974 the Church experienced a 1.6 percent decrease in income under 1973, the first negative growth in the Church's history. It fell another 4.8 percent the following year (*The Worldwide News—Special Edition*, June 24, 1985, p. 3).

HERMAN HOEH AND RAYMOND COLE TAKE SIDES

Where did Herman Hoeh and Raymond Cole fall philosophically during these volatile years? They both were considered conservative "old timers," and therefore neither was part of the progressive camp. Mr. Herbert Armstrong himself was viewed by these progressives as an obstacle to their "new truths," and stodgy lieutenants like Herman Hoeh and Raymond Cole were seen as strengthening him *to remain recalcitrant* against any change. Garner Ted Armstrong and his contingent were desperately seeking a way to get his father's approval for the changes they considered imperative. Yet, when the doctrinal debates finally came to a head in 1974, Raymond Cole and Herman Hoeh would wind up on opposing sides.

What follows is an accounting of events as testified by Raymond Cole and others who were involved with the 1974 doctrinal committee in Pasadena, CA, summarized from an article entitled, *The Doctrine of Divorce and Remarriage—How and Why It Was Changed* (Church of God, The Eternal, 1975, pp. 5–6).

A TALE OF TWO STUDENTS   327

Recall that Herman Hoeh had made his reputation as a serious scholar since his days in Ambassador College. Having been awarded a doctoral degree in religion by Mr. Armstrong in the early 1960s, Dr. Hoeh emerged very early as the church's most respected "biblical authority." Although the fundamental teaching on major doctrines had emanated from Herbert Armstrong, it was Dr. Herman Hoeh who added *technical credibility* to many of them through his skill in research and exegesis. Mr. Armstrong had come to value highly and lean upon Herman Hoeh to provide scholarly defense for the most controversial teachings, including the marriage doctrine. And even through March 1974, Herman Hoeh had held firm in stating that, biblically, there was *no possible justification* for such a change. In this, he and Raymond Cole were much agreed.

By early 1974, Mr. Armstrong was under enormous pressure. He was being told by senior ministers that many members were withholding tithes and offerings, waiting for the "relaxation" of specific teachings, especially the marriage doctrine. The income was indeed down drastically. Membership had fallen by 1.4%—the first such loss in church history. As Executive Vice President, his son, Garner Ted Armstrong, and his hand-picked "Doctrinal Committee" were clamoring for the changes that would ease this pressure and save the day. Yet it appeared Mr. Armstrong was still not willing to compromise his principles, seeing no biblical evidence whatsoever to justify the changes being advocated. How convenient it would be if someone discovered a "legitimate" new argument to permit members to divorce and remarry, but there simply was none. That is, not until Dr. Herman Hoeh provided the solution.

Through March 1974, members of the Doctrinal Committee continued to wrack their collective brains to come up with some "credible" technical argument that would convince Mr. Armstrong to make the change. Since argumentation over the meaning of Greek and Hebrew words was not working, they had to come up with a better ploy. In mid-April, while the committee was toying with a new—but even weaker—plan, Herman Hoeh unexpectedly provided them the "magic bullet" they had been waiting for. This scintillating new argument was so clever, it provided exactly the kind of logic that would appeal to Mr. Armstrong and give him cover for approving the change. But most importantly, it would relieve the increasing pressure upon ministry and laity alike, which presumably threatened to destroy the whole church.

When asked afterwards by another prominent minister why he made such an about-face in his position, Herman Hoeh stated, "Why, I never knew what Mr. Armstrong wanted. When I knew, I gave it to him." In other words, once he understood that Mr. Armstrong (even under great duress) would actually *relish* an immediate solution to the problem, Dr. Hoeh was very willing to feed the Doctrinal Committee a clever technical argument to make it happen. And that is just what he did.

Less than two weeks later, near the beginning of May, a clandestine group of evangelists led by Garner Ted Armstrong appeared at his father's home one evening to lay out their new "evidence" for a change in the marriage doctrine. Discovering that Herman Hoeh was the source of this "new truth" was actually a major selling point to Mr. Armstrong. The men left that night with "a sell," and the announcement of a major revision of church doctrine was delivered days later at the annual Ministerial Conference.

How did Raymond Cole react? Here are his own words on the matter:

> For the conference, nearly every minister, elder, and even some lead men in church areas had been flown into Pasadena. Something definitely was in the making. There were, according to my best recall, about 700 men and their wives present for the opening session. The first order of business was the dedication of the newly constructed Ambassador College Auditorium. With these celebratory events out of the way, the conference quickly turned sober and anticipatory. Nearly everyone was deeply concerned about projected doctrinal decisions. The anticipated day came. Mr. H. W. Armstrong began attempting to explain the proposed change for the doctrine of divorce and remarriage.

A Tale of Two Students   329

He could not do it. He quickly yielded the floor to his son. You are aware of the information distributed. Succinctly, the conclusion was that many marriages were never marriages and that divorce was acceptable.

To say the least, I was stunned. The preparatory work of the committee had already been written, duplicated, and distributed to all the ministers with the exception of myself. I heard the conclusion for the first time in that fateful meeting. So shocked was I that I experienced one of the severest headaches of my life—for some three days. It was incredulous. I could not believe my ears. The thought flashed through my mind, "Now nothing will be restrained from them." The way was paved. Doctrine after doctrine will fall at the hands of those who had no love for the truth. I knew my days within Worldwide Church of God were limited (*An Open Letter From Raymond C. Cole*, December 1999).

By the end of that same year, because he refused to go along with this and other changes to long-held doctrines—even though approved by his beloved mentor and Pastor General, Herbert Armstrong—Raymond Cole was put out of the church, having his ministerial credentials in the Worldwide Church of God officially revoked. Ironically, it was Herman Hoeh who was sent to visit Raymond Cole at his home in Coquille, Oregon, in November 1974 to assess where he stood, and whether there was a chance he might "come around" and accept the new church doctrines after all. Herman Hoeh was accompanied on that visit by another senior minister, Raymond McNair (who was likewise one of the earliest graduates of Ambassador College and ordained by Mr. Armstrong—along with Herman Hoeh and Raymond Cole—in 1952). Even after the dust had settled for several months since the May announcement, Raymond Cole was adamant that he would never accept or teach those "perverted" new doctrines. Based upon that face-to-face interchange between two old friends, the die was cast.

330   A PECULIAR TREASURE

Herman Hoeh, by comparison, survived and thrived during those volatile times, negotiating his way through the political minefields between the "liberal" and "conservative" camps, and preserving his reputation among all as the church's most scholarly authority.

If Herman Hoeh and Raymond Cole had had so much in common, especially their joint mentorship under Mr. Armstrong through the early years of the church and Ambassador College, how and why would they have taken such different paths in 1974? The answer to that question may be found in another part of the early history we have not yet examined. Let us go back now and look a little deeper into some very influential and telling events that occurred in the late 1940s.

YOUTHFUL CONTENTIONS WITH HERBERT ARMSTRONG

What was not previously mentioned is that both Herman Hoeh and Raymond Cole had *personal contentions* with Mr. Armstrong as young men which offer additional insight into their strengths and weaknesses, and which events certainly came to inform their later choices.

First, Mr. Armstrong reveals an early story about Herman Hoeh that very few today have ever heard:

> Since I could do no other, I was forced to choose instructors trained in the prevailing system of education. But I sought those of outstanding qualifications and adequate degrees. I wanted the best!
>
> There was the woman professor of English. She had at least two Ph. Ds.—some eight degrees altogether. This surely sounded like the best. She had taught many years in India. I did not know, when Mr. Dillon and I employed her, that she was filled and saturated with Hindu philosophies, occultism, and eastern beliefs. She highly respected insects—especially butterflies.
>
> Professor Mauler-Hiennecey frequently jested with her.

A Tale of Two Students

331

"Well," he would say, "what have you decided this morning you are going to be in your next life—a butterfly, bed bug, or beetle?"

Soon I found that our English professor was introducing all kinds of Hindu or Indian expressions and philosophies into her teaching. Now it so happened that the 18-year-old Herman Hoeh had begun, prior to coming to college, to delve into occultism. It had pricked his curiosity. And he had a scholarly mind with a good degree of intellectual curiosity. This interest in the direction of occultism disturbed me greatly.

I realized at once that this young man was a very important potential, but still immature and inclined to get off balance on some tangent, unless taught the necessity of sound balance. I went immediately to work on this problem. I now had to combat both his intellectual interest, and the influence of our new English professor.

I had a very serious talk with Mr. Hoeh. I did not try to refute or even discredit occultism or mystic Indian teachings. I was afraid this might drive him to it the more. Instead I reasoned that it was better to take up one field of study at a time. I tried to show him that what I was going to teach him at Ambassador College was BASIC knowledge—that, to lay his researches into the occult fields on the shelf for the time being, and acquire this FOUNDATION of knowledge would be the proper *preparation* preliminary to his study of the mystic fields.

In other words, I did not ask him *not* to delve into this thought, but tried to persuade him to arrange a time-order system in his study.

"And since you have now enrolled at Ambassador College," I reasoned, "why not put this first, now you are here, and then take that up *later?*"

He agreed. And thus, instead of getting off balance prior to full mental maturity, I was able to steer Herman Hoeh on the track of intellectual BALANCE and sound-mindedness. He

332   A PECULIAR TREASURE

had been gifted with an extraordinarily intellectual mind.
Now it was being anchored to the course of sound balance
and right UNDERSTANDING. And *what an asset it has become
to God's Work!* ("The Autobiography of Herbert W.
Armstrong," *The Plain Truth*, July 1963, p. 14)

This enlightening story about the young Herman Hoeh is found
only in the *original version* of the "The Autobiography of Herbert W.
Armstrong" written in serial form in *The Plain Truth*, and was never
included in the book version later published in 1973, and certainly
not the further revision of 1986. One might be led to wonder why.
Was it the fact that Herman Hoeh had editorial authority over the
republishing of these very works through the 1970s and wished to
de-emphasize this potentially embarrassing personal history? We
cannot say.   But what is fact is that Mr. Armstrong's
original—unabridged—accounts of these events cannot be found in
the repackaged versions distributed by the church during the 1970s
and later.

In any case, we learn that Herman Hoeh had been fascinated
with the occult and with Eastern religion, but to Mr. Armstrong's
understanding, he had renounced all such leanings through his
studies at Ambassador College. Notice Mr. Armstrong's comments
at the end of the story, providing another contrast between these two
young students:

As time went on, it became evident to both Raymond Cole
and Herman Hoeh that our English professor was not at all
in harmony with the real objectives of Ambassador College.
She expressed later in the year that she still felt there was
some hope for Mr. Hoeh, but she had given Mr. Cole up as
hopeless. However, Mr. Hoeh stuck loyally to his agreement
to pursue his studies into the Bible under me first. So he
proved hopeless, too, for her.

Along about March in that school year, Mr. Hoeh and Mr.
Cole came to me together about this instructor. Mr. Hoeh
reported that she had told him she was *sent* to Ambassador

A TALE OF TWO STUDENTS

College by invisible forces in the east, for the purpose of *destroying* the college before it could get fairly started—and that she had said that if she could have just six more weeks' time, "there won't be a grease-spot left of this college."

So that was one of the oppositions from within, at the outset of the college ("The Autobiography of Herbert W. Armstrong," *The Plain Truth*, July 1963, p. 14).

So Raymond Cole apparently had no interest whatsoever in Eastern religion and was considered "hopeless" by this Hindu professor, while Herman Hoeh had shown "some hope" which had nonetheless been dashed by the aggressive influence of Herbert Armstrong.

But Raymond Cole himself had a much more prickly contention with Mr. Armstrong during that same time period, which likewise tells us much about the man. His problem was not one of dabbling with Eastern religions alongside the Bible, but one of coming to grips with *the real source* of all spiritual Truth. What follows is Raymond Cole's own description of his early indoctrination concerning Passover, and the volatile episodes with Mr. Armstrong that led to his changing his whole orientation toward Bible truth:

My future maternal grandfather and his brother for unusual reasons became aggressively interested in the Bible at a very young age. As a result of their study they became aware of the significance of Palestine in the scheme of world affairs. They left their parents, and home state of Michigan and traveled to Palestine—while the country was still a mandate of Great Britain. Shortly after arrival in Palestine my grandfather-to-be became acquainted with the daughter of a British journalist.

The two boys continued their Biblical endeavor. They became acquainted with a number of Jewish religious bodies. One, the Essenes, had a considerable influence upon their thinking. That particular group with whom they associated kept "the Passover" on the night of the 15th of the first month instead of on the 14th. They were quite strongly convinced. Consequently, after my grandfather, his new bride, and his brother returned to the United States they strongly believed and continued to keep "Passover" on the night of the 15th. In the process of time I, too, was indoctrinated with the same concept. . . .

Now a point made earlier comes into play. College was going well. I thought I was intensely satisfied. But, by the spring of 1948, I was facing the approach of Passover. Mr. Armstrong being aware of the family belief, made a gentle approach in attempting to teach me the error of "observing Passover" on the 15th. After a number of rather lengthy discussions on the subject, Mr. Armstrong felt that a truce was best for that year. But the issue was not yet settled. I returned to college in the fall of 1948. The spring of 1949, bringing Passover, inevitably came. That year the subject took on a different dimension. On many occasions Mr. Armstrong had vociferously insisted that God revealed to him the truth he was preaching.

A circumstance about which I am not proud and for which I apologized to Mr. H. W. Armstrong, and repented before God, perhaps will help some to understand the gravity of this matter of divine revelation. I was very much technically oriented. I wanted facts. Logic must rule. Because of these fundamental differences in philosophy, conflict loomed large. Mr. Armstrong was emphatically insisting that God had revealed His truths to him. I, on the other hand, wanted to see tangible and technical proof. The conflict all too frequently took on an ugly dimension. Both of us being very aggressive and vocal, our conversations became strained and cutting. For days Mr. Armstrong continually insisted God had revealed to him that which he was preaching. My concepts respecting Passover—the 14th or

15th, the 31 A.D. issue and other less significant subjects—being stripped away, I was left with a single decision to make. Was I going to protect the self, or was I willing to accept in faith and absolute conviction that which had been demonstrated—divine revelation. One of the greatest psychological releases I have ever experienced came at the moment when I decided Mr. Armstrong was right—God reveals His Truth to a chosen servant. It, therefore, is absolute and cannot change. Now can you understand why I was so troubled by the changes which constituted the apostasy of 1972–74? (*An Open Letter From Raymond C. Cole*, December 1999)

Indeed, this helps explain very well why Raymond Cole and Herman Hoeh each approached the crisis of 1974—twenty-five years later—in very different ways. Many today will argue that the young Raymond Cole was foolish to allow Herbert Armstrong to *bully him* into abandoning his commitment to "scholarly proof" for every biblical teaching, replacing it instead with "blind faith in a man." But that is beside the point at this juncture. Given that this transformational experience *did take place*—but only for *one* of these young students and not the other—it helps answer why these two with so much in common took very divergent paths under pressure years later.

As we saw, Herman Hoeh retained a devotion to *technical human scholarship* as his underlying confidence, while Raymond Cole traded this very same reverence for scholarship for belief in *the invisible operation of God through the divine inspiration of a chosen servant.* Furthermore, it would appear that the ideological "rightness" of any technical doctrine was less important to Herman Hoeh than to Raymond Cole, given Mr. Hoeh's willingness in 1974 to "change sides" concerning doctrine if it helped to solve a momentary physical crisis in the church.

What appears to be true is that Herman Hoeh manifested a *personal devotion* to Herbert Armstrong, *the man*. If Herbert Armstrong insisted rigidly upon defending a teaching as having come

336   A PECULIAR TREASURE

to him by God's divine inspiration, Herman Hoeh would gladly
provide the technical "Bible proof" to make that position credible
within scholarly circles. But if Mr. Armstrong changed his mind for
whatever reason, Dr. Hoeh was equally willing to rework the
technical exegesis to support the new doctrinal position. Once he
knew what Mr. Armstrong wanted, he was there like a *Bible scholar
for hire* to provide the "evidence" to give that position legitimacy.

Raymond Cole, by comparison, became *an ideological zealot*,
convinced that all Truth is absolute and comes by the specific and
purposeful inspiration of God. He believed that God works through
a hand-picked servant to reveal that absolute Truth, and that
Herbert Armstrong was such an instrument in the twentieth century.
Ironically, even though Raymond Cole and Herman Hoeh had vastly
different ideas about *the source of spiritual Truth*, both of these men
were walking *side-by-side* in support of their mutual mentor as long
as Mr. Armstrong held firm to his original convictions about
doctrine. This was the case for over twenty-five years. On the
surface, it would have appeared to most that both men were devout
"Armstrongites."

But here is the twist: Unlike Herman Hoeh, Raymond Cole did
not believe Herbert Armstrong had the authority of God to change
doctrine. It was Herbert Armstrong who had *hammered that into
his young mind* by claiming the authority of Jesus Christ for the
things he was teaching! And so Raymond Cole came to believe
strongly that no man—not even a *bona fide* apostle of God—has
authority to change doctrines already revealed, because Truth comes
from Jesus Christ, and Christ is absolutely dependable in giving real
Truth, when it is given at all. Here is how he summarized that
conviction:

> After much reading, studying, and praying I had accepted
> the idea of divine revelation. And, though never specifically
> discussed, the concept of revealed Truth that could never be
> changed or altered took on a special meaning to me. I lived
> with the absolute conviction that the Truth had been given to
> him [Herbert Armstrong] and that it could not, nor ever

A TALE OF TWO STUDENTS

337

would, be changed. From my study of God's Word I knew that revealed Truth was absolute (*An Open Letter From Raymond C. Cole*, December 1999).

It was that very different orientation toward spiritual Truth that led to the divergent choices of Herman Hoeh and Raymond Cole in 1974. While Herman Hoeh proved his loyalty to *the man*—no matter what edicts he made concerning doctrine—Raymond Cole proved "disloyal" to the man, by choosing his conviction about *doctrinal certainty* over any *change of expediency*, even when the change came from his beloved mentor whom he believed was God's instrument on earth.

The Lasting Critical Dynamic

Some might view this story as an interesting little piece of church history, but not much more. They would be wrong. As mentioned before, the *underlying dynamic* that manifested in the pressure cooker of the 1974 crisis within the Worldwide Church of God is *the very same one* that would play out again twenty years later, in 1994. The only difference is, by then, Mr. Armstrong was dead and the newest doctrinal changes were being implemented by a successive Pastor General.

At the time Herbert Armstrong died in January 1986, Raymond Cole was still leading a small remnant group which had formed in early 1975, and was holding fast to the same doctrines first taught by Mr. Armstrong so many years before, including the sanctity of marriage. It is ironic indeed that although vilified by his former ministerial colleagues and considered a traitor by Mr. Armstrong himself, Raymond Cole refused to make any derogatory comments in return, believing yet that although Mr. Armstrong had erred in approving changes to doctrine at the behest of the liberals, he was still due respect as the man through whom God had made that priceless Way of Life available to all during the twentieth century.

Conversely, in January 1986, Herman Hoeh was still a highly-respected Evangelist within the WCG, absolutely loyal to his mentor till the end. He had survived the purge of 1978, when Garner Ted Armstrong—along with other high-ranking "liberal" ministers—was finally put out of the church by his father. He thrived during the days of the church legal problems with the State of California, and the "*back on track*" years when some of the original "conservative" doctrines (like avoidance of makeup for women) were re-instituted, changed, and then changed back again. He was there to provide the technical justification for every doctrinal position at every moment, whatever it might be, as long as he knew what Mr. Armstrong wanted.

After Mr. Armstrong's death, his appointed successor, Joseph Tkach, Sr., began to change more and more of the church teachings over the ensuing years. By 1994, the heart of Herbert Armstrong's fundamental teachings had been virtually gutted, and many of the long-time ministers who had been loyal to Mr. Armstrong refused to tolerate any more. You see, even though Mr. Armstrong had appointed Joseph Tkach—and he theoretically carried *the very same authority* as Pastor General of *God's true Church* as had Mr. Armstrong himself—recognition of that authority obviously had its practical limits. Somehow, the idea of the Pastor General being able to change major doctrines (like Mr. Armstrong had begun to exercise in 1974) was tolerated only to a certain point. When the new man began to do away with the seventh-day Sabbath, the annual Holy Days, and to embrace many Protestant doctrines as well, the conservative ministers finally balked. Refusing to tolerate these changes in doctrine, they were forced out of the Worldwide Church of God and began to minister to brethren who likewise loved the original doctrines and refused to accept these new changes.

Oh, wait a minute! Does that not sound familiar? Where have we heard about a long-time minister of the church who refused in conscience to accept changes to major doctrines, rejecting the notion that any man—even the Pastor General, under God—had such authority? Yes indeed, it was 1974 all over again! But this time, the very same ministers who had labeled Raymond Cole as a traitor for defying the authority of "God's chosen servant" by rejecting strange new doctrines, *were now themselves* defying "God's chosen servant"—Joseph Tkach—in order to avoid accepting strange new doctrines! Amazing.

Of course, they crafted their explanation around the premise that Herbert Armstrong—as an apostle—had authority that his successor never possessed. But that is quite a stretch of credibility. The underlying fact is this: From the time that Herbert Armstrong began to give in to those who convinced him *under duress* to compromise the core teachings (which he even possibly still believed were true), a new precedent was set that would make it *impossible* over time to hold back the floods of radical change! In 1974, the die had been cast, and even though it took twenty years to play out completely, the overturning *of even one doctrine* on the basis of "human scholarship over divine revelation" was the beginning of the end.

The Final Chapter

But what about Herman Hoeh? What did he do during the late 1980s, after Mr. Armstrong's death, when his mentor's legacy was being systematically annulled by the new Pastor General, and the Worldwide Church of God was turning into a Protestant assembly? Surely he sided with one or more of the other senior ministers to defend Mr. Armstrong's teachings? No, actually. He remained loyal to the physical organization (which became a member of the National Association of Evangelicals and began to teach the Trinity—a doctrine that Herbert Armstrong despised), continued to remain above the political fray, and collected his pension from the church until he died in November 2004. From all of the eulogies written about him after his death, the common sentiment emphasized his kind, down-to-earth approach to people, his ability to avoid taking sides, and his relations with everyone on all sides, in spite of doctrinal disputes. Here is one particular eulogy written by Raymond McNair which is telling:

> Although I often spoke to Dr. Hoeh through the years, in more recent years (after I left the WCG in 1993), I did not have much contact with him. He would write or phone me

from time to time, and I did the same. But during the last few years, I had very little contact with him. So far as I know, he continued to work with the men at Headquarters during these times, apparently feeling that, for personal reasons, he did not need to sever his relationship with the leaders of the WCG, because of the sweeping doctrinal changes which the Church leaders were making at Pasadena. He seemed to want to maintain cordial relations with people in the various Churches of God (including many of the Church leaders), and would discuss various matters with some of them from time to time. [He also had close ties with some of the leaders of the Buddhist faith.]

This last bracketed statement by Mr. McNair is true, for Herman Hoeh was known from the 1970s on to have had ties with Buddhists of Southern California and in Thailand in connection with humanitarian projects. Members of the Wat Thai Temple of Los Angeles, California, attended his memorial service and eulogized him. Whether he had actually embraced any of their religious ideologies, or not, is much debated. But the history of his fascination with Eastern religion as a young man certainly has kept the speculation alive. What is fact is that he did not feel compelled to defend the teachings of Herbert Armstrong publicly in his later years. Perhaps he still believed them and practiced them privately, but his choices make this all very much a mystery.

Raymond Cole died in his home in September 2001. There was no doubt at all what he believed until his dying day. He remained adamant about the idea of Truth revealed by Jesus Christ alone through a chosen servant, and the conviction that Herbert Armstrong was indeed such a servant in this age. Although he was likewise known for his kindness and acts of personal sacrifice in dealing with individuals, his uncompromising defense of unalterable truths from the pulpit certainly cost him among those who demanded *compromise and conciliation* as the price for their favor.

Rigid adherence to uncompromising doctrinal "truths" at any cost, on one side; flexible elasticity and progressive evolution of beliefs on the other side. Two polar extremes that defined the divergent end points of two men who seemingly had begun together in unison. It is the very same set of forces that affected *everyone else* in that organization to a lesser or greater degree over the decades. Why were certain individuals originally attracted to Herbert Armstrong's brand of religion in the first place? When difficulties arose over time, why did so many react in such radically different ways? The history of Herman Hoeh and Raymond Cole together provides one of the best laboratories for isolating those hidden dynamic forces at play.

PART V

IF IT WAS GOD'S *PECULIAR TREASURE*,
WHERE IS IT TODAY?

CHAPTER EIGHTEEN
CURRENT STATE OF HIS LEGACY

By the time Herbert Armstrong died in 1986, rather than having *solidified* the church foundation to provide *a durable platform* for preserving his doctrines and convictions, the stage had been set instead for *even more volatile changes* which would ultimately tear that church apart before the next decade was out.

After so much turmoil over so many decades, where does that church stand today? What follows is a generalized snapshot of the current state of *Armstrongism* in the early twenty-first century. (Please note that although "Armstrongism" is considered by many to be a derogatory term, it is used here merely to identify the movement at large, as viewed from the perspective of the outside world.)

WHERE DID THE CHURCH GO?

Because the past writings of Herbert Armstrong are readily available and easy to stumble upon today—especially on the internet—new generations of Bible students are still discovering them for the first time. But what a shock when they seek to contact the church that originally published all that material. What happened to the Worldwide Church of God? After some digging, they discover that there is no longer a church by that name, but rather a residual organization that was *renamed* Grace Communion International (GCI), in 2009. Upon further examination they find that this church embraces mainstream Protestant theology (it now is a member of the National Association of Evangelicals) and no longer supports the teachings of Herbert Armstrong in any way. Being moved to *reject* Protestant theology, these new students find that they have simply been led in a circle right back to where they began. If one desires affiliation with a church professing born-again

Trinitarianism and which abolishes the Law of God, why join GCI when there are dozens of local denominations in every town where such doctrines are promoted? OK then, so now what? Is there anyone else teaching what Herbert Armstrong describes in these fascinating books and articles?

Next, emerging onto the scene are other church names seemingly associated with the Worldwide Church of God and claiming Herbert Armstrong as their source of inspiration. But not just one or two churches: hundreds of them! What is all of this about? Begin to examine a few of the most prominent groups and it becomes even more confusing. At first blush, they seem to be very similar in beliefs, and they even portray themselves with a very similar style. Why then are they not all together in one fellowship?

Out of a single, dynamic and unified church under Herbert Armstrong, how did it ever come to this? Do any of these remnant groups have any potential legitimacy? Most of them claim to be "the one," to the exclusion of all others. How would one even begin to assess them? Perhaps the very fact of their *splintered confusion* is evidence that the whole concept of "Armstrongism" was a farce from the beginning. Maybe it thrived only as long as a "master svengali" pulled the puppet strings to promote and sustain the movement. Perhaps after Mr. Armstrong died, his whole theology collapsed under its own weight, finally having been exposed as one great unsustainable personality cult. These are the kinds of questions and considerations confronting potential converts, not to mention many thousands of confused former members.

For those who resist throwing up their hands and just walking away in disgust—because there is still something *just too compelling* about Armstrongism to escape its orbital pull—how could they even begin to proceed to sift through the current confusion?

A Demographic Snapshot

It would be much easier to catalogue all of the remnant fellowships spawned from the Worldwide Church of God over the

CURRENT STATE OF HIS LEGACY

last forty years if they would all just "stay put" for a while. But there is nothing remotely static about this collection of churches. While a certain percentage of them have remained fairly stable over time, many others have come and gone like ducks on a pond. New groups spring up continually, and former groups disappear just as rapidly. How many total groups are there today claiming some portion of "Armstrong doctrines"? In spite of the perpetual volatility, there still *seems* to remain at least three hundred registered groups.

A number of individuals have tried to create directories of the splinter groups during the last twenty years. Those lists are never accurate for very long (if ever). Grace Communion International once provided a directory on their website based upon information available to them back in 1997. That list included over one hundred registered churches. Within ten years, other online directories listed more than three hundred, even though some of those groups have website addresses that seem to have been suspended. With such a volatile life-cycle for many fellowships, the total number of groups that *ever once existed* or *may still exist* could be much greater. Note, too, that this does not include many small groups that have resisted public attention but still exist in some kind of organized structure within local areas.

The advent of the internet in the mid-1990s provided the first opportunity to begin capturing demographic information more readily. As groups began to use the internet to promote their "works," it became easier to find and document many of them. It is also interesting to note that the largest proliferation of new groups began to surface at the very same time that the internet began catching on—right after the Worldwide Church of God rejected the seventh-day Sabbath and openly embraced Protestant tenets in 1994. Prior to this time, the total number of breakaway groups (mostly formed in the 1970s) was relatively small and more easily identified. But after 1994 it was a very different story. Once the "mass exodus" from the Worldwide Church of God started that year, an explosion of new groups began appearing.

There are about twenty distinct groups which claim to have at least 300 or more members. The single largest of these claimed about 20,000 members until a few years ago, but internal strife caused a major split in 2011 which is still cascading. The next largest groups claim about 8,000, 6,000, and 4,000 members respectively. Below that, the next four in size claim anywhere from 1,000 to 2,000 members, but after that it quickly drops off to groups having between 300 and 500 members. Please note that all of these estimates are "self-reported" or anecdotal, which is anything but reliable. There is much incentive to appear stronger in numbers as a way to claim credibility as the *true heir* to Herbert Armstrong's legacy. It is also very likely that some of the *very same* people are being counted as members by multiple groups. There are many today who receive literature from multiple organizations and fellowship with various groups on a round-robin basis.

But for those who truly seek to evaluate the differences in ideology, is there any way to sort these groups into more manageable categories for classification? Most certainly. While many of them claim to be absolutely unique, there are specific ideologies and philosophies that engender natural sub-groupings. If you keep these *major identifiers* in mind, it becomes much easier to overcome the confusion and to make some sense of the current landscape.

What are some of these distinctive ideologies that permit us to make more sense of what is left of Armstrongism today?

GOVERNMENT AND INDIVIDUALISM

Perhaps the first, best way to identify a key philosophical difference between these remaining groups is to ask about their concept of church government. It is also something that most of them readily disclose. It is probably the most sensitive and charged topic among former members of the Worldwide Church of God, and also likely the catalyst that is most responsible for the proliferation of so many remnant groups to begin with.

Some defend the kind of *top-down government* that prevailed under Mr. Armstrong for fifty years. Others absolutely reject that "hierarchical" structure. From the inception of the Radio Church of God in 1934, Mr. Armstrong was never "subject" to a board of directors, but always held the authority to make every final decision unilaterally as the head (later confirmed under his title as Pastor General). These decisions included ecclesiastical as well as administrative judgments as sole leader of that physical organization. Most remnant groups today are either steadfast in supporting that same (or similar) structure, or else in repudiating it entirely. There is very little middle ground. So if one is personally adamant about church government from his own interpretation of the Bible—from either viewpoint—this is the first best litmus test which can be applied to begin to classify the remnant groups.

On one side are those who came to view "one man rule" as *the great evil* which destroyed the church. Within this category are those who had trusted *Mr. Armstrong himself* to wield such power, but no one else. If the man at the top is sincere and defends the doctrine, then such power in his hands is a good thing, they believe. But after Mr. Armstrong's death in 1986, that same unilateral power passed directly into the hands of a successor who did not share his predecessor's love of the doctrine. Within eight years, Joseph Tkach—followed by his son, Joseph Tkach, Jr.—repudiated the entire foundation of Armstrong doctrine, and because of the church's governmental structure, there was nothing anyone could do to stop it. No board had the power to veto the Pastor General's unilateral changes. Therefore, one of the major new ideologies emerging in the 1990s was the need for *a democratic governing board* at the top to prevent the possibility of repeating that same history. If a quorum of elected church elders was required to approve any major changes, then there would be some built-in protection against treacherous, unilateral actions.

By contrast, some of these new groups were started by men who defended the original governmental structure of the church, rejecting any form of democracy as being against biblical principles, no matter how well-intentioned. They have established themselves with authority over their new churches in a manner similar to Mr. Armstrong's example.

There are others who reject the former top-down structure for personal reasons. Having been victims of "abuse" by ministers in the parent organization who used their authority unkindly and unwisely, the whole concept of ministerial authority became anathema to many. While Mr. Armstrong was still alive, many labored under that *heavy-handed* administrative philosophy because they believed this was "God's Church," and to leave that church would be to leave God. However, they were accumulating progressively a closet full of resentments and hurt feelings because of the way they had been treated under that institutional hierarchy. The dam held in large part while Mr. Armstrong was still alive, but once those members who rejected the new Protestantism of the 1990s were forced out of the "new" WCG, the waters could be restrained no longer, and many newly-forming remnant groups decided to solve the *government problem* while they were at it. These groups go out of their way to advertise themselves as being more open and inclusive—sharing the ministerial stage with many individuals—and governing themselves with democratic policies. To them, "hierarchy" is a dirty word, and any top-down structure is totally incompatible with "servant-based" leadership.

Among hundreds of ministers of the former Worldwide Church of God who were forced out in order to preserve fundamental Armstrong teachings in the 1990s, there was no clear "heir apparent" for the laity to embrace. Many of these ministers therefore decided to stake their own claim to the mantle of *successor* and "hang out a shingle," set up shop, and begin to do business. What was the effect? Many of these long-term members of the parent church who had no other option than to "stay put," suddenly found themselves presented with *a whole new smorgasbord* of options. Close-held personal views about church government became—for many—the number-one criterion used for selecting a new fellowship. The "hierarchical top-downers" picked a group whose leader defended

CURRENT STATE OF HIS LEGACY   351

the "old" system, while those who resented ministerial authority in general exclaimed, "Never again!" and promptly chose a group that celebrated *individualism*.

THE EMERGENCE OF CHOICE

Note that the 1990s did not produce the first instances of this phenomenon within the Worldwide Church of God. Remnant groups had already begun to form—separate and apart from the parent body—from the early 1970s while Mr. Armstrong was still alive and leading the church. Those early traumas hinged upon doctrinal disputes as high-ranking ministers under Mr. Armstrong lined up either to preserve long-held teachings or else to "relax" them, according to either their liberal or conservative leanings. Some "liberals" left because they did not get sufficient changes fast enough, while other "conservatives" were forced out for their unwillingness to countenance *any change* to doctrines that they attributed to God's divine revelation. Mr. Armstrong began approving significant changes in 1974 to appease the liberals, especially his own son, Garner Ted Armstrong. Yet by 1978, that gulf in doctrinal ideology was still far too wide, and the son was finally forced out. While past breakaway groups had been relatively small and largely invisible to the public, once Garner Ted Armstrong used his public image to found a new church in 1978, for the very first time in church history there was a significant rival body to offer members *a choice* in fellowship. No longer was there only *one place* to go to practice some form of Armstrongism. The 1970s fostered *the first major fractures* that would ultimately turn into wide and gaping chasms twenty years later.

Ultimately, there evolved a marketplace for any and all viewpoints, so thousands divided themselves along ideological lines and picked a new fellowship according to their personal preferences. Never had these members within one, regimented parent body been handed so much *freedom to choose*.

Another consequence of having so many new fellowship choices was that many members inadvertently became *transients*. Where once they had been rooted so strongly in the parent church and unwilling to budge—no matter what adversity they experienced—after they endured *the first trauma of separation*, followed swiftly by *the liberation of choice*, it became much harder for many of them to ever put down solid roots again. Some certainly did so, but many lost their former willingness to tolerate *any level of negativity* that might arise (and is common within all organized fellowships). Become upset with any minister, laymember, doctrine, or administrative ruling? Simply decide to "vote with your feet" and separate once again. After all, why commit to one particular group and put up with its inevitable internal "people problems" when it is so easy just to pick up and move to another? With so many groups to choose from now, there is no need to grasp onto any single one like the sole-remaining life raft. And so "churning of membership" became a new reality among these remnant groups.

Today, it hardly requires any past celebrity recognition or ministerial credentials (such as Garner Ted Armstrong enjoyed) to start your own remnant church. Especially since the advent of the internet, all one needs is a low-budget website and the personal conviction that he (or she) has been called by God to "do a Work," and then it's *off to the races*! If a former minister—or even a laymember—of the church becomes disgruntled with his current fellowship, and if no other existing remnant group strikes his fancy, not to worry. Just start one of your own! This is precisely the mentality that has predominated since the breakup of the parent body and *freedom of choice* has been popularized. Over the last thirty years we have seen the *number of groups* growing in large part because of "splits from splits of splits." This does not imply at all that the total number of members practicing some form of Armstrongism is increasing, but more likely that the groups over time simply continue to splinter further and to divide the faithful into ever smaller fellowships. As a side note, if one cares at all about the *relative credibility* of the leader of a particular group he may be

CURRENT STATE OF HIS LEGACY

considering, examination of his *ordination history and resumé* under Herbert Armstrong and the Worldwide Church of God is another good test that might make a difference to some in classifying the remnants.

OPINIONS ABOUT THE PATRIARCH

Another key measure to help distinguish these hundreds of remnant fellowships is their individual view about Mr. Herbert Armstrong himself. Was he an apostle? If so, what does that imply? If not, what was his real contribution as a servant of God? And what influence, if any, does his legacy have in affecting future policies of the church? Evaluating how each remnant group answers these questions will highlight very strong distinctions in ideology.

On one side are those who believe Herbert Armstrong was an "apostle," which to them means that every decision he ever made—whether doctrinal or administrative—was backed up by God. Among some of these groups, a key test for membership is the requirement to pledge acceptance of Herbert Armstrong in this light. Some add the requirement of accepting that he was also the "last-day Elijah," fulfilling a specific prophetic office before the return of Jesus Christ. Although they would never admit it—and in fact resent the comparison—there is little difference between their view of Herbert Armstrong's scope of authority and that of the Pope within the Catholic Church. In both cases, they believe that a designated man has the power to "bind and loose" any doctrine or judgment, and that God will back it up absolutely. Common also to these particular fellowships are leaders who claim the same unlimited powers, now that they are the "successors" to Mr. Armstrong. If Mr. Armstrong was the modern-day Elijah, then the successor can be the modern-day Elisha, the prophet to whom the mantle was passed in antiquity. And along with that transfer passes all the authority of the predecessor, to bind and to loose with infallibility. Those leaders who add the claim of being a prophet likewise expand their authority to include making certified predictions about specifics of the future.

It is also not uncommon to hear some of these church leaders claim to be one of the *Two Witnesses* of the Book of Revelation (Revelation 11:3), or one of many other prophetic titles. Among some of the largest of the splinter groups with this general philosophy are ones attempting to duplicate everything Mr. Armstrong did. Mr. Armstrong began a college, so they begin colleges. Mr. Armstrong had a grand auditorium, so they seek to build one also. Mr. Armstrong sought to warn the world to fulfill Matthew 24:14 through radio, TV, and glossy print media , so they must likewise *take up the torch* to complete his work. On this extreme side of the equation are those groups whose works definitely resemble that of a "personality cult." The focus is on *a man* in some way, whether it be Herbert Armstrong or the current successor.

At the other extreme are fellowships that reject that Herbert Armstrong was an apostle, let alone a prophet. Their writing and speaking exudes an underlying animosity for him, which is ironic. Ironic, because they hold many key doctrines in their foundations that were unique to the ministry of Herbert Armstrong, although they are loath to admit it. For instance, they may preserve and teach the seven-thousand-year plan of God as depicted in the weekly Sabbath and annual Holy Days, as well as many aspects of the nature of God and man which made Herbert Armstrong stand out from all other religious figures. They especially are likely to believe and preach that the purpose for human creation is the hope of being born into the God Family—to become "God, as God is." That is a teaching found *in no other church* except the one formed under Herbert Armstrong. Yet these groups simultaneously claim that Herbert Armstrong was no true Bible scholar, that his teachings were not inspired by God at all, and that he merely assembled doctrines according to his personal whims of the moment. Leaders in many of these groups put much emphasis upon "credentials," pointing to superior education, degrees, and training as a confirmation of their access to "real truth." In the end, what it means is that they give themselves license to pick and choose what doctrines are valid, based upon their "superior" skills. Among these groups are leaders who are "doctors," and ones who write and teach as historical scholars. To them, any nuggets of truth Herbert Armstrong possessed, he acquired quite by accident, and these same truths would have been uncovered by more scholarly men sooner or later, with or without him. In essence, on this extreme side of the equation, the basis of the group's very existence derives from the work of Herbert Armstrong, but in actuality that patriarch is resented and despised. Fascinating.

JEWISH ROOTS MOVEMENT

Another major category that has emerged today is Messianic Judaism, or the Jewish Roots movement. A significant number of former members of the Worldwide Church of God have gravitated toward this philosophy, and in fact a number of the remnant groups forming out of that parent organization have embraced key concepts from it.

Their philosophy centers on preserving many of the customs and practices of Judaism while at the same time accepting Jesus Christ as the true Messiah, which traditional Judaism would never countenance. It is easy to understand why this pre-existing movement would have become so attractive to so many members of the Worldwide Church of God after it began to disintegrate. Armstrongism and Messianic Judaism share in common the belief that accepting Jesus Christ as Savior does not mean abolishing the "Law of God." So these "Christians" mutually keep the seventh-day Sabbath and the annual Holy Days of Leviticus 23. They both adhere to the laws of clean and unclean meats, and many other beliefs. But they differ very strongly in many other ways. Herbert Armstrong rejected the validity of many "Jewish customs" as being those which Christ condemned as "the commandments of men" (Mark 7:7). It is a distinction in defining what is part of God's *spiritual Law*, vs. *uninspired human tradition*. One prominently disputed teaching is the "Sacred Name." Many of these Jewish Roots groups believe that the only proper way to address the Creator is by His Hebrew name. It is interesting that Herbert Armstrong vociferously rejected this

356　　　　　　　　　　　　　　　　　　　　A PECULIAR TREASURE

teaching from the earliest years as being superstitious nonsense. That was a position that he held without wavering until his death (*The Worldwide News—Special Edition*, June 24, 1985). Therefore, former members of the WCG who eventually joined existing Sacred Name fellowships (or new groups with similar tenets begun by former WCG ministers), certainly had to repudiate many doctrines of Herbert Armstrong in order to do so.

TREATMENT OF THE CALENDAR

Another key teaching that has emerged to distinguish many remnant groups concerns the calendar. Which calendar has real legitimacy to tell us *which days* are God's intended annual Holy Days? Herbert Armstrong confirmed the legitimacy of the Jewish calendar as the single calendar inspired and preserved by God. He taught that the Jews were in error *in their use of that calendar* to assign the dates for holy observances (like Passover and Pentecost), but that the calendar itself was inspired and preserved in the very same way that God made sure to preserve the authentic books of the Bible and to bring them down through history.

Many of the splinter groups today choose to define themselves by their beliefs about God's calendar. It is a prominent point of distinction. In one camp are those who defend the Hebrew calendar used by Mr. Armstrong. This is probably still the most prevalent position. The Jewish Roots groups certainly agree on the validity of that calendar, but they often keep their holy days differently than did the WCG. Why? Because they disagree with Mr. Armstrong that the Jews were in error in their assignment of Passover and Pentecost. So they not only defend the calendar itself, but the authority of the Jews to *use* that calendar.

In the other camp, a number of new groups that formed from the WCG reject the Jewish calendar altogether in favor of their own creations. They assert that God never inspired "the Hillel calendar" at all, but that it likewise is one of those "commandments of men." They seek instead to document "the calendar God gave Moses," even

CURRENT STATE OF HIS LEGACY

357

though they hardly agree on exactly what that calendar is or how it should operate. Because of such heated disagreement on this particular topic and wide promulgation of so many unique calendar formulas, this single doctrinal dispute constitutes *a major cause* for the existence of so many different fellowships today. After all, one of the strongest bases for unity is observance of Sabbaths and Holy Days. Groups that cannot meet together on the same holy occasions can hardly be part of the same fellowship. Today, besides church government, one of the first questions one can ask to help categorize these groups is to clarify which calendar they use, and how they use it. It is interesting that for so many thousands who were first taught by Herbert Armstrong to begin keeping those "Jewish Sabbaths," since his death those Holy Days are being kept *on many different days in many different months*, according to a variety of customized calendar rules. It is another example of *newfound freedoms* and the smorgasbord of options confronting those who seek *to preserve—or to adopt*—some form of Armstrongism today.

STAY-AT-HOME ADHERENTS

Another very significant category within Armstrongism today includes those who are not part of any organized fellowship whatsoever. This is the segment of adherents that is least possible to quantify. They have no internet websites and seek to do no proselytizing "works." But they value many teachings of Herbert Armstrong and quietly practice them as best they can on their own.

The motivations for avoiding formal membership in any particular group are varied. For some, it relates to the church government issue. A significant number of former members are so "turned off" by authority and hierarchy issues in the "corporate churches" that they refuse ever to be part of one of them again as a matter of principle. That does not mean that they are not involved. There are many "floaters" who dabble with a number of different groups, listening to their recorded sermons and reading their articles (either by subscribing to multiple mailing lists or by anonymous consumption of website content). Some may attend the meetings of many different fellowships on Holy Days throughout the year, not as members, but as "visitors." During the fall festival of Tabernacles—which includes meetings on eight consecutive days—individuals in this category may "make the rounds" to several different groups that are hosting feast sites in the same general area. A common denominator of thought among individuals within this category is: 1) belief that God is not working through any one organized body today, so there is no necessity of "joining up" in order to please God; 2) belief that there are *snippets of truth* that can be gleaned from many different ministries, hence the sampling from a wide variety; and 3) belief that the individual has the unilateral power and prerogative to "sift and sort" what concepts have value and are to be kept versus what is to be discarded.

For others, the reason they are sitting at home is not because they are certain that God wants them to do so, but because they are simply confused about what they should do. For these, it is especially frustrating because they are hardly satisfied with the status quo. On one side, a nagging feeling makes them yearn to fellowship with others, especially to fulfill the "obligation" to appear before God on His commanded days. But on the other side, they are totally confused by the proliferation of so many groups out there, and unsure how even to begin to distinguish between them all. In that case, it is easier to "do nothing" than to wade into the swirling rapids of the river.

This is certainly not an exhaustive or even a scientific portrayal of the current state of that church, but it should provide an accurate snapshot of the issues of mind and motivations that are yet playing out among those still attracted in some way to the unique principles taught by Herbert Armstrong in the twentieth century.

CHAPTER NINETEEN
WHAT ABOUT MISTAKES AND BAD BEHAVIOR?

If the Worldwide Church of God was not God's true Church—His *peculiar treasure*—then where might it be, and what would it actually look like? What are you looking for, and how will you know if you find it?

Will the true work of Jesus Christ through human beings be ideal, physically? Will it exist in a state of near-perfect unity among all participants, without doctrinal dispute, and having human leaders who will always reflect the character of Jesus Christ Himself? Is that what you are looking for? Good luck in finding it! That is not a flippant statement to denigrate the possibility of finding Christ's Work on this earth. But it is an admonition against using *a faulty yardstick* that will *never* lead you to find real Truth. Why? Because that has never been the way Christ described the actual behavior of His *peculiar treasure*! Such a yardstick will *never* reveal *any physical assembly* that will ever measure up.

Oh yes, the Body of Jesus Christ will be known for love and unity (John 13:35). It will be known for faithful defense of revealed doctrine (John 14:15). But this is speaking of the *spiritual organism* in which the Holy Spirit is dominant in each true member. However, God's church has always existed physically as *a mixed multitude*, made up of all kinds of people in varying states of spiritual conversion (or lack thereof). At best, the physical assembly of those called by God is a hodgepodge of fallible human beings working to cast off the burdens of their ingrained wretched habits and carnal inclinations. At best, it is *a hard slog* to put off the flesh, to let Jesus Christ truly *begin to rule in our lives* and to manifest the fruits of His Spirit. Some ministers and laymembers do so, but many in the end do not.

What Are You Seeking?

Those looking primarily for a church that is filled with "nice people" can go to any number of corner churches. It is especially easy among groups that believe God's Law is done away and that a person does not really have to change to be saved. Where there is no pressure or expectation of personal overcoming, there is a very "low bar" of expectation that makes it much easier for members to pat each other on the back and believe that they are all OK in God's sight. No pressure. Just "be nice." Everybody goes to heaven.

But that is not how the Bible defines the expectation for real salvation, and neither is it how the physical members of the "true church" are described by Christ. If no murderers, whoremongers, sorcerers, liars, idolaters, or abominable people will be allowed into God's Kingdom—and that is exactly what Jesus Christ said in Revelation 21:8, reinforcing *the hold* of the Ten Commandments—then the true Church, wherever it is found, will be made up of individuals *who know* that God requires them to *change their behavior*, because He will not accept them *just as they are.* Such individuals who are schooled in the need to become "overcomers" recognize that salvation is not really as easy as falling off a log. It requires the crucifixion of our natural impulses and concepts of mind, and the need to actually *walk in the footsteps* of Jesus Christ, not just to spout a lot of religious platitudes.

Now then, take a group of called individuals *like that*, put them in a physical assembly with others who are tasked with the very same quest, mix in a lot of individuals who are not really serious about the quest at all, and a dash of others who are actually there for more nefarious reasons, and you have *a perfect stew* of potential and predictable drama. *That* is the kind of church that Jesus Christ chose to assemble in the flesh. What is the evidence?

Just read the epistles of Paul, Peter, and John from the first century, and examine the problems that they were grappling with within *the true churches of God* at the time! Where is the blissful harmony? Oh yes, the Book of Acts records an initial flush of unity

WHAT ABOUT MISTAKES AND BAD BEHAVIOR?

and oneness that prevailed when the church first began (Acts 2:44–47; 4:32–34). But that was very short-lived indeed (like a honeymoon period), replaced within just a few years with all kinds of internal strife, gross personal sins of weakness, doctrinal argumentation, political debate, and the misbehavior of shepherds who did not remain loyal to the revealed Truth.

> And I, brethren, could not speak unto you as unto spiritual, but as unto carnal, even as unto babes in Christ. I have fed you with milk, and not with meat: for hitherto ye were not able to bear it, neither yet now are ye able. For ye are yet carnal: for whereas there is among you envying, and strife, and divisions, are ye not carnal, and walk as men? (1 Corinthians 3:1–3)

> It is reported commonly that there is fornication among you, and such fornication as is not so much as named among the Gentiles, that one should have his father's wife. And ye are puffed up, and have not rather mourned, that he that hath done this deed might be taken away from among you (1 Corinthians 5:1–2).

> For I know this, that after my departing shall grievous wolves enter in among you, not sparing the flock. Also of your own selves shall men arise, speaking perverse things, to draw away disciples after them. Therefore watch, and remember, that by the space of three years I ceased not to warn every one night and day with tears (Acts 20:29–31).

That is the New Testament record God gave to us to describe His *peculiar treasure* of the day! Sadly, in spite of having access to the power of the Holy Spirit to help them behave differently, many of them instead followed in the very footsteps of the ancient Israelites—God's *church in the wilderness* (Acts 7:38)—the first

362   A PECULIAR TREASURE

rendition of His *peculiar treasure.* Is this shocking? It should not be if we simply read the entire biblical record with open eyes.

By the end of the first century, very few had held firm to the true Faith. The physical—organized—church had been taken over by men who did not love the original revelation. By the 90s A.D., the Apostle John had been *put out* of his own church!

> I wrote unto the church: but Diotrephes, who loveth to have the preeminence among them, receiveth us not. Wherefore, if I come, I will remember his deeds which he doeth, prating against us with malicious words: and not content therewith, neither doth he himself receive the brethren, and forbiddeth them that would, and casteth them out of the church (3 John 9–10).

But Jesus Christ did not orchestrate all of this for our failure. All of it is part of His *ingenious program* to produce *real spiritual character* out of a crucible of serious trial. Salvation is not easy, but it is very much *achievable*—possible for any of those called ones who come to *love that Way* enough to fight for it.

What then can help make such a *wobbly construct* of a physical church—like the one Christ assembled—successful? Firstly, the power of God's Holy Spirit helping many to be transformed in mind *in spite of the negative pressures*—pressures both inside and outside of the body. Secondly, *good leadership* of shepherds who are applying *real wisdom* in the administration of their duties. The whole enterprise, as Christ designed it, is very much like a house of cards—extremely fragile and merely *one wrong move away* from disaster. But it can stand, nevertheless, if Christ's rules for both laymember and minister are followed. Often, those rules *are not followed,* and that is why bad fruits manifest. But wherever Christ is truly working, there will indeed be a *vestige of legitimacy,* even if you have to look more closely to find it.

Is the WCG Ruled Out?

According to *a realistic measure* in evaluating the *physical* assembly of God's true church, the Worldwide Church of God cannot be discounted at all. The fact that this organization over time became wracked with division, infighting, bad behavior of many ministers and laymembers alike, watering down of revealed doctrines, and the ultimate implosion of its empire, does not prove that it *could not have been* God's true church. Many have drawn that conclusion, citing documented "bad fruits." But in fact, it actually makes it *more credible* that this might actually have been the church that God raised up in the twentieth century! If that seems the reverse of good logic, then pray tell, where is the biblical evidence for the *fairytale manifestation* of a *physical church* that many have demanded to see? It simply does not exist that way. It never did exist that way in the past, and God prophesied that His last-day church would do *all of the very things* that the WCG ended up doing. Here are just a few examples:

Jesus said He would build a church, the leadership of that church would bear His authority, and that this church would never perish (Matthew 16:18–19). The WCG was built as an unusual and amazing church from the 1930s through the 1960s, Herbert Armstrong claimed God's authority to guide that church, and remnants of that work still survive today because his teachings which have *intrinsic value* have never been eradicated.

That Church was to proclaim the Gospel of Jesus Christ—His inspired message and instructions (Mark 16:15). Herbert Armstrong proclaimed the Gospel—the *Good News* of the coming Kingdom of God—and that message touched thousands around the globe.

That very Church that Christ built would go astray—apostatize from revealed Truth (Acts 20:28–31; Jude 4, 18; 2 Timothy 3:1, 5; 4:3–4; 2 Peter 3:3–4). The WCG changed its foundational teachings which had been so blessed during its first forty-year history, reverting over the ensuing twenty-year period to *the very same false teachings* that original members had initially renounced as *empty and unsatisfying*.

This is what Jesus said His church would be like, and what it would eventually do, and that is exactly what the WCG was like, and what it eventually did. What other religious denomination that you know of today fits that model nearly as well? There is none!

When a *legitimate church* that God raises up *falls away* from Him and separates from revealed Truth, there is a reason. It would never happen if the ministry and its core members insisted upon remaining faithful. The only way such a *prophesied apostasy* can take place is for serious mistakes to occur, God's Holy Spirit as a guiding force to be quenched, gross negligence to ensue, and serious sins to overtake those who were once faithful.

You can never *apostatize* (fall away) from Truth, if you did not first *possess Truth*! Deceived peoples of the world cannot commit apostasy. They have never yet had that Truth revealed to them. What is the only group of people who can possibly fulfill the very prophecy that Christ said would befall His own church? It must be His own called—legitimate—sheep! They are the only ones who can fulfill this prophecy. There is no other possibility.

With that premise in place, let us now examine the tabloid accusations that have been leveled against Herbert Armstrong and the Worldwide Church of God over the past fifty years.

Anatomy of Accusation

For many years there have been provocative and salacious accusations made against key figures within the Worldwide Church of God, and Mr. Herbert Armstrong in particular. Once internal strife broke out in the 1970s and ministers and members alike began to defect *en masse*, a number of "tell-all books" and other tabloid-style publications began to crop up. Especially heading into the 1980s and beyond, newsletters, books, and other media items began to be distributed by former members and ministers who now sought

WHAT ABOUT MISTAKES AND BAD BEHAVIOR? 365

to destroy the very church they had once served with loyalty. The internet is rife today with all manner of "Armstrong hate sites."

Understand this distinction: There had always been detractors of Herbert Armstrong and his religious enterprise, but until the 1970s it had largely come from other Christian denominations that considered the WCG a dangerous cult. They sought to denigrate the doctrines (biblical exegesis) of Herbert Armstrong which challenged their "orthodox" interpretation of Scripture and which often set *mainstream* scholars back on their heels. But this *new brand* of hater was very different.

There is no adversary like the one who begins as a devoted follower but then flips one-hundred-eighty degrees. In chapter fifteen we spotlighted the main categories of individuals who became members over the years, including the ones who were there primarily out of fear of future world events—seeking to *save their skins*. But when the world did not end in the 1970s, leadership judgment began to be questioned, and then when the misbehavior of certain prominent church icons began to be divulged, many who had followed previously with blind faith now reacted with feelings of betrayal, disappointment, and embarrassment that they had ever been so "duped." Many just left the fellowship and faded back into the world, but some responded with greater volatility.

In some cases, ministers (or minister wannabes) who found themselves "outside the fold" sought a following of their own. One of the best ways to poach members from your former affiliation is to begin a campaign to vilify the parent body, sow discord, and thereby *shake loose* vulnerable members for your own new group.

Others just seemed to need a kind of *cathartic outlet* to cope with their own deep disappointments and hurt feelings. They became crusaders—as a "public service"—to try to expose the *real danger* of that *Armstrong cult* so that other unsuspecting people could be spared from being abused and taken advantage of as they now believe they had been. They became warriors for a new *humanitarian cause*.

366   A PECULIAR TREASURE

Still others found solace in attacking the WCG for a different reason: Having separated for whatever *outward reason*, they carried with them a real sense of guilt that perhaps—just maybe—they had abandoned *the real Faith* and were now estranged from God. That is a terrible feeling, whether rational or not, and if it persists in the mind it becomes devastating. One solution was to return to that former faith in some way. But if that was not an option (for whatever reason), the only way for some to try to dispel the persistent guilt was to *convince themselves* that it *really was not* God's Church at all. If I can *convince myself* that it really was just a man-made cult, I am safe with God. Conscience clear. Therefore, let me become a consumer of every salacious accusation I can find against that church, and let me practice self-psychotherapy by sharing with others my own horror stories from my past affiliation. In so doing, maybe I can eventually convince myself that I did not really do the wrong thing.

That is just a brief summary of some (not all) of the motivations behind much of the anti-Armstrong literature that began to surface in the 1970s and beyond.

ARE EXPOSÉS OK WITH GOD?

In general, what is a true Christian supposed to do if he/she finds out about the *private sins* of someone else? Is it a godly principle to expose secret sins as a way to *help defeat* hypocrisy through a *militant purge*? Hardly. Oh yes, there are many biblical texts that emphasize the need to "call out" sin for what it is, but this is always speaking of *heresy*—blatant sin being espoused to try to teach God's people that wrong is actually right; to espouse something that threatens *the entire body*. That is very different than *a sin of personal weakness* that one has not yet been able to overcome. If you do not understand the difference between heresy (spreading false doctrine) and personal weakness, then you will make serious mistakes in trying to apply God's instructions. He commanded that we do both—*show mercy* and *resist sin.* You cannot do both of them correctly without knowing the difference in application.

In any case, because all of God's commandments are *expressions of love*, wisdom to know when to reveal a sin vs. when to *cover* (not *cover up*) a sin requires one to have a sincere desire to create peace and harmony within the church. If someone is rabble-rousing within a group—being contentious and robbing the church of peace—that must not be tolerated. Call it for what it is and get rid of that cancerous influence. But if it is merely the weakness of a brother or sister of the faith—a weakness that one has not yet been able to master, though acknowledging it as sin—it would be a direct violation of godly wisdom to "expose" that person's private mistakes and not to provide time and patience for true repentance. Jesus indicted those who were hardhearted and cruel—lacking sincere love—and thereby becoming guilty of hanging a millstone around the necks of His dear children (Matthew 18:6).

> A talebearer revealeth secrets: but he that is of a faithful spirit concealeth the matter (Proverbs 11:13).

> He that covereth a transgression seeketh love; but he that repeateth a matter separateth very friends (Proverbs 17:9).

> And above all things have fervent charity among yourselves: for charity shall cover the multitude of sins (1 Peter 4:8).

> Brethren, if a man be overtaken in a fault, ye which are spiritual, restore such an one in the spirit of meekness; considering thyself, lest thou also be tempted. Bear ye one another's burdens, and so fulfil the law of Christ (Galatians 6:1–2).

So the question is, concerning these individuals who have written tell-all books to reveal private sins of their targets within the WCG, is this very premise even remotely an expression of God's love? In

368 A PECULIAR TREASURE

other words, is that what Jesus would have done? You be the judge. Just understand that if you believe you need to read every salacious accusation written against Herbert Armstrong to complete your investigation *of his legitimacy,* then at least recognize that you are choosing to *receive testimony* from individuals who are proving that they do not reflect God's Spirit or anything resembling a *Christian mind.* Anyone who would *choose to write* such a publication is proving an *inherent lack of moral character.* So just be careful not to be duped by their claims of innocence and *altruistic public service.*

And if it is necessary to put Herbert Armstrong *under the microscope* in order to be totally objective about him, how about applying *the very same standard* to these detractors? Perhaps we should be willing to delve into their personal histories to discover what "hidden secrets" existed in their lives which account for their taking part in such endeavors. After all, what's good for the goose is good for the gander. Who is to say they are credible? Maybe there are people who knew *them,* who will testify, third or fourth hand, about things somebody else saw or "witnessed." Should that kind of *hearsay testimony* not also be weighed, if you think as a general principle it is appropriate and needful to *find out all the dirt*?

Did They Ever Believe?

Part of anyone's credibility is showing a foundation of reliability. Many of these critical authors once chose to join the Worldwide Church of God—to become baptized and to devote themselves to seeking salvation in God's Kingdom. The official church doctrine always emphasized that making this commitment was *a very serious matter,* and should never be undertaken by anyone who is not absolutely sure. Prospective members were strongly advised to *count the cost* (Luke 14:28), and to be certain to *prove all things* (1 Thessalonians 5:21). Herbert Armstrong often repeated to his audiences, "Don't believe me; believe your Bibles!" Therefore, anyone who chose to get baptized into that faith was one who claimed to have performed that comprehensive *due diligence* and was *convinced* that it really was God's revealed Way of Life.

And yet, within a few years' time, these very ones who separated from the church and then began to make accusations, also began to claim they had been duped by a charlatan from the beginning. Well, if they are correct—and Herbert Armstrong was merely an opportunistic snake oil salesman—then what else does that prove? These individuals had *never really proven the Truth at all*! They were admonished to check out in their Bibles everything Herbert Armstrong preached and to verify if it were so. They supposedly did so and became convinced—by their own diligent investigation—that what he taught was the *real Truth*! But if, in the end, it was not the real Truth, why then did they not discover that during their own initial study? They had all of the tools. They were told to prove it for themselves!

Perhaps they never really did the work to put those teachings to the test. Instead, they must have subscribed to those church tenets because they were enamored by *the personality* of Herbert Armstrong, Garner Ted Armstrong, or some other *physical aspect* of that organization. Otherwise, if he has truly searched the Scriptures to verify the truth (like the Bereans did; Acts 17:10–11), then it matters not what any man does, minister or otherwise. Truth is truth! If he has proven it, then he believes it *no matter what another human being does*, now or in the future. And if instead, his commitment to a belief system is *ever contingent upon the future actions* of a minister, another laymember, an organization, etc., it is *glaring proof* that the command of 1 Thessalonians 5:21 was never really followed.

The *true believers* were the ones who discovered value in those doctrines taught by Herbert Armstrong which were found in *no other church*! They really did prove their veracity, especially by *practicing* those teachings. If you prove something *by living it* and you verify that blessings from God *actually derive from following His commandments*, then who should ever be able to take that "evidence" away from you in the future? No one!

So what do we say about those who supposedly proved it, followed it for a time, but then changed their minds and became enemies of that very same church—enough so to seek to destroy what they once professed to believe? Someone was either not diligent enough in their initial study, or else they allowed *superficial attractions* to bring them into the church rather than real interest in God's salvation plan.

The third category is also one that God warned about—legitimate children who *did indeed prove it*, but then later *forgot* all of those proofs because of severe tribulation (Psalm 78). Regardless of which reason it may be, whose fault is that? God will hold each individual accountable for himself.

Move Along—Nothing to See Here?

If you conclude that you are being advised *to ignore and to suppress* knowledge of gross impropriety in leaders of the Worldwide Church of God, and to refuse to consider that some (even many) might have done some really bad things, you are mistaken. That is not the point here at all.

This particular work—like no other before it—has attempted to show you the facts of what happened without resorting to salacious gossip to make a point. It has shown you evidence that *plenty of mistakes* were made over the years, but without attacking or maligning the good intentions of those involved. When possible, a summary of documented facts has been cast in the light of *possible motivations* behind the scenes, but without claiming the ability to read anyone's heart or mind.

That is why when addressing Herbert Armstrong's actions, you have seen most of the analysis taken from his own words. There is always much that is revealing, even without resorting to the testimony of avowed enemies. To discover what is truly important, it simply is not necessary to get down into the cesspits of character assassination. This assertion is not a way to try to deflect attention away from potential serious personal failings, but to point out the futility in trying to chase *real truth* by probing gossip and presumptions that come from others—especially those who are unreliable because they have an axe to grind.

Even in assessing the actions of Joseph Tkach, this work has focused upon *his actions and his own explanations of his actions*, rather than implying any evil intent. He may have been very sincere in what he did. Why not allow for that? It has *no bearing* on whether he was right or wrong in his doctrinal conclusions. Why not stick to *the issues*? It is all about judging the value of any religious doctrine on the basis of soundness of rationale from the Bible, rather than just attempting to "win" by attacking someone else's *personal character*. We have plenty of politicians who engage in *scorched-earth defamation of character* to try to "win power." They do not care if their opponent is really guilty of being "evil" or not. It is only about winning the prize. In those circles, trampling someone's character and reputation is considered *part of the price* of winning.

For us, why not instead stick to evaluating doctrinal issues? The *fundamentals of belief* of the Radio Church of God should either stand or fall based upon their own merits. If that church just might have been God's *peculiar treasure* in our time, then it will have redeeming value in its explanation of God's plan for human salvation, irrespective of the weaknesses of those who first brought those truths to our attention.

Do not forget that being innocent provides no firewall against personal attacks. If it were so, then Jesus, being perfect, would never have been maligned as a mentally unbalanced, carousing, gluttonous drunkard (Matthew 11:18–19; John 7:20). That point is not to try to change the subject or to obfuscate any man's mistakes. It is just a reminder that if you insist upon believing always that *where there's smoke there's fire*, then you likewise would have rejected the Savior because He was accused without mercy by His enemies. Just be very careful about taking personal accusations at face value. Consider the source.

The Very Greatest Indictment

If it is true that the Radio Church of God was indeed raised up by Jesus Christ as His *peculiar treasure* in our time—founded upon the revelation of *true doctrine* to a called people—then the very most serious sin that Herbert Armstrong committed as physical head of that church was allowing, while on his watch, God's Truth to be besmirched and abandoned by covetous underlings. It was a mistake that permitted the personal faith of thousands to be destroyed, and it set in motion all of the chaos that resulted over the next twenty years. And lest you believe that this assertion in itself is an uncorroborated personal attack, again, weigh it from Mr. Armstrong's own words:

> So I will just tell you now, that I myself, cannot see one scintilla of an argument so far that is going to overthrow the teaching of God's Church on divorce and remarriage. . . If we would do that, brethren, do you know what would happen in less than another three months? I'll bet you nearly hundreds and hundreds of members of the Worldwide Church of God would divorce and they would go out and marry someone else. And that would be the *end of the Worldwide Church of God*—and Jesus Christ would spue us out of His mouth. And anyone who does go and do that will get spued out. I have to warn you (Transcribed from audio recording of Herbert Armstrong Bible study on Divorce and Remarriage; Ambassador College Gymnasium; Pasadena, California; April 13, 1973).

Either this statement in 1973 is true, or else it is not true. You need no salacious personal exposé to confirm this as a mistake, if it was indeed the fulfillment of God's prophecy that His true church would go into apostasy (Malachi 2:14–16). You have already seen the public evidence of it from the history highlighted in Part II of this work. You only need to decide if you think it matters.

It would be so much nicer to believe that Herbert Armstrong made no serious mistakes in leading the church, and that the "real trouble" came only after he died. Again, there are plenty of other written works out there to reinforce that particular notion. But every one of those versions leaves much to be desired, and they do not address many nagging questions at the heart of the story which you have seen highlighted here. The point is this: Our confidence in the validity of Herbert Armstrong's legitimacy as a servant of God *is not dependent upon* making him out to have been virtually perfect. We need not chase every personal attack against him and then rebut it. Whether he secretly engaged in personal behaviors that were wrong is not germane to our belief that he offered us *something of immense value.* That doctrine he taught to the exclusion of all other religionists has value in and of itself.

As for the rest, God will indeed be the Judge of every one of us, and He knows what those secret intents of heart and mind have always been.

A BELIEVER IN HAPPY ENDINGS

What if it is true that God purposely called and used a man in our time to establish His Church, but a man who had natural weaknesses that would manifest under pressure in his old age? What if God did this *intentionally* to assure that His prophecy of *a falling away* would come to pass as stated (2 Thessalonians 2:3)? What if God allowed this to happen for reason—*to verify* whether each member of that church was actually there because of *love for the revealed Truth*, or whether they were only following a man or a physical organization? What if God decided that there is no better way to show *what is truly in each member's heart* than to allow the very man through whom that Way of Life was preached to fall prey to a character weakness in his old age and permit the church to go astray? What if God could have prevented that personal weakness from manifesting by choosing to keep strong defenders of the faith surrounding Mr. Armstrong, like his faithful son Richard Armstrong, and his wife, Loma? What if it were possible—by taking a liberal influence like Garner Ted Armstrong *out of the way* instead of Richard—that the church might have had stronger leadership in the 1970s in order to rebuff attempts to water down God's Truth? What if God intentionally allowed that liberal son (and others) to gain power in that organization in order to help precipitate the prophesied challenge to sound doctrine?

And what if Herbert Armstrong was actually very sincere in his heart, and what if he came to recognize his error before he died and to repent bitterly before God, even if he was too weak physically by that time to be able to bring the church back to the original revelation (on doctrines like Pentecost, divorce and remarriage, etc.)?

Again, none of us can read hearts and minds. But because *the real legacy* of Herbert Armstrong is found in God's true plan of salvation—which we received by his preaching and no one else's—this author chooses to hope for that outcome, and to continue to respect and to defend his memory for all of the blessings that we received through his work. It truly changed our lives for the good.

CHAPTER TWENTY
WHAT ABOUT A WORK TODAY?

We have seen a snapshot of that scattered church today, as well as some of the major ideologies that distinguish many of the hundreds of remnant fellowships. If you are one who comes to believe that what Herbert and Loma Armstrong produced was indeed God's *peculiar treasure* in this age, what will you choose to do now?

If you seek to find a legitimate remnant of that work where you will feel at home, how will you sift between all of those making claims today? It all depends upon which yardstick you use. But even if you narrow your search to groups that share a respect for Herbert Armstrong as a true servant of God, you will still be faced with many competing fellowships. Now what?

You are sure to come across groups that claim they are carrying on the commission given to Herbert Armstrong, and they will tell you very quickly how to rule out more imposters. What is their yardstick? They will tell you that any faithful remnant must be doing two specific things:

1) They must be doing a "Work"— carrying the gospel to the nations like Mr. Armstrong did, and
2) They must have enough "numbers" of members to prove that God is blessing them as the "heir apparent" to Mr. Armstrong's work.

So according to these standards, a faithful remnant in God's eyes today cannot be "small in numbers," and it cannot be failing to do a major evangelical outreach program to *warn the world* and to *gain new converts.*

It is interesting that this two-pronged criteria for evaluating and confirming the work of God is actually very prevalent among *many*

376   A PECULIAR TREASURE

former members of the parent body. How did that come to be so?
How did so many become conditioned to look at *growth in numbers*
and *a worldwide work* as their basis for finding God?

GOD CONFIRMED MR. ARMSTRONG'S WORK
THROUGH GROWTH

There is no question that one of the key ways God proved His
support and favor for the efforts of Mr. Herbert Armstrong and the
Radio Church of God was by blessing it with incredible growth over
several decades. What started as a small and vulnerable operation
by Mr. and Mrs. Armstrong alone, grew consistently by leaps and
bounds from 1933 through 1968. As a refresher, notice again just a
few of Mr. Armstrong's own comments about the source of that
unparalleled and monumental result. First, from the *Co-Worker
Letter,* July 27, 1966:

> This is not MY Work--nor even ours--except that the
> Creator God grants us the glorious PRIVILEGE of being used
> as His instruments in what <u>HE is doing</u>! It is GOD'S WORK
> here on earth. And God has put the <u>living</u> Jesus Christ at the
> HEAD of it. He guides, directs, inspires, and blesses this
> Work. And for 32 years, He has caused this Work to GROW
> at the rate (on the average) of <u>30% every year</u> over the
> preceding year!

> EVERY YEAR He has caused <u>HIS</u> Gospel to be heard by
> 30% more people than the year before. Today, approximately
> <u>FORTY MILLION</u> people are hearing it EVERY WEEK--over
> every continent on earth! Every year the living Christ has
> caused 30% more precious lives to be CONVERTED--
> CHANGED--begotten as children of God--made HEIRS of
> the KINGDOM OF GOD and <u>eternal life</u>--than the year
> before! NOW several THOUSAND are converted annually

WHAT ABOUT A WORK TODAY?   377

through this very Work! The POWER OF GOD is in it! The
SPIRIT of the living God EMPOWERS IT!

Next from *The Autobiography of Herbert W. Armstrong*:

The only reason this work survived—and grew—is that I
was not, after all, "on my own."
Pitifully small as this effort was during those first few
years . . . still it was, though assuredly not then apparent, the
very WORK OF THE LIVING GOD. The divinely-imparted dynamic
spark was in it. People have asked, in recent years, what makes
this now great work "tick." The vital energy and life that the
living CHRIST has imparted is what makes it tick! . . .
    Looking back, now, over the actual physical
circumstances, conditions, and happenings of those years, it
seems utterly incredible that a work started in such a humble,
crude manner without any visible backing could have
survived, let alone continued to grow at the pace of 30% a
year. . . .
Of course this work did not double in size every day, every
week, or even every year. But doubling in number of people
reached, in number of precious lives converted, in radio
power, and in scope of operation every two years and seven
and a half months is, after all, a very rapid and almost
unheard-of rate of growth. And that rate of redoubling has
continued for 28 years! (*The Plain Truth*, December 1961,
pp. 20–21)

Yes,   truly,   this   has   been   "Mission
Impossible"—ACCOMPLISHED! And still being accomplished
in ever-increasing magnitude! It has been and is, as stated
above, an example of what the living God can do, has done,
and is doing through human instrumentalities yielded to Him
and obedient to HIS WAYS! (*Autobiography of Herbert W.
Armstrong*, Vol. 1, 1986, Introduction, p. 5)

378   A PECULIAR TREASURE

But, from that moment when we began to rely solely on God for financial support not only, but also for guidance, direction, and results, the Work began a phenomenal yearly increase of nearly 30% for the next 35 years. It doubled in size, scope and power on the average of every 2 2/3 years. It multiplied eight times every eight years—64 times in 16 years. Today it is an immensely larger and greater Work than then.

WHY has this Work leaped from virtually *nothing* to worldwide power and scope, multiplying itself continually over and over again?

Certainly I had not the ability, the resources within myself, to have planned, directed, and accomplished anything remotely like the phenomenal development into the worldwide enterprises that is reality today. . . .

The DIFFERENCE between *THIS* Work of GOD and others is *just that*—this is the Work of *GOD* and not of MEN. It started, and continued, to rely on GOD, not on MAN (*Autobiography of Herbert W. Armstrong*, Vol. 1, 1986, pp. 526–527).

So we see that Mr. Armstrong asserted repeatedly that it was the work of God—not man—and that a substantiation of the divine nature of its results was found in monumental growth, as that message was carried to the whole world with great power. Over the years, when challenges were made to Mr. Armstrong's teachings or authority, he very often pointed to those very things as substantiation of his credibility. He would challenge anyone to identify another work that was going out boldly to proclaim Jesus Christ's Gospel of God's coming Kingdom, or that was producing the fruits of 30% average annual growth, year after year.

No wonder then that most members of the church had these two tenets—necessity to do a worldwide work and confidence in membership growth—drilled into their thinking. Those two pillars were thundered by Mr. Armstrong as the proof of *his own authority*

How Was That Great Work Later Destroyed?

Remember that the Bible is very clear that an apostasy—a departure from Truth—would occur in the last-day church of God, even as God's people historically have always departed from the original revelation. The ancient Israelites did it time and time again, and were never able to remain faithful to what God, from the beginning, gave to them. Neither could the first-century church hold on, having corrupted the original teachings of the Apostles within the first forty years (Acts 20:28–30). Likewise, the last-day church proved it could be no more faithful than any of its predecessors. "Let no man deceive you by any means: for that day shall not come, except there come a falling away [apostasy] first . . ." (2 Thessalonians 2:3). As we came to understand, apostasy does not mean departing from *membership in a physical organization.* It means literally a departure from *the Truth!* Most had no idea that the physical organization they identified as God's Church would itself turn from God's revealed doctrines. When the first major doctrinal changes began to be implemented in the early 1970s—including a change in Pentecost from Monday to Sunday, and allowance for divorce and remarriage—most members accepted these by apostolic authority. After all, they were strongly admonished that leaving the WCG would be synonymous with leaving the Church—the spiritual organism that is Christ's Body. They were also told that if the ministry is wrong, God is the one who will correct them in time. The laity was responsible only for upholding obedience to church government. Therefore, the majority continued to stay, even when more and more fruits of that organization became increasingly distressing.

Finally, after Mr. Armstrong's death in early 1986, the repudiation of other core teachings came in short order, including abandonment of the Sabbath and the nature of God doctrines. Many could no longer stomach this flagrant corruption of God's Truth and did what they thought they never would: They "left the church"!

Since the early 1990s, many of these "new groups" have been vigorously attempting to do what Mr. Armstrong did—prove their authenticity and authority by 1) doing a great evangelistic work to the world, and 2) seeking exponential growth in membership. They feel that if they can duplicate the success Mr. Armstrong experienced in these two ways, they can make a case for being the legitimate continuation of his spiritual work.

From the time certain long-time members of the WCG were forced out in the 1970s—because, in conscience, they could not go along with the change in Pentecost and the new definition of adultery—they were consistently quizzed by former brethren about their credibility in gathering within a small remnant. The two most prevalent questions asked were: "What *kind of Work* is your minister doing?" and "How many members do you have?" For most people, the lack of one or the other was an automatic indication that a remnant fellowship could not be an authorized body. But are these two criteria really the appropriate yardstick for proving where God may be working today?

ASSUMPTIONS ABOUT GOD'S WORK

The problem begins by accepting major assertions that have no biblical substantiation: First, that any legitimate assembly of God must at all times be doing a worldwide, warning work, and second, that a legitimate continuation of Mr. Armstrong's work will be growing exponentially today, even as it did in the early years. Let us address each one of these assumptions in turn.

Does every individual becoming a Christian have a right to attach himself to Christ's command in Matthew 28, and go out to do a grand work? What did Jesus Christ actually say, and to whom was He speaking?

WHAT ABOUT A WORK TODAY? 381

And Jesus came and spake *unto them*, saying, All power is given unto me in heaven and in earth. *Go ye* therefore, and teach all nations, baptizing them in the name of the Father, and of the Son, and of the Holy [Spirit]: Teaching them to observe all things whatsoever I have commanded you: and, lo, I am with you alway, even unto the end of the world. Amen (Matthew 28:18–20) [emphasis mine].

Who was the "them" to whom Christ was speaking when He said "go ye"? Did that apply to every Tom, Dick, and Harry who volunteered to become a teacher in Christ's name? Or do we accept that Christ has the prerogative to commission *whomever He chooses*? Yes, God has the same right to selectively commission those who will speak in His name, even as you and I would reserve the right to hand-pick someone acting as our personal agent. We would never allow someone to tell us that he is *making himself* our agent. Certainly, that would be ludicrous. No one has the authority to speak on your behalf unless you approve. Does not God have the same authority? Or is He duty-bound to back up everyone who appoints himself to do a "work" in His name? It simply does not make sense. How would there ever be such a thing as a "false prophet" if all were truly authorized to do God's work?

No, Jesus Christ specifically was addressing His hand-picked disciples, *the ones He had worked with personally* for three years and prepared to become apostles. Jesus said, "I speak not of you all: I know whom I have chosen . . ." (John 13:18). It is to apostles *only* that this task was assigned—to go out and to proclaim that Truth to the world, making converts of those God would call. The Apostle Paul also became such an authorized agent because he was personally selected by Christ for that commission, taught directly in the wilderness through divine revelation, and then sent to his assigned area with a specific and definable mission (Galatians 1:15–18). These are all attributes of authentic apostles and will exist wherever an authentic "work" is truly commencing in God's name.

If Herbert Armstrong was likewise a commissioned apostle in

these last days, it is because he also was called and selected by God, given direct—divine—inspiration concerning the plan of salvation and coming Kingdom of God, and then commissioned to proclaim that same gospel to the world. And as we have already noted, the fruit of that grand work certainly seems to confirm that his commission was authentic—and was believed by many whose lives were changed by that incredible message.

How Long Does God Support a Chosen Servant?

How long does a commissioned servant continue to be blessed and backed by God? Once chosen, does he have "tenure for life"? Or does God support that servant only as long as he holds true to the *inspired* message? What about Jesus Christ's own ministry? Christ said:

> For I have not spoken of myself; but the Father which sent me, he gave me a commandment, what I should say, and what I should speak. And I know that his commandment is life everlasting: whatsoever I speak therefore, even as the Father said unto me, so I speak (John 12:49–50).

What if Jesus had decided to amend His Father's message and customize it to fit the times and circumstances of human beings He encountered in Jerusalem during the first century? Would the Father have been duty-bound to back up such customization? Remember, if the initial message really emanates from God, that message must be right and true as it is first revealed, or else we accuse God of being fickle and shifty. Jesus had no need to amend the message from His Father. It was the perfect representation of Truth *as given*! Therefore, the only test was whether Jesus—as fully human and having a carnal mind, yet possessing a full measure of the Holy Spirit—could resist the urge to corrupt the revealed message, and instead to remain a true Ambassador of the Father. By speaking that revealed message faithfully—without corruption—He

WHAT ABOUT A WORK TODAY? 383

proved His worthiness. A faithful ambassador delivers the message *as given* by his master. He never arrogates to himself the right to amend it in any way.

Likewise, notice again the strict command Christ gave to those trained disciples whom He had selected to become apostles:

> Go ye therefore, and teach all nations, baptizing them in the name of the Father, and of the Son, and of the Holy [Spirit]: *Teaching them to observe all things whatsoever I have commanded you*: and, lo, I am with you alway, even unto the end of the world. Amen (Matthew 28:19–20) [emphasis mine].

Once each of these men was ordained to the office of apostle, did he then receive authorization from Christ to modify doctrines in future years according to Matthew 16:19? Or did Jesus Christ mean just what He said— "teaching them to observe all things *whatsoever I have commanded you*"? Notice the condemnation of those pastors who were certainly legitimate shepherds of Israel, but who turned away from teaching what God had given to them:

> Woe be unto the pastors that destroy and scatter the sheep of my pasture! saith the LORD . . . Thus saith the LORD of hosts, *Hearken not unto the words of the prophets that prophesy unto you*: they make you vain: they speak a vision of their own heart, and not out of the mouth of the LORD. They say still unto them that despise me, The LORD hath said, Ye shall have peace; and they say unto every one that walketh after the imagination of his own heart, No evil shall come upon you. For who hath stood in the counsel of the LORD, and hath perceived and heard his word? who hath marked his word, and heard it? (Jeremiah 23:1, 16–18) [emphasis mine]

That God of the Old Testament is the very same Being who became Jesus Christ. How can any prophet or apostle ever take the

384 A PECULIAR TREASURE

liberty of changing the message of that God? Even the Apostle Paul confirmed he had no such authority from Jesus Christ, his Master!

> I marvel that ye are so soon removed from him that called you into the grace of Christ unto another gospel: Which is not another; but there be some that trouble you, and would pervert the gospel of Christ. But though we, or an angel from heaven, preach any other gospel unto you than that which we have preached unto you, let him be accursed. As we said before, so say I now again, If any man preach any other gospel unto you than that ye have received, let him be accursed. For do I now persuade men, or God? or do I seek to please men? for if I yet pleased men, I should not be the servant of Christ. But I certify you, brethren, that the gospel which was preached of me is not after man. For I neither received it of man, neither was I taught it, but by the revelation of Jesus Christ (Galatians 1:6–12).

If Herbert Armstrong was likewise an authentic apostle in these last days, then it is true because he received *divine doctrine* directly from Jesus Christ *by revelation*. That is the way *all* legitimate servants have *always* been commissioned. Those arguing that he taught us a mixture of truth and error from the beginning are only building a case to reject him as a false prophet altogether. But if you believe Mr. Armstrong was legitimately a chosen servant of God, then that means the message he taught us *from the beginning* was not his own, even as Paul's was not his own, and Christ's was not His own. That continuity *must* be there, or else we have no spiritual foundation whatsoever!

When Did God's Initial Last-day Work End?

If it is then true that Mr. Armstrong was a legitimate apostle, what must we conclude about his decision in 1974 to approve the change of Pentecost and divorce and remarriage at the urging of

WHAT ABOUT A WORK TODAY? 385

liberal ministers? He resisted those attempting to strong-arm him in his old age—including his own son—for quite some time.

Ultimately, he capitulated and signed off on those perverted teachings that he had condemned so strongly before. After that, the church did *then* begin a downward spiral that eventually ended in a repudiation of almost every foundational doctrine it had once held dear. It took twenty years for that deterioration to progress to the point that most members could recognize it, but it happened nevertheless, exactly as Mr. Armstrong prophesied it would.

The problem is, very few recognized when that departure from God actually occurred. Until his death in 1986, most accepted the changes in doctrine Mr. Armstrong had approved under "apostolic authority," but rejected those initiated by his successors thereafter. They think the prophesied apostasy occurred in the early 1990s! But as more of them are having to face as time goes on, the roots of that corruption began *twenty years previously*, under the watch of their own beloved apostle! As mentioned in chapter nineteen, although no one but God knows what was in his heart, we think it possible that Mr. Armstrong may have repented of allowing those changes, even if it was too late for him to truly bring that organization back to God in the 1980s. In any case, we will always hold him in high esteem for the powerful work God did accomplish through him in building the last-day church.

WHAT ABOUT "THE WORK" AFTER 1973?

God never continues to sanction a chosen servant who allows the perversion of his mission to uphold the Truth. From the time Jesus Christ was rejected in 1974 as the Revelator of Truth to the Church—and human scholarship was elevated instead—God ceased to bless and inspire that work. Even Paul confirmed it was not impossible for an apostle to fail. He had to be ever vigilant to keep himself in check. "I therefore so run, not as uncertainly; so fight I, not as one that beateth the air: But I keep under my body, and bring it into subjection: lest that by any means, when I have preached to others, I myself should be a castaway" (1 Corinthians 9:26–27). This shows that even an end-time apostle must likewise keep himself in subjection, or else lose the inspiration and blessings of God. Did that happen with Mr. Armstrong? You decide.

In the June 19, 1978, edition of *The Good News* magazine, Mr. Armstrong provides a chart showing the actual percentages of growth in the church as far back as 1955. This chart confirms that the monumental growth of 30% annually ended in 1968. What else is amazing is that the first year the church actually *declined* in membership was 1973, just months before the announcement of the Pentecost change. From 1968 to 1977, the church experienced an average annual *decline* of 1.8%! Of course, this was explained at the time as being a result of his liberal son being in charge in Pasadena. But what steward can ever blame his subordinate when the ultimate approval for each of those doctrines was made by he himself personally? Yes, it is also true that the High Priest Eli was handicapped by age and a father's weakness for his sons, but that did not absolve him of responsibility for failure in the eyes of God. Notice the condemnation God uttered toward Eli through Samuel: "For I have told him that I will judge his house for ever for the iniquity *which he knoweth*; because his sons made themselves vile, and *he restrained them not*" (1 Samuel 3:13) [emphasis mine]. So the High Priest was responsible for allowing God's house to become corrupted, even as the last-day apostle was held responsible for the destruction of God's temple on his watch. Mr. Armstrong showed a strong desire to fix it, but it was not to be. Is it any wonder the evidence now points to the winding down and ultimate termination of that grand work beginning in the early 1970s?

Support for Any Work Contingent Upon Obedience

The work of God to spread the gospel requires a commissioned servant to proclaim the *unadulterated* words of God. That is such a simple concept, but one that most seem to overlook. How can one go out as an authorized agent of Jesus Christ, yet proclaim a

WHAT ABOUT A WORK TODAY? 387

corrupted message not reflective of God's true character? From the time Mr. Armstrong approved doctrinal corruption in 1974 by accepting a Sunday Pentecost, God withdrew His Holy Spirit—which, ironically, is the very significance of that Holy Day. This marked the end of God's blessing of that grand and glorious work. With fits and starts of attempted resurgence—which tried to recapture the past glory through efforts like "*back on track*" in the 1980s—the Worldwide Church of God nevertheless continued on a steady decline. The effort during those same years to do the work of Elijah—to warn the kings of the world in preparation for Christ's return—was equally lacking in legitimate fruit. None of those kings ever received a real warning at all! And not a one of them was ever left shaking in his boots, the way Ahab did after the original Elijah's visit. The fruit of those visits was to make the WCG more visible and acceptable to the pagan world, not to warn that world of its need to repent. His fruits made a strong case for his having been an apostle raised up by God to build His Church of the last days. *That* he absolutely accomplished. But he did not fulfill that unique commission *yet to be given*, to prepare the way for the literal return of Jesus Christ.

WILL THE FAITHFUL REMNANT GROW EXPONENTIALLY?

We have seen that a legitimate work of God must be predicated upon a revealed and uncorrupted message from God, and proclaimed by an authorized *and faithful* instrument. Lacking either initial authorization, or adherence to the revealed doctrines of God invalidates any "work" as having God's blessing, no matter whose it is.

But what about a remnant still holding fast to *the faith once delivered* (Jude 3)? Is the proof of such a remnant the continuation of monumental growth on an annual basis? Not at all! Notice that God prophesied that the church would be scattered, and it would become difficult to find *any faithful vestige* of Truth whatsoever.

Your country is desolate, your cities are burned with fire: your land, strangers devour it in your presence, and it is desolate, as overthrown by strangers. And the daughter of Zion is left as a cottage in a vineyard, as a lodge in a garden of cucumbers, as a besieged city. Except the LORD of hosts had left unto us *a very small remnant*, we should have been as Sodom, and we should have been like unto Gomorrah (Isaiah 1:7–9) [emphasis mine].

This is a prophecy for Israel of the last days! God confirms that the body of those holding fast to the original revelation would be *very few* in number. "Because strait is the gate, and narrow is the way, which leadeth unto life, and few there be that find it" (Matthew 7:14).

This author believes that God used Mr. Armstrong as an apostle to do a grand work to *build* the last-day Church. But that major construction ceased in the late 1960s! Yes, many more were called after that time, but never to the extent seen in its earlier heyday. And of all those men now trying to duplicate Mr. Armstrong's work, which of them have works that are growing at 30% per year? Not a one. The WCG stopped growing like that, and not even one since then has grown like that either. That phase of God's work ended according to His will. The reality is, most of these men have tied their own credibility to growth in numbers, so they now feel great pressure to deliver, even though God is not blessing. For all of their claimed growth in new members, the truth is, nearly as many people are *leaving by the back door* as are *coming in the front*. They are all spinning their wheels, desperate to prove that they are the ones God is blessing with growth, yet failing in every way by their own measure of success.

The truth is, the Bible shows that the prophesied remnant of God's people is never pictured as having the carbon-copy growth pattern of its early parent organization. All who have assumed that the continuation of God's faithful today—after the prophesied apostasy—would be *many* in number and *growing* exponentially, are truly misguided. We are now in a very dark period of time for God's church. The remnant is just that—a small piece of the original, leftover and remaining. God never asserted that after the parent body went apostate, a very large remnant would come out of it with thousands of members, and then begin growing by leaps and bounds, doing a warning work to the world. In fact, just the opposite. What was the prophesied result of that apostasy?

> But there were false prophets also among the people, even as there shall be false teachers among you, who privily shall bring in damnable heresies, even denying the Lord that bought them, and bring upon themselves swift destruction. And *many shall follow their pernicious ways*; by reason of whom the way of truth shall be evil spoken of. And through covetousness shall they with feigned words make merchandise of you: whose judgment now of a long time lingereth not, and their damnation slumbereth not (2 Peter 2:1–3) [emphasis mine].

Was it only *a few* who were to be deceived by the introduction of false doctrines into the church by the ministry, or was it the many—the majority? It was the many. And yes, God's Truth *did* become "evil spoken of" by men who had put their trust in human scholarship rather than the divine revelation of Jesus Christ. They belittled Mr. Armstrong by saying that he was not a scholar, and therefore did not understand how to decipher proper doctrine regarding the Pentecost count and the technicalities of divorce and remarriage. And unfortunately, Mr. Armstrong, in his old age, lost confidence in the fact that God had *given him* that Truth as a gift, irrespective of man's scholastic abilities and credentials. The majority of God's people bought into that deception, unfortunately, and followed a man into error under the false notion of adhering to church government. It was only a very small remnant that, after being forced out, held fast to the original teachings Christ had delivered. And it is still few indeed who have been able to put all those pieces together and get it right.

Since 1974, God's last-day church has been in a spiritual wilderness, and a legitimate manifestation of the Truth has been very scarce and difficult to find. However, God said the gates of hell would not prevail against His Church, and so, in spite of the mass corruption of doctrine by the majority, a small remnant must have been preserved, if it is true that Mr. Armstrong's work was legitimate. But a remnant today cannot be verified by the false expectation of finding it doing another grand warning work to the world, and having thousands of members. Note how God recorded the state of His church in the last days, after the apostasy commenced:

> And I will turn your feasts into mourning, and all your songs into lamentation; and I will bring up sackcloth upon all loins, and baldness upon every head; and I will make it as the mourning of an only son, and the end thereof as a bitter day. Behold, the days come, saith the Lord GOD, that I will send a famine in the land, not a famine of bread, nor a thirst for water, but of hearing the words of the LORD: And they shall wander from sea to sea, and from the north even to the east, they shall run to and fro to seek the word of the LORD, and shall not find it (Amos 8:10–12).

There has truly been a famine of the hearing of the Word since 1974, even though the physical organization took twenty years to fully implode. There was not a total *absence* of that Word, but it certainly became more scarce, and often mixed with false notions of men. God ceased to back and support that parent organization, and God's unadulterated doctrines—from that time forward—continued to be preserved only by a very small remnant, somewhere.

WHAT ABOUT A WORK TODAY?   391

WHAT IS THE REAL WORK OF THE REMNANT?

If we should not be trying to duplicate Mr. Armstrong's apostolic commission to go to the world, what is the work of a faithful remnant in these dark times? Let Jesus Christ answer that, as He did when asked how to do a legitimate "work" in God's name.

> Then said they unto him, What shall we do, that we might work the works of God? Jesus answered and said unto them, *This is the work of God*, that ye *believe on him whom he hath sent* (John 6:28–29) [emphasis mine].

Christ confirmed that the first and most important work is to *believe* Him! How do we believe Him? Is it just by saying the words, "I believe"? No, the proof of one who truly believes Christ, is that he acknowledges that God puts doctrine into the Church by revelation, and then he believes that God never lies!

> Hereby know ye the Spirit of God: Every spirit that confesseth that Jesus Christ *is come* in the flesh is of God: And every spirit that confesseth not that Jesus Christ *is come* in the flesh is not of God: and this is that spirit of antichrist, whereof ye have heard that it should come; and even now already is it in the world (1 John 4:2–3) [emphasis mine].

The Apostle John was not saying that the proof was in agreeing that Christ *had come* to this earth almost 2,000 years ago. The test is admitting that "Christ *is come* in the flesh." The term is definitely present tense in the Greek, not past tense. It is an admonition for the last-day church—upon whom the ends of the world are come (1 Corinthians 10:11)—that we accept that Christ *did* manifest Himself *by the divine inspiration of a chosen human servant* in these last days, and that His revelation was true from the beginning of that work. All those now claiming we had to change doctrine forty years later to correct errors made by Mr. Armstrong are only admitting that they think it was a man's work all along, and not God's work after all. Whether they know it or not, they are actually saying that they do not believe Jesus Christ *is come* in this last time, having put His doctrine into the Church! And that is calling Him a liar.

By contrast, a truly faithful remnant first believes that Christ is the one who established the last-day Church in this time, building it upon a foundation of Truth—His own Truth! All others who have accepted a Sunday Pentecost, the allowance of divorce and remarriage, and every other perverted doctrinal change since the early 1970s, are calling Christ a liar, and they can never represent Him in doing a work. He will not allow it. The legitimate remnant is therefore holding on to *the faith once delivered*, first and foremost. They refuse to corrupt what God revealed, and they count it as a pearl of great price. Furthermore, that faithful remnant is then doing its work to reach out to the lost and scattered sheep who have been so decimated by the apostasy over these many decades.

If your first criterion is to find "a large church," and one that is spending time and effort on radio, TV, and printing magazines that imitate Herbert Armstrong's evangelical Work, then you will miss the first, most important criterion for finding a remnant that God is inspiring. The real work is to believe what He revealed, and to hold fast to it, no matter what.

CHAPTER TWENTY-ONE
HALLMARKS OF A FAITHFUL REMNANT

If you are still reading at this point, it may be because you believe it possible that the work of Herbert Armstrong *just might have been* the Work of Jesus Christ, and that the church raised up under him in the twentieth century *just might have been* God's peculiar treasure. If that is true, it means that all of the mistakes and failures documented in earlier chapters—which took place in that organization in the areas of prophecy speculation, unwise administration, and unauthorized doctrinal changes—have still not dissuaded you from recognizing some intrinsic value in *the substance of teaching* that made Mr. Armstrong's interpretation of Bible truths come to life like no other. If that is true, then you may be one who is faced with a serious dilemma. What do I do now?

With so many groups—and individual leaders of those groups—claiming authority to speak and to act in the name of Jesus Christ today, how can sincere children of God sift through all the claims of competing factions and know with confidence where God truly is abiding and working? In the early twentieth century it was much easier. No one but Herbert Armstrong was proclaiming *that Way.* Not so today. And yet, the truly sincere need never be confused.

They All Look and Sound So Much Alike

An increasing number of former members of God's church seem to be seeking to reconnect with their spiritual roots. Having been scattered to the four winds by the traumatic events that destroyed the unified parent body, many simply disappeared for a time into the woodwork, becoming discouraged and choosing either to forsake it outright or slowly to drift away. But finding that there really is no resting place for them in this world, and discovering through hard experience the emptiness of a life cut off from God and His true Way of Life, more and more of them have been seeking to come out of that spiritual wilderness once more. Add to these the trickle of new converts who continue to come out of this world through first-time exposure to the preserved writings of Mr. Armstrong, and we have a modern-day contingent of *called ones* looking for a spiritual home.

But where will they go? To whom will they turn to help reestablish their spiritual foundations? The parent organization from whence they all came no longer teaches those things, and in fact is embarrassed that it ever did. So these wandering sheep have no choice but to turn to a host of competing daughter groups—hundreds of them—all vying for supremacy as the standard-bearer of Herbert Armstrong.

For most, it is a daunting challenge. What is the real difference between all of these groups? Is there any? If so, how much scrounging is required to get to the heart of those differences? After all, on the surface, many of them look and sound so much alike. Many are claiming to respect the legacy of Mr. Armstrong and champion the idea of defending his teachings. So many voices. Is it even possible to distinguish if one or more of them is truly legitimate?

The easiest response is the one that many others have adopted: When faced with confusing choices they would prefer not to make, find a way to avoid making a decision at all. The best way to do this is to claim that all (or many) of the groups are legitimate and mutually-favored instruments of God. Become official members of none, but associate with many. Subscribe to literature and sermon programs of various groups, send tithes and offerings in rotation to a number of them, and attend Sabbath and Holy Days with different fellowships throughout the year. This is understandably an attractive response to the current dilemma, but it still reflects nothing of the way that God told His people to make these decisions historically:

If any man will do his will, he shall know of the doctrine
(John 7:17).

Can two walk together, except they be agreed? (Amos 3:3)

That we henceforth be no more children, tossed to and fro,
and carried about with every wind of doctrine, by the sleight
of men, and cunning craftiness, whereby they lie in wait to
deceive (Ephesians 4:14).

These are only a very few samples that reflect the mind of God on
the issue of fellowship and affiliation. Holding to *the* correct
doctrine is paramount. Like it or not, there is no biblical evidence to
justify flitting between multiple groups that hold doctrinal teachings
at variance with one another, claiming that they are all acting to
some degree with God's favor. It surely would be nice if that were
true, because then one could avoid doing the *due diligence* necessary
to discern the differences among all of these groups and making
concrete decisions about where God is residing. But it is not God's
will to let any of us off the hook. No, quite the contrary, it is His
express will to force us to use the instructions He provided in His
Holy Scripture and to demonstrate the tenacity to make a decision,
and then commit to it. It would be nice if we could just sit on the
fence, but when has God's character ever been reflected in fence-
sitting and double-mindedness?

But let him ask in faith, nothing wavering. For he that
wavereth is like a wave of the sea driven with the wind and
tossed. For let not that man think that he shall receive any
thing of the Lord. A double minded man is unstable in all his
ways (James 1:6–8).

So once again, for those who are willing to engage in the process
of discerning among the competing factions—because they know
God requires it—how will they do so? What formula is available to

help one distinguish among so many which on the surface seem credible? Is there really a way for God's children to make such evaluations, and then to know without doubt?

The Hardest Question of All

One of the best ways to begin to "cull the herd" and to separate those with potential legitimacy from many of the pretenders, is to ask the question that many of these group leaders dread: By what authority do you now lead a church and claim to represent God in this age?

This question is posed very often by former members of the church who are now very bitter and who seek to denigrate any and all groups out there that claim to be carrying on God's work. No longer believing that Mr. Armstrong was a legitimate servant of God, they seek to make sport out of anyone who still believes that he actually was. They treat all of these remnant group leaders like mental-ward patients claiming to be the reincarnation of Napoleon Bonaparte. And the very best way to have the most fun with them is to question their fundamental authority for doing what they are doing. Why is this angle of attack so effective? Because many of these remnant group leaders have absolutely nothing to call upon to substantiate themselves. The recalcitrant mockers love to see so many of them squirm. But is this kind of ploy something new to our age? Actually, it is the very same tactic that has been used throughout human history to demean and to ridicule.

Moses feared to accept God's commission because he was afraid he would not credibly be able to answer this very same question:

And Moses said unto God, Who am I, that I should go unto Pharaoh, and that I should bring forth the children of Israel out of Egypt? . . . And Moses said unto God, Behold, when I come unto the children of Israel, and shall say unto them, The God of your fathers hath sent me unto you; and they shall say to me, What is his name? what shall I say unto them? . . . And Moses answered and said, But, behold, they will not believe me, nor hearken unto my voice: for they will say, The LORD hath not appeared unto thee (Exodus 3:11, 13; 4:1).

God provided the means for Moses to overcome these doubts in his introduction to the leaders of Israel in Egypt, but the very same spirit of questioning and doubt continued to plague him, even years later:

And they gathered themselves together against Moses and against Aaron, and said unto them, Ye take too much upon you, seeing all the congregation are holy, every one of them, and the LORD is among them: *wherefore then lift ye up yourselves above the congregation of the LORD?* (Numbers 16:3) [emphasis mine]

They were really asking—through the same flippant sarcasm—by what authority do you claim to be a legitimate spokesman for God any more than are we? Notice that it was the very same spirit manifested in the questioning of Jesus Christ Himself by the leaders of this same Israelite nation centuries later:

And when he was come into the temple, the chief priests and the elders of the people came unto him as he was teaching, and said, By what authority doest thou these things? and who gave thee this authority? (Matthew 21:23)

In this particular instance, Jesus refused to answer them, because He knew they were not interested in a serious explanation. Their minds were not open at all to the possibility that He might actually be the emissary of God. That is why He answered in a way that revealed their hypocrisy. But that does not mean that the question, when asked from a heartfelt desire to know the Truth, is wrong. In fact, it is very legitimate—even necessary—for all of God's people to ask that question of anyone claiming to represent God. With so many counterfeits out there in the world, we are commanded to try the spirits and to discern the difference (1 John 4:1). The errancy of many of these pretenders is made known by the shallowness manifested in their answers to this very basic question of authority.

How Then Should We Evaluate?

If it is not only permissible, but mandatory, to verify the authority by which any man claims to speak in the name of God, how are we supposed to go about doing that? After all, they all have an answer of some kind. But what should we look for in discerning the legitimate from the fraudulent? And how should a truly legitimate remnant group be able to answer the irreverent taunts of the naysayers?

Given that some of you still reading this final chapter *may believe* that Mr. Herbert Armstrong was indeed the servant whom God raised up in this age to begin His last-day work, we will start with that presumption of his legitimacy. After all, how would anyone ever accept one of the groups spawned by the Worldwide Church of God if he has first rejected the legitimacy of that group's very founder? So if Herbert Armstrong was truly an apostle sent by God and inspired with the authority of Jesus Christ to speak in His name, where do we go from there?

Mr. Armstrong died in 1986. If we also believe that God did not lie when He promised that the gates of hell would not prevail against His church (Matthew 16:18), how will we identify a legitimate remnant that is carrying on today (Isaiah 1:9; 37:31–32; Zephaniah 3:13; Matthew 24:45–46; Romans 11:4–5)?

Is He Truly Ordained of God?

The first criteria of any legitimate remnant is having a leader who can trace his ordination to a legitimate origin. In spite of so many of

God's people today who have rejected the faith once delivered on the topic of church government, the process for becoming a true minister to represent Jesus Christ is quite clear. No man can take that authority to himself. Jesus Christ specifically selects those who will represent Him. It is a false Protestant concept that any true "Christian" can go out and begin "a ministry" and do God's work. Jesus Christ said quite the opposite:

> Ye have not chosen me, but *I have chosen you, and ordained you*, that ye should go and bring forth fruit, and that your fruit should remain: that whatsoever ye shall ask of the Father in my name, he may give it you (John 15:16) [emphasis mine].

God also contrasted His authorized agents with those who have presumed to do a work in His name without proper authority:

> The anger of the LORD shall not return, until he have executed, and till he have performed the thoughts of his heart: in the latter days ye shall consider it perfectly. I have not sent these prophets, yet they ran: I have not spoken to them, yet they prophesied (Jeremiah 23:20–21).

We understand that any man—or organization—has the right to determine who will represent him. We would never allow someone to assume the right to speak for us if we did not authorize it, would we? No, you and I are quite particular about whom we trust to represent our interests. Does it make sense to believe that Jesus Christ is any less careful? As already mentioned, do we really think it is OK for any Tom, Dick, or Harry off the street to make himself a minister and go out to represent Christ? Notice this example of the severe consequences that can result from such bald-faced presumption:

Then certain of the vagabond Jews, exorcists, took upon them to call over them which had evil spirits the name of the Lord Jesus, saying, We adjure you by Jesus whom Paul preacheth. And there were seven sons of one Sceva, a Jew, and chief of the priests, which did so. And the evil spirit answered and said, Jesus I know, and Paul I know; but who are ye? And the man in whom the evil spirit was leaped on them, and overcame them, and prevailed against them, so that they fled out of that house naked and wounded (Acts 19:13–16).

God made a very explicit example out of these pretenders. They had no authority to act in the name of Jesus Christ because they had never been commissioned through a legitimate process. What is that process? Ordination through the laying on of hands! Jesus Christ personally ordained those men who were to become apostles sent out to raise up the true Church. There were no apostles except for those whom Christ Himself specifically appointed. There were the Twelve whom Christ called and appointed during His own ministry, there was the replacement of Judas Iscariot through the casting of lots to confirm Christ's specific appointment, not man's (Acts 1:26), and there was the appointment of Paul, likewise directly by Jesus Christ in the Spirit—not by man (Galatians 1:15–17).

The Bible does not clarify the specifics of how Christ conducted that ordination process for those apostles. We cannot therefore conclude with certainty that He did so by the laying on of His own hands in an ordination ceremony, but given the many other examples in the Bible of this procedure, it is certainly very likely. Even as the ordination process for Paul as an apostle is not specifically recorded, we have no doubt he was "ordained" to that office by Christ (1 Timothy 2:7). Likewise, as already stated, at this point we are presuming the acceptance of Herbert Armstrong as a legitimate apostle. The question is, how are any other men—besides apostles—confirmed into their offices? For that, we have very definite instructions and examples given to certify God's expectations.

Laying on of Hands

One of the most significant authorities granted to those apostles by God was the process of inducting newly-called members into the Body of Christ. All baptisms must be conducted with the laying on of hands to be legitimate.

> Then laid they their hands on them, and they received the Holy [Spirit]. And when Simon saw that through laying on of the apostles' hands the Holy [Spirit] was given, he offered them money, Saying, Give me also this power, that on whomsoever I lay hands, he may receive the Holy [Spirit] (Acts 8:17–19).

The only way for any man—other than an apostle—to have this authority to baptize is if he himself has been ordained through a legitimate delegation order from an apostle. All other men who were called to become ministers were appointed under the authority of one of the apostles. It was to each apostle that a jurisdiction was assigned by God to raise up churches. All other ministers derived their authority as *delegated helpers* of those apostles. There is no evidence that a separate work during the New Testament Church era was raised up under a "non-apostle." Notice confirmation of the purpose for all other ministerial ordinations:

> Wherefore I put thee in remembrance that thou stir up the gift of God, which is in thee by the putting on of my hands. ... Who hath saved us, and called us with an holy calling, not according to our works, but according to his own purpose and grace, which was given us in Christ Jesus before the world began. ... Whereunto I am appointed a preacher, and an apostle, and a teacher of the Gentiles. ... That good thing

which was committed unto thee keep by the Holy [Spirit] which dwelleth in us (2 Timothy 1:6, 9, 11, 14).

To Titus, mine own son after the common faith: Grace, mercy, and peace, from God the Father and the Lord Jesus Christ our Saviour. For this cause left I thee in Crete, that thou shouldest set in order the things that are wanting, and ordain elders in every city, as I had appointed thee (Titus 1:4–5).

So Paul appointed Timothy and Titus to become his delegated representatives. Titus was instructed to ordain other men to become his helpers in local jurisdictions. Timothy was likewise instructed concerning the selection of local elders for ordination (1 Timothy 3:10; 5:22). But all such men—ordained either directly by the apostle himself or by one of those men later ordained by an apostle, like Timothy and Titus—fall under the jurisdiction assigned by Jesus Christ to the original apostle. It is a chain of delegation for the purpose of fulfilling that single mission.

A Last-day Apostolic Work

Why is this principle important? It confirms the very fundamental requirement that must be true as much today for the Church as it was in the first century. There is only one apostle that we recognize by the fruits of his doctrine and work as having been raised up by God in this age, and that is Mr. Herbert Armstrong. He is the only one who taught that complete plan of salvation from the Bible which we have come to recognize as the revelation of Jesus Christ. Therefore, for any other men to hold legitimate claims of being true ministers of Jesus Christ today, they must have been ordained either directly by Mr. Armstrong, or through one of those men who were themselves ordained by Mr. Armstrong.

Many individuals in the past have stumbled at this principle, and many more yet will stumble. Having been a pastor or teacher in a

HALLMARKS OF A FAITHFUL REMNANT

403

former church—or desiring to be a minister in their new affiliation—it is sometimes hard to give up the idea of holding that office, and some have actually aborted their entrance into the faith taught by Mr. Armstrong once they discovered their past ministerial credentials would not be accepted, or that they were not being looked upon as a future minister. But those kinds of personal decisions are also telling.

What about the ordinations of ministers within groups today that *did indeed* come out of that parent organization? Are they legitimate? Again, if those men can trace their ordinations back to Mr. Armstrong, then they have passed this primary criterion test. (Just recognize that this is only *the first* of several tests to complete the *full formula* for identifying all imposters and pretenders.) An example would be a man who was ordained by Mr. Armstrong while in the parent body, but then separated and began ministering to his own group (for whatever reason). His ordination is not annulled just because he is no longer with the original body. He still carries legitimate authority to be a minister. The ordination of God is for life. The same is true of any man ordained by that minister—whether while he was still in the parent body or even once he is separated—if that man's own ordination included the power to ordain others. A deacon (one ordained to manage only physical duties for the church) does not have the authority to baptize or to anoint, and he certainly does not have the authority to ordain any others to the ministry. Only one who was ordained with these "full spiritual powers" is in a position to ordain other men, even as Timothy and Titus were given by Paul.

This is the first acid test that can be applied to all of those claiming the authority of Jesus Christ today. Therefore, any man who was never ordained in this manner, and simply appointed himself as a teacher (based on a claim of divine calling or whatever it may be) is automatically eliminated. Likewise, any man who was ordained by someone who lacked *real authority* to ordain in the name of Jesus Christ is eliminated as well.

But there are many men today who pass this particular test. We have culled only a small percentage of the ones out there claiming to carry the banner of Mr. Armstrong. Yet these remaining men still disagree with each other and contend one against the other. What then is the next test we should administer?

GLORY TO GOD OR TO MAN?

The next test is one that Jesus Christ gave by His own example. Here is what He stated as a test of His own legitimacy:

> I can of mine own self do nothing: as I hear, I judge: and my judgment is just; because I seek not mine own will, but the will of the Father which hath sent me. If I bear witness of myself, my witness is not true (John 5:30–31).

> He that speaketh of himself seeketh his own glory: but he that seeketh his glory that sent him, the same is true, and no unrighteousness is in him (John 7:18).

> Believest thou not that I am in the Father, and the Father in me? the words that I speak unto you I speak not of myself: but the Father that dwelleth in me, he doeth the works (John 14:10).

Therefore, the next test we should administer to any group leader claiming the authority of Jesus Christ is this: What is his true motivation for doing what he is doing? Is he simply making a good living off of his religion? Is he leading a group to satiate his desire for personal attention and the accolades of others? Is he using his position to advance new doctrinal teachings which he claims as his own new inspiration from God—especially those that contradict past church teachings? Who gets the real glory for his work: God or himself?

Evaluate the history of each minister. When did he come into the church, and when was he ordained? What did he accept and teach doctrinally at that time? When did he finally separate from the parent organization (if he was ever a member), and why did he leave? Many stayed as long as they could to protect their positions and their salaries. In spite of the perversion of God's Truth, they held their peace and supported the new party line, for a time trading their conscience for physical security. Only when things in the parent body became bad enough that a critical mass of brethren were unwilling to accept more changes, these men stepped out "boldly" to defend the faith, starting their own groups to "preserve the truth." How convenient to wait until they could count upon enough members to follow them and provide a source of income to keep them in the standard of living to which they had become accustomed—and a following significant enough to preserve their sense of self-importance.

Examine the history of these new groups—what they teach and how they behave. By their words and their actions, is God really getting all of the glory, or are decisions being made that seek to spotlight the man as something special? Do not be fooled by outward statements of self-deprecation or honor for God. Talk is cheap. Look beyond the surface and examine what the deeper message of that ministry is really all about. What is its real motivation and conviction based upon the history of its formation and its progress over time? Are you seeing a work that seeks to build up a man as something special, or is it a work that is truly pointing to God and encouraging the flock to build faith in Jesus Christ alone? What might likely happen if the leader of that group dies? Is the whole basis of unity in that group predicated upon a man, or is there substance beyond the personality of one or more human beings?

Applying this second acid test should help cull quite a few more claimants to authority in these last days. Some of the past actions of these men tell the story very plainly—what they really care about, and why they are doing what they are doing. Yet, in other cases it may be hard to verify for sure. You may not be able to confirm from

406   A PECULIAR TREASURE

available documentation what a man's real motivation has been. You may be suspicious, but have to keep him on the short list of possible servants who are legitimate because there is no iron-clad evidence otherwise. In that case, where do you go from there?

WHAT ARE THEY TEACHING?

The ultimate test of legitimacy is what they are teaching as *the Truth*. This criterion applies to *all* ministers, including apostles.

> I marvel that ye are so soon removed from him that called you into the grace of Christ unto another gospel: Which is not another; but there be some that trouble you, and would pervert the gospel of Christ. But *though we*, or an angel from heaven, *preach any other gospel unto you than that which we have preached unto you*, let him be accursed. As we said before, so say I now again, If any man preach any other gospel unto you than that ye have received, let him be accursed (Galatians 1:6–9) [emphasis mine].

Paul was an apostle. Yet he said that not even he himself (by saying "though we," he included himself in this test) had the authority to change *anything* that God had revealed to the Church through him. However, this is the single most critical principle that most of God's people today have still not fathomed. They grasp that Moses did not have the authority to tinker with the Ten Commandments just because God used him as the messenger to deliver those precepts to Israel. They grasp that the Twelve had no authority to amend or to pervert anything that Jesus Christ had taught them during His three-year ministry. And they have the words of Paul through the Holy Spirit to show that it applies likewise to any apostle—like himself whom Christ taught in the Spirit for three years in the Arabian desert. The apostles never taught that they had authority to change doctrine and that God would back them up. Such an idea violates the very essence of these works being inspired and founded upon Jesus Christ.

Yet, why then do many of these same brethren believe that Herbert Armstrong had the authority to make changes to the doctrines revealed by God through him just because he was an apostle? It makes no sense at all. Yet that is exactly what many of these other groups profess and teach to their members today. They claim that Mr. Armstrong—being an apostle—had the authority to change doctrine and that God backed him up, but that no one else could do it. Therefore, they basically embrace all of the changed doctrines made in the Worldwide Church of God up until Mr. Armstrong died in 1986, but then refuse to accept any changes made by his successors.

How does that make any sense at all? It is an outright rejection of the very clear instructions given by Jesus Christ to the Church!

> If any man will do his will, he shall *know of the doctrine, whether it be of God, or whether I speak of myself.* He that speaketh of himself seeketh his own glory: but he that seeketh his glory that sent him, the same is true, and no unrighteousness is in him (John 7:17–18) [emphasis mine].

Upon whom was this church founded, Herbert Armstrong or Jesus Christ? Those who claim that Mr. Armstrong got some of his doctrines wrong in the early years because he was never a true Bible scholar (doctrines like Monday Pentecost, divorce and remarriage, the nature of man, divine healing, etc.), are really saying that they do not believe Jesus Christ was truly the foundation of that great work after all. Jesus Christ is the same, yesterday, today and forever (Hebrews 13:8). He never lies, and He never makes a mistake, even when He works through fallible human servants. By a miracle, He has always made sure that the church (whether ancient Israel—the church in the wilderness—or the New Testament Church) has been founded upon *real Truth!*

I have not written unto you because ye know not the truth, but because ye know it, and that no lie is of the truth. .... *Let that therefore abide in you, which ye have heard from the beginning.* If that which ye have heard from the beginning shall remain in you, ye also shall continue in the Son, and in the Father. And this is the promise that he hath promised us, even eternal life. These things have I written unto you concerning them that seduce you. But the anointing which ye have received of him abideth in you, and ye need not that any man teach you: but as the same anointing teacheth you of all things, and is truth, and is no lie, and *even as it hath taught you,* ye shall abide in him (1 John 2:21, 24–27) [emphasis mine].

So what is our third and most powerful test to distinguish the legitimate ministers from the perverse? Anyone who tells you that Mr. Armstrong or any other man had the authority to change what Christ revealed is lying. He should be rejected. Anyone who is justifying repudiation of original doctrinal teachings under the guise of "better scholarship" is denying that Christ is the foundation.

Divine Revelation Is the Key

The reason that most of the groups that came out of the WCG are themselves continuing to embrace more and more false doctrine as the years go by is that they are not rooted in the belief that Jesus Christ revealed His Truth in the last days through a chosen servant, and that this revelation can never change! *Divine revelation* is the solitary concept that undergirds *real Truth.*

In that hour Jesus rejoiced in spirit, and said, I thank thee, O Father, Lord of heaven and earth, that thou hast hid these things from the wise and prudent, and hast *revealed them* unto babes: even so, Father; for so it seemed good in thy sight. All things are *delivered to me* of my Father: and no man knoweth who the Son is, but the Father; and who the Father is, but the Son, *and he to whom the Son will reveal him*. And he turned him unto his disciples, and said privately, Blessed are the eyes which see the things that ye see: For I tell you, that many prophets and kings have desired to see those things which ye see, and have not seen them; and to hear those things which ye hear, and have not heard them (Luke 10:21–24) [emphasis mine].

But we speak the wisdom of God in a mystery, even the hidden wisdom, which God ordained before the world unto our glory: Which none of the princes of this world knew: for had they known it, they would not have crucified the Lord of glory. But as it is written, Eye hath not seen, nor ear heard, neither have entered into the heart of man, the things which God hath prepared for them that love him. But God hath *revealed them unto us by his Spirit*: for the Spirit searcheth all things, yea, the deep things of God (1 Corinthians 2:7–10) [emphasis mine].

Not only was the Truth uniquely hidden from the wise men and scholars of the world—that revelation to the Church came not by the individual Bible study of each one called—but it came through a chosen servant who was commissioned as an instrument of God to preach that Way.

For this cause I Paul, the prisoner of Jesus Christ for you Gentiles, If ye have heard of the dispensation of the grace of God which is *given me to you-ward*: How that by revelation *he made known unto me* the mystery; (as I wrote afore in few words, Whereby, when ye read, ye may understand my knowledge in the mystery of Christ) Which in other ages was not made known unto the sons of men, as it is now revealed *unto his holy apostles and prophets* by the Spirit (Ephesians 3:1–5) [emphasis mine].

For after that in the wisdom of God the world by wisdom
knew not God, it pleased God by the foolishness of preaching
to save them that believe (1 Corinthians 1:21).

Yes, Mr. Armstrong always challenged people to prove it from
their own Bibles, but they would never have known where to look, or
even what questions to ask, if they had not been instructed by a
commissioned servant of God. We can attempt to deny these facts
all we want. This is precisely what most have done. But then, are
not their sickly fruits proof that they have constructed inferior
foundations, having rejected the real Christ and His Holy Spirit?
Many remnant groups that came out of the Worldwide Church of
God are traveling the very same road as their parent organization,
howbeit at a much slower pace. Why? Because they have likewise
embraced the liberal, perverted doctrines of the 1970s—including a
Sunday Pentecost and the acceptance of adulterous relationships
they call marriages—rejecting the idea that Jesus Christ gave His
Truth to the Body from the very beginning, through the initial
teachings of Mr. Armstrong.

But What About Convenience of Fellowship?

But did we not just see that many of the ministers of these groups
still have a very valid ordination? Even if they have changed some of
the teachings, are we not approved in attending their worship
services, and will not God honor our spiritual offerings made in
those convocations? Again, let Jesus Christ Himself clarify the
principle:

Then spake Jesus to the multitude, and to his disciples,
Saying, The scribes and the Pharisees sit in Moses' seat: All
therefore whatsoever they bid you observe, that observe and
do; but do not ye after their works: for they say, and do not
(Matthew 23:1–3).

HALLMARKS OF A FAITHFUL REMNANT

Christ is certifying that those scribes and Pharisees did indeed have a right to the offices they held, being legitimate leaders of the nation. They were not illegitimate usurpers. Those offices must be respected (even the office that Satan holds today is a God-given position and requires our respect; Jude 9–10). But He warned that this did not mean the people were to follow all that they did, because they were not holding fast to God's Truth at all, being hypocrites.

> *If any man teach otherwise* [no matter who he is], and consent not to wholesome words, even the words of our Lord Jesus Christ, and to the doctrine which is according to godliness; He is proud, knowing nothing, but doting about questions and strifes of words, whereof cometh envy, strife, railings, evil surmisings, Perverse disputings of men of corrupt minds, and *destitute of the truth*, supposing that gain is godliness: *from such withdraw thyself* (1 Timothy 6:3–5) [emphasis mine].

> Now we command you, brethren, in the name of our Lord Jesus Christ, that ye withdraw yourselves from every brother that walketh disorderly, and not after the tradition which he received of us (2 Thessalonians 3:6).

Someone within Israel (the church) is sponsoring Sabbath and Holy Day convocations that God will not honor, and in fact, He hates.

> To what purpose is the multitude of your sacrifices unto me? saith the LORD: I am full of the burnt offerings of rams, and the fat of fed beasts; and I delight not in the blood of bullocks, or of lambs, or of he goats. When ye come to appear before me, who hath required this at your hand, to tread my courts? Bring no more vain oblations; incense is an abomination unto me; the new moons and sabbaths, the calling of assemblies, I cannot away with; it is iniquity, even

the solemn meeting. Your new moons and your appointed feasts my soul hateth: they are a trouble unto me; I am weary to bear them. And when ye spread forth your hands, I will hide mine eyes from you: yea, when ye make many prayers, I will not hear: your hands are full of blood (Isaiah 1:11–15).

I hate, I despise your feast days, and I will not smell in your solemn assemblies. Though ye offer me burnt offerings and your meat offerings, I will not accept them: neither will I regard the peace offerings of your fat beasts. Take thou away from me the noise of thy songs; for I will not hear the melody of thy viols (Amos 5:21–23).

Thus saith the Lord GOD; Woe unto the foolish prophets, that follow their own spirit, and have seen nothing! O Israel, thy prophets are like the foxes in the deserts. Ye have not gone up into the gaps, neither made up the hedge for the house of Israel to stand in the battle in the day of the LORD. They have seen vanity and lying divination, saying, The LORD saith: and the LORD hath not sent them: and they have made others to hope that they would confirm the word. Have ye not seen a vain vision, and have ye not spoken a lying divination, whereas ye say, The LORD saith it; albeit I have not spoken? Therefore thus saith the Lord GOD; Because ye have spoken vanity, and seen lies, therefore, behold, I am against you, saith the Lord GOD (Ezekiel 13:3–8).

God did not reject the offerings of His people because the priests and prophets were not legitimate office-holders. No, he rejected their offerings because those leaders had perverted the commands of God and had begun to teach their own concepts. There is no way to fulfill the command to keep Sabbaths and Holy Days in the midst of those particular groups that have rejected God's divine revelation and turned to doctrines based upon the wisdom of human scholars.

What they claim to be the product of "growing in grace and knowledge," God calls the rejection of His very revelation.

> Remember therefore from whence thou art fallen, and repent, and *do the first works*; or else I will come unto thee quickly, and will remove thy candlestick out of his place, except thou repent (Revelation 2:5) [emphasis mine].

So these are just a few principles that should be considered, if you are earnest in seeking a fellowship where you hope that God may still be preserving *a peculiar treasure*.

IS THERE A FAITHFUL REMNANT TODAY?

Jesus Christ promised that the gates of hell would not prevail against His Church (Matthew 16:18). Isaiah also was inspired to write a prophecy concerning the survival of a faithful remnant, after the apostasy of the visible church. "And the daughter of Zion is left as a cottage in a vineyard, as a lodge in a garden of cucumbers, as a besieged city. Except the LORD of hosts had left unto us a very small remnant, we should have been as Sodom, and we should have been like unto Gomorrah" (Isaiah 1:8–9).

Many of those who reject the substance of this promise presume and assert that there is no faithful ministry left today that can be looked to as inspired servants of God. It is fashionable instead to believe that we are left to ourselves to determine what is truth. Many are now jumping onto this bandwagon, content to sit at home, subscribing to various religious publications, and selecting nuggets from each one that *they decide* has value. Many even make it their personal mission to write and tell various ministers what they need to do to be right in the eyes of God, as if they have now somehow become the source of divine inspiration. But this whole premise is a rejection of the promise Jesus Christ gave to His disciples before His ascension.

414   A PECULIAR TREASURE

And Jesus came and spake unto them, saying, All power is given unto me in heaven and in earth. Go ye therefore, and teach all nations, baptizing them in the name of the Father, and of the Son, and of the Holy [Spirit]: Teaching them to observe all things whatsoever I have commanded you: and, lo, *I am with you alway, even unto the end of the world.* Amen (Matthew 28:18–20) [emphasis mine].

Christ promised He would be manifesting Himself *somewhere* in the last days, even as He was preparing to work through the Twelve in the first century. And this promise cannot be made void by claiming He is simply fulfilling it in each individual Christian, as He leads us personally through the Holy Spirit.

Who then is a faithful and wise servant, whom his lord hath made ruler over his household, to give them meat in due season? Blessed is that servant, whom his lord *when he cometh shall find so doing* (Matthew 24:45–46) [emphasis mine].

Someone was commissioned to preach with authority in the name of Jesus Christ. The called of God were expected to hear that voice—the voice of Christ Himself *through that human agent*—and to respond. Even though that servant God used to raise up His Church in these last days approved corrupted doctrine in his old age as a fulfillment of prophecy—allowed by God to test the whole church—Christ's promise to preserve a faithful remnant *and a faithful ministry* has not been broken. Jesus Christ did not lie. The only legitimate question is, where is that remnant, and who are those faithful servants still feeding the sheep?

Was that great religious work, initiated through Herbert and Loma Armstrong in the 1930s, a divine operation of God? If it was, then Jesus Christ was the One who truly sponsored it, inspired it, and made it His very own *peculiar treasure.*

And if all of that is actually true, then in spite of the confusion and splintering that has resulted in recent decades, there is still a legitimate vestige of that *divine work* extant someplace today. Herbert and Loma Armstrong did indeed leave us a valuable legacy. Many today cannot see it. But perhaps, now, you are one who does.